# Managing Values and Beliefs in Organisations

**PEARSON**
Education

We work with leading authors to develop the strongest educational materials in business, bringing cutting-edge thinking and best learning practice to a global market.

Under a range of well-known imprints, including Financial Times Prentice Hall, we craft high quality print and electronic publications which help readers to understand and apply their content, whether studying or at work.

To find out more about the complete range of our publishing please visit us on the World Wide Web at: www.pearsoneduc.com

Tom McEwan

# Managing Values and Beliefs in Organisations

 Prentice Hall
FINANCIAL TIMES

*An imprint of* **Pearson Education**

Harlow, England • London • New York • Boston • San Francisco • Toronto • Sydney • Singapore • Hong Kong
Tokyo • Seoul • Taipei • New Delhi • Cape Town • Madrid • Mexico City • Amsterdam • Munich • Paris • Milan

**Pearson Education Limited**
Edinburgh Gate
Harlow
Essex CM20 2JE
England

and Associated Companies throughout the world

*Visit us on the World Wide Web at:*
http://www.pearsoned.co.uk

---

First published 2001

ISBN-10: 0-273-64340-1
ISBN-13: 978-0-273-64340-1

*British Library Cataloguing-in-Publication Data*
A catalogue record for this book is available from the British Library

*Library of Congress Cataloging-in-Publication Data*
McEwan, Tom.
    Managing values and beliefs in organisations / Tom McEwan.
        p.   cm.
    Includes bibliographical references and index.
    ISBN 0–273–64340–1
    1. Business ethics.   I. Title.
    HF5387.M42  2001
    174′.4—dc21                               00–069169

10  9  8  7  6
07   06

Typeset by 35 in 10/12½pt Sabon
Printed in Malaysia, PJB

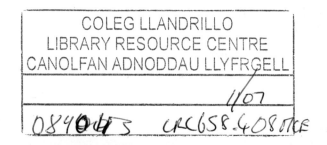

# Contents

# Preface

Numerous books are available that treat corporate social responsibility, business ethics and corporate governance as separate subjects. There are also other texts that explore common features of corporate social responsibility and business ethics. A few writers (Harvey[1], Goodpaster and Mathews[2], and Mahoney[3]) also cover shareholder issues, but without discussing corporate governance in detail. An explanation of why the task of integrating corporate social responsibility, business ethics and corporate governance has been undertaken in this book therefore seems necessary.

Corporate social responsibility, business ethics and corporate governance were imported into Britain from the United States as separate academic subjects over the last thirty years and one or more is taught on most business education programmes. A sociologist or political scientist might observe that the original separation of these subjects occurred as a result of attempts to provide different perspectives on the management capitalism model described by Burnham[4]. Burnham's main conclusions are that capitalism has been transformed because a managerial elite has steadily acquired two forms of power over shareholders, employees and consumers. The first resulted in control over the means of producing goods and services, and the second ensured 'preferential treatment' for this elite in the distribution of money and goods resulting from these profitable activities. Whether Burnham's analysis is valid half a century later is a question which is discussed in Chapter 2. It also has moral implications when the further question is asked about why attempts to prevent abuses of the managerial capitalism model, by adopting the Cadbury, Greenbury and Hampel recommendations on corporate governance and directors' remuneration, have been largely ineffective in Britain.

Corporate social responsibility and business ethics have longer histories than corporate governance. Each reflects an earlier attempt to balance economic decisions against ethical judgements and explore the impact of these on the complex relationship between the business world and the rest of society. Corporate social responsibility, for example, emerged first at the start of the last century when the American writer, Ida Tarbell, published a series of critical essays on the methods used by John D. Rockefeller to create a monopoly in the US oil industry. After Tarbell's revelations, what had been a largely unknown example of dubious business strategy soon became a matter of national importance, which led to the intervention of President Teddy Roosevelt and ended with a narrow judgment against Rockefeller's Standard Oil corporation in the US Supreme Court.

Business ethics emerged in the 1970s under a broader umbrella of social concerns which, to name but four, included issues such as unrest about US involvement in the Vietnam War; the emerging civil rights movement; concerns about environmental pollution; and the impact of computer technology on work practices in what came to be known as post-industrial society. This time, however, business ethics adopted a more critical global perspective on business practices from the standpoint of different stakeholders or constituencies. These were usually divided into 'internal constituencies' (including shareholders, employers, directors and management) and 'external constituencies' (including consumers, suppliers, government agencies, the local community and host countries) with which the corporation entered into socioeconomic relationships.

## Aims of this book

The main aims of this book are to summarise the separate histories of corporate social responsibility, business ethics and corporate governance before developing a method of enquiry which attempts to integrate the three different perspectives on business. This methodology consists of three broad levels of enquiry. First, a *descriptive* approach is presented that draws attention to the values and beliefs of people from different cultures and societies which influence their attitudes towards the various activities of business in their home countries and abroad.

Secondly, a *normative* approach is presented which identifies sets of values and beliefs which can be defended as a basis for making ethical decisions at the individual, group or senior management level in an organisation. For example, at the individual level, emphasis might be placed on practising the 'virtues' of honesty and loyalty, as opposed to the 'vices' of lying and fraud. At the management level, however, the emphasis would be on displaying professional rather than unprofessional behaviour towards an organisation's various stakeholders.

Finally, an *analytical* approach is also presented which attempts to explore the relationship between these normative values and beliefs and other value-systems or ideologies such as political or religious beliefs and culture or other social customs.

To assist the reader in developing these different levels of enquiry, other important aims of this book include:

- Providing opportunities for identifying ethical problems and developing skills in evaluating these issues, by analysing the case studies at the end of each chapter on actual organisations which include issues that have failed to meet the demands and expectations of various stakeholders.
- Providing opportunities to explore personal responses to leading ethical perspectives by completing the Moral Compass instrument presented after each Part, which is explained in the Appendix at the end of the book.

## Who should read this book?

This book should be of interest to all readers who regard themselves as actual or potential stakeholders in any organisation (e.g. a university or college student, an employee of a profit-seeking or public sector organisation, a member of a local community, club, church or political organisation). A more specific intention is to provide an introduction to the impact of corporate social responsibility, business ethics and corporate governance on the policies and procedures of different institutions in the private and public sectors of the economy. It should therefore appeal to:

- *Undergraduates* on business studies, related social science, technical, or modular degree programmes, as no prior knowledge of ethics or moral philosophy is assumed.
- *MBA and postgraduate candidates* on other specialist masters degree programmes, who should also find that it provides them with well-rounded historical and critical evaluation of the emergence of corporate social responsibility, business ethics and corporate governance as legitimate fields of study.

## Distinctive features

**A modular approach**

In keeping with the trend in higher education for academic terms to be replaced with semesters, and courses by modules, this book sets out to include a discussion of topics which are widely recognised as a requirement of any comprehensive study of corporate social responsibility, business ethics and corporate governance. Each Part is written as a self-contained module and each chapter should therefore be regarded as a free-standing unit of study. Some repetition of references is unavoidable and whenever this occurs it should be regarded positively as an aid to learning and also as an indication of the overriding need to integrate sources of study material, supported by research findings and other relevant academic literature.

**Questions, case studies, assignments and other exercises**

Readers are invited to test their understanding of the contents by attempting to answer the various questions and short assignments which appear at the end of each chapter. These exercises are not intended to expose areas of misunderstanding but have the positive aim of providing indicators of progress achieved through revision, especially with examinations or other tests in mind.

The case study at the end of each chapter is based on real events in actual organisations rather than the 'armchair' variety which is concocted to reinforce particular values and beliefs. The aim is to encourage the reader to explore specific issues so that an individual rationale is developed, supported by case material provided, and new information acquired, which helps to justify one loosely argued judgement in preference to another. Such evaluations usually become more 'concrete' for the reader if supported by relevant examples or applications from organisations where he/she is employed or has work-placement experience, provided these judgements can be defended during discussions with fellow students with comparable experiences, or with tutors, at a college or university.

The importance of peer-group discussion and analysis is emphasised by the inclusion of an original Moral Compass instrument at the end of each Part of the book. Two versions of the instrument (i.e. simple and detailed) are included for completion by the reader depending on the level of personal interest or time available. Both versions of the instrument consist of statements on ethical aspects of behaviour which should be evaluated using the Likert scale provided. Details of how to record, collate and interpret overall scores for the two versions of the Moral Compass instrument appear in the Appendix. The aim of the Moral Compass instrument is twofold; namely, to enable the reader to establish his/her personal evaluations in private of the main ethical perspectives which have influenced business development in the West and internationally.

Secondly, to encourage discussion with fellow students or colleagues of Moral Compass 'scores' so that a fuller understanding of the moral perspectives of others may emerge as a basis for achieving consensus when ethical issues arise in actual organisations.

**Analysing case studies**

Cases and case histories were regarded as important ways of applying theory to practice in the study of law and medicine long before the 'methodology' was adapted as case studies by the Harvard Business School almost ninety years ago. Since then, thousands of case studies have been written on every aspect of organisational and business activity. Useful guides on how to analyse case studies [5,6] are so plentiful that it would be hard to add anything original on the subject, except perhaps to urge the reader to read a case study with a questioning mind, seeking confirmation for any assumption or decision reported in the text, and supporting or challenging any conclusion with her/his own analysis, based on actual experience where possible and on other observations obtained from reliable sources of data.

**Avoidance of 'right' answers to moral issues in organisations**

Most people living in a multicultural society like Britain realise how difficult it is to arrive at a single 'right' answer to the various moral questions that arise in working with others in different organisations. For some, the absence of reassuring, clear-cut answers to problems at work or in other situations can be frustrating and even hurtful. For others, the challenge of being involved in uncertain *ad hoc* situations allows them to exercise imagination, intelligence and personal integrity, and 'find their own voice' by contributing to the resolution of complicated or embarrassing ethical issues in a working environment.

As the following chapters make clear, there are no easy ways of reconciling rival viewpoints, especially for those who see themselves as members of a pluralistic, democratic society in which each individual is entitled to freedom of thought and belief; and to be heard in a courteous, open manner, regardless of gender, age, race, creed, qualification, years of experience, or position in an organisational hierarchy. For those who may be studying corporate social responsibility, business ethics and corporate governance for the first time, however, various references are included to relevant study material in standard works in business education such as Laurie J. Mullins' *Management and Organisational Behaviour*, 5th edition, 1999 and Chris Fill's *Marketing Communications: Contexts, contents and strategies*, 2nd edition, 1995, both of which are published by Financial Times Pitman Publishing.

**Chapter summaries**

A synopsis is presented at the end of each chapter which summarises key issues under bullet points, as a revision aid for students.

**Selected further readings**

Further reading materials are listed as appropriate in the Notes and References section at the end of each chapter so that the reader is able to explore topics and related issues in more detail.

**Lecturer Resources**

An Instructor's Manual is published separately for lecturers who prescribe this textbook for use by students. It includes relevant commentaries on each chapter and other selected materials which can be distributed to students for revision purposes. Overhead Transparency Masters are also available. These resources can be downloaded from a companion website to the text at www.booksites.net/mcewan.

| **Review and discussion questions** | The various questions which appear in these sections at the end of each chapter are mainly intended to test the reader's knowledge and understanding of key issues and topics covered in the preceding text. The opportunity is also provided for the reader to apply his/her own experience and personal values and beliefs in explaining why a particular perspective is stressed in answering specific questions. |

*Tom McEwan*

## Notes and references

1. Harvey, B., ed., *Business Ethics: A European approach*, London, Prentice Hall, 1994.
2. Goodpaster, K.E. and Mathews, J.B., Can a Corporation have a Conscience?, *Harvard Business Review*, 1982, January–February, 132–41.
3. Mahoney, J., *Mastering Management*, London, Financial Times Pitman Publishing, 1997.
4. Burnham, J., *The Managerial Revolution*, London, Putnam, 1942, 56–7.
5. Mullins, L.J., *Management and Organisational Behaviour*, 5th edn, London, Financial Times Pitman Publishing, 1999, 10–12.
6. Easton, G., *Learning from Case Studies*, 2nd edn, London, Prentice Hall, 1992.

# About the author

Tom McEwan was employed in the frozen food industry for over 15 years in four countries as a quality controller, production manager and operations director. He graduated in systematic and history of philosophy and was awarded his MBA and PhD from the University of Cranfield School of Management. He left industry to take up the post of senior lecturer, then principal lecturer, deputy head of department and finally international director at the University of Portsmouth Business School. He was appointed Professor of Business Administration at the University of Natal, Pietermaritzburg, South Africa, from 1996 to 1999. Since returning to Britain to take up writing, he has been appointed as an associate lecturer at the Open University Business School.

# Author's acknowledgements

Two groups of people almost six thousand miles apart have helped me with this book. Linking them both has been my family and I must first express my affectionate gratitude to Kathleen, Lucy and Susan, for their encouragement and remarkable tolerance of my nocturnal semester in front of a computer screen working on this book. Special thanks are also due to Professors David Maughan Brown, Ahmed Bawa and Ron Nicholson at the University of Natal, Pietermaritzburg, for reducing the heavy teaching and administrative commitment during the last six months of my appointment as Professor of Business Administration in the Faculty of Commerce, when I was able to lay down the foundations of this book. Clare O'Neill, Nhlanhla Moses Ndlovu and Margaret Sandwith, of the same university, were particularly helpful in locating databases, assisting with diagrams, and in tracing references after my return to Britain. They, and Julia Dyall, who typed and collated materials, are all warmly thanked for their generous assistance.

Since returning to Britain, I have received invaluable help on numerous occasions in converting draft materials into a publishable format from Peter Hobden, with some sound advice from Jeremy Empson, and thank both accordingly. Professor Richard Welford, University of Huddersfield, is also thanked for his theoretical contribution to the survey instrument in Chapter 11. I owe a debt of gratitude to two former TEMPUS students from the University of Tirana, Albania, Hortense Tomina and Dr Julinda Nuri, now of the University of Surrey, for their enthusiastic help in analysing the longer version of the Moral Compass instrument pilot survey in 1993. Judith Samenkovic, Portsmouth Business School librarian and the staff at Nettleham and Lincoln Central libraries are also thanked for obtaining information on changes in UK business that occurred during my four years in South Africa. Jane Powell, Sadie McClelland, Elaine Richardson and Geraldine Lyons of Pearson Education must also be thanked for the professional way they ensured that I kept to agreed deadlines.

Finally, I must pay tribute to two writers, one American the other British, whom I have never met, who have played a major part in placing business ethics on the curriculum of business education programmes in the USA and UK, respectively. I refer to Richard De George and Professor Jack Mahoney, whose writings have influenced my own views on the subjects they developed. Where their analyses are quoted in the pages that follow, it is simply because a book on moral issues in business would be much the poorer if these had been excluded. Any misinterpretation of their views must, however, remain my full responsibility.

# Publisher's acknowledgements

We are grateful to the following for permission to reproduce copyright material:

Academic Press New York, adapted extracts 'Professional Ethics' by T. Airaksinen, in *Encyclopaedia of Applied Ethics*, vol 3 1998 pp 671–682, 'Sexual Equality' by S. Dodds in *Encyclopaedia of Applied Ethics*, vol 4 1998 pp 53–63, 'Reputation Management' by C Fombrun in *Encyclopaedia of Applied Ethics*, 1998 pp 829–834, 'Computer and Information Ethics' by S. Rogerson in *Encyclopaedia of Applied Ethics*, vol 1 1998 pp 563–570, and 'Corporate Responsibility' by C. Wells in *Encyclopaedia of Applied Ethics*, 1998 pp 653–660; American Management Association for an adapted extract from 'Whistleblowers: Who's the real bad guy?' by B. Etorre in *Management Review*, 1994 pp 18–23; Business Horizons for an adapted extract from 'Five Propositions for Social Responsibility' by K. Davis & R.L. Blomstrom in *Business Horizons* June 1975 pp 19–24; the author Terrell Bynum, for an adapted extract from Rogerson, S. and Bynum, T.W. (eds) *A Reader in Information Ethic* edited by S. Rogerson & T.W. Bynum, Oxford; Blackwell, 1997 pp 563–70; Jon Carpenter Publishing, Charlbury for an adapted extract from *Ethical Investment: A Saver's Guide* by P. Lang 1996 pp 86, 87–105; CCC for adapted extracts from 'A Stakeholder Framework for Analysing and Evaluating Corporate Social Performance' by M.B.E. Clarkson in *Academy of Management Review* 1995 vol 20.1 pp 92–117 and an adapted extract from 'A Three-dimensional conceptual model of corporate social performance' by A.B. Carroll in *Academy of Management Review* 4, 1979 pp 497–506; The Economist Newspapers Ltd for adapted extracts from the article 'Storm over Globalization and the Battle in Seattle' in *The Economist* 27.11.99; Harvard Business School Publishing Corporation for an adapted extract from 'The Working Group on Corporate Governance' in *A New Compact for Owners and Directors* July–Aug 1991 pp 17–18; International Thomson Publishing Services for adapted extract from 'Corporate Governance' by J. Lorsch and S.K. Graff in *International Encyclopaedia of Business Management* edited by M. Warner 1996 pp 772–781; Kluwer Academic Publishers and the authors for adapted extracts from 'An Islamic Perspective on Business' by M.C. Bassiouni, 'Christianity and Business Ethics' by S. Hosaka, S. & Y. Nagayasu, 'Christianity and Business Ethics' by J. Mahoney, 'A Jewish perspective for Modern business morality' by M. Tarnari, all in *The Ethics of a Business in a Global Economy* edited by P.M. Minus 1993 London: Kluwer pp 117–122, pp 99–103, pp 111–116, pp 105–109; Macmillan Inc for adapted extracts from *Moral Issues in Business* by T.R. De George 3rd edition 1990 pp 14–16, pp 32–36, pp 287–306, pp 17–18, pp 63–86, pp 217–241, pp 182–186, pp 308–355, pp 79–81 © New York: Macmillan 1990, and an adapted extract from 'Business and Environmental Ethics' by W.M. Hoffman in *Business Ethics Quarterly*, 1 April 1991; McGraw Hill Inc for adapted extracts from 'Business and the Changing Society' by G.C. Lodge and 'The Corporate Impact' by R. Nader *Issues in Business and*

*Society* by G.A. Steiner and J.F. Steiner 2nd Edition 1977 pp 22–35, 132–152; Massachusetts Institute of Technology for extract reprinted from The Ethical Side of Enterprise by V.E. Henderson, *Sloan Management Review*, 23, 1990, pp 37–47 by Sloan Management Review Association. All rights reserved; Nations Business for an adapted extract from 'Clamping down on employee crime' by R.T. Gray in *Nations Business* April 1997 pp 44–45 copyright 1997 US Chamber of Commerce; University of Notre Dame Press for an adapted extract from *Ethics and Problems of the 21st Century* edited by K.M. Sayre and K.E. Goodpaster © 1979 by University of Notre Dame Press; Oxford University Press for an adapted extract from *Our Common Future* 1987 pp 1–23 © World Commission on Environment and Development 1987; Oxford University Press Inc for adapted extracts by L. Kohlberg and C. Gilligan in *Business Institutions and Ethics: Text with Cases and Readings* 2000 by J.W. Dienhart pp 64–69, 74–79 © Copyright 1999 by John Dienhart; Pearson Education Ltd for adapted extracts from 'The Ethical Context' by R. Christie and C. Fill in *Marketing Communications: Contexts and Strategies* 2nd edition 1995 pp 47–69, *National Cultures of Capitalism* by G. Hofstede 1993 pp 31–33, *Mastering Management* by J. Mahoney 1997 151–152, *Management and Organizational Behaviour* by L.J. Mullins 5th edition 1999 Financial Times/Pitman Publishing, London pp 652–654, 661–663, 663–669, *Operations Management* by N. Slack, S. Chambers, C. Harland, A. Harrison and R. Johnston 2nd edition, 1998 pp 547–587, 760–794; Salem Press for adapted extracts from 'Animal Research' by B.C. Auday pp 36–37; 'Professional Ethics' by S.F. Barker pp 703–706, 'Machiavellian Ethics' by A.R. Brunello, 'Character' by R. Clouse pp 127–128, 'Integrity' by R. Forrest pp 441–442, 'Hindu Ethics' by K. Francis pp 376–377, 'Jewish Ethics' by P.J. Haas pp 464–465, 'Lying' by R. Kagan pp 514–515, 'Social Darwinism' by T.A. Murad pp 817–818, 'Bribery' by P. O'Neill pp 103–104, 'Communitarianism' by G.E. Paul pp 172–173, 'Buddhist Ethics' by P.L. Redditt pp 99–110, 'Marketing and Ethics' by J.E. Richardson pp 529–530, 'Intellectual Property' by D.R. Francischetti pp 441–443, 'Natural Law' by R.A. Spinello pp 599–602, 'Computer Crime' by C.E. Sutphen pp 177–178, 'Sexual abuse and harassment' by S.C. Taylor pp 792–793, 'Sexual stereotypes' by M. Vandendorpe pp 794–795, 'Animal Rights' by G.F. Varner pp 37–40. All in *Ethics* edited by J.K. Roth. Copyright 1994 by Salem Press, Inc; Sloan Management Review Association for an adapted extract from the article 'The Ethical Side of Enterprise' by V.E. Henderson in *Sloan Management Review* 1990, 23 pp 37–47 © Sloan Management Review Association 1990; Joseph Spieler Agency for adapted extract from *The Seven Cultures of Capitalism* by C. Hampden-Turner and A. Trompenaars, published by Doubleday 1993 pp 11–12; UCLA Extension Press for adapted extract from 'Stockholders and Stakeholders', New Verso Ltd for an adapted extract from ch 1–4 *The Long Twentieth Century* by G. Arrighi 1994 London, Verso; Box 1.1 from *Journal of Business Ethics*, 4 (1985) pages 377–383, 'Defining Business Ethics' by Lewis, A., fig. 1.2 by permission of Kluwer Academic Publishers; Fig. 15.2 reprinted with the permission of The Free Press, a division of Simon & Schuster, Inc., from *Communication Networks* by Everett M. Rogers and D. Lawrence Kincaid. Copyright© 1981 by The Free Press.

# PART I

# Corporate social responsibility, business ethics and corporate governance

# The integration of corporate social responsibility, business ethics and corporate governance

*Gentlemen: You have undertaken to cheat me. I will not sue you, for law takes too long. I will ruin you. Sincerely yours, Cornelius Vanderbilt. And he did.*

Max Josephson, *The Robber Barons*, 2nd edition, New York, Harvest/HBJ Books, 1962, p. 15

## Learning objectives

After reading this chapter you should be able to:

■ summarise the origins of corporate social responsibility, business ethics and corporate governance;

■ evaluate the case for and against each of these subjects;

■ identify a domain of ethical issues which is common to all three subjects;

## Introduction[1]

Chiefly because they appeared at different times during the last century, corporate social responsibility, business ethics and corporate governance are treated as separate subjects in this book. Because of their different histories, each subject is introduced and evaluated in chronological order. The main aim of this chapter, however, is to show that these three subjects should be treated in the same academic domain, as other writers have shown that the topics discussed under each subject are, in fact, interrelated. Integration in the USA and UK has been held back by the narrow reappraisal of corporate governance. However, this seems likely to change as organisations and stock exchanges consolidate and, in expanding activities across international boundaries, have to accommodate different approaches to corporate social responsibility, business ethics and corporate governance in different cultures.

## The rise of corporate social responsibility

The emergence of corporate social responsibility in the USA was in reaction to the rapid growth of capitalism during the thirty years following the American Civil War (1861–5). The USA succeeded Britain as the world's largest industrial power during this period which was partly due to the entrepreneurial activities of a group of men identified by Josephson[2] as the 'robber barons'. Hofstadter[3] confirms that modern corporate social responsibility arguments date back to the anti-trust movement against the robber barons.

Politically, this began with the Sherman Anti-trust Act in 1890 which was implemented against the Standard Oil company trust by President Teddy Roosevelt in 1904. The rationale was that the new industrial trusts and corporations had become too powerful, wasted resources, were politically dangerous and socially irresponsible. The remedy was to alter the industrial structure, reassert the power of government and create more competition. Roosevelt's intervention was influenced by the social effects of the long US recession from 1873 to 1895, and by public response to six critical articles on the rise of Standard Oil by Tarbell[4]. Her critique of the monopolistic practices of John D. Rockefeller laid down criteria for evaluating the social responsibilities of the new corporations throughout the twentieth century.

## Renewed calls for corporate social responsibility

Almost 70 years after Tarbell, the call for increased corporate social responsibility was restated by Nader *et al.*[5] They traced the source of the conflict that affected the business community, government and civil society in the USA to the American Constitution of 1787, which 'does not mention the business corporation'. It was almost 120 years later that the US Supreme Court ruled that: 'The corporation is a creature of the state. It is presumed to be incorporated for the benefit of the public. It receives certain special privileges and franchises, and hold [sic] them subject to proper government supervision' (*Hale* v. *Henkle* (1906) 201 US 74). Nader *et al.* concede that American corporations probably became more aware of their public responsibilities following the Supreme Court judgment, yet add that the United States Constitution, which governs every state, county and local authority, 'is silent about the giant corporations which govern our economy'.

Their concerns are that giant corporations have both the size and the power to undermine the major classical economic argument in favour of capitalism. That is, if only the government would mind its own business, a self-correcting market would result, with the gross national product as the proper barometer of US wealth. They cite the views of Berle and Means[6] and Galbraith[7] to support their view that the power of 'the giant corporation [is] more like a private government'. They add that in the twenty years up to 1974, the number of US corporations owning more than half of the total assets of the remaining two million smaller businesses fell from 200 to 100.

Consolidation continued over the next twenty years and in 1997 the number of American multinationals holding over half of the assets of the remaining two million corporations fell from 100 to 80 corporations.[8] The leading 50 global economies in 1991 included 13 major global corporations with greater assets than several Western countries. The leading six American corporations were General Motors, Ford Motor Company, Exxon Corporation, IBM Corporation, General Electric Company and Mobil Corporation. The remainder included three Japanese (Tokyo Motor Corporation, Hitachi Limited and Matsushita Electric); two British or Anglo-Dutch (Royal Dutch/Shell and British Petroleum); one German (Daimler-Benz); and one Italian corporation (Fiat).

Nader *et al.*'s critique of big corporations is a useful starting point for exploring corporate social responsibility developments as the issues they raised are still regarded as examples of the excluded social costs of production and the hidden costs incurred by society in living alongside large corporations in the twenty-first century:

- industrial pollution and toxic waste;
- racial and sexual discrimination;
- management burn-out/white collar blues;
- political influence of powerful corporations;
- invasion of employees' privacy (e.g. 27 per cent of employee e-mail is read surreptitiously by US managers (BBC World Report, 8 April 1999);
- deceptive information in marketing (i.e. TV advertising etc.);
- product safety of manufactured goods;
- the price of technology, including effects of pesticides, aerosols and nuclear power;
- multinational corporation exploitation of less developed countries;
- increasing concentration of wealth and income in fewer hands;
- business crime.

Nader *et al.* conclude by noting that large business firms, as creators of wealth and jobs, are a major reason why the US real per capita income tripled between 1930 and 1970. They also recognise that corporate philanthropy totals US$1 billion annually, or 6 per cent of all charitable contributions in the USA. Yet when the costs are added up, the social balance sheet of big business contains enormous debts to society. This leads them to enquire: 'Where is the law? When confronted with social or economic wrongdoing, presumably the law – that reflection of democratic will – can provide a remedy? Has it historically done so?' They conclude that the weight of evidence is on their side and that the law should be changed to bring big business more within the public purview.

## The case against corporate social responsibility

Milton Friedman[9], criticised corporate social responsibility arguments, by stating that: 'Few trends could so thoroughly undermine the very foundations of our free society as the acceptance by our corporate officials of a social responsibility other than to make as much money for their stockholders as possible.' For Friedman, the corporate executive is 'an agent of the individuals who own the corporation . . . and his primary responsibility is to them'. He is entirely free to spend his own money on worthy causes in the community but when his 'social responsibility' contributions 'reduce returns to stockholders, he is spending their money . . . raise the price to customers, he is spending the customers' money . . . lower the wages of some employees, he is spending their money'. Instead of acting as the agent of the stockholders, customers or the employees, in a different way than they would have spent it, 'he is in effect imposing taxes on the one hand, and deciding how the tax proceeds shall be spent on the other'. In dealing with the concerns raised by supporters of corporate social responsibility, he calls for more measures to strengthen competition, particularly the enforcement of anti-trust laws against price fixing by cartels, but also urges businesspeople to reassert their responsibilities, as agents of their shareholders, in the single-minded pursuit of profits within the law.

Kelso and Adler[10] also insist that the sole function of any company is to generate and diffuse capital for the benefit of its shareholders. This would be put at risk by the growing separation of management control, which tends to dilute responsibility and leads to an increase in social expenditures. Hence, their remedy is that tax laws should be changed so that all surplus company income is distributed to the shareholders, coupled with more aggressive anti-trust laws and strict enforcement of property legislation. Like Friedman, they call for substantial curbs on managerial freedom within companies. This view is shared by Rostow[11] who proposes that directors should be legally required to concentrate on their primary role as sole trustees of the economic interests of their shareholders.

Two points are worth noting, which will be returned to later. First, the distinction between corporate social responsibility and corporate governance is not recognised by the above critics. In short, they may reject what was regarded as an unwarranted attack on business activity, but end up by calling for more rigorous corporate governance by imposing more controls over the activities of corporate executives and directors. Secondly, Friedman's attack on corporate social responsibility is not confined to economic grounds but strays into the field of political criticism. Hence, Mulligan[12] notes that:

> Friedman's most emphatic language is devoted to his position that the advocates of social responsibility in a free-enterprise system are 'preaching pure and unadulterated socialism'. . . . the doctrine of social responsibility . . . does not differ from the most explicitly collectivist doctrine.

## The rise of business ethics

The rise of business ethics is linked by Lodge[13] to the radical social changes that first occurred in the post-war American way of life, before spreading to Europe and to other parts of the world. From an American perspective, he links the Watergate scandal, which led to the impeachment and resignation of President Nixon, with growing public disillusionment with government. This was followed by the 'disclosure that scores of America's most important corporations had violated the Corrupt Practices Act, making illegal contributions to political campaigns and payoffs to many politicians for presumed favours'. These revelations, in the context of other critical issues mentioned below, reshaped American public opinion leading to the emergence of a new ideology:

- the assassinations of President Kennedy and his Attorney-General brother, Robert;
- disillusionment following the US withdrawal from Vietnam;
- the growing civil rights movement amongst black Americans;
- the assassination of Martin Luther King which resulted in corporations examining their policies on equality, discrimination and affirmative action;
- the rise of the feminist movement which challenged traditional values in corporations on the grounds of sexism and discrimination;
- growing secular interest in ecology and environmental pollution, following the publication of Rachel Carson's books *The Sea Around Us* (1951) and *Silent Spring* (1962);
- greater tolerance of the use of 'soft' drugs by American middle-class intellectuals and college students, due to the increased commercial power of 'the affluent society'[7] and the spread of American pop culture in arts and music;

■ the switch from traditional mass production to electronic computer-aided manufacturing processes with the corresponding reduction and de-skilling of labour and the creation of what the Harvard sociologist, Daniel Bell, identified as 'post-industrial society'.

Lodge[14] concludes that the combined impact of these societal changes has resulted in an emerging new American ideology, which rejects the Puritan work ethic of its founding fathers in favour of one based on a major shift from:

■ individualism to communitarianism (see Chapter 4);
■ exclusive property rights to inclusive membership rights;
■ competitive markets, which determine consumer needs, to a broader societal evaluation of community needs;
■ limited expansion to more extensive planning in the community;
■ scientific specialisation in favour of a holistic utilisation of knowledge.

## Reconciling differences between corporate social responsibility and business ethics

As noted in the Preface, understanding the differences between corporate social responsibility and business ethics is not helped by the reluctance of writers to discuss both subjects. Harvey[15] is an exception, although a clearer distinction could have been made between corporate social responsibility, as concerned with 'the debate about the social role of, especially, large business enterprises' and 'the raised profile in the public mind of business behaviour and the responsibilities of the corporation – in effect to questions of right and wrong – namely business ethics'. Mahoney[16] defines business ethics as:

> the application of ordinary human ethical values or principles in the conduct of business, . . . business ethics is no different from other branches of applied ethics, such as medical . . . social . . . or sexual ethics, which all submit various fields of human behaviour to ethical and moral analysis and evaluation.

He adds that a concern for 'social responsibility' is a second characteristic of contemporary business ethics after considering the conditions under which modern business is conducted. The growing conviction that the two subjects were introduced at different historical periods to investigate similar areas of enquiry is supported by Lewis[17], whose principal component approach towards defining business ethics is summarised below.

Lewis identified 38 concepts in over 250 articles containing definitions of business ethics. To save space, only the 10 most common concepts or practical activities which appeared in two-thirds of these definitions, are listed in Table 1.1. It is worth noting that the same concepts are also used in US definitions of corporate social responsibility. This is hardly surprising as De George[18] notes that business ethics generally involves four principles:

■ the application of general ethical principles to particular business cases or practices;
■ consideration of the *metaethical* aspects of business ethics, which entail deciding whether the moral terms used to describe individual actions can be applied to collectivities such as profit-seeking and public sector organisations;

**Table 1.1 The ten most common concepts used in business ethics definitions**

| Concept | Frequency (%) |
|---|---|
| Rules, standards or codes governing individual behaviour at work | 16 |
| Moral principles developed in the course of a lifetime | 8 |
| What is right and wrong in specific work situations | 8 |
| Telling the truth | 7 |
| A belief in social responsibility | 6 |
| What is fair and above board | 5 |
| Honesty | 5 |
| The Golden Rule | 4 |
| Sets of values | 3 |
| What is in accord with one's religious beliefs | 3 |
| **Total** | **65** |

Source: P.V. Lewis, Defining 'Business Ethics': Like nailing jello to a wall, *Journal of Business Ethics*, 4, 1985, 377–83.

- analysis of the moral presuppositions of business which operate within an economic system (i.e. capitalism) that has been transformed by the prevailing culture in various industrialised nations, to provide different perspectives on how non-moral, instrumental aspects such as property, competition and efficiency should be evaluated;
- a pluralist perspective on business ethics has emerged in response to macro-moral issues that may have to be addressed nationally and internationally. This means that enquiries often have to go beyond the field of ethics into other domains of knowledge, such as economics, political science or organisational behaviour, to enable other perspectives to be taken into consideration.

## The case against business ethics

Carr[19] attacks business ethics using arguments based on experience and the analogy of playing poker. Examples are cited of executives who are 'almost compelled, in the interests of their companies or themselves, to practice some form of deception when negotiating with customers, dealers, labour unions, government officials, or even other departments of their companies'. This is because the individual experiences difficulty in adjusting to the rules of the 'business game' and suffers when he has to enact policies 'that challenge his conception of himself as an ethical man'. To succeed in the business game, he must play to win and, if offered from time to time, 'a choice between certain loss or bluffing within the rules of the game, then if he is not resigned to losing, if he wants to rise in his company and industry, then in such a crisis he will bluff – and bluff hard'.

Carr's comparison of expedient behaviour in business with poker is refuted in Bok's[20] argument against people engaging in such minor deceptions

> that those who begin with white lies can come to resort to more frequent and more serious ones. Because lines are hard to draw, the indiscriminate use of such lies can lead to other deceptive practices. The aggregate harm from a large number of marginally harmful instances may, therefore, be highly undesirable in the end – for liars, those deceived, and honesty and trust more generally.

The latter are discussed in Chapter 6.

Drucker[21] compares business ethics dismissively with medieval casuistry, or the study of the reasoning through which cases of seemingly conflicting duties are resolved often by use of sophistry (i.e. fallacious reasoning), although his criticism appears wider of the mark than Webley's[22] observation that some managers see business ethics as a waste of time, because business is already regulated by law. Consequently, they may also regard the introduction of codes of business ethics as a 'second best' option if an individual's values are acquired during childhood.

The question of the need for business ethics, if business is regulated by law, was addressed by De George[23] who notes that morality is broader than legality, but that not everything that is immoral should be made illegal, since public opinion is not expressed only in law, therefore improper business activities should be challenged in the marketplace, as well as in the ballot box or in the legislature. In short, a pluralist perspective on business ethics is needed because its wide area of application covers related subjects such as economics, politics, law, religion and the other social sciences.

## The rise of corporate governance

The growing importance attached to reappraising the governance of modern businesses was in response to public concern about increases in corporate failures, due to allegations of fraud etc., and the questionably large remuneration 'packages' offered to senior managers often without the approval of shareholders. Charkham[24] and Lorsch and Graff[25] provide helpful descriptive accounts which compare and contrast corporate governance procedures in leading G7 countries.

Setting aside legal questions about the responsibilities of the directors and senior managers of business and other types of organisation, the case for corporate governance has been largely influenced by the spectacular corporate collapses which have occurred in the United States and Britain due to fraud or mismanagement since the 1980s.

### US congressional hearings

Congressional hearings into corporate fraud in the 1980s prompted the *Harvard Business Review* to set up a Working Group on Corporate Governance in 1990. Matters investigated included investors' rights and management accountability, the roles of executive and non-executive directors in both monitoring management's performance and representing shareholders' interests, and matters relating to remuneration and the conditions of employment agreed with managers. The Harvard Working Group's findings were published as a new Compact for Owners and Directors, comprising the following recommendations for shareholders and directors.[26]

■ Directors should evaluate the performance of chief executives regularly to ensure agreed strategies are implemented.

- Evaluations should be carried out by appointed non-executive directors, who should meet at least once per year under an independent chairperson.
- Qualifications of current and prospective board members should be set by directors and communicated to shareholders for approval.
- Board candidates should be screened by non-executive directors and recommended for approval against agreed qualifications.
- Institutional shareholders should see themselves as the owners, and not just as investors, in the company, but should refrain from intruding in the company's day-to-day activities.
- Shareholders should also carry out an independent evaluation of the performance of directors on a regular basis and need to be informed about the company's activities in order to conduct their evaluation effectively.
- Shareholders should also recognise and respect that their only common commitment with each other is the ongoing prosperity of the company.

The Harvard Compact had considerable influence on the main recommendations of the Cadbury Report[27] on 'The Financial Aspects of Corporate Governance', which was mentioned in the Preface, and received a lukewarm reception in *The Times*, *The Independent* and *Financial Times*' editorials on 28 May 1992. The main recommendations appear in Box 1.1.

---

**Box 1.1**

## The main recommendations of the Cadbury Committee

1 Boards should have separate audit and remuneration committees made up entirely of independent directors.
2 Audit committees should meet with the external auditors at least once a year and without the presence of executive directors.
3 The full remuneration package of all directors, including performance-related elements, should be disclosed in annual reports.
4 Directors' terms of office should run for no more than three years without shareholders' approval for reappointment.
5 Companies should make funds available to non-executive directors who wish to obtain independent advice on governance-related issues.
6 The board must meet regularly.
7 The board should have a formal schedule of matters for consideration.
8 Independent directors should be appointed for specified terms.
9 Independent directors should be appointed through a formal process.
10 Independent directors should have a standing outside the company which ensures that their views carry weight.
11 Independent directors should be fully independent and free from links with the company other than fees and shareholdings.
12 Fees for independent directors should reflect the time they spend on company business.
13 There should be an accepted division at the head of the company, which will ensure a balance of power and authority such that no one individual has unfettered powers of decision. Where the chairman is also chief executive, there should be a strong independent element on the board with an independent leader.

---

## The case for corporate governance

Research by Stiles and Taylor[28] on six key guidelines in the Cadbury Code found that 73 per cent of the largest 100 UK companies were conforming with at least four of these six compliance criteria. Surprisingly, some prestigious and successful British companies were found to have implemented only one or two of the criteria, while one had introduced none. All told, an estimated 93 per cent of British companies have complied with the Cadbury guidelines, possibly to avoid stronger legislation being implemented by the government, although the Department of Trade and Industry regards self-regulation as the most effective method of achieving effective governance procedures.

In defending the Cadbury recommendations, Stiles and Taylor argue that the leadership task in governance must be stressed if good practice is to become secure in companies. Whilst accepting that the benefits of tighter internal controls will not improve profitability, they note Sir Adrian Cadbury's comment that 'if companies which have gone down the drain [are examined], none of them have the kind of [governance] structure we have recommended'.

## The case against corporate governance

The main criticisms of the Cadbury Code are that it cannot guarantee good business conduct, has little impact on company performance, and no influence on earnings per share, does not encourage enterprise, and would not have prevented the collapse of the Maxwell companies or similar financial scandals. As to the criticism that the Cadbury Code does not encourage enterprise, the latter fell outside the remit of the Committee, which was required to examine financial aspects of corporate governance, and concentrate on issues relating to accountability, disclosure and monitoring procedures. To dismiss the Report as neglecting to encourage enterprise is simply to aim at the wrong target. Sir Adrian Cadbury responded to the specific charge that the Code should have been robust enough to prevent the scandalous collapse of the Maxwell group of companies, reminding the British business community that

> the sad fact . . . is that public warnings were given by the Board of Trade reporting in 1971, yet shareholders were prepared of their own volition to support the company. Directors were prepared to go on its board and bankers were prepared to lend to it.[29]

Other arguments against corporate governance came from those who thought the recommendations intrude too much on the primary relationship between shareholders, as owners, and directors, as their agents. Criticism ranged from statements about corporate governance 'running out of control' by Sir Stanley Kalms[30], chairman of Dixons, the high street retailers, to more detailed research by Clarke, Conyon and Peck[31], whose survey of 342 chairmen of 1,200 London-based companies obtained views on accountability, business prosperity, rewarding non-executive directors, and relations with shareholders.

Their main finding was that almost three-quarters of respondents agreed that the corporate governance debate in the UK has been too preoccupied with issues of accountability rather than business prosperity; with only 8 per cent of respondents disagreeing with this verdict. A further 43 per cent agreed that details of remuneration disclosure in UK annual reports had led to a 'ratcheting-up' effect on directors' pay. This is confirmed in a separate study by Ezzamel and Watson[32] which concluded that public disclosure of pay levels is more likely to result in executives paid below the market rate having their remuneration increased, while those receiving above the prevailing market rate are less likely to have their compensation reduced.

## Integrating corporate social responsibility, business ethics and corporate governance

Sheridan and Kendall[33] are also critical of the Cadbury Report's recommendations for not going far enough. After dismissing the Report as 'a mouse roars', they propose to widen the definition of corporate governance, as a system of structuring, operating and controlling a company to achieve the following five objectives:

- fulfil the long-term strategic goals of the owners;
- consider and care for the interests of employees, past, present and future;
- take account of the needs of the environment and the local community;
- work to maintain excellent relations with customers and suppliers; and
- maintain proper compliance with all the applicable and regulatory requirements under which the company is carrying out its activities.

The five objectives in their 'better definition' of corporate governance expand the Cadbury recommendations to give company directors and senior managers additional responsibility for specific corporate social responsibility and business ethics issues raised by Nader *et al.* as aspects of corporate social responsibility, and by De George as legitimate concerns of business ethics.

These topics are incorporated in Box 1.2, which is an amended version of the list proposed by Webley[22] for inclusion in codes of business ethics by UK companies.

| Box 1.2 | Integrated list of corporate social responsibility, business ethics and corporate governance topics |
| --- | --- |

| | |
| --- | --- |
| ■ personal ethics | ■ organisational responsibilities |
| ■ workers' rights | ■ workers' responsibilities |
| ■ discrimination | ■ relations with trade unions |
| ■ codes of conduct | ■ 'whistleblowing' by employees |
| ■ consumer safety | ■ computer data and privacy |
| ■ accounting practices | ■ industrial espionage |
| ■ insider dealing | ■ directors' responsibilities |
| ■ relations with shareholders | ■ executive compensation |
| ■ takeovers and mergers | ■ global business |
| ■ company 'perks' | ■ corrupt practices |
| ■ environmental protection | ■ energy utilisation |
| ■ famine and Third World countries | ■ animal rights |

Sheridan and Kendall's proposed five objectives of corporate governance raise a fundamental question about the role of company directors in UK listed companies. Namely, if it is argued that corporate social responsibility and business ethics issues do not fall within a broader definition of corporate governance, then who is accountable in UK quoted companies? Furthermore, a failure to address these issues by company directors and senior managers could lead to further legislation being introduced as governments respond to public concern about violations of current civil liberties, consumer and environmental protection policies.

The latter issue is likely to take on added importance if the London stock exchange merges with either its Swedish or German counterparts. In Germany, for example, Charkham[24] notes that a different mode of corporate governance prevails than that adopted in Britain. Furthermore, Giddens[34] is surely correct when he states that globalisation is not a force of nature because 'States, business corporations and other groups have actively promoted its advance'. If this is the case, and national economies begin to converge more rapidly, new ways of adapting to the contrasting attitudes towards corporate social responsibility and business ethics matters in different nations and cultures will begin to preoccupy the directors and senior managers of UK companies.

The Cadbury Report was followed by the Greenbury Committee Report on 'Directors' Remuneration' (1995)[35] which was unenthusiastically received by the Institute of Directors and City analysts. More criticism followed after *The Economist*[36] revealed that the Committee chairman had failed to implement a key recommendation in the Cadbury Report, by relinquishing one of his dual roles as chairman and chief executive of the British retailer, Marks & Spencer Plc. In addition, generous remuneration packages for the main board directors had been approved prior to the company's recent run of disappointing financial results. A further report summarising codes of best practice in corporate governance adopted in various countries outside the UK, was published as an interim document by the Hampel Committee, under the chairmanship of Sir Ronald Hampel, former chairman of ICI, in 1997 before a final report appeared in 1998.[37]

## Synopsis

- The three subjects, corporate social responsibility, business ethics and corporate governance, have developed separately, yet the central argument of this chapter is that they are more alike than different and should be integrated as a single academic domain.
- The origins of modern corporate social responsibility date back about a hundred years and led to US government action under the Sherman Anti-Trust Act against the monopolistic practices of the Standard Oil company trusts.
- New corporate social responsibility legislation was proposed by Nader *et al.* in 1977 who noted that the failure to include business corporations in the American Constitution allowed them to expand in size, power and pervasive influence, to become massive global corporations which increasingly behave like unelected private governments.

- The case against corporate social responsibility is advanced by Friedman who argues that it distracts managers from their primary task of maximising shareholder profits and also undermines the foundations of a free society.
- The rise of business ethics reflected a shift in social values which occurred in the 1960s and led to public demands for US companies to eradicate policies that violated civil rights, consumer protection and environmental pollution, etc. both nationally and abroad.
- Critics of business ethics point to its unrealistic aims which fail to recognise that individuals may have to 'cut corners' if they are to succeed in a competitive environment. Ethical codes in business are also a 'second best' option if an individual's values are acquired during childhood, since business is already regulated by law.
- Acceptance of corporate governance recommendations has resulted in improved accountability of directors, more transparent auditing and remuneration provisions, increasing responsibilities for independent directors, and a division of the roles of chairman and chief executive implemented in most UK quoted companies which have implemented the Cadbury, Greenbury and Hampel Committees' recommendations.
- Critics of corporate governance argue that it results in accountability being given priority over business prosperity, does not guarantee good business conduct, has little impact on company performance, fails to increase earnings per share, and has not prevented the collapse of companies as a result of financial scandals.
- Other critics argue that corporate governance requirements should include corporate social responsibility and business ethics issues which, if not addressed by company directors and senior managers, could lead to further legislation as governments respond to public concern about civil liberties, consumer and environmental protection.

## Review and discussion questions

1 What reasons would you give for or against the argument that corporate social responsibility, business ethics and corporate governance should be studied as related subjects under the same academic 'umbrella'?

2 What arguments would you give for deciding for or against the Friedman statement that the sole responsibility of management is to maximise profits for the shareholders within the law?

3 After considering the case put forward by Lodge for the rise of business ethics in the USA, what reasons would you suggest have influenced the introduction of this subject in the UK?

4 What reasons would you give for supporting or opposing the argument that the brief of the Cadbury Committee should have been confined only to examining financial aspects of corporate governance in the UK?

# Case study
# Keeping Auntie on the straight and narrow!

'Auntie' is the affectionate name by which the BBC has been known for most of its history. This is because the BBC, founded in 1924, led the way internationally in establishing standards of respectable and reliable public service broadcasting under the stern, paternalistic leadership of its first director-general, John, later Lord, Reith.

In the changed social environment of the late 1990s, the 11 members of the executive committee responsible for running the BBC were finding it more difficult to provide relevant programmes for an increasingly fragmented audience under a mounting barrage of public criticism. The *Daily Mail*, which purports to speak for middle England, asked in an editorial at the time: 'Is there anyone who seriously believes that the BBC is offering the quality that it once did?' Even *The Times* took the unprecedented step of including successive leaders which opposed the recent appointment of its latest director-general, Mr Greg Dyke. The paper's stance was supported by the leader of the official opposition party, Mr William Hague, who questioned Mr Dyke's appointment on the grounds that he had once made a substantial political donation to the ruling Labour Party and could therefore not exercise neutrality in carrying out his responsibilities.

The problems confronting the BBC precede Greg Dyke's appointment, however, and are a direct consequence of a change in strategy introduced during the period when the outgoing director-general, Sir John Birt, was in office. These have led to public criticism of the BBC including questions about whether the government should continue to sanction its traditional source of revenue, namely, the £100-plus television licence fee that the British public pays annually for turning on their TV sets and radios. Critics like Diana Coyle[38] regard this fee as a 'poll tax' which people cannot avoid without risk of prosecution.

The question that irks most critics is the apparent lack of public accountability of the BBC executive committee which is formally responsible to an independent Board of Governors, made up of members of the so-called 'great and the good' of British society. In practice, the control exercised by the governors appears to be more at 'arm's length' than would be found in a profit-seeking media company that had implemented the Cadbury guidelines on corporate governance. Criticism of the BBC falls under the following headings.

**Executive pay awards**

High executive pay awards appear to have damaged staff morale within the corporation. For example, Coyle notes: 'You pay their salaries (and pay them rather well)', before posing the question, 'But are the BBC top brass worth it?' The facts are clear enough. The BBC has an annual income from television licence fees of over £2 billion. It employs about 23,000 people who are responsible to an executive board. The board is paid over £3 million annually in salaries and awarded itself increases of between 12.6 and 23 per cent in 1999. One executive committee member received a

£50,000 'golden hello' on joining the BBC in 1998 to run its commercial activities. Another executive also received a £19,000 long-service 'loyalty' award in 1998, as though he was likely to join a rival organisation after 25 years' service with the BBC.

The majority of employees received average increases of approximately 2 per cent during the same period. These dissatisfied employees were already unhappy with the outcome of the BBC's plan, introduced in the late 1980s and early 1990s to save national insurance and pension payments, which required staff to accept freelance contracts. This policy was introduced without first taking legal advice on the future tax implications for employees and it has since been challenged by the Inland Revenue who have forced the BBC to withdraw the scheme. The climbdown has embittered lower-paid employees, who have lost long-service and pension rights during the period when the policy was in place which they can ill afford, unlike executive committee members on far higher salaries; and a legal challenge is under consideration.

**A lack of public accountability**

A lack of public accountability is apparently condoned by the Board of Governors. For example, falling TV and radio ratings occurred in 1998/1999 due to increased competition, which raises questions about how the executive committee could justify allocating its members such attractive pay awards. Leadership at the BBC also appears to have vacillated between its traditional public service commitments, which have been enshrined in its corporate charter since the days of Lord Reith. Yet there are public demands for more mainstream sitcoms, soap operas and game shows alongside its flagship programmes like the *News* and internationally praised programmes like *Panorama* and *The Money Programme*.

Added to this demand, the BBC is finding that its two TV channels, five national radio networks, 40 local radio services and 24-hour news offerings are increasingly expensive to run. Hence, deciding where and how to economise is a difficult task when the average viewer watches over 25 hours of television each week, but only spends two hours per week tuned into BBC programmes. More cuts appear unavoidable but what irritates critics is that these should be accompanied by a fall in the quality of the service. For example, the audience share of BBC1, the main BBC channel, recently fell below 30 per cent for the first time, accompanied by the loss of popular sports programmes originally launched by the BBC such as Test Match cricket coverage, Formula One Grand Prix car races, England Five Nation rugby matches, and highlights of English Premier League games in its long-running *Match of the Day* programme. These sporting events have all been lost to higher bids from competing commercial TV and satellite services. These and other losses have prompted critics to question whether the licence fee is too high a price to pay for a poorer quality TV without commercials.

**A failure to fulfil its public service role**

There are also increasing signs that the BBC is unable to fulfil its public service role to all sections of Britain's pluralistic society. Critics argue that this is because the BBC has lost its way under its outgoing director-general, whom they insist has abandoned its traditional public service role to engage in a loss-making competition for viewers with the richer commercial channels. At the same time, expensive BBC networks have been expanded internationally. In 1997, for example, four cable and satellite commercial TV channels were launched. A few months later, a 24-hour news channel was inaugurated to compete with CNN and Sky News. A costly Internet site has since been developed and partnerships have also been established with US broadcasting networks to sell popular programmes from BBC archives around the globe. The short-term problem with this strategy is that British viewers perceive that the quality of programmes has fallen to pay for this expansion and they object to millions being spent on developing these global networks without any benefits being seen or heard on TV and radio networks in Britain.

The BBC executive committee insists that it is listening to complaints but staunchly defends its global diversification strategy on the grounds that profit-making ventures will eventually enable the BBC to offer more choice to its licence payers. In unveiling its new 'millennium' programme schedules, the BBC confirmed that it would withdraw from the ratings war with its commercial rival, ITV, and would focus more on providing educational programmes and high quality drama in future. Critics insist that the strategic and financial policies of the executive committee are still not transparent enough or accountable to licence payers in the same way that the directors of a profit-making organisation are responsible to shareholders. They argue that it is time for the executive committee to lead a less privileged, sheltered existence.

On 27 May 2000 *The Times* reported that the outgoing director-general, Lord Birt, was to receive almost £400,000 in cash and benefits for leaving the BBC before retirement age. The payment was controversial because the former director-general's departure was his own choice and was agreed well in advance by him and the corporation. Under his contract arrangements, however, he was entitled to a compensation payment of one year's salary, about £320,000, plus a pension benefit equivalent to £50,000, which would increase his pension to about £115,000 a year when he reaches retirement age at 60. A spokesman for the broadcasting union, Bectu, condemned the severance payment, pointing out that 'John Birt wasn't made redundant, he resigned'. He added: 'There are 60,000 people working for the BBC on fixed-term, one-year contracts who are barred from entering the pension scheme, even though some of them may have five years' service, all on fixed-term contracts.' The BBC said that the 'package was intended to make up for the fact that unlike executives in private companies, he received no share options'. Lord Birt joined the BBC from ITV and missed the LWT share bonanza.

The government has recently applied the principle which requires public sector executives to be more directly accountable to the UK taxpayer. Even the Governor of the Bank of England is required to give a public explanation if agreed inflation targets are not met. Government-approved regulators of the privatised gas, electricity and water companies have powers to block executive pay awards if published performance targets are not achieved. Critics question why similar regulation has yet to be extended to the BBC. At the time of writing the government is reviewing public broadcasting policy in Britain. Meanwhile, critics have enquired why the BBC Board of Governors is not more active in monitoring executive committee decisions on controversial issues such as global diversification, public service broadcasting, programme quality standards, executive remuneration awards, and the contractual arrangements and employment benefits of its non-executive employees.

**Questions**

1 As a BBC governor, what steps would you take to ensure that effective corporate governance is introduced at the BBC before the proposed government review of public broadcasting in Britain is published (in 2001)?

2 What reasons would you give for (a) supporting or (b) opposing the view that the BBC should maintain its expensive public service role, assuming that a rising amount would have to be paid for out of an increased licence fee?

## Notes and references

1. See McEwan, T., for a short treatment of these subjects in Mullins, L.J., *Management and Organisational Behaviour*, 5th edn, Financial Times Pitman Publishing, 1999, 142–61.
2. Josephson, M., *The Robber Barons*, 2nd edn, New York, Harvest/HBJ Books, 1962.
3. Hofstadter, R., What Happened to the Antitrust Movement? in *The Business Establishment*, ed. E.F. Cheit, Wiley, 1964, 113–51.
4. Tarbell, I., History of Standard Oil Company, New York, *McClure's Magazine*, 1904.
5. Nader, R., Green, M. and Seligman, J., The Corporate Impact, in Steiner, G.A. and Steiner, J.F., *Issues in Business and Society*, 2nd edn, New York, Random House, 1977, 22–35.
6. Berle, A.A. and Means, G.C., *The Modern Corporation and Private Property*, New York, Macmillan, 1932.
7. Galbraith, J.G., The Emerging Public Corporation, *Business and Society Review*, 1972, Spring (1), 54–6.
8. Fortune 500, *Forbes Magazine Supplement*, New York, 26 April 1999, 86–156; and Rugman, A.M. and Hodgetts, R.M., *International Business: A strategic management approach*, New York, McGraw-Hill, 1995, Appendix 2F, 59.
9. Friedman, M., The Social Responsibility of Business is to Increase its Profits, *New York Times Magazine*, 13 September 1970.
10. Kelso, L.D. and Adler, M.J., *The Capitalist Manifesto*, New York, Random House, 1958.
11. Rostow, E.V., To Whom and for What Ends is Corporate Management Responsible?, in *The Corporation and Modern Society*, Harvard University Press, 1959.
12. Mulligan, T., A Critique of Milton Friedman's Essay 'The Social Responsibility of Business is to Increase Profits', *Journal of Business Ethics*, 1986, 5, 265–9.
13. Lodge, G.C., Business and the Changing Society, in Steiner, G.A. and Steiner, J.F., *Issues in Business and Society*, 2nd edn, New York, Random House, 1977, 132–52.
14. Lodge, G.C., *The New American Ideology*, New York, Knopf, 1979.
15. Harvey, B., ed., Business Ethics: A European approach, London, Prentice Hall, 1994, 3–5.
16. Mahoney, J., Business Ethics, in *International Encyclopaedia of Business and Management*, ed. M. Warner, London, Routledge, 1996, vol. 1, 474–82.
17. Lewis, P.V., Defining 'Business Ethics': Like nailing jello to a wall, *Journal of Business Ethics*, 4, 1985, 377–83.
18. De George, R., *Moral Issues in Business*, New York, Macmillan, 1995, 17–18.
19. Carr, A.Z., Is Business Bluffing Ethical?, in Steiner, G.A. and Steiner, J.F., *Issues in Business and Society*, 2nd edn, New York, Random House, 1977, 236–47.
20. Bok, S., *Lying: Moral choice in public and private life*, New York, Pantheon Books, 1978, 19, 31.
21. Drucker, P., Ethical Chic, *Forbes*, 14 September 1981, 160–73.
22. Webley, S., *Codes of Business Ethics: Why companies should develop them – and how*, London, Institute of Business Ethics, 1993.
23. De George, R.T., Moral Issues in Business, in *Ethics, Free Enterprise and Public Policy*, (ed.) R.T. De George and J.R. Pilcher, New York, Oxford University Press, 1978.
24. Charkham, J., *Keeping Good Company*, Oxford University Press, 1995.

25. Lorsch, J. and Graff, S.K., Corporate Governance, in *International Encyclopaedia of Business and Management*, ed. M. Warner, London, Routledge, 1996, vol. 1, 772–81.

26. The Working Group on Corporate Governance: A new compact for owners and directors, *Harvard Business Review*, July–August 1991, 141–3.

27. Cadbury, A., *Report of the Committee on the Financial Aspects of Corporate Governance*, London, Gee, 1992.

28. Stiles, P. and Taylor, B., Benchmarking Corporate Governance: The impact of the Cadbury Code, *Long Range Planning*, vol. 26, no. 5, 1993, 61–71.

29. Cadbury, A., in Stiles, P. and Taylor, B., ibid., p. 69.

30. Kalms, S., A Guide to Corporate Governance, in *Mastering Management*, Financial Times Pitman Publishing, 1997.

31. Clarke, R.N., Conyon, M.J. and Peck, S.I., Corporate Governance and Directors' Remuneration, etc., *Business Strategy Review*, 9, 4, 1998, 21–30.

32. Ezzamel, M. and Watson, R., Market Comparison Earnings and the Bidding-Up of Executive Cash Compensation: Evidence from the United Kingdom, *Academy of Management Journal*, 41, 1998, 221–31.

33. Sheridan, T. and Kendall, N., *Corporate Governance*, Financial Times Pitman Publishing 1992, ch. 7.

34. Giddens, A., *The Third Way: The renewal of social democracy*, Oxford, Polity Press, 1998, 33.

35. Greenbury, R., *Directors' Remuneration: Report of a study group chaired by Sir Richard Greenbury*, London, Gee, 1995.

36. Face Value, *The Economist*, 21 November 1998, 94.

37. Hampel, R., *Committee on Corporate Governance: Final report*, London, Gee, 1998.

38. Coyle, D., Nice Work if You Can Get it, *The Tuesday Review, The Independent*, 13 July 1999, 13.

# 2 Moral reasoning and applied ethics

*When a person goes from a protected home into the stress of competitive business and finds that moral standards which apply in one do not hold in the other . . . if (s)he tries to face the conflict in thought, (s)he will search for a reasonable principle by which to decide where the right really lies. In so doing, (s)he enters into the domain of moral theory.*

J. Dewey and J. Tufts, *Ethics*, New York, Holt, 1932, p. 173

### Learning objectives

After reading this chapter you should be able to:

■ explain the meaning of moral reasoning and its importance in individual moral behaviour based on valid moral arguments;

■ explore the differences between subjective and objective morality and the relevance of excusing conditions and other factors affecting individual moral responsibility.

■ consider whether different levels of moral development occur in males and females, and examine some of the implications for the business community;

■ consider the different meanings of morality as a basis for exploring the myth of amoral business;

## Introduction

Moral reasoning is probably rarely discussed at work yet is just as important as keeping accurate records. Most of the latter are computed automatically anyway, but this has not prevented profitable businesses collapsing because management failed to act in an open, morally responsible way. Companies normally employ people whose moral development ensures that tasks are performed according to approved procedures, even if company auditing did not exist. Yet little is known about individual moral reasoning and research into its development is also controversial. Similarly, whether moral behaviour by individuals can be aggregated into meaningful notions of group or organisational morality is also open to question. Without such assumptions, however, conventional morality would probably be replaced by the myth of amoral business. Ethical strategic decision making by managers would increasingly be undermined by groupthink behaviour, probably leading to more business scandals and a further loss of public confidence in company management.

## Moral reasoning

### False reasoning

It is possible to distinguish between simple true and false arguments without the need to study formal logic. The reader will quickly recognise the false 'reasoning' of the fictitious professor, whose response to a friend's concern about his heavy drinking was to record his intake over five consecutive evenings. On Monday, he drank whisky and soda water; brandy and soda water on Tuesday; rum and soda water on Wednesday; gin and soda water on Thursday; and vodka and soda water on Friday. Consequently, on the Saturday, he took his friend's advice and gave up drinking soda water.[1]

The professor's argument is flawed because it draws the wrong conclusion from previously stated information, or premises. The following argument contains two conclusions to show the differences between valid and invalid arguments:

> P1. A person who is a father is a male;
> P2. Harry is a father;
> C1. Therefore, Harry is a male; *or*
> C2. Therefore, Harry is *not* a male.

The premises P1 and P2 limit what can appear in the conclusion. Hence, if P1 and P2 are true, then the conclusion C1 is also true. This is a *valid* argument. If both P1, P2 and the conclusion C2 are true, a contradiction occurs, since these conflicting statements cannot all be true at the same time. This is, therefore, an *invalid* argument.

### Definition of moral reasoning

De George[2] recommends that a similar approach is adopted in moral reasoning which may be defined as 'arguments containing moral judgements, or other statements, about the actions of a person, a group, or an organisation, in their conclusions'. For example:

*Moral judgements or statements about a person*:

> P1. Mary is a regular churchgoer;
> P2. She would not vote for an atheist politician;
> C. Therefore, Mary is a good woman.

There are several inconsistencies in the above argument. First, it cannot be assumed that Mary would not vote for an atheist politician because she is a regular churchgoer. Secondly, more information is needed before it can be concluded that she is a good woman. Finally, any suggestion that an atheistic politician, who presumably does not attend church, may not be a good person, is also invalid. Examples of moral judgements about group activity and organisational behaviour follow.

*Moral judgements or assertions about a group activity*:

> P1. Any action that breaks the law is morally wrong;
> P2. Civil protests by any minority group break the law;
> C1. Therefore, civil protests by any minority group are morally wrong.

*Moral judgements or assertions about organisational behaviour*:

P1.  KornFlak Ltd produces good quality cereals and claims to be seriously committed to protecting the environment;

P2.  Over 90 per cent of KornFlak's packaging is made from recycled materials;

C2.  Therefore, KornFlak Ltd's assurance that 'people and the environment receive good value from its products' is valid.

The P1 premises in both cases declare a moral principle. The P2 premises could be checked to ensure these statements are factual in each case. Finally, moral judgements are included in both conclusions. In the case of C1, the conclusion is invalid and may be accepted or rejected by different people with contrasting views about civil protests and minority groups. In the second example, the conclusion, C2, is probably valid but more information is required about KornFlak's environmental protection policy. The statement may be welcomed by those who think any action is better than none at all, but rejected as a public relations exercise by those in favour of more rigorous legislation. The point to note here is that this sort of argument is usually easier to accept or reject as valid in examples dealing with individual moral reasoning. When similar arguments are extended to groups or organisations, made up of aggregates of individual viewpoints, 'exceptions to the rule' are more likely to cast doubt on the validity of any conclusions.

## Different meanings of morality

The word morality has different meanings in different contexts as the following three examples indicate:

- Morality refers to *a set of principles or standards* in which a person may believe.
- Morality raises the notion of *sincerity, consistency or goodness*, in the sense that a moral person's behaviour is influenced by certain principles or standards.
- Morality also describes the *degree of conformity* with a set of principles, in the sense that an individual may pray at a chosen place of worship on a particular day.

The fact that morality has three meanings is further complicated by the use of first person and third person judgements in what is known as *subjective* and *objective* morality.

## Subjective and objective morality

Subjective and objective morality focus on the human tendency to apply dual/double standards in making moral judgements. In first person, or 'subjective' moral judgements, an individual may evaluate or justify an individual action or belief less severely according to his/her conscience. In third person, or 'objective' moral judgements, an individual tends to evaluate the actions or beliefs of others more severely without possessing knowledge of the subjective states of the other person(s). Simple examples of both moral positions are contrasted in Table 2.1.

**Table 2.1 Comparisons between subjective and objective morality**

| Type of morality | Moral action | Immoral action |
|---|---|---|
| **Subjective morality** | I accept a complimentary glass of wine at a party. | I take a few bottles later but tell myself it was not theft. |
| **Objective morality** | I watch a colleague 'fiddle' an expenses claim. | I keep quiet but inform his boss anonymously. |

## Requirements of moral reasoning

De George[2] proposes that valid arguments in moral reasoning should be:

- logical;
- supported by factual evidence, wherever possible;
- derived from valid moral principles.

**Logical argument**    Moral arguments or judgements need to be logical and not based on personal opinion, emotion or sentiment, if the aim is to convince others of their validity.

**Fact-based arguments**    Moral arguments should ultimately relate to human activities in the real world. Supportive information should also refer to actual events or experiences otherwise any evaluation will be invalid. In the KornFlak example above, evaluation of the moral argument may need to reflect the views of experts on the conversion of trees into wood pulp, the packaging industry and recycling costs, and environmental protection legislation.

**Valid moral principles**    Moral judgements also have to be based on standards or principles that stand up to rational scrutiny and criticism if they are to be regarded as valid. That said, and this applies especially to moral judgements about groups and organisations, no universal tests exist for deciding on the validity of moral principles. This means that, ultimately, we make private judgements, although moral philosophers mostly agree that these judgements should only be regarded as valid if they satisfy the following criteria:

- the argument has a clear form;
- it displays consistency;
- it expresses a belief that possesses universality, that is a rational content that is the same if stated by another person (e.g. Spanish people are more excitable than Danes);
- it includes only a priori reasoning, which is not based on past experience;
- it has a conclusion, arrived at rationally rather than in an emotional state of mind.

## The categorical imperative

The above criteria are requirements of the 'categorical imperative', as proclaimed by the German idealist philosopher, Immanuel Kant[3] (1724–1804). He stated that every person possesses an innate will to do good, rather than pursue self-interest, and is therefore bound by a duty to obey universal moral laws according to the principle: 'Act so that . . . you are treating mankind also as an end, and never merely as a means.' This achieved, the categorical imperative urges individuals to: 'Act only according to a maxim by which you can simultaneously will that it [your behaviour] shall become a general law.'

## Rules/principles of a common morality

The influence of Kant's categorical imperative is evident in Gert's[4] 10 ethical rules/ principles of a common morality which follow:

| | |
|---|---|
| 1 Don't kill. | 6 Don't deceive. |
| 2 Don't cause pain. | 7 Keep your promises. |
| 3 Don't disable. | 8 Don't cheat. |
| 4 Don't deprive of freedom. | 9 Obey the law. |
| 5 Don't deprive of pleasure. | 10 Do your duty. |

An important question is whether Kant's categorical imperative and Gert's ethical rules apply to all human beings, such as young children or those whose powers of reason are impaired through illness or old age? Legal systems around the world generally treat these examples as exceptional cases and apply the law accordingly. But what about other individuals?

## Causal and moral responsibility

It is also clear that despite the problems of deciding what morality means, and distinguishing between its subjective and objective forms, this fails to stop countless people performing what they understand to be numerous moral responsibilities every day. They may do so as parents towards their children, citizens who belong to voluntary organisations, honest employers, reliable employees, or responsible members of professional bodies. As De George[2] notes, in each of these roles, the notion of obligation is expressed by the individual carrying out some assumed or prescribed duties on the basis of being causally responsible for his/her actions, and morally responsible for any act and its consequences. The question is why should any person be required to act differently as a member of an organisation than they ever would away from their working environment as a morally responsible member of the community?

*Causal responsibility*, as De George (p. 87) explains, occurs in the twin concepts of legal and moral responsibility for an action. For example, in a business organisation's hierarchy, a manager may have a legal responsibility for authorising a particular decision, which a supervisor organises, so that operatives eventually carry out a particular activity. Exactly how responsibility is allocated down the three hierarchical levels may be determined in the job specifications of the sets of employees involved. Alternatively, if responsibility is not established in advance and a serious accident occurs, legal responsibility may have to be decided in a court of law.

*Moral responsibility* is assumed to follow the same causal chain as legal responsibility, providing it can be established that each party in the hierarchy knowingly and willingly approved of the action and intentionally wanted to carry it out, or actually did so. Moral responsibility does not apply if one of the parties was forced to approve of, or carry out, the action. Nor does it apply if an individual did not exercise choice and was unaware of what the action entailed, or was unsure what the consequences might be, or did not deliberately act to ensure that the action was implemented. In short, varying levels of knowledge and deliberation may arise which are referred to as excusing conditions.

## Excusing conditions

Excusing conditions refer to any circumstances that reduce, mitigate or eradicate moral responsibility for a particular action. As De George (p. 88) notes, these conditions either prevent the action or make it impracticable; reduce or exclude the availability of required knowledge; or eliminate or reduce the freedom required to carry out the action satisfactorily. In each case, complete moral responsibility is lessened or inapplicable if freedom to choose how to carry out an action is impaired in any way.

For excusing conditions to apply, there should also be no alternatives to the one available; no lack of personal control which might alter the outcome of the action in some way; no external 'pressure', coercion or compulsion to prevent an alternative course of action being taken; and no internal coercion to prevent a person from carrying out an alternative action, which may be due to a clinical condition or an unexpected change in normal behaviour.

## Liability and moral responsibility

Moral responsibility is often regarded as a minefield because it includes concepts other than those of obligation and duty, possibility, knowledge, freedom and choice discussed above. De George (p. 92) presents an extensive list from which liability, accountability and agency are explored below because of their direct relevance to the working environment.

**Liability**
Moral responsibility is influenced by the legal distinction that exists between strict liability, where no excusing conditions are applicable, and limited liability, when the owners or shareholders of a company are liable for any claim on their assets equivalent to the amount of their shares in the organisation. Whether strict liability should ever apply to a limited company is a contentious moral issue in the USA and the UK.

**Accountability**
This is a more complicated concept which stipulates that a person is bound, obliged or willing, if called upon, to give an account of personal responsibility or liability for an action, or to make explicable any involvement in the action. Moral accountability consists of being prepared to give an account of an action carried out by a person either on his/her own behalf or as the agent of another party. As in the example of causal liability above, moral accountability is normally structured at different levels of hierarchical responsibility in most business organisations.

**Agency**

As a sole ownership enterprise expands to employ directors, managers, supervisors and operatives, the organisation increasingly adopts a hierarchical structure with one person acting as the agent of the individual above him/her. Each relationship between two people at different levels in the hierarchy is known as agent responsibility. The two main forms of agency responsibility are *simple agency* and *moral responsibility*. Simple agency occurs in straightforward transactions such as the sale of a house, when an estate agent and a solicitor act as agents for the vendor. Their tasks are bound by a contract that sets out the client's requirements which can result in claims for financial compensation, if broken. In this example, both agents have moral responsibilities to their client, which cannot be evaded simply because they are not acting for themselves, but as agents of their client. The solicitor, for instance, cannot act against his/her own moral or professional standards simply because s/he is the agent of another person (i.e. his/her client).

**Role moral responsibility**

This relationship was discussed above in the example where people carry out different roles at various levels in an organisational hierarchy. The line responsibility of a manager is obviously different from that of an operative, although both have clear moral responsibilities. Assume, for example, that a new policy is approved by a board of directors and communicated to senior management for implementation. The decision is passed down the hierarchy until operatives carry out a policy that contravenes prevailing health and safety legislation, resulting in a serious accident and injury to several employees. The moral implications may be complicated by the senior managers in the hierarchy claiming that they were either absent or doing something else at the time of the accident. Meanwhile, operatives who were present when the accident occurred may insist that they were simply carrying out orders from above. In short, the issue of moral responsibility is in danger of bouncing round the organisation, like a golf ball in a washing machine at full spin.

**The moral hindsight question**

What is in danger of being overlooked in the above example is that several innocent parties were seriously injured, so the issue of role moral responsibility will not go away. To start from this stubborn fact, no amount of delegation of authority can relieve members of the organisation at every level in the hierarchy of some moral responsibility for the consequences of an inept policy. The executives and managers who initiated and approved the policy, together with the supervisors and operatives who implemented their orders, must bear moral responsibility for the accident. As De George points out, doubts about whether different members of the organisation were morally responsible can be settled by a simple response to the 'moral hindsight' question: Would you have authorised the policy, had you been able to witness the consequences of your decision beforehand, or carried out the order had it been left to your own judgement, specialist knowledge and previous experience?

Those who give a negative answer to the moral hindsight question, irrespective of their position in the organisation, are role agents who have to bear some moral responsibility for the action that resulted in the serious accident. Agency and role moral responsibility clearly raise perplexing issues for all members of organisations, not least those who carry out dual roles involving professional responsibilities such as accountants and certified engineers in organisations.

## Levels of moral development

Questions of moral responsibility hinge on the assumption that human beings are capable of moral behaviour in the first place. In a multicultural society, more complicated questions about which version of morality should be used as a benchmark to assess compliance are also important, and are addressed in the following chapters. The immediate aim below is to consider whether individuals within the same culture or society display the same levels of moral development in carrying out their duties and responsibilities as rational human beings. Two Harvard psychologists, Lawrence Kohlberg[5] and Carol Gilligan[6], who investigated this research question in separate studies, reached different conclusions, which created some controversy that still persists in the USA.

### Rationality-based moral development

Kohlberg's research is based on the cognitive development theory in psychology and adopts a functional perspective on ethical behaviour which assumes that:

- individual behaviour is directed by moral beliefs;
- moral beliefs enable individuals to understand and evaluate the behaviour of others.

His research consisted of an 18-year longitudinal study, begun in the late 1950s, of 50 US males from the ages of 10 to 28 years. This research and other studies led Kohlberg to conclude that moral beliefs are obtained in a rational and predictable manner. Shared ethical values occur because individuals use the same rational behaviour to select them, rather than learning them at random from their social environment. Three levels of moral development with two stages at each level are identified by Kohlberg. Each stage corresponds to a set of beliefs about rules and principles that needs to be interpreted and related to received facts, as shown in Box 2.1.

| Box 2.1 | Levels and stages of moral development |
| --- | --- |
| Level I: The preconventional level | Stage 1: reaction to punishment stage <br> Stage 2: reward seeking stage |
| Level II: The conventional level | Stage 1: 'Good boy/nice girl' morality stage <br> Stage 2: The 'law and order' stage |
| Level III: The post-conventional, autonomous or principled level | Stage 1: contract and individual rights <br> Stage 2: rational defence of moral actions stage |

**Level I: preconventional level**

Individuals at Stage 1 are unable fully to understand how rules define and constrain the behaviour of others. They also justify their actions according to the actual consequences on themselves. Most are unable to focus on anything but their own self-interests. Moral judgements are made on the basis of ignoring the interests of family members and friends and 'right' acts are those that escape punishment. At Stage 2, the importance of cooperation and reciprocity is grasped as subjects slowly learn that avoiding punishment does not yield the higher benefits of cooperative behaviour. A basic form of cost–benefit analysis behaviour occurs. Family and friends are viewed instrumentally in terms of any delayed gratification resulting in a reward large enough to compensate for the immediate loss and smaller immediate reward.

**Level II: conventional level**

Individuals learn how institutions, such as families and governments, apply rules to bind individuals into cohesive groups. Right acts are expressed by individuals keeping or breaking these rules. Self-sacrifice of rewards is recognised and evaluated in terms of the resulting benefits to the group, which is viewed as morally superior to other groups. At Stage 1, right acts comply with rules that enhance the good of the group and receive approval from those in authority. At Stage 2, the individual's moral orientation extends beyond the immediate small group to focus on a larger institution such as a country. Loyalty to the leader (e.g. The Queen) and compliance with the laws of the land are viewed as a moral development of similar behaviour to that shown to the family in Stage 1.

**Level III: post-conventional level**

Individuals are able to accept or reject wider universal moral standards and their impartiality, common to Stages 1 and 2, is replaced by a moral detachment that regards all human beings as of equal value. Individuals also consciously reformulate their views on institutional values, which are regarded as social constructions for the first time. By identifying these core institutional values, they seek to adapt institutions to meet new needs, etc., of society, believing that if enough people act similarly, institutions change accordingly. At Stage 1, right acts and policies that enhance the well-being of those affected in an equitable way may also be distinguished, as the individual recognises that all the institutions, which inspired loyalty at Level II, can behave unjustly and loyalty to rules and groups is conditional on a respect for human beings being maintained.

At Stage 2, the individual rejects the good of all as a moral standard, in favour of right acts that respect the universal principle of human dignity, as previously held loyalties to laws and groups are rejected. Kohlberg accepted that not all individuals achieve all three levels of moral development. Hence, one individual may have advanced to the third level, as a second person is at the first level, and so on. This variability complicates the study of moral development but has the benefit of allowing one individual's level of moral development to be compared with those of other people.

## Care-based moral development

Kohlberg's model has since been challenged by Carol Gilligan, who found three levels of moral reasoning based on care, similar in structure to Kohlberg's three levels of moral reasoning, which she states fail to show how women take moral decisions. She provides evidence that about one-third of women took these decisions based on care and compassion. Here, a care perspective on moral behaviour emphasises personal relationships, responsibility and care. This is in contrast with Kohlberg's model which interprets morality development in terms of individuality, rules and rights. According to Gilligan, women place more emphasis on relationships, caring roles and responsibility for others. This is in contrast to males, who are more influenced by principles of justice, abstract rules and a need to adopt an 'impartial' viewpoint.

**Level I**
**differences**

Individuals at Kohlberg's and Gilligan's Level I, respectively, both show the same behaviour but they interpret this self-interest differently. Kohlberg's research shows that individuals use institutions and rules to advance their self-interest by punishing or benefiting from others. Gilligan found that individual self-interest led to relationships which ward off loneliness and offer the prospect of friendship.

**Level II**
**differences**

At Level II, individuals in both studies relied on institutions to define right and wrong moral behaviour. Care-oriented individuals in the Gilligan study showed more concern about how these institutions structured relations amongst members compared with those in Kohlberg's study who were concerned with rights and duties.

**Level III**
**differences**

At Level III, women in the Gilligan study viewed care reasoning in terms of mutual care, at least when participants are equals in the care relationship, which some women developed to the point that their own interests were neglected and they could no longer help others. Gilligan's Level III findings also indicated that the majority of women regard non-violence and compassion as universal standards whereas Kohlberg's findings reveal that males took fairness, justice and the good of all as universal standards.

## Similarities between the studies

Despite the above differences, significant similarities between the two studies include the following:

- agreement that at the first level of moral reasoning, individuals focus on themselves;
- at the second level, attention switches to institutions and groups; and
- at the third level, individuals focus on universal standards to evaluate their own moral judgements. They also examine the roles, rules and principles underpinning institutions. Both sets adopt new strategies to cope with conflicts in an institutional context but retain successful beliefs and strategies as part of their moral development.

Critics have tended to focus on differences rather than similarities between these studies of moral development as the former are regarded as controversial by those who doubt they can be reconciled. For example, in an organisational context, differences have been used to justify the 'glass ceiling' in corporations which, historically, has prevented women from reaching the most senior positions in commerce and industry. (See Chapter 9 for further discussion of this topic.)

## The legal and moral status of organisations

Moral responsibility has so far been considered from the standpoint of the individual. This is because there is less uncertainty about issues of individual moral responsibility than when moral standards are applied to organisations. Argandoña[7] notes that companies operate within a legal and institutional framework that helps or hinders their activities. The latter are governed by regulations, codes, and customs and practices created over time by society, within a legal framework created by the state to ensure the consistency and legitimacy of these norms and regulations.

Laws which do not abuse individual freedom and are applied in a consistent and humane way are also morally binding on the individual because the aim of the company is also to attain the good of society and of its members. Since companies also contribute to this common good through economic means they, or their agents (i.e. managers), must also obey the law. The multitude of possible legal relationships between companies and other members of society is so complex, that separate study is required. It is covered under business, company and employment law on undergraduate business education courses.

Suffice it to say, therefore, that in the socioeconomic infrastructure in which companies operate, the legal framework created by the state varies from country to country, although a long process of harmonisation is under way in the member countries of the EU. As a general rule, the relationship between morality and the law, which gives legal meaning to corporate responsibility when applied to organisations, is defined in contracts. These are regulated by employment law as they refer to formal relationships with individuals, and by commercial law as they apply to relationships with other institutions. These legal relationships may refer to property rights; relationships covered by contracts between buyers and suppliers of goods and services; the distribution of information as in the media and its compliance with agreed standards; and market structures which eradicate cartels to ensure free and fair competition.

## Conventional morality and groupthink

**Conventional morality**

A member of a group in an organisation might describe conventional morality in an offhand way as 'the way we do things around here'. This simple statement implies that considerable agreement exists about how the organisation's designated activities are being carried out by its members. Several other assumptions can be made, otherwise the way things are done may suddenly be subjected to considerable change. First, a broad consensus presumably exists among the organisation's various stakeholders that the company is prospering and its reputation is not about to be damaged by complaints of unsatisfactory goods or services, or inept financial management. Secondly, this loose coalition of shareholders, employees, customers, suppliers, government agencies and members of the community also feel assured that no laws are deliberately being broken by senior management or others legally associated with the company. Finally, they also believe that public opinion is not being ignored, or the rights of innocent people violated, without breaking the law, by those responsible for running the company.

It is still possible that without conventional morality being flouted, situations may arise in which a company fails to comply with one of the above economic, legal or ethical assumptions without the knowledge or approval of its stakeholders. This may occur for a number of reasons, not all unethical, but when a consensus is reached by senior management to deliberately misinform or lie to stakeholders, a process known as 'groupthink' has probably occurred.

**Groupthink**    Janis[8], borrowing from George Orwell's *1984*, identified groupthink behaviour in government institutions as 'a deterioration of mental efficiency, reality testing and moral judgement that results from in-group pressures'. Trevino[9] and Gioia and Poole[10] also found evidence of groupthink in profit-seeking organisations which acted as a barrier to ethical decision making. This usually occurs when unforeseen situations arise in groups or organisations and conventional morality, which is characterised by the conscious performance of expected behaviour, is disturbed.

Gioia and Poole conclude that the group does not intentionally create a system that makes it difficult to identify ethical issues. Rather, the group deals with novel or infrequent situations through 'controlled or automatic processing'. Controlled processing occurs in less typical situations when doubts about proposed responses are raised at meetings or interviews. 'Scripts' of appropriate actions are agreed and modified if necessary, to deal with specific situations and contexts. Although no illegal or unethical behaviour may occur, the prospect of group members evaluating novel situations by using scripts based on past experiences identifies an obvious danger of groupthink behaviour.

More typically, 'automatic processing' is used, often informally, to resolve ethical problems which arise in situations where partially stereotypical or stereotypical forms of groupthink behaviour occur. These are called 'schema' by Gioia and Poole, which are 'cognitive frameworks that people use to impose structure, upon information, situations, and expectations, to facilitate understanding'. Related research by Kanter and Mishel[11] identifies what perhaps can best be described as 'mindless' behaviour, when the necessity of further active discussion is precluded, which allows virtually effortless interpretation of information and events. Gioia and Poole propose various strategies for dealing with groupthink, which may have to be modified in response to specific organisational situations and contexts, but include revision of job descriptions and management development training 'to include ethical considerations'.

The obvious danger of groupthink behaviour is that it is most likely to flourish when people are in novel situations and uncertain about what is right or wrong, and may be unable to give valid reasons for taking particular decisions. It then becomes convenient or expedient to hide their doubts behind generalisations such as 'All morality is ultimately subjective' or 'There is no such thing as objective morality', or to quote De George's example in the old American adage: 'Business and ethics don't mix: Nor do heaven and businessmen', a piece of American folk knowledge which forms part of a popular view he calls the 'myth of amoral business'.

## The myth of amoral business

DeGeorge[2] begins his explication of moral issues in business by exposing the shortcomings of the myth of amoral business before expressing optimism that the latter is slowly waning in the USA. He provides reasons for this change which have resonances in the UK: 'businesses act immorally not because of a desire to do evil, but simply because they want to make a profit and therefore disregard some of the consequences of their actions' (p. 4). The myth, which could be seen as an example of groupthink, is perpetuated because it represents the way many of those involved (and those outside business) perceive business, 'but also the way many would like to continue to perceive business'. De George's findings are summarised as follows:

- Increased reporting of business scandals in the USA (and the UK) has led to an unsympathetic response from the public.
- Action groups, especially those concerned with environmental and consumer affairs, monitor business performance and put pressure on government and international agencies to bring about required change. This change is examined in more detail in Chapters 10 and 13.
- There is increasing evidence that the US business community wishes to be seen as 'a good neighbour/citizen' in dealing with the general public. This commitment is expected to result in more transparency by managers in addressing problems of mutual concern to companies and communities at conferences, and in journal and newspaper articles; and an implementation of more rigorous codes of conduct, supported by additional staff training on issues of concern to consumers and the wider community.

Whether De George's optimism is fully justified is open to doubt, if only because it appeared before public reaction against well-publicised business scandals in both the USA and UK at the end of the 1980s. As noted in the previous chapter, this public concern led to the introduction of corporate governance guidelines in both countries. Yet the persistent nature of these problems raises fundamental questions about the role of management in the running of companies which only serve to perpetuate the myth of amoral business in Britain.

## Perpetuating the amoral business myth in the UK

Pared down to its essentials, corporate governance is about the control of power in listed companies. The issue is not new and dates back over a hundred years in the USA to the Sherman Act and the subsequent Supreme Court ruling of 1906 on the legal relationship between the corporation and the state which were discussed in the previous chapter. According to Handy[12], uncertainty about the legal status of listed companies still exists in Britain and this anomaly was first raised over fifty years ago by Percy[13] who observed that 'the most urgent challenge to political invention ever offered to the jurist and the statesman [is that] the human association which in fact produces and distributes wealth, the association of workmen, managers, technicians and directors, is not an association recognised in law'.

### Berle and Means' study of US corporations

In the 1930s, in the USA, Berle and Means[14] concluded their classic study of US corporations by stating that increasing share dispersion had left power vested in senior management, who enjoyed both security in office and considerable freedom in their own strategic goals. When Berle[15] re-examined the issue in 1959, he noted that US corporations were virtually free of outside control from capital markets, which had traditionally provided them with capital. Funds for investment were increasingly provided by 'retained earnings' which were allocated by senior management. Financial institutions owned an increasing portion of shareholdings from investing the proceeds of pension funds, insurance policies, mortgages and unit trust investments of millions of private citizens who had no say in the running of these corporations.

## Management capitalism

Burnham[16] called this acquisition of power in listed companies 'management capitalism', noting that traditional capitalism had been transformed through the increasing control of a managerial elite, which has gradually acquired two forms of power over shareholders, employees and consumers. The first was to gain control over the means of producing goods and services and the second was to ensure 'preferential treatment' in the distribution of money and goods resulting from these profitable activities. The relevant question is whether Burnham's analysis still holds over fifty years later. The answer is a resoundingly positive one and the indications are that, as business is transformed by the rapid technological exchange of information, the first form of managerial control will also expand in the new global economy.

For example, the *FT Survey of International Mergers and Acquisitions*[17] reports that the top 10 global deals between January and June 2000 amounted to about US$530 billion. The actual amount was much larger as 1,452 smaller mergers and acquisitions carried out by just the leading 10 global financial corporations during the same six-month period, not including smaller finance houses, have been excluded. As to the second form of managerial power, Burnham explains 'preferential treatment' by observing that 'the easiest way to discover what the ruling group is in any society is usually to see what group gets the biggest incomes'. That the average Premier League footballer earns more than the senior managers of most British companies may, at first sight, contradict this guideline.

Yet when share options and other benefits are factored into this remuneration equation, it becomes clearer why the President of the Board of Trade in 1995 reportedly advised the then Prime Minister against an inquiry into executive pay 'for fear of further damaging revelations'.[18] Not that the election of a rival political party appears to have changed much as, five years later, a report in the same newspaper states: 'The fat cats are back, purring excuses as they lap up rich rewards for their work.'[19] Meanwhile, an independent survey[20] revealed that the average director's pay increased over six times more than the UK inflation rate in 1999/2000. In short, US and UK evidence suggests that management has allocated itself more preferential treatment over the last two decades than Burnham could possibly have envisaged nearly sixty years ago.

## Power holding and public consensus

Without directly mentioning the management capitalism model, Mahoney's[21] concern about reducing 'the too-wide gap between management and ownership by increasing management accountability to owners and also by encouraging owners to pay the ethical dues of ownership, which extend beyond financial risk' led to the idea of ownership responsibility by shareholders being rejected by the UK Institute of Directors 'as "simplistic" on the strange logic that there are frequently too many shareholders for them to act responsibly'. Berle[15] concludes his study of the legitimacy (i.e. 'the rightful possession of power') of the management capitalism model by asserting that: 'The real legitimacy of power-holding at base depends on acceptance by the public consensus.'

It was the threat that this consensus might be withdrawn – after eminent 'outsiders' from religion, the arts and political journalism had criticised business practices in the UK[22,23,24] – that the Cadbury, Greenbury and Hampel recommendations on corporate governance and executive remuneration were introduced during the 1990s. Whether these measures will succeed in eradicating the myth of amoral business in the public perception of UK listed companies, only time will tell. If Henry Ford II is a reliable prophet: 'The successful companies will be those that anticipate what their customers, dealers, and their many other publics will want in the future, instead of giving them what they wanted in the past. . . . These are the companies that will earn the highest profits for their stockholders by discharging their responsibilities to society.'[25] Meanwhile, the immediate task in the next chapter is to explore the origins of these rival perspectives on the complex relationship between business and society as expressions of different value and belief systems.

## Moral evaluation of actions

De George[2] anticipates the need to integrate corporate social responsibility, business ethics and, presumably, corporate governance issues (since the latter did not appear in the USA until a year later). He notes that it is possible to evaluate actions as either moral or immoral at the personal level (irrespective of individual roles), the company level, and at the levels of nation-state and transnational organisations. Not to concede this argument would result in the unacceptable alternative that it is morally acceptable for companies and other institutions to condone lying, stealing, exploitation, or even violent crimes, but unacceptable for individuals to act in similar ways on behalf of these institutions.

Organisations and individuals are not the same and therefore cannot be expected to act as similar moral agencies, but it is entirely reasonable to expect organisations not to approve or implement any action or policy that is morally prohibited. It is equally reasonable to expect different role players, such as senior executives, not to evade their moral responsibilities, hiding behind the notion of corporate moral neutrality to execute actions in the organisation's name that would be condemned by civil society, which could never be justified as moral actions if executed by them as individuals in the community.

## Synopsis

- Moral reasoning refers to arguments with moral judgements as conclusions about behaviour, or activities performed by individuals, or on behalf of groups and organisations. This assumes that a member employed at any level in an organisation knowingly approves of an action, intends it to happen, or actually carries it out.
- Differences between subjective and objective morality are influenced by personal considerations as opposed to views about others. Moral reasoning should therefore possess a clear form and be logical, factual, based on valid moral principles, consistent, universally applicable, rational and not based on personal experience.
- These requirements of moral reasoning underpin Kant's 'categorical imperative' which has been converted by Gert into 10 principles of common morality.

- Causal and moral responsibility raise important questions about the relationship between legal responsibility and morality. Moral responsibility does not apply to an individual who is forced to condone or carry out an action if his/her autonomy and independence are rejected.

- Strict liability does not always imply individual moral responsibility, as excusing moral conditions may limit a person's liability according to his/her level of accountability in the organisations and whether simple or moral agency applies is a specific situation.

- Moral hindsight is a useful yardstick for establishing moral responsibility based on the assumption that if the individual would have altered his/her behaviour with hindsight, then moral responsibility should be accepted for the behaviour that would have been changed.

- Kohlberg's rationality-based theory of moral development states that individuals may advance on three levels and six stages from self-centred preconventional morality to concern for 'right' acts that respect the principle of human dignity, at the post-conventional level.

- Kohlberg's research has been challenged by Gilligan's care-based theory which found that at Level I individual self-interest led some women to seek relationships which ward off loneliness and offer the prospect of friendship. At Level II, care-oriented individuals showed more concern about how institutions structured relations between members; and at Level III, some women viewed care reasoning in terms of mutual care, at least when participants are equals in the care relationship.

- There are many similarities between Kohlberg's and Gilligan's studies but differences have been interpreted controversially to problems such as the 'glass ceiling' which prevents women reaching the top positions in organisations.

- Conventional morality implies that considerable agreement exists about how the organisation's designated activities are being carried out by its members, otherwise things may suddenly be subjected to change, if stakeholders believe that public opinion is being ignored, or the rights of innocent people violated, without breaking the law, by those responsible for running the company.

- This might occur as a result of groupthink behaviour, which is a deterioration of mental efficiency, reality testing and moral judgement that results from in-group pressures, which may act as a barrier to ethical decision making.

- There is a myth of amoral business whereby businesses act immorally not because of a desire to do evil, but because in pursuing profit they may disregard the consequences of their actions. This represents the way business is often perceived and many would like to continue to perceive it.

- Groupthink and the amoral business actions are more likely to thrive in companies where management capitalism is established and management's control over the production of goods and services leads to excessive preferential treatment in terms of remuneration and other benefits.

- Organisations and individuals are clearly different and cannot act as similar moral agencies; nevertheless, morally dubious activities should not be approved or implemented on behalf of organisations by members who evade moral responsibility for approving or executing an action by hiding behind the principle of corporate moral neutrality.

## Review and discussion questions

**1** Summarise the key points in Kant's categorical imperative and explain its relevance to the notion of moral responsibility as it might apply to a manager or a supervisor.

**2** State Gert's 10 ethical rules and comment on their similarities and differences from any other code of moral behaviour with which you are familiar.

**3** What are the key levels and stages in Kohlberg's model of moral development and how does this model differ from the one put forward by Gilligan? Explain your views on either set of findings and comment on the implications for removing the 'glass ceiling' in UK companies.

**4** What is meant by subjective and objective morality? How might use of these moral distinctions have clarified a conflict situation at work with which you are familiar?

**5** Summarise the myth of amoral business and comment on the argument that it remains an obstacle to the implementation of good governance in British companies.

## Case study
## National disasters, corporate liability and moral responsibility in the UK

Major accidents involving loss of life and serious injuries to the public are, sadly, fairly regular occurrences in the UK and around the world. Since 1987, for example, four national disasters which have occurred in Britain, or claimed the lives of UK citizens outside this country, have aroused a powerful emotional response from the public. These were the capsizing of the *Herald of Free Enterprise* in the sea off Zeebrugge in Belgium in March 1987, the Clapham rail disaster in September 1988, the Southall rail crash in 1997, and the Ladbroke Grove/Paddington rail crash in 1999. These disasters are summarised from an applied ethics standpoint with regard to the professional and corporate responsibilities of the people and companies involved, because the legal complexities involved prevented charges of corporate liability for manslaughter being brought against either the companies or employees involved in these accidents.

What undoubtedly added considerable anger and frustration in the aftermath of each disaster was not being able to bring successful prosecutions against the owners, or the surviving operators, of the different forms of public transport on a charge of corporate liability for manslaughter. Independent public inquiries were established by the Government's Department of Transport or the Health and Safety Executive to investigate the causes of each accident and make detailed recommendations which would prevent their recurrence.

Discussion of how effective such official procedures are in satisfying legitimate interest in the provision of safer public transport lies outside the scope of this case study. What is open to question, however, is why it has not been possible to extend the concept of corporate liability in the UK, in line with developments in the USA and The Netherlands, so that the agents of the offending companies could answer the charge of corporate liability in the public interest. After all, some 30,000 UK citizens have been killed in similar disasters since the 1960s, yet only a handful of companies have been prosecuted for corporate negligence, of which a mere two cases were successful.

**The *Herald of Free Enterprise* disaster**

The car and passenger ferry capsized about a mile outside the Belgian port of Zeebrugge in March 1987 after had it put to sea with its bow doors open. This allowed water to pour into the car deck, causing the ferry to roll over and sink within minutes of leaving port at 7 pm. An initial estimate of 200 passengers, including many cross-channel day trippers, were feared drowned. However, 187 people were finally recorded as 'unlawfully killed' at the official inquest in October 1987. This verdict led the then Transport Minister to announce that nobody was immune from possible prosecution, adding that the Department of Public Prosecutions (DPP) would decide whether or not charges should be made. The prospect that the ferry operator, Townsend Thorensen, or their parent company, P & O European Ferries (Dover) Ltd, would be prosecuted with corporate manslaughter seemed more likely after the official inquiry into the disaster was informed on the first day that inherently dangerous orders had been issued to the ship's crew. The P & O company was further criticised for 'sloppiness from top to bottom' by the inquiry, which also recommended that its directors should be charged with corporate negligence leading to the disaster. A national memorial service was held for the victims of the tragedy and a Zeebrugge Disaster Fund was launched and generously supported by the public. Many who took part in the rescue attempt received awards for bravery in the New Year's Honours List in 1988.

A charge of corporate liability for manslaughter was brought against P & O European Ferries (Dover) Ltd by the Department of Public Prosecutions in 1991. As Ridley and Dunford[26] observe, for a charge of manslaughter to succeed at the time the prosecution had to show that the defendant created an obvious and serious risk, and that he then proceeded with a course of action either having recognised the risk involved, or without having given any thought to its possibility. Without delving into legal aspects of the case, three relevant points need to be made: first, lawyers acting on behalf of the company were able to convince the judge to drop the recommended charge against P & O European Ferries (Dover) Ltd. Instead, a charge of manslaughter proceeded against the marine and engineering personnel who were operationally involved in the accident.

Secondly, the revised manslaughter charge also failed after the trial judge expressed doubt about whether it could be established that sailing with the bow doors open had created an obvious and serious risk, in view of the frequency with which this had occurred before without any mishap. In brief, the court ruled that all the accused possessed professional expertise in their respective fields. In the case of the ferry door operator, for example, any decision about whether or not there was a risk to passenger safety depended on his expert judgement rather than on the standards of an ordinary layperson. In brief, even if a layperson concluded that sailing a ferry with the bow doors open could endanger life, this was immaterial. What was crucial was whether or not the bow doors' operator regarded this as hazardous prior to the accident outside Zeebrugge harbour.

The third critical point was the failure of the DPP to convince the court that the manslaughter charge against P & O should have been couched in terms of its failure to establish and maintain an adequate safety policy. The initial problem was one of attribution and, citing Fisse and Braithwaite (1988), Ridley and Dunford note that the prevailing view of the English courts was that 'companies don't commit crimes, people do'. Shortly after the DPP's case failed, the remaining 'Herald' range of vessels in the cross-channel fleet were withdrawn from service and sold abroad. The company's name, Townsend Thorensen, was replaced by that of its parent company, P & O Ferries, which is currently the largest passenger ferry operator in Western Europe with more than 50 ferries on over 20 European routes. These have undoubtedly provided high standards of passenger safety as no major incidents have involved their vessels since the tragic *Herald of Free Enterprise* disaster.

**The Clapham rail crash**

Shortly after 8 am on 12 December 1988, two trains packed with over 1,000 commuters piled into each other outside Clapham Junction, one of the largest railway interchanges of its kind in the world. Seconds later, an empty train ploughed into the wreckage and only quick thinking by a train guard prevented a fourth train from speeding into the pile-up. As a result, 35 people died and over 100 more were badly injured, in Britain's worst rail disaster for over twenty years. A public inquiry was immediately authorised by the government and the inquest returned a verdict of unlawful killing in September 1989, which was confirmed by the inquiry's finding that the accident was due to a major signal failure.

The driver of one of the commuter trains was killed in the crash and the DPP decided not to proceed with a charge of corporate liability for manslaughter against the railway operating company. The inquiry also made over 80 recommendations which, if implemented, would help reduce the risk of similar accidents in future. The most critical of these was the recommendation that ATP (Automatic Train Protection) accident prevention technology should be fitted on every commuter train without delay. However, after years of what the *Railway Magazine* describes as 'political procrastination' (December 1999), the government decided in 1995 against installing the ATP system on grounds of cost, but rail operating companies were urged to search for a cheaper system.

**The Southall rail crash**

On the morning of 19 September 1997, a crowded passenger train crashed into another train outside Southall railway station at a speed of 70 mph, resulting in the deaths of seven people. Over 100 other passengers were injured, including the chief executive of Great Western Rail, the company that operated the passenger train involved in the crash. The accident was promptly investigated by the railway police service and a public inquiry was authorised by the Health and Safety Executive. The DPP decided to prosecute both the driver of the train and the rail operating company on separate charges of manslaughter. The basis for these prosecutions was that the train driver was twice recorded as stating that he had been 'packing his bag' at the time of the accident, and there was also evidence that the ATP equipment on the train had not been operating prior to the crash.

The chief executive of Great Western was advised by lawyers not to appear in court to answer the DPP charge of corporate manslaughter, to which the company pleaded guilty and for which it was fined a record £1.5 million for corporate negligence.

However, as in previous cases, the judge ruled that Great Western could not be charged with corporate liability. The court was also informed that Great Western had been sold to a rival company and the media later reported that the chief executive had recorded a personal profit of over £3 million, or twice the imposed fine on the company, from this transaction.

The trade union representing the driver engaged a leading law practice to defend its member against the charge of manslaughter, arguing that he was an employee earning less than 5 per cent of the chief executive's salary and should not be held solely responsible for an accident which was also partly due to negligence by the rail operating company. The DPP was persuaded to drop the charge of manslaughter against the train driver. The public inquiry was informed by the driver that he could not remember seeing two yellow warning lights alerting him to slow down the train, nor did the warning ATP klaxon sound in his cab because the system was not fully operational, prior to him seeing the red signal when it was too late to bring the train to a halt. He added that he had been packing his time-sheet paper in his overnight bag, which took a few seconds, immediately prior to seeing the red signal and did not feel personally responsible for the crash.

The Great Western chief executive broke down while giving evidence to the inquiry but confirmed that the ATP system, which was regarded as 'unreliable', had not been working prior to the accident and that train drivers were not trained in its use. The public inquiry, which could not proceed until the aborted trials of manslaughter were withdrawn, lasted 12 weeks and finally issued its report in February 2000, in which it concluded that driver failure to respond to the two yellow warning lights was the primary cause of the accident, which had been exacerbated by the failure of the rail operating company to implement its mandatory safety regulations. While the inquiry was in session, its proceedings were overshadowed by a more serious loss of life as a result of the Ladbroke Grove/Paddington rail disaster in October 1999.

**The Ladbroke Grove/Paddington rail crash**

Britain's worst train crash since the Clapham rail disaster of 1988 resulted in the deaths of 30 passengers and crew, including both drivers, after a head-on collision between two trains at a combined speed of 120 mph. The accident occurred in the morning rush-hour when a packed Great Western high-speed train (HST) and a turbo-diesel train collided after the driver of the latter train inexplicably drove through a danger signal having ignored two yellow warning lights. The diesel oil caught fire on impact, trapping passengers, and safety experts agreed later that the death toll and the total of 245 injured passengers could have been far higher.

A public inquiry was immediately authorised by the Transport Secretary and, unusually, the Health and Safety Executive released an interim report within three days of the accident. In addition to the negligence of the driver of the Thames Trains Class 165 Turbo train, it was noted that 'experience had shown ATP to suffer from reliability problems and the equipment in the HST cab was switched off because it was not operational'. The HSE belief was that 'a systems failure' was responsible for the crash and 'any action or omission on the part of the driver was only one factor . . . [but] the signalling equipment is unlikely to have been at fault' (*Railway Magazine*, December 1999, p. 7). The accident is still subject to a judicial inquiry and a decision about any enforcement action, including prosecution, could still be taken if evidence of gross negligence is established. In that event, the case would have to be referred to the DPP to bring a charge of manslaughter against the designated parties.

Four topics have since emerged for consideration. First, the diesel train driver had been qualified less than six weeks and had previously received just 32 weeks of training, compared with the 20–30 years prior training as a fireman under training arrangements in place before 'privatisation' of the nationalised British Rail system. Secondly, there is still confusion about which version of the ATP safety system recommended by the Clapham Junction crash inquiry should be installed by the various rail operating companies. The original ATP system was rejected by the previous government as being 'too expensive on a cost–benefit analysis basis. In crude terms, that means the value of each human life it would save is estimated at £14 million – and politicians feel that is "unacceptable"' (*Railway Magazine*, December 1999, p. 10). Of two alternative systems available, the more advanced is the digital method known as ETCS (European Train Control System), which is widely used in continental Europe and is likely to become mandatory on the UK routes that form part of the proposed Trans-European Network.

The immediate problem is one of cost, as the ETCS would cost an estimated £3 billion, or three times the cost of the recommended ATP system, and rail operating companies favour the use of the TPWS (Train Protection & Warning System) which automatically stops a train if it has passed a signal or is travelling too quickly. At a cost of £200 million, it is said to deliver 80 per cent of the benefits at 20 per cent of the cost, but has the major drawback that it will not stop a train travelling at more than 70 mph, which would prevent its use on all high-speed trains in the UK. The Transport Secretary had stated after the crash that '£1 billion is not a lot to save lives' (*Railway Magazine*, December 1999, p. 10), but, when pressed whether the government planned to invest this amount, he appeared to back-track by indicating that funds should be provided out of Railtrack's profits. This was confirmed by the Railtrack CEO who said that the rail infrastructure company was willing to foot the bill from profits for a train protection system. It was not clear whether he had been referring to the full ATP or ETCS system, although a Railtrack spokesperson confirmed later that the CEO had been referring to the cheapest TPWS system.

Thirdly, the elimination of communication problems between rail operating companies whose trains shared tracks was one of the recommendations of the Clapham Junction crash inquiry, a recommendation which had apparently not been implemented at the time of the Ladbroke Grove disaster. For example, it was revealed that three embargoed passenger coaches, severely damaged in the Southall crash, formed part of the diesel train that was totally destroyed in the Ladbroke Grove disaster. Finally, the British Transport Police service informed the Southall rail crash inquiry that it had been restricted in its investigations by an unwillingness of managers and engineers in all rail companies to provide relevant information about matters related to driver training, signalling and use of ATP accident prevention systems. Nevertheless, the inquiry recommended that the investigation of future accidents should be carried out by Railtrack's own accident investigation unit. The objective would be to obtain vital information about the causes of accidents more rapidly. However, according to a senior Transport Police investigating officer this recommendation would be self-defeating as the prevailing railway culture did not encourage managers to air safety problems in public.

**Questions**

**1** What are the moral and legal arguments (a) for and (b) against introducing a charge of corporate liability, or corporate manslaughter, against the director(s) responsible for public safety of transport companies involved in accidents leading to loss of life?

**2** What moral and commercial arguments could be used to (a) justify or (b) criticise the Railtrack chief executive officer's announcement at a press conference that the cheapest TWPS system would be introduced as soon as possible?

**3** Give reasons why you (a) agree or (b) disagree with the argument that the train driver in the Southall rail crash, who was charged with manslaughter, should not be held solely responsible for an accident which was also partly due to negligence by the rail operating company.

## Notes and references

1. I cannot trace the source of this example but think it may have been included in one of Irving Copi's excellent books on Logic, read many years ago.
2. De George, R.T., *Moral Issues in Business*, New York, Macmillan, 1995, ch. 4.
3. Kant, Immanuel, *Lectures on Ethics*, trans. Louis Infield, Indianapolis, Ind., Hackett, 1980, 44.
4. Gert, B., *Morality*, New York, Oxford University Press, 1988, 157.
5. Kohlberg, L., Revisions in the Theory and Practice of Moral Development, *Moral Development*, San Francisco, Josey-Bass, 1978, no. 2, 86.
6. Gilligan, C., *In a Different Voice*, Cambridge, Mass., Harvard University Press, 1982, 2, 84–91, 166–72. For a detailed evaluation of Kohlberg's and Gilligan's research, see J.W. Dienhart, *Business, Institutions and Ethics*, New York, Oxford University Press, 2000, ch. 2, 64–92.
7. Argandoña, A., Business, Law and Regulation: Ethical issues, in *Business Ethics: a European Approach*, ed. B. Harvey, London, Prentice Hall, 1994, 124–53.
8. Janis, I., *'Groupthink': A diagnostic approach to organisational behaviour*, Boston, Allyn and Bacon, 1983, 454.
9. Trevino, L., Ethical Decision Making in Organisations: A person–situation interactionist model, *Academy of Management Review*, 1986, 11 (3), 603–13.
10. Gioia, D. and Poole, P., Scripts in Organisational Behaviour, *Academy of Management Review*, 1984, 9 (1), 454.
11. See Best, J., *Moral Development: Advances in Research and Theory*, New York, Praeger, 1986, 385.
12. Handy, C., What is a Company For? *Royal Society of Arts Journal*, 1991, March.
13. Percy, E., Lord, *The Unknown State*, Oxford University Press, London, 1944.
14. Berle A.A. and Means, G.C., *The Modern Corporation and Private Property*, New York, Harcourt Brace, 1932.
15. Berle, A.A., *Power Without Property*, New York, Harcourt Brace, 1959.
16. Burnham, J., *The Managerial Revolution*, London, Putnam, 1942, 56–7.
17. *FT Survey of International Mergers and Acquisitions*, 30 June 2000, 1.
18. *The Independent*, 14 March 1995, 6.
19. *The Independent*, 25 July 2000, 3.
20. Imbucon/The Guardian Senior Executives' Pay Survey for 1999, *The Guardian*, 22 August 2000.
21. Mahoney, J., *Mastering Management*, London, Financial Times Pitman Publishing, 1997.
22. Dr George Ramsay, Archbishop of Canterbury's Easter Message on gap between rich and poor, 3 April 1994.

23. Royal Society of Arts, Tomorrow's Company Conference, London, 1995.
24. Hutton, W., *The State We're In*, London, Cape, 1995.
25. Henry Ford II, *The Human Environment and Business*, New York, Weybridge and Talley, 1970, 63.
26. Ridley, A. and Dunford, L., Corporate Liability for Manslaughter: The art of the possible, *International Journal of the Sociology of Law*, vol. 22, 1994, 309–28.

# 3  Values, beliefs and ideologies

*What is most important is that management must consider the impact of every policy and business action upon society. It has to consider whether this action is likely to promote the public good, to advance the basic beliefs of our society, and contribute to its stability, strength and harmony.*

Peter Drucker, *The Practice of Management*, London, Pan Books, 1968, p. 461

## Learning objectives

After reading this chapter you should be able to:

- explain the meaning of values, beliefs and ideologies;
- explore the origins of the ideologies of capitalism, liberalism and socialism;
- examine the impact of these ideologies on individual values and beliefs as expressed in the world's major religions and the rise of secularism;
- briefly consider how managers of organisations in multicultural societies might accommodate differences in individual value systems by adopting the 'Golden Mean' or humanistic perspective.

## Introduction

As technology continues to transform national and international working environments, involving more people from different cultural backgrounds, the values, beliefs and ideologies of individual employees, consumers and other 'constituents' have assumed added importance for management. A useful starting point would be to understand the rise of capitalism and rival ideologies during the nineteenth century, and explore the possible impact of these on the religious and secular beliefs of their various constituents. This should enable management to understand whether the complex relationships between socioeconomic and other cultural changes in pluralistic democratic societies complement the operational and strategic plans of organisations in an emerging global economy.

## Values, beliefs and ideologies

**Values**

The word 'value' has different meanings in English, depending on the context in which it is used. It may describe a thing's worth, desirability, usefulness, or qualities which influence these judgements. In economics, value refers to the purchasing power of goods or services to acquire something else. In mathematics, physics and biology, it indicates an amount or its ranking in a classification system. For the purposes of this book, however, a value refers to *the principles or standards that people use, individually or collectively, to make judgements about what is important or valuable in their lives.*

**Belief**

A belief has fewer meanings than a value and is usually defined as a statement or proposition that is held to be true. More formally, a belief is the 'mental acceptance of a proposition, statement, or fact, as true on the ground of authority or evidence.' (*OED*). This also applies when what is believed cannot be observed, or is based on another's testimony.

**Ideology**

This word was first used in 1795 by Antoine Destutt, Compte de Tracy (1754–1836), a French Enlightenment thinker, who proposed that the philosophy of mind, or analysis of mental events, should be known as 'ideology'. His ambitious proposal to provide 'a plan of ideology' to deduce the first principles of all other branches of knowledge was never completed. Nevertheless, most nineteenth century thinkers accepted that human knowledge would always remain uncertain unless based on sound first principles. Ball and Dagger[1] observe that underpinning the word 'ideology' are the familiar features of ideas and power which, in turn, influence the values and beliefs of people either as individuals or as members of organisations. A similar observation was made earlier by Marx and Engels[2] who used the word to criticise the characteristics of class-divided societies and their followers.

A single definition of ideology is hard to find, however, and Hamilton[3] identifies 27 different versions from 85 sources. Because of these numerous meanings, the word ideology is sometimes used to defend or criticise political, economic and religious beliefs and values. Whether religion should be regarded as an ideology is a contentious issue which is considered briefly below.

## The impact of three ideologies on organisations

In Britain during the 1980s, it became fashionable to call for a return to 'Victorian values'. Anyone interested in setting up a small business might have benefited from the writings of Samuel Smiles (1812–1904) on 'Self-Help' (1859), 'Thrift' (1875) and 'Duty' (1880). These works stressed the 'gospel' of prudence, hard work and other Victorian values. This ideology strongly influenced the entrepreneurial ambitions of William Hesketh Lever (1851–1925), the co-founder of Unilever, the Anglo-Dutch conglomerate, and those of the Scottish-born, American steel tycoon, Andrew Carnegie, whose business activities are summarised in the case study at the end of this chapter. Whatever the merits of these Victorian values, enough people were oppressed by poverty, unemployment and poor health during the nineteenth century to support alternative economic systems to capitalism. The legacy of the three major ideologies is still to be found in the different functions, activities, values and beliefs of those employed in modern profit-seeking and public sector organisations. The three ideologies are:

- capitalism;
- liberalism;
- socialism.

## Capitalism

Capitalism was first used by Karl Marx to describe the free enterprise system which had emerged in Europe in the thirteenth century. The economic basis of capitalism is founded on the three principles of:

- private ownership of property, and the means of producing goods and services;
- primacy of the consumer, who is regarded as free to buy as (s)he chooses;
- individual rewards for producers whose goods and services satisfy consumer needs.

Free competition between producers is not an essential principle of capitalism. For example, Bill Gates' Microsoft Corporation has been challenged in the courts by the US government which argues that the company's monopoly in computer software is against the public interest.

Critics of capitalism regard the above three principles as ideological because economic goals cannot be achieved in isolation. Capitalism also flourishes in many countries with populations of different races, creeds and political viewpoints. Whether its spread is related to the influence of one religion more than another is open to question, although Weber[4] and Tawney[5] both noted the important contribution of the Protestant religion and the 'Protestant work ethic' in the rise of capitalism in northern Europe and the USA.

Other economic historians argue that this view ignores the origins of capitalism in Asia and its emergence in a form recognisable today in fourteenth century Catholic Italy, about a hundred years before Protestantism was established elsewhere in Europe. Prior to this, after its movement from Asia to the Middle East, an invaluable contribution was made by Jewish people to the spread of capitalism from southern to northern Europe, first to The Netherlands and later to England in the seventeenth and eighteenth centuries.

## The rise of modern capitalism

Braudell[6], Cox[7] and Arrighi[8] separate the rise of modern capitalism into the Italian phase, the Dutch phase, the English phase, and the American phase.

**The Italian phase**  Modern capitalism developed in Europe in the latter half of the fourteenth century when Genoese merchants with surplus capital began financing the profitable public debts of the city-states of Venice, Florence and Milan. Their success led to the Casa San Georgio bank being opened in 1407 which was 'not to be parallelled in effectiveness or sophistication until the Bank of England was established almost three centuries later' (Arrighi, p. 110). Capitalism flourished by financing hired mercenaries from outside Italy and McNeill[9] notes that this 'protection' industry became self-sufficient when city-states fell out with each other. Surplus capital from taxes was used to hire soldiers but the costs were soon transformed into revenue once the mercenaries, who were far from home, spent their pay in the local community.

**The Dutch phase**  The second phase of capitalism occurred in the sixteenth century when these Italian city-states were forced into alliances by the more powerful France and Spain. Genoa became a Spanish protectorate and acquired most of the silver landed in Seville from

Spain's South American colonies, in exchange for shipping gold to Antwerp where the Spanish Imperial Army was based. This arrangement broke down in 1566 after Spain failed to enforce taxes on the Dutch which provoked the Dutch War of Independence. The Dutch navy retreated to the Baltic and for the next 80 years seriously weakened the Spanish economy through privateering and piracy.

The Dutch also cornered the Baltic grain trade, essential to feed European armies, and they soon became immensely wealthy. They protected these interests by shrewdly drawing other European nations into their long-running conflict with Spain. A famous example was the Dutch support for England in the defeat of the Spanish Armada in 1588. Throughout this period, Schama[10] notes that capitalism flourished because of a self-perpetuating policy of encouraging conflict in Europe, which increased Dutch profits from their Baltic trade. This not only created an 'embarrassment of riches' for the Dutch, but also resulted in the transfer of an expanding capitalist system from Catholic into Protestant hands.

## The English phase

The third phase in capital accumulation occurred during the eighteenth century after London overtook Amsterdam as a financial centre. Relations between the two nations deteriorated when the English navy destroyed the Dutch fleet for supporting America in the Wars of Independence (1775–83). Part of the Dutch East Indies empire was also lost, leading to the near collapse of the Amsterdam market when many Jewish financiers decided to settle in London. The impact of war on the growth of capitalism has already been noted and was later repeated during the French Wars when Britain's public expenditure rose from £22 million to £123 million between 1792 and 1815.

Growth accelerated from the unique expansion of the iron industry as Britain's wartime manufacturing capacity exceeded its peacetime needs. New uses were found for these furnaces in the production of iron ships and railways, which Jenks[11] observes came to be built: 'because contracting organisations needed work, iron masters orders, bankers and business organisers a project to work upon'. As the British Empire expanded, increased exports prevented these furnaces being shut down at home. A similar policy transformed the mechanisation of the textile industry and, by the early 1840s, liberalisation policies created conditions for an unprecedented boom in world trade and production. This two-way system of trade allowed British finished goods to supply ready markets across the world which were paid for, or the debts incurred were serviced by, increasing the supply of raw materials to Britain. As Hobsbawm[12] observes, 'From 1847 to 1857, no dramatic new discoveries were made, yet for practical purposes an entirely new economic world was added to the old and integrated into it.'

This new economic order would certainly have foundered but for the creation of 'merchant' banks which occurred after increased flows of money for overseas contracts placed embarrassing 'calls' on the Bank of England. To maintain the Bank's reputation for 'sound money', the government allowed London merchants to operate privately as merchant bankers. As a result, most of the costs of the Napoleonic Wars were met by merchants who used foreign contacts to purchase uniforms, small arms, horses and soldiers' rations for delivery to prearranged European destinations. Few of these merchant banks would have succeeded without support from the Jewish financial community in London which possessed expert knowledge of international trade, having established reliable organisations and rapid communication with European business capitals.

The English phase of capitalism took over 350 years to develop into a complex economic system that enabled Britain to dominate foreign investment until its decline in the 1920s and 1930s. Keynes[13] summarises this era vividly by noting that Elizabeth I used the booty Drake brought back on the *Golden Hind* (about £600,000) to redeem England's national debt and invest £42,000 in the Levant Company for overseas trade. Gains from the latter provided capital which financed more successful foreign investments during the seventeenth and eighteenth centuries. As Keynes concludes: 'Assuming an annual rate of return of 6½ per cent and a 50 per cent rate of reinvestment on these returns, the £42,000 of 1580 were sufficient to generate the entire . . . capital of the East India Company, Royal African Company, and Hudson Bay Company . . . and . . . close to £4,000 million that constituted the entire stock of British investments in 1913.'

**The American phase**

The fourth cycle of capital accumulation began in the USA after the Civil War (1861–5) between the southern and northern states ended decisively with the latter's victory. The defeated southern states had wanted to retain closer trading links with Britain's world market system; however, the victorious 'northern states favoured a reorientation of US strategic concerns with outward territorial expansion to the integration of the acquired territories into a cohesive national economy' (Arrighi[8], p. 291). This policy heightened the economic struggle between Britain and the USA which had already swung in the latter's favour after land purchases and conquests doubled US territory between 1803 and 1853. Further territorial expansion occurred after the Civil War when the government achieved its military aim of annexing the native Indian tribes on the reservations.

Thereafter, settlement of the west proceeded rapidly through the exploitation of agriculture, development of a transcontinental railway and telegraph system, and the rapid inflow of European immigrants. The US banking system was centralised and domestic industries were supported by imposing a 'protectionist' barrier mainly against British and other European imports. The outcome was that 'by 1895, more land was occupied by farmers, cattle-breeders and speculators in the 30 years that followed the Civil War than in the previous three centuries' (Arrighi, p. 291).

Probably the unique American contribution to the growth of capitalism was the creation of corporate institutions, which played a powerful role in undermining the global markets structures assembled by Britain. It was 'economies of speed', not 'economies of size', which increased efficiency and enabled vertically integrated, multi-unit organisations to operate more profitably in the US than in Europe. Capital accumulated as mass marketeers (e.g. retailers, chain stores, mail-order houses) reorganised distribution across the USA, handling 'the myriad of transactions involved in moving a high-volume flow of goods directly from thousands of producers to hundreds of thousands of consumers' (Chandler[14], p. 236).

These new organisations soon crossed national boundaries. Hymer[15] explains how easy it was for successful US corporations to expand abroad, since the economics were regarded as a simple extension of the learning acquired in creating a national corporation. Domestic and international expansion of these vertically integrated businesses could not have occurred without simultaneous growth of bureaucratic organisational hierarchies. These new structures gave the prospect of stability and continued growth. Thereafter, Chandler (p. 236) notes:

> the modern business enterprise took on a life of its own. . . . The hierarchies that came to manage the new multi-unit enterprises had a permanence beyond that of any individual or group of individuals. . . . Men came and went. The institution and its offices remained.

## Liberalism

Liberalism is a general term for a variety of political ideologies, derived from the Spanish *Liberales*, after the political party that opposed absolute monarchy in Spain in the early nineteenth century. According to Flathman[16], liberal perspectives are probably best understood in terms of the distinction between *agency-oriented* and *virtue-oriented* liberalism.

**Libertarianism**  Agency theory-oriented liberals are also known as libertarians[17] and take the view that the origins of classical liberalism are rooted in an ancient principle, enshrined in Magna Carta. They also believe in the notion of individualism associated with John Locke's (1632–1704) philosophy of individual rights. The rights identified by Locke are regarded as *negative* and *natural*. They are negative in that a person is diminished, damaged, possibly allowed to die, as a result of these rights being violated. Individual privacy is therefore valued above all else as the sovereign right of the individual to be undisturbed and left alone. These rights are also natural because human beings are assumed to be born with them as separate individuals and, therefore, should retain them throughout life, independently of any social conventions or political institutions.

Locke's theory of liberty is deceptively simple in urging us to refrain from interfering with others. Beyond this, he insists, we have no social obligations to do anything for others, nor is anyone else obliged to do anything positive for us. In return, we have no right to be provided with paid employment or with any other material necessities of life. This insistence on individual rights imposes severe constraints on how we may act towards others and means that we cannot morally impose on another's rights for any purpose. Others, therefore, may not intrude on an individual's liberty for the common good (as proposed in utilitarianism, see Chapter 4) or for the general welfare of society (as argued under 'Socialism' below). These constraints apply even if either alternative could be shown to reduce the total number of occasions when the rights of others might be violated.

This inviolate right to be free from the intervention of others is morally justified if the individual fully respects the uniqueness of his or her own life and also extends the same right to other people. It is regarded as most at risk when arbitrary power is assumed by a monarchy or government, although libertarians support the notion that liberty and elitism can be reconciled within the traditional hierarchies of the state's numerous institutions. It is therefore possible for a libertarian to oppose slavery and the employment of children in factories, and support self-determination of smaller nations, universal suffrage, press freedom, the legalisation of trade unions and religious tolerance, but all within the context of an elitist hierarchy based on privilege.

## Applications in economics and business

Locke's atomistic view of society influenced the ideas of Adam Smith[18] and other so-called physiocrats, like David Ricardo, Karl Marx and John Stuart Mill. Smith argued, in his book of the same name, that the wealth of nations was the sum of all the activities of individual members of the state. His starting point was that each individual could be expected to act rationally in his/her own self-interest. This meant that government should refrain from attempting to regulate business activity. Smith's insistence on *laissez-faire*, or the absence of government intervention, became the main tenet of classical economics, which encouraged free trade in Britain and the USA in the nineteenth century.

The role of the state was not just to avoid any interference in these transactions but, more positively, to remove all bureaucratic interventions that prevented economic advantage from being maximised. Famously, in explaining how individual efforts are aggregated for the benefit of others in society, Smith introduced the metaphor of intervention by a 'hidden hand' to ensure that the earth's goods and services are distributed equitably for the greatest possible benefit of mankind. This assumed that each individual could be relied upon to act out of his/her own self-interest. If so, by dint of a dubious circular argument, the proposition that government should refrain from regulating individual business transactions was justified.

Friedman's critique of corporate social responsibility, mentioned in Chapter 1, is derived from Smith's analysis, as is his contribution to the moral defence of capitalism mentioned below.

## Classical liberalism

Virtue-oriented liberals, such as de Tocqueville (1805–1859) and T.H. Green (1836–1882), employed classical Greek ideas to provide moral alternatives to the individualism associated with John Locke. They rejected Locke's analysis as condoning brutal and degenerate behaviour. Starting from Aristotle's works, de Tocqueville presented what came to be known as 'virtue theory' (see Chapter 4) to promote his belief in the need for a civil religion comprising a network of voluntary, liberal democratic societies. Green's 'communitarian' alternative (also discussed in Chapter 4) also draws on Aristotle in advancing the notion of a democratic, pluralistic society, composed of numerous voluntary organisations, that is also 'anti-statist', meaning its followers would vigorously oppose undue intervention by government bureaucracy.

## Socialism

The most severe criticism of capitalism was launched by followers of socialism, which emerged in two forms, utopian socialism and revolutionary socialism, during the late eighteenth and nineteenth centuries.

Utopian socialism takes its name from the title of the sixteenth century book *Utopia*[19] by Thomas More, which advocated the common sharing, or community of property. As the Industrial Revolution spread from Britain to France, supporters of utopian socialism widened their appeals for public ownership of the means of production and provision of goods and services. This new ideology became known as utopian communism and its followers called for all industrial machinery to be relocated in centralised factories on collectively owned land. Their unrealised aim was that these communes would practise the revolutionary principles of 'true Christianity' in reaction to the severe economic and social conditions imposed by the Industrial Revolution.

## The rise of revolutionary socialism

Following the collapse of utopian socialism, Karl Marx and Friedrich Engels[20,21] published their *Manifest der Kommunistischen Partei* in 1848, advocating a radical form of revolutionary socialism, called communism, which was influenced by empirical evidence of the economic exploitation following the Industrial Revolution, collected by Engels[22], in working-class districts of Manchester.

Morally, capitalism and revolutionary socialism are opposed because Marx and Engels rejected the basic principle of private property as a force for good in society. Neither writer was concerned with moral philosophy, however, and each regarded the fundamental factor in society as economic production from which follows every cultural change in politics, religion, philosophy and the arts. Society is also divided into classes defined by their economic roles; and religious, racial, gender and other conflicts between these classes are ultimately based on economic differences. The state, as the controlling institution of political and legal authority, also has a class character which can be changed through peaceful or violent means. Marx and Engels predicted that this conflict between the classes would continue until the economic forces in society were liberated from the pursuit of continuous profit, when the economic exploitation of mankind due to capitalism would also end. Their main criticisms of capitalism are summarised below.

**Exploitation of the workforce**

A major failing of capitalism occurs because the majority of people have only their labour to sell. They are exploited because entrepreneurs regard labour as a component of production that can be bought and sold like any other commodity. However, all commodities are the product of human activity. Only human labour is sold below its real value. This is because the difference between the amount received by labour as wages is less than the value of what is produced. This surplus value is also the profit of the employer whose sole reason for hiring labour is, in modern jargon, to create 'added value'. If profits are to be maximised, employers must pay labour the minimum wages. Profit maximisation therefore depends on the exploitation of labour, who have to choose between exploitation by one employer or a rival in order to survive.

**Alienation**

Capitalism depends on labour being used as a means to increase profits, not as human beings or as ends in themselves. The principle of 'divide and rule' is used to encourage one class of people to control the activities of another in the workplace. Each time labour carries out monotonous, repetitive tasks to produce goods in return for wages, creativity is suppressed. This leads to alienation whenever the individual is separated from, or unable to purchase or use, the products of his/her labour. In modern parlance, this occurs whenever work is 'de-skilled', or simplified by technology, which creates surplus labour to carry out any related routine tasks. As the demand for labour falls, real wages fall progressively. Increasing reliance on machines and technology also devalues the character/dignity of work. Labour is alienated as it becomes an appendage of the machine, which is unjust, unfair and undemocratic for the majority of people in society.

**Protection of vested interests**

Earlier societies always rewarded one sector, or class, at the expense of another through the acquisition and retention of private property, which later occurred through ownership of the means of production. A minority has always owned property, which means that in order to survive those without had to enter into master/servant, lord/serf or bourgeois/worker relationships, based on inequality. Class conflict was necessary to ensure that a just and equal society is created, and would continue until this social injustice was removed.

**The effects of over-production**

Capitalism is a fundamentally unstable economic system since it cannot provide the workforce with regular employment and higher living standards at the same time as it maximises profits for entrepreneurs. These outcomes are all subject to market conditions. Yet labour typically bargains from a position of weakness since its savings are so small that paid employment is essential. In contrast, entrepreneurs have substantial personal savings. The workforce therefore suffers more when market fluctuations result in production surpluses as this leaves them liable to unemployment and ensuing poverty without warning.

**Widening of inequalities**

Traditional institutions – such as monarchies, religions, landowners, industrial entrepreneurs, speculators, political parties, banks and other financial organisations – are created to support economic exploitation in society. To prevent this, committed workers and communists needed to join together to fight for their class interests across the world, irrespective of nationality, race or gender. The only solution was the overthrow of these institutions by revolution for the benefit of the people. Workers needed to take power for themselves to prevent other forms of government trying to maintain class rule, so that the ethical principles of justice and equality could be upheld through the abolition of capitalism.

## The moral justification of capitalism

Acton[23], Novak[24], Rand[25], Renne[26] and De George[27] have all defended capitalism and the free enterprise system against Marxist criticism on either moral, religious, theological or business ethics grounds. Their arguments are derived from libertarian or liberal perspectives and assert that capitalism is morally preferable to socialism because it:

- safeguards and enhances the moral value of individual freedom;
- safeguards and enhances the moral value of thrift and efficiency;
- provides greater wealth for more people;
- increases the distribution of goods and services.

There is also the suggestion that capitalism is preferred by people who are free to choose their own economic system.

De George rebuts Marxist criticism of capitalism in more detail. First, the charge that labour is exploited by entrepreneurs is countered by pointing out that the labour theory of value never criticises the payment of minimum wages to labour by entrepreneurs as being immoral behaviour. In short, if they were paid their replacement value, then they would be earning what they were worth in the marketplace. Or, if labour rather than the entrepreneur paid for someone to invent and install the machines that replace labour, plus the latter's wages when the former are in use, it would be entitled to the added value, rather than the entrepreneur who takes the risk of the venture being successful or ending in failure.

The second Marxist argument that, if not theft, the owner's profit is excessive and amounts to exploitation of labour, is challenged by reference to the actions of unions and government in ensuring fairer wages, profit sharing, shorter hours and other benefits. De George extends the argument to defend the transfer of manufacturing to underdeveloped countries where the charge of exploitation, as payment of lower wages, cannot be justified if these are comparable with living costs, etc. in that country. His extension of this argument to raw materials imported from underdeveloped countries is less convincing since the greater portion of 'added value' occurs in the importing country.

The third criticism, that capitalism has led to the alienation of labour from other individuals employed in the mass production process, is generally conceded. The notion 'that they are the result of private ownership of the means of production and will disappear with the disappearance of such ownership' is rejected as 'clearly not to be true' (p. 142). This argument is also unconvincing, as no supportive evidence exists either way, as is the case in the argument that: 'Injuries to pedestrians from accidents involving private motorists will disappear when the latter are replaced by public transport.' Of course they would, if only public transport were available, but that has not occurred, whereas the ethical issues resulting from people being injured in accidents involving private motorists are a tragic reality in modern society.

## Values and beliefs in religion

Most people acquire political and economic ideas with the gaining of literacy and some formal education. Yet the values and beliefs of approximately 60 per cent of the world's six billion (and counting) people are based on a religious faith, acquired during an individual's formative years and shared with family members and other members of the community. This is the case with the 'great religions' such as Buddhism, Christianity, Hinduism, Islam and Judaism, which as Nisbet[28] observes are universal because: 'the emphasis [in these religions] rests on a belief or set of beliefs available to everyone without regard to nationality, race, sex or locality'.

Clearly, when a religion becomes the dominant influence in an individual's life more than strictly doctrinal or ideological elements become involved. The belief may dominate all the social and cultural conditions affecting the individual, who feels more fulfilled by these experiences. As Durkheim[29] observes: 'The believer who has communicated with his god is not merely a man who sees new truths of which the unbeliever is ignorant; he is a man who is stronger. He feels within him more force either to endure the trials of existence, or to conquer them.'

## Essential characteristics of religions

The five characteristics discussed below are common to all religious communities but especially to the universal religions that have endured for many centuries.

- *Charisma.* Max Weber[30] noted that a fundamental aspect of the world's great religions was the presence and influence at the start of a charismatic person such as Moses, Buddha, Jesus, Mohammed, who communicated in diverse ways with disciples and other followers.
- *The Sacred.* Durkheim[29] observes that another essential of the great religions, irrespective of their beliefs and organisation, is the contrast between the sacred and the profane. The sacred becomes meaningful by drawing attention to all the beings, objects, images and values that are believed to have a supernatural quality of either good or evil beyond the world of ordinary experience. The profane is rejected because it denies all of these sacred properties.
- *Dogma.* A third essential is dogma, which includes any proposition about the universe, society or human behaviour that is held to be right or true, irrespective of the need for supporting proof or confirmation. It is enough to believe in one or more of these propositions unquestioningly, or to believe strongly in the possibility of proof or verification, given sufficient time or means, through rational or empirical methods of investigation.
- *Rites.* A fourth characteristic is the rites which Nisbet[28] notes include behaviours that reflect the sacred or the dogmatic in some fixed ceremony or ritual. A rite is therefore an 'external' mode of behaviour which signifies or relates to an 'internal' dogma accepted by believers.
- *The Cult.* The final element is the cult, or the smallest social structure, capable of sustaining the sacred rites and dogmas after the departure or death of the charismatic individual who founded the religion. Durkheim notes that: 'it is the cult which gives rise to those impressions of joy, of interior peace, serenity, of enthusiasm, which are, for the believer, an experiential proof of his beliefs' (p. 417).

## The main universal religions

Summaries of how capitalist values underpinning business activity are evaluated by the world's main religions appear below. Those which contain no direct references to business activity have been excluded. However, humanism, which provides an alternative value-system for many without religious beliefs, is also briefly mentioned. Mahoney[31] introduces the concept of 'ethics resource management' which includes religion as a possible resource that 'can provide scope among its adherents for agreement on the acceptance of certain basic values at the level of . . . strategic ethical awareness' (p. 35). An understanding of the world's leading religious beliefs, which are well established in multicultural societies like Britain, should assist managers in achieving this objective. Differences and similarities in these religious and agnostic value-systems are more likely to influence formal and informal exchanges among managers, and between management and other members of organisations, in multicultural societies at home and overseas as contacts between organisations increase in the global economy.

## Buddhism

The ultimate goal of Buddhism[32,33,34,35] is nirvana, which is achieved by a person through goodness but not during his/her lifetime. Hence, a cycle of karma and rebirth has to be endured during which a person may be reborn many times. Karma affects the way people will be reborn in future lives on their journey towards nirvana. Goodness achieved in this life enhances the future lives of a person, and vice versa. Buddhists believe that the things of the world are transient and will pass away over time. They also believe that life in the world should be taken seriously.

Followers of the 'way' should not try too hard to change things, but should develop acceptance and forbearance through spiritual exercises. Buddhist ethics are based on the four noble truths: life is suffering; suffering has a cause; the cause of suffering is individual self-seeking desire; a way of escape is available on the eightfold path guided by five precepts. These steps include right knowledge, right thinking, recognition of the above four noble truths, and a willingness to abandon anything that interferes with personal liberation.

Right behaviour involves practising the following ethical teachings, known as the five precepts, by refraining from taking any form of life, which is why most Buddhists are vegetarians; abstaining from taking what is not given, by practising charity, and avoiding sexual misconduct through self-control; practising right speech by refraining from lying and malicious gossip; abstaining from intoxicating drinks and drugs; and finding a 'right livelihood' which would prevent a believer from taking up any occupation which interferes with the achievement of these precepts.

The four 'cardinal virtues' emphasised in Buddhism are love, compassion, joy and equanimity (or the absence of greed, hatred and envy), which are all derived from the basic insight that, since there is no underlying self, self-seeking is futile. Other virtues include generosity, righteousness, patience and wisdom, but the greatest virtue is compassion for others, which enables a Buddhist to reach salvation.

Links between Buddhism and economics are discussed by Schumacher[34], who summarises the differences in attitudes between a modern European and a Buddhist economist as follows:

> Just as a modern European economist would not consider it a great economic achievement if all European art treasures were sold to America at attractive prices, so the Buddhist economist would insist that a population basing its economic life on non-renewable fuels is living parasitically, on capital instead of income. (p. 34)

Welford's[35] paper on the application of Buddhist economics in evaluating sustainable development issues in business concludes:

> management systems, cultural change within the company, education and whatever else has been proposed within the current Western economic framework is, in fact, unlikely to be enough. Buddhism is the way to achieve much that we need to achieve [in] sustainable development. It provides an alternative to the extremes of free market capitalism and state socialism. But it also adds something new . . . it provides meaning to our lives. (pp. 35–6)

## Christianity

Christianity has about 1.7 billion followers worldwide and its principal aim is the salvation of human beings created by God 'in his own image'. Human beings lead sinful lives, however, and are not able to behave as they should without the grace of God which becomes available through redemption by a saviour, Jesus Christ. Christians try to lead good lives according to principles given by Christ which include loving God above all else, and loving one's neighbour as oneself.

Mahoney's[36] account of the ethical implications of Christianity on the business activities of those employed in profit-seeking organisations is summarised as follows. Christian attitudes towards business are based on the contrasting detached or participatory views about life on earth. The 'detached' view compares human existence unfavourably with the promise of eternal life hereafter. Adherents, such as religious contemplatives, often withdraw from involvement in worldly affairs, including business. The 'participatory' view of most Christians is to assist in completing God's work by creating more just economic and social conditions so that all people on earth can live better lives, worthy of their destiny in the life hereafter.

Both approaches are based on the belief that human activities are flawed by sin, which most Christians see as a dominant characteristic of society, including the business community. Many Christians also believe that humanity is in constant need of salvation and forgiveness due to its inherent selfishness, pride and self-reliance which may result in the pursuit of wealth and success as, for example, in business activity. Other Christians are less critical of society because of the goodness of creation, which inspires human motivation and enterprise. Business activity is therefore viewed positively as cooperating with God in developing natural and human resources for the common good.

The moral dilemma for Christians is evaluating that which business does, or has the potential for doing well, against justifiable concern about business activities that fail to promote human well-being as the legitimate aim of society. This aim is expressed in the moral imperative to love one's neighbour and, when in doubt, to give priority to those most in need. Christianity opposes all political, social or economic ideologies that encourage elitism, alienation or conflict; and any government that opposes the notion of a common human destiny which offers shared access for all to the benefits of God's creation.

Christians also respect the inalienable fact of human individuality which has moral consequences for how humans should treat and respect each other in social situations, especially when opportunities arise for developing individual potential in business. Many Christians also believe that individual potential is expressed as a vocation, or a unique 'call' to serve God in a particular way. In business, such a vocation includes any occupation that provides opportunities for individuals to carry out God's work diligently according to the values inherent in the 'Protestant work ethic'.

Mahoney also compares the contributions of the Judaeo-Christian tradition, Protestant Christianity and Catholic Christianity, as separate ethics resources in business, but expresses concern about whether 'such values can be agreed upon with others in society as common ground on which to base the conduct of business' (p. 35).

## Hinduism

The aim of Hindu[37] teachings and religious practices, which have about 700,000 followers worldwide, is to achieve 'liberation', or *moksha*, which is a way of seeing clearly that may be partly achieved through good actions, otherwise a person cannot begin to follow the way. Like Buddhists, Hindus also believe in rebirth, known as *samsara*. This is possible because human beings possess indestructible souls which enter new bodies whenever a person dies. This cycle of rebirth continues until a particular soul achieves liberation and becomes part of the 'ultimate being', or 'Brahman', and escapes from the world. As part of this cycle, the actions of this life affect the future lives of any soul through what is known as *karma*. Hindu ethics have evolved over four thousand years in the world's oldest known literature, the Vedas. These differ from Western ethics in exploring the direct link between social and spiritual life.

In business activity, the Vedas would advocate righteous and moral actions such as honesty, friendship, charity, truthfulness and modesty in dealing with others, supported by the practice of celibacy, religious worship, purity of heart, and *ahimsa*, the principle of non-violence, associated with the teachings of Mohandas K. Gandhi, as a personal morality. These necessary virtues are to be pursued to avoid the vices of bad intentions, swearing, falsehood, gambling, egoism, cruelty, adultery, theft and injury to life. The central text of Hinduism, the *Bhagavadgita*, provides specific ethical advice about how to achieve *moksa* as the goal of life, though a strict code of spiritual discipline.

## Islam

According to Islam[38], which has over one billion followers worldwide, all God's creation is good; therefore wrong behaviour can only arise through human disobedience of the code of law called the 'Sharī'a', which is based on two sources, the Qur'ān and the Sunna. The former contains the scripture revealed to Muhammad, and the latter sets out the 'way of life' of the Prophet, which is recorded in the 'Hadith' ('the tradition'). Muslims believe that God has provided all the necessary guidance to live a life of good conduct and it is up to all believers to follow this guidance in their private and public lives.

Bassiouni[39] summarises the holistic approach of Islam in three essential tenets which include the unity of God, the unity of human beings and the unity of religion. These tenets combine to make Islam a universal and timeless faith, which applies to all peoples in all places, as a continuation of divine revelations from Abraham to Muhammad, the last of the prophets. The Qur'ān explicitly states that it is the continuation and conclusion of the Creator's religion given to humankind. The Sharī'à, or the law of Islam, is based on the Qur'ān. The most universal ethical prescriptions of the Sharī'à require a Muslim to act without exception in a decent and benevolent way; to refrain from wrongdoing; not to harm others; to deal with others as one would wish them to deal with oneself.

The New Testament's golden rule to 'Do unto others as you would have them do unto you' is also a fundamental tenet of Islam. In addition, the Sharī'à regulates almost every relationship, from the spiritual relationship between the Creator and human beings to the most intimate of interpersonal relations. The Sharī'à is also a comprehensive legal system regulating all aspects of Muslim society which have developed across the centuries.

The Islamic ethical tradition as it extends to commerce and business is based on a long history of international trade. For want of unified legislative and judicial authorities, Muslims have developed diverse customs and practices including a free enterprise, private sector approach to economic and business practices which is, however, subject to limitations for the greater benefit of the community. The right to private property is upheld in the Sharí'à providing the community's right to what is called the 'eminent domain' and other collective interests are not threatened and the abuse and waste of private property is avoided. Private profit is a valid reward of Islamic business activity if it is obtained in a permissible way without compromising the duties of brotherhood, solidarity, charity, or payment of 'Zakat', which is a particular tax imposed upon Muslims.

Over all, the 'Halal' and the 'Haram' distinction between legitimate and illegal profits must be maintained. The latter, known as 'riba', includes money lending, which is prohibited, although payment of a reasonable predetermined fixed amount of interest is acceptable. Muslims may also profit from their own work or, if capital is involved, whenever the risk of loss is shared. Undue profiteering from the poverty or misery of others is prohibited under the Islamic Code. Stock market speculation is a contentious issue for many Muslims and is only acceptable if a distinction is made between legitimate risk taking and gambling, which is prohibited.

The most important commercial bond for regulating financial activity between Muslims, and also with non-Muslims, is the contract. All contractual obligations must be based on honesty and taking unfair advantage of others is not permissible. Fairness is regarded as the means and end of all human transactions, irrespective of circumstances, because honesty is not just a virtue but a requirement of every Muslim. Investment in mutual funds or other financial ventures is also acceptable if the investors share the risk of potential loss.

## Judaism

Meir Tamari[40] states that Jews believe that Israel is the chosen land of God on earth. The task of the Jews is to show God's 'righteousness' and 'holiness' on earth. The righteousness of God is found as 'commandments' in the Torah which, with the Talmud (a collection of teachings by the rabbis), are the chief books of guidance, although right and wrong actions for Jewish people are ultimately decided by God's laws.

In the fields of commerce and economics, Judaism states that there is nothing wrong or immoral with the possession of wealth and the acquisition of material goods, which ensure economic needs are satisfied through human endeavour, as there is no spiritual value or redemption in poverty. The pursuit of economic wealth is morally legitimate and essential for the survival and welfare of the human race. Human greed is so powerful and all-pervasive, however, it can result in unethical behaviour leading to injustice and oppression. Greed increases with fear of economic uncertainty which human beings always try to avoid by minimising business risks through legitimate or immoral means. In a world where people knew their future needs and had the means of satisfying them, there would be no fraud, exploitation or business immorality.

This view assures believers that God will provide for all needs thereby freeing human beings from having to seek unethical ways of eliminating future uncertainty by denying the private property rights of others. Judaism rejects the concept of 'let the buyer beware' in favour of full disclosure by the seller, because of a belief in God's ability to see and know everything. The spiritual damage to the performer of unethical business behaviour is always regarded as greater than the financial damage suffered by the victim because the perpetrator of an unethical act loses sight of God, the Provider, from whom all wealth originates. Wealth provided by God is primarily for satisfying the needs and wants of individuals who remain responsible for helping the poor, old, weak and even lazy members of society, providing human greed does not devalue their acts of charity and philanthropy. Society is therefore entitled to a property right on individual wealth through compulsory taxation to provide for the social and charitable needs of its members. Recognition of the divine source of wealth promotes an 'economics of enough' viewpoint as Judaism encourages moderation in demand, expressed in the biblical response: 'I have all I need' to the economic proposition that 'more is better than less'.

Charity is regarded as the voluntary sharing of wealth to meet the claims of the poor and weak, whereas compulsory involvement in the communal provision of funds for these needs is an act of justice. Non-participation in these communal activities is viewed as akin to theft from both those in need and those who have to provide a greater share as a consequence. This is because the divine insistence on using private wealth for the needs of others makes this holy money, which can neither be wasted nor abused. Finally, with regard to the environment, as its custodian, the individual must safeguard natural resources so that use does not overlook the anticipated needs of future generations through which human beings become partners in divine creation.

## Religious values in the working environment

There may be an understandable reluctance to accept that religious values have a role in profit-seeking organisations which are committed to instrumental goals such as increased profits, costs reduction, or some measure of improved effectiveness. Ettorre[41] acknowledges the validity of this rationale but questions whether management can maintain a neutral stance in a multicultural society, where it may be unrealistic to expect people to leave their religious values in the office foyer or at the factory gate. For some people, their religious (or political) beliefs may influence every aspect of their lives including employment so the question for management is whether these views, if sincerely held, intrude on the privacy of other employees. Assuming that problem is resolved, Ettorre adds that management should satisfy itself that the values of its employees are broadly reflected (and certainly never challenged) in the organisation's mission statement. Shaw and Barry[42] observe that possible misunderstandings or conflicts can be averted if management accept that the core values of the world's leading religions are included in the 'Golden Mean/Rule'[43], which encourages understanding and tolerance of the cultural diversity of others according to the 'Do unto others as you would have them do unto you' principle.

## Humanism

According to Radest[44], modern humanism is a product of the European Enlightenment, although its origins are found in classical Greek thought. Humanism's main beliefs are that 'man is the measure of all things' and that life and the world should be viewed from a naturalistic standpoint, rather than interpreted from a supernatural perspective. Parallel beliefs, found in India, Japan and China, are expressed in some forms of Buddhism and Confucianism. Humanism, however, flourished in Europe from the nineteenth century onwards in response to the development of science and liberal democracy and the spread of a secular society.

Humanism is a philosophy which views individuals as rational agents living in a world that both sustains and constrains human behaviour. Instead of decrying fate or resorting to a belief in a more secure supernatural world offered by some religions, the humanist strives to endure, enjoy and work within these constraints as an autonomous moral agent. As such, he/she exercises both freedom and responsibility by acknowledging an obligation to judge, choose and act in taking every opportunity to make a rational difference to him/herself and to the world around. This is often achieved through a commitment to democracy and education, as the means of developing human competence, and to science as the outcome of organised intelligence. From these springs a scepticism about belief in a supernatural being or beings and a rejection of authoritarian religions and political ideologies.

## Synopsis

- Knowledge of the values, beliefs and ideologies of individuals in organisations can lead to a greater understanding of the impact of complex economic, socio-political and cultural relationships on the emergence of more pluralistic democratic societies in an increasingly global and technological environment.
- As a starting point, understanding the reasons why the rise of modern capitalism is supported by libertarianism and challenged by liberalism and socialism, provides grounds for acknowledging that belief in any of these ideologies may have a moral basis rather than being grounded in greed or envy.
- The world's major religions present no insurmountable opposition to business activity providing it does not exploit others in the community or in underdeveloped countries. The 'great religions' share a dual belief in the uniqueness of the individual and his/her place in the community, which requires each person engaged in business activity to contribute to the needs of the community and live by its norms.
- These religions also have a distinct set of moral values but whether these can be integrated as a form of ethical resource management in a multifarious society remains an open question, as ways would have to be found of reconciling different religious beliefs, and the secular values of humanism, with the material goals of profit-seeking organisations.
- Prudent managers may wish to minimise the impact of political or religious beliefs on these legitimate goals, which may not always be possible in a multicultural society. An appropriate strategy would ensure that different belief-systems are not opposed, but accommodated by adoption of the 'Golden Rule/Mean' principle in the mission statement.

## Case study
## The rise and fall of America's robber barons[45,46]

**Introduction**

The massive development of the US economy during the nineteenth century was accompanied by a corresponding rise in the urban population and the spread of large bureaucratic organisations to meet the increased demand for employment and the supply of goods and services. New corporations sprang up with thousands of shareholders, employees and managers, to utilise an expanding transport system for supplying goods from the emerging coal/coke, steel, oil and food industries, supported by new banks and insurance companies. While the impact of these new corporations on the US economy is indisputable, it is often overlooked that many were preceded by dubious financial 'trusts' which were run by the notorious 'robber barons'. In the 30 years after the American Civil War, much of the population consisted of an impoverished workforce, abused consumers and exploited investors, because the nation's savings, natural environment and human resources were mismanaged by these ruthless speculators, many of whom lived to become generous philanthropists. The 'tyranny of wealth' they imposed was only curbed at the start of the twentieth century when President Teddy Roosevelt invoked the Sherman Anti-trust Act of 1890 against the best known of these entrepreneurs, John D. Rockefeller, and the Standard Oil trust which he had created.

This case study briefly examines the lives of just a few of some twenty leading robber barons, who were born within a few years of each other and came to prominence in the massive expansion of the US economy that followed the Civil War, and whose innovations still influence modern American business. For all their shortcomings, the demise of the robber barons was not widely welcomed and it is sometimes forgotten that the US Supreme Court only approved Roosevelt's legislation by a narrow 5:4 majority vote.

This vote reflected public opinion at the time which, on the one hand, condemned the unprecedented greed of these robber barons yet, on the other, admired their energetic and competitive individualism. This competitiveness was later extended into personal rivalries over who could become the greatest philanthropist as the dubiously acquired fortunes of most robber barons were used to create public foundations from which American and international communities have benefited. Nearer our own time, the merits of the Sherman Anti-trust Act have been strongly criticised by Alan Greenspan (1962) who, as the influential chairman of the US Federal Reserve Bank, has been called the third most powerful person in the USA after President Clinton and Bill Gates, CEO of Microsoft (source: *Time Magazine*, 17 June 1996, p. 47). Ironically, Bill Gates has since become locked into a protracted legal dispute with the US government over the same anti-trust issues which led to the invocation of the Sherman Act against Standard Oil almost a hundred years ago.

**Andrew Carnegie (1835–1919)**

Andrew Carnegie was a Scottish-born American industrialist who pioneered the enormous expansion of the US steel industry in the late nineteenth century and, like the Rockefellers, was a leading philanthropist of this era. Carnegie's father was a handloom weaver and an active Chartist who became impoverished after the power loom was invented. The family emigrated to the USA in 1848 and settled into the Scottish community outside Pittsburgh, where Andrew started work, aged 12, in a cotton factory. The family became naturalised American citizens and Andrew advanced rapidly thereafter through self-education at night school.

Aged 14, Carnegie became a messenger in a telegraph office, where he was appointed private secretary to the superintendent of the Pennsylvania Railroad within four years, becoming superintendent himself at the age of 24. He shrewdly invested in the Woodruff Sleeping Car Company (holder of the Pullman patents) and introduced the first successful sleeping car on American railroads. Anticipating the growing importance of heavy industry, he also invested in diverse industrial companies including the Keystone Bridge Company, Superior Rail Mill and Blast Furnaces, the Union Iron Mills, the Pittsburgh Locomotive Works, and also in a Pennsylvania oilfield. These were financed by Carnegie taking several trips to Europe to sell railroad securities and his annual income was $50,000 by the age of 30.

During these trips he also met steelmakers in Britain, and he anticipated increased future demand for iron and steel in the USA. He left the Pennsylvania Railroad in 1865 to manage the Keystone Bridge Company. Thereafter, he concentrated on steel production, founding the J. Edgar Thomson Steel Works, later the Carnegie Steel Company, near Pittsburgh where he installed the first Bessemer steel processing plants in the USA, which he copied from Britain along with the more efficient open-hearth process in the 1890s. Carnegie's great achievements, which allowed him to overtake his UK rivals, were detailed cost and production accounting procedures to increase efficiency, coupled with vertical integration which he achieved by purchasing coke fields and iron ore deposits to provide raw materials, and ships and railroads to transport supplies to his steel mills. Carnegie also probably first introduced a system of 'interlocking directorates', being assisted by only three senior managers, namely Henry Clay Frick, Captain Bill Jones and his own brother, Thomas Carnegie.

So successful was the Carnegie Steel Company that by 1890, American steel production exceeded that of Great Britain for the first time. Variations of Carnegie's system of vertical integration were introduced across US industry. However, despite increasing annual profits, the Carnegie Steel Company's reputation suffered a severe setback during the depression of 1892 when the Homestead plant strike resulted in unnecessary deaths and bloodshed. In public, Carnegie professed support for the rights of unions but, in practice, he and Frick were implacably opposed to collective bargaining. Without being directly involved, Carnegie approved of Frick's decision to shut down the Homestead steel plant in 1892 and re-open it five days later, employing only non-union labour. This action was supposedly based on 'the inviolability of property and the life and liberty guaranteed by the Constitution' and, without waiting for the legal support of the police or militia, Frick brought in a battalion of armed Pinkerton guards to remove striking Amalgamated Association of Iron, Steel, and Tin Workers from the Homestead steel works, resulting in unnecessary bloodshed. The workforce was given the stark choice of returning to work but only if they gave up union membership. Rioting followed during which guards and workers were killed or tortured and the Homestead plant was occupied by workers for five months before being successfully stormed by government soldiers. Public sympathy mostly favoured the workforce but swung rapidly behind the Carnegie management after

Frick narrowly avoided public assassination by a leading anarchist. The strike broken, most of the workforce was reinstated at subsistence wages of $358–400 per year which remained unchanged for the next eight years, allegedly to recoup the $2 million cost of the strike even though the Carnegie company achieved profits of over $4 million, or a 16 per cent return on capital employed, during the same year. By 1900, Carnegie Steel Corporation's profits were $40 million, of which Carnegie's share was $25 million. His public reputation damaged, he never fully recovered from the aftermath of the Homestead strike, and sold his company to J.P. Morgan's new United States Steel Corporation for $250 million in 1901.

Carnegie subsequently retired from business and devoted himself to his philanthropic activities and writing. His most famous article, 'Wealth', appeared in the June 1889 issue of the *North American Review*, in which he outlined his Gospel of Wealth. In summary, he insisted that a man who accumulates great wealth is clearly exceptional, having used his talents and energy for the advancement of society by providing employment. However, his further duty was to use any surplus wealth for the philanthropic 'improvement of mankind' since 'a man who dies rich, dies disgraced'. Carnegie undoubtedly abided by his own Gospel of Wealth and distributed about $350 million, of which $62 million included notable benefactions in the USA. His remaining wealth was used to create 'trusts' or charitable foundations to create and expand four Scottish universities and provide financial aid for Scottish students. Other benefactions maintained and improved educational and cultural institutions in the UK through the building of libraries, theatres, child welfare centres, etc., and similar institutions were founded in Pittsburgh.

The Carnegie Institution for Medical Research was founded in Washington, while the Carnegie Foundation for the Advancement of Teaching provided free pensions for college professors. The Carnegie Endowment for International Peace funded the World Court and Palace of Peace in The Netherlands and his largest benefaction supported 'the advancement and diffusion of knowledge and understanding among the people of the United States' and also in Canada and the British Commonwealth, by providing financial aid to colleges, universities and libraries, as well as research and training in law, economics and medicine.

**Jason (Jay) Gould (1836–1892)** Jay Gould was a financier, speculator and important railroad developer, who was widely regarded as probably the most unscrupulous robber baron in nineteenth century America. Gould left school with only a basic education before being employed as a surveyor and later as a tannery manager until 1859 when he began speculating in small railways securities. Taking advantage of new transport opportunities during the American Civil War, he became manager of the Rensselaer and Saratoga Railway, using his position to buy and reorganise the Rutland and Washington Railway and also became a director of the Erie Railroad in 1867. Two other notorious robber barons, Daniel Drew and Jim Fisk, persuaded Gould to join them in 1868 as they struggled to keep another baron, Cornelius Vanderbilt, from gaining control of this railroad. Gould's response was to issue fraudulent shares and then bribe New York state legislators to legalise their sale, enabling him to gain control of the railroad. Gould and Fisk then joined forces with William 'Boss' Tweed and Peter Sweeney to profit from further unscrupulous speculations using additional Erie shares. The four men next attempted to corner the New York gold market and caused the panic of

'Black Friday' in September 1869, which was only resolved by the direct intervention of the US Treasury, by which time many investors had been ruined.

The public outcry forced Gould to relinquish control of the Erie Railroad in 1872, after Fisk's death. When the infamous Tweed Ring of insider traders in New York was also broken up, Gould walked away with a fortune of $25 million which he used to buy shares in Union Pacific Railroad, acquiring control in 1874. Smaller railway lines were also bought and at its peak in 1881, Gould owned the largest railroad empire in America, which extended 15,800 miles (25,500 km) and included 15 per cent of the total railway network. Again, Gould made huge profits by manipulating the company's shares before he sold his Union Pacific interests in 1882. He next began building a new railway network system centred around the struggling Missouri Pacific Railroad until he owned half of the south-west railway network by 1890. Once more, Gould made massive profits after persuading gullible investors to purchase the overvalued shares in his railroad.

Gould had already gained control of the Western Union Telegraph Company in 1881, by buying its shares at low prices after first weakening the company by personally financing cut-throat competition from his own smaller telegraph companies. He used the same dubious practice to purchase the New York *World* in 1879 until state legislators forced him to sell the newspaper, again for a large profit, in 1883. Three years later, he acquired the Manhattan Elevated Railroad and held a monopoly over New York City's elevated railways until his death in 1901. The unscrupulous Gould scorned the philanthropic gestures of his fellow tycoons and remained ruthlessly single-minded and friendless until his sudden early death, when he left an estimated $77 million to his eldest son.

**John D(avison)
Rockefeller
(1839–1937)**

John D. Rockefeller was an outstanding US industrialist, philanthropist and founder of the Standard Oil company, which dominated the oil industry and became the first great business trust in the USA. Rockefeller came from a poor family that moved to Cleveland in 1853, where he established his first enterprise at the age of 20, before building an oil refinery near Cleveland in 1863, which became the largest plant in the area within two years, and was incorporated as the Standard Oil company (Ohio) in 1870. Because of its greater economic efficiency, Standard Oil prospered, and bought out its main competitors until it controlled most refineries in Cleveland by 1872. This monopoly power enabled Rockefeller to negotiate rock bottom rates with railroads on his oil shipments. Standard Oil used these profits to acquire more pipelines and terminal facilities, purchasing competing refineries in other cities, and rapidly expanding its markets in the United States and abroad. Within 10 years, it had a near monopoly of the oil business in the United States. To maintain overall control, Rockefeller placed the stock of Standard of Ohio and its associate companies in other states under the control of a corporate board of nine trustees, with Rockefeller as its head, which was registered as the first major United States 'trust', creating a new type of organisation that other monopolies quickly copied.

The aggressive competitive practices of Standard Oil and other trusts attracted growing public hostility. This led some US states to implement anti-monopoly laws which culminated in the passage of the Sherman Anti-trust Act by the US Congress in 1890. Two years later, the Ohio Supreme Court ruled that the Standard Oil trust had violated a law prohibiting monopolies. Rockefeller reacted by dissolving the trust in Ohio and transferred its assets to Standard Oil companies in other states which had no anti-monopoly legislation. To maintain overall control, he also created a system of interlocking directorates so that the same nine men controlled the operations of all the affiliated companies as a single consolidated holding company, Standard Oil company (New Jersey), which existed until 1911 when the United States Supreme Court declared it to be in violation of the Sherman Anti-trust Act, and ordered it to be broken up. Rockefeller responded by restructuring Standard Oil into the separate oil companies Amoco, Chevron, Exxon and Mobil, which still operate successfully. Ironically, as the major shareholder in Standard Oil, Rockefeller immediately became far richer by complying with the Supreme Court ruling than he had been beforehand. An intensely private entrepreneur, Rockefeller was implacably opposed to trade unions and, if not in direct executive control, at least condoned the so-called Ludlow Massacre (20 April 1914), in which over 40 sit-in strikers at the Rockefeller-owned Colorado Fuel and Iron Company were shot dead by the Colorado state militia. Public anger was intense and only subsided after Rockefeller agreed to the formation of the first company unions in the USA, which were all controlled by management.

Rockefeller was a devout Baptist and, once his immense fortune easily exceeded his personal needs, devoted himself entirely to philanthropy. In 1892, his generosity helped found the University of Chicago and his donations eventually exceeded $80 million. In association with his son, John D. Rockefeller Jr, he provided funding for the Rockefeller Institute for Medical Research (renamed Rockefeller University) in New York in 1901; the General Education Board in 1902; and the Rockefeller Foundation in 1913. Additional benefactions by the Rockefeller Foundation included the United Service Organisations (USO), an agency for the aid of members of the United States military and their dependants, during World War II. After the war, his son donated the land for the United Nations headquarters and $5 million for the Lincoln Center for the Performing Arts, both in New York City. His other philanthropic works included restoration of colonial Williamsburg and the construction of low-rent housing in the poorer areas of New York. During his lifetime, Rockefeller senior's public donations totalled more than $500 million, while those of his son and principal heir exceeded $2,500 million before his death in 1955.

**Conclusion**

All the so-called robber barons discussed above engaged in dubious monopolistic practices which were either outlawed under the Sherman Anti-trust Act, or would have been had the legislation been in place prior to 1890. The trusts came into existence, according to Greenspan[47], because 'they were the most efficient units in those industries which, being relatively new, were too small to support more than one company'. This was because the general development of industry has historically begun with a few small firms. Over time, these merged to increase efficiency and profits. As demand increased, the entry of yet more firms reduced the market share of the dominant firm. Greenspan adds that

> The observable tendency of an industry's dominant firms eventually to lose part of their share of the market, is not caused by antitrust legislation, but by the fact that is difficult to prevent new firms from entering the field when the demand for a certain product increases.

For Greenspan, the Sherman Act may have made sense during the nineteenth century when fear and economic ignorance prevailed, yet it is 'utter nonsense in the context of today's economic knowledge'. Greenspan summarises his criticism of the entire structure of anti-trust statutes by arguing that they are based on economic irrationality and ignorance, seriously misinterpret the history of industrial development, and are based on a naive and unrealistic grasp of economics. He also criticises the argument that at least the anti-trust laws have done no harm because, even if competition inhibits the spread of coercive monopolies, it is only being prudent to declare this economic activity illegal in the first place. The flaw with this argument, he insists, is that 'no one will ever know what new products, processes, machines and cost-saving mergers failed to come into existence, killed by the Sherman Act before they were born'.

**Questions**

**1** What arguments would you raise in favour of, or against, Greenspan's argument that anti-trust legislation may have made sense in the nineteenth century but is 'utter nonsense in the context of today's economic knowledge'?

**2** To what extent can the activities of a market leader like the Microsoft Corporation, which at the time of writing is engaged in an anti-trust legal battle with the US government, be justified because, to paraphrase Greenspan, 'it is the most efficient unit in a relatively new industry, which is too small to support more than one company'?

**3** Can you suggest any industry or public sector organisation which already benefits society more (or would do) from the presence of a single provider; and what reasons would you give to support your case?

**4** To what extent do you think Greenspan uses objective and impartial arguments when he states: 'no one will ever know what new products, processes, machines and cost-saving mergers failed to come into existence, killed by the Sherman Act before they were born'?

## Notes and references

1. Ball, T. and Dagger, R., *Ideals and Ideologies*, New York, Longman, 1999, 4.
2. Marx, K. and Engels, F., *Collected Works*, vol. 5, London, Lawrence & Wishart, 1976, 586–7.
3. Hamilton, M.B., The Elements of the Concept of Ideology, *Political Studies*, 35, 1987, 38.
4. Weber, M., *The Protestant Ethic and the Spirit of Capitalism*, New York, Scribner, 1958, 181.
5. Tawney, R.H., *Religion and the Rise of Capitalism*, New York, Harcourt Brace, 1926.
6. Braudell, F., *The Perspective of the World*, New York, Harper & Row, 1984, 120–1.
7. Cox, O.C., *The Foundations of Capitalism*, New York Philosophical Library, 1959, chs 2–5.
8. Arrighi, G., *The Long Twentieth Century*, London, Verso, 1994, chs 1–4.
9. McNeill, W., *The Pursuit of Power: Technology, armed force and society since* AD1000, Chicago, University of Chicago Press, 1984, 74.
10. Schama, S., *The Embarrassment of Riches: An interpretation of Dutch culture in the Golden Age*, Berkeley, University of California Press, 1988.
11. Jenks, L.H., *Accumulation of British Capital to 1875*, London, Knopf, 1938, 133–4.
12. Hobsbawm, E., *Growth of Capital 1848–1875*, New York, New American Library, 1979, 32, 38, 50–1.
13. Keynes, J.M., *A Treatise on Money*, vol. 2, London, Macmillan, 1930, 156–7.
14. Chandler, A., *The Visible Hand: The managerial revolution in American business*, Cambridge, Mass., Belknap Press, 1977.
15. Hymer, S. The Multinational Corporation and the Law of Uneven Development, in J.N. Bhagnati, *Economics and World Order*, New York, Macmillan, 1972.

16. Flathman, R.E., Liberalism, *Encyclopaedia of Ethics*, ed. L.C. and C.B. Becker, New York, Garland, 1992, 698–702.

17. Steiner, H., Libertarianism, *Encyclopaedia of Ethics*, ed. L.C. and C.B. Becker, New York, Garland, 1992, 702–4.

18. Smith, A., *The Wealth of Nations*, Edinburgh, 1776.

19. More, Sir Thomas, *Utopia*, London, Penguin Books, 1965.

20. Drennen, D.A., *Karl Marx's Communist Manifesto*, Woodbury, New York, Barron, 1972.

21. Marx, K. and Engels, F.T., *The Communist Manifesto*, Chicago, Kerr, 1940.

22. Engels, F., *Condition of the Working Class in England* (1844), London, Penguin, 1988.

23. Acton, H.B., *The Morals of Markets: An ethical exploration*, London, Longman, 1971.

24. Novak, M., *The Spirit of Democratic Capitalism*, New York, Touchstone, 1982.

25. Rand, A., *Capitalism: The unknown ideal*, New York, New American Library, 1967.

26. Renne, R., *The Ethic of Democratic Capitalism*, Philadelphia, Fortress Press, 1981.

27. De George, R.T., *Moral Issues in Business*, New York, Macmillan 1990, 133–5, 282–3, 314–15.

28. Nisbet, R., *The Social Philosophers: Community and conflict in Western thought*, London, Heinemann, 1974.

29. Durkheim, E., *The Elementary Forms of Religious Life*, trans. J.W. Swain, Glencoe, Ill., Free Press, 1947, 416.

30. Weber, M., *The Protestant Ethic and the Spirit of Capitalism*, New York, Scribner, 1958, 181.

31. Mahoney, J., How to be Ethical: Ethics resource management, in *Business Ethics: A European Approach*, ed. B. Harvey, London, Prentice Hall, 1994, 32–55.

32. Redditt, P.L., Buddhist Ethics, *International Encyclopaedia of Ethics*, ed. J.K. Roth, London, Fitzroy-Dearborn, 1995, 109–10.

33. Hosaka, Shunji and Nagayasu, Yukimasa, Buddhism and Japanese Economic Ethics, in *The Ethics of Business in a Global Economy*, ed. Paul M. Minus, London, Kluwer, 1993, 99–103.

34. Schumacher, E.F., Buddhist Economics, in *Small is Beautiful*, London, Abacus Books, 1973, ch. 4, 44–51.

35. Welford, R., *Creating the Sustainable Business: A Buddhist Path*, Bradford, ERP Briefings, 1999, 2, 1–37.

36. Mahoney, J., Christianity and Business Ethics, in *The Ethics of Business in a Global Economy*, ed. Paul M. Minus, London, Kluwer, 1993, 111–16.

37. Francis, K., Hindu Ethics, *International Encyclopaedia of Ethics*, ed. J.K. Roth, London, Fitzroy-Dearborn, 1995, 376–7.

38. Islam, *International Encyclopaedia of Ethics*, ed. J.K. Roth, London, Fitzroy-Dearborn, 1995, 109–10.

39. Bassiouni, M.C., An Islamic Perspective on Business, in *The Ethics of Business in a Global Economy*, ed. Paul M. Minus, London, Kluwer, 1993, 117–22.

40. Tamari, Meir, A Jewish Perspective for Modern Business Morality, in *The Ethics of Business in a Global Economy*, ed. Paul M. Minus, London, Kluwer, 1993, 105–9. See also Haas, P.J., Jewish Ethics, *International Encyclopaedia of Ethics*, ed. J.K. Roth, London, Fitzroy-Dearborn, 1995, 464–5.

41. Ettorre, B., Religion in the Workplace: Implications for managers, *Management Review*, December 1996, 15–18.

42. Shaw, W.H. and Barry, V., *Moral Issues in Business*, 7th edn, Belmont, Calif., Wadsworth, 1998, 40.

43. Slomski, G., The Golden Mean, *International Encyclopaedia of Ethics*, ed. J.K. Roth, London, Fitzroy-Dearborn, 1995, 353–4.

44. Radest, H.B., Humanism, *International Encyclopaedia of Ethics*, ed. J. K. Roth, Fitzroy-Dearborn, London, 1995, 411–12.

45. Chernow, R., *Titan: The life of John D. Rockefeller, Snr*, New York, Little, Brown & Co., 1995.

46. Josephson, M. *The Robber Barons*, 2nd edn, New York, Harvest/HBJ Books, 1962, chs 2–5.

47. Greenspan, A., The Assault on Integrity, in A. Rand, *Capitalism: The unknown ideal*, New York, Signet Books, 1967, 118–21.

# 4

# Means/ends analysis and its practical applications

*The end cannot justify the means, for the simple and obvious reason that the means employed determine the nature of the ends produced.*

Aldous Huxley, *Ends and Means*, London, Chatto & Windus, 1937, C.1

### Learning objectives

After reading this chapter you should be able to:

- explain the ethical basis of means/ends analysis and its practical applications in an organisational context;
- distinguish between alternative descriptive and analytical approaches to ethics;
- appreciate how these different ethical positions can be criticised for lacking either rational consistency or practical applications;
- recognise the historical contribution and current applications of these ethical positions in the social sciences, organisational behaviour and management;
- understand how various descriptive positions can be evaluated in an original Moral Compass exercise, which is presented in simple and detailed versions.

## Introduction

Means/ends analysis is a powerful way of evaluating complicated problems in applied ethics. However, some critics regard this method as too mechanistic and propose instead that different ethical positions should be considered from descriptive and analytical standpoints. The main advantage of the latter approach is that a wider spectrum of ethical views can be evaluated. A systematic method of completing this comparative analysis is proposed in which various ethical positions are shown as 'points' on a Moral Compass. Evaluation by the reader is possible after key elements are summarised and criticised, and practical applications in subjects such as organisational behaviour are discussed.

## Ethical values as means and ends

The maxim 'The end justifies the means' is probably familiar to many who are not aware of its origins in means/ends analysis in ethics and application in political science. On the positive side, the reader may be aware of its indirect application in organisational behaviour and management theory. A relevant application occurs in 'systems theory' (see Mullins[1], pp. 99–101) in the simple concepts of 'inputs' and 'outputs', which are derived from means/ends analysis in ethics. This link should become clear when 'means' are regarded as equivalent to 'inputs' and 'ends' as 'outputs'. Means/ends analysis in ethics is concerned with comparative evaluation, just as input/output analysis in a production process is concerned with the output yielded from a known input. The difference lies in the various meanings and uses of the word 'value' which is essential in any comparative evaluation, as the following examples should indicate.

A company producing frozen chips from raw potatoes may use quantitative 'values' in several different ways. First, a simple way to establish the efficiency of the process would be to calculate a value called the 'yield' by comparing the weight of the 'input' of raw potatoes with the weight of the frozen chips as 'output' over a given period. A second monetary value could be calculated by comparing the labour costs of the inputs and outputs on Day 1 with those on Day 2. Yet a third, more complicated 'value' could be calculated if details are known of the costs of freezing, cold storage, distribution, retailer's profits, and the selling price of the frozen chips. These could be used to compute the 'added value' over an agreed financial period (e.g. one year), as a measure which is used by management in calculating the overall profitability of the frozen chip company.

*Means/ends analysis in ethics* is concerned with comparative evaluation of the moral value of human behaviour. For example, the maxim 'The end justifies the means' is meaningless unless an action precedes an outcome. This then allows the moral value of the outcome to be assessed by comparing the merits of the action with the merits of the outcome. This evaluation is based on the rationale that a 'good' end justifies a 'bad' means, since a 'good' end achieved through 'good' means presumably needs no justification and a 'bad' end, irrespective of the means used, probably deserves none at all. With the frozen chip manufacturing example in mind, this is similar to arguing that a high yield of good quality frozen chips from a bad quality batch of raw potatoes is justifiable, whereas a high yield of good quality chips from a good batch of raw potatoes is only to be expected. However, a high yield of bad quality chips from either good or bad quality potatoes would be impossible for a reputable company to justify, since the ends (e.g. customer complaints, loss of profit, loss of goodwill, etc.) would be damaging to its reputation and future sales.

If ethical means/ends analysis is examined more closely, the emphasis is on the outcome because a moral act is assumed to be the one that achieves the greatest good for the greatest number of consumers, citizens, etc. A reasonable question, therefore, is whether the means/ends equation can be extended to justify an immoral action if it results in a greater good being accomplished? For example, should a person tell a lie in the hope of stopping hijackers killing other passengers? This type of argument has been criticised by those who argue that the relative merits of the means and the end are secondary compared with the circumstances that affect a specific situation.

However, even this criticism is not without its ethical problems. The main problem is that *outcomes can never be predicted precisely as ends, in advance of any action and can only be known with hindsight*. To return to the example in the last paragraph, telling a hatful of lies may not save a single passenger and may even put more lives in greater danger, if one of these lies is detected. Despite this problem, means/ends analysis provides a robust form of moral argument which has been adapted and is widely used in cost–benefit analysis exercises by profit-seeking and public sector organisations (see 'Utilitarianism' below).

## Means (as deontology) and ends (as teleology) analysis

There are probably no ethical theories that satisfy all the criteria of those who study ethics as moral philosophy or in applied forms such as business ethics. Broad agreement exists on two different approaches which address many of the moral issues that people are confronted with. These were identified in pre-Christian times by the Ancient Greeks and are known as deontological and teleological approaches to ethics.

### The deontological approach

In its fundamental form, the basic moral objective of this approach is to carry out one's duty irrespective of the consequences, or ends, of any action. Deontological morality is clear-cut because an action is right or good, if it possesses one set of characteristics, and wrong or bad, if it does not. Concerns about what sort of good, or how much may occur from a specific action are irrelevant. Duty is simply doing what is morally right and avoiding what it is morally wrong, regardless of the outcomes. The deontological approach draws on the classical Greek and the Judaeo-Christian traditions (see Chapter 3) and is also concerned with justice and human rights, although mostly from the standpoint of the individual.

### The teleological approach

The other major broad category of ethical theories derives its name from the Greek word *telos*, which means an end or goal. Aristotle[2] argued:

> Now if there is an end which as moral agents we seek for its own sake, and which is the cause of our seeking all the other ends . . . it is clear that this must be the good, that is the absolutely good. May we not then argue from this that a knowledge of the good is a great advantage to us in the conduct of our lives?

Aristotle also maintained that knowledge of human good is the outcome of exercising the human faculty of reason. Teleological ethics usually include all ethical theories that base the rightness of actions, or the moral value of individual traits, on the ends or goals they promote or bring about, as in hedonism or utilitarianism.

The contrast between teleological and deontological theories has been explored by Frankena[3] and Rawls[4] who argue that the two basic concepts in ethics are the *right* (the rightness or obligatoriness of actions) and the *good* (the intrinsic goodness or value of things, or states of affairs). Teleological theories give priority to the good over the right. The right is separately defined as that which maximises the good. Although various forms of teleological ethics provide important landmarks in moral thinking, these have been criticised for devaluing the sovereignty of the individual, especially when individual rights are threatened to promote the greatest amount of good for the greatest number of people (see 'Libertarianism' in Chapter 3, pp. 50–1, and below).

## Descriptive and analytical ethics

De George[5] describes three main ways of generalising about ethical theories by classifying them as descriptive, normative or metaethical approaches. However, it is increasingly common for the metaethical approach to be discussed under the heading of *analytical* ethics (pp. 14–16). Descriptive ethics reflects developments in the social sciences of economics, anthropology, psychology, sociology and politics. As such, it employs a similar 'scientific' method by comparing and contrasting different systems of morals, ethical codes, professional and organisational practices, and other applications of individual and collective values. It also includes the study of comparative morality, culture and their impacts on society; and how these change over time. Relevant applications might include comparisons between corporate social responsibility, business ethics and corporate governance and their relationship to other fields of study such as organisational behaviour, business administration and management.

The chief characteristic of normative ethics is an attempt to provide a moral perspective or system consisting of specific norms, values and beliefs, without which the moral system would lose its essential coherence and justification in the opinion of its adherents. Contrasting examples of normative ethics might include pacifism and totalitarianism. The core aims of normative ethics are, first, to achieve a consistent and coherent set of values and beliefs. Second, to identify an essential principle from which relevant norms and beliefs are derived (e.g. the pacifist principle of not taking life through warfare or other forms of aggressive behaviour). Third, to discover ways of defending core beliefs against critics.

Metaethics is the original form of analytical ethics which examines the meaning of moral terms, such as good and bad, and seeks to examine the validity, or identify inconsistencies, in statements of principles made by practitioners of descriptive and normative; and also in the practical applications of these two branches of ethics. Suffice it to state, that the limitations of continuing with a more detailed account of the differences between these three approaches to ethics are recognised. Hence, a more practical approach is adopted below which attempts to introduce the reader to various forms of normative ethics. These are then appraised from a descriptive ethics standpoint, by including critical summaries together with examples of how each has either been adopted, or rejected, in the fields of business, economics and management. Finally, the reader is invited to develop his/her skills in analytical ethics by evaluating each normative perspective in the following Moral Compass exercise.

## The Moral Compass exercise

Various ethical theories, relating to corporate social responsibility, business ethics and corporate governance, are presented in descriptive and analytical contexts below. The traditional maritime compass model is used to locate similar and opposing ethical theories at four 'cardinal points' (i.e. north, south, east and west) and four 'semi-cardinal points' (north-east, south-east, south-west and north-west). The traditional 360° maritime compass is divided into 32 equal points but, as it would be difficult to identify 32 ethical theories which have appropriate business applications, only 16 theories are presented below. For those who may find the prospect of evaluating 16 theories too daunting, a simple version of the Moral Compass exercise which includes only eight theories is first presented for evaluation.

## Simple and detailed versions of the Moral Compass

The Moral Compass exercise is presented in two forms, the *simple* and *detailed* versions. The simple Moral Compass depicts eight major ethical theories at each of the four cardinal and four semi-cardinal points mentioned above. The detailed Moral Compass extends the simple version by including an additional eight ethical theories in the appropriate quadrants at 16 points on the Moral Compass in total. It is left to the reader to decide whether to complete the simple 8-point or detailed 16-point Moral Compass questionnaires, which appear at the end of each part of the book. The Moral Compass is:

- divided vertically into two semi-circles which separate the deontological/means normative theories from the teleological/ends theories of ethics, as shown in Figure 4.1;
- further divided horizontally into four quadrants which separate normative theories of ethics concerned with individual behaviour from those concerned with group/organisational, or collective perspectives, as shown in Figure 4.2;
- subdivided diagonally to show eight theories of ethics at the four cardinal and four semi-cardinal points. The simple 8-point Moral Compass is shown in Figure 4.3;

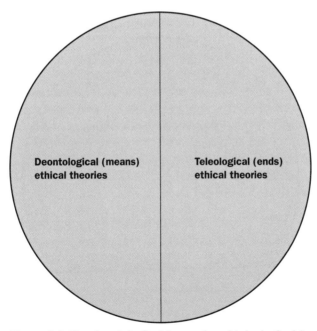

**Deontological (means) ethical theories**

**Teleological (ends) ethical theories**

**Figure 4.1 The deontological (means) and teleological (ends) 'hemispheres' of the Moral Compass**

© T. McEwan 1993, 2000

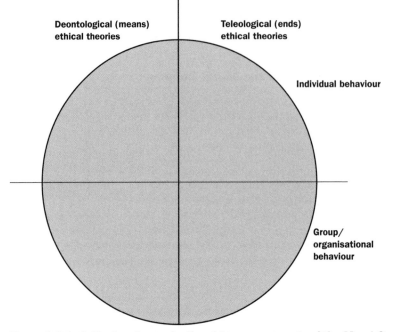

**Figure 4.2 Individual and organisational/group segments of the Moral Compass**
© T. McEwan 1993, 2000

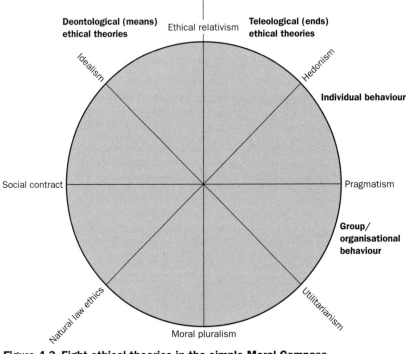

**Figure 4.3 Eight ethical theories in the simple Moral Compass**
© T. McEwan 1993, 2000

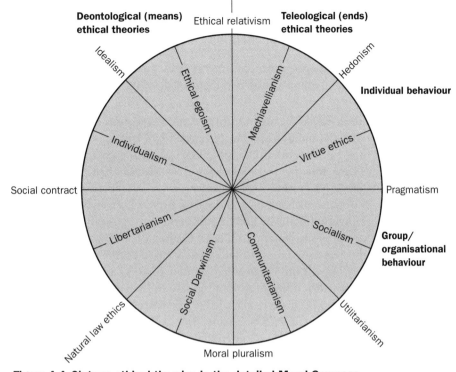

**Figure 4.4 Sixteen ethical theories in the detailed Moral Compass**
© T. McEwan 1993, 2000

■ further subdivided diagonally to include eight more ethical theories in appropriate quadrants in the 16-point detailed Moral Compass shown in Figure 4.4.

As noted above, summaries of each of the ethical theories are presented below. Lickert-type questionnaires are also included at the end of this chapter, and at the end of each part of the book so that personal evaluations of statements on these theories can be recorded.

## Objectives of the Moral Compass

The Moral Compass has three main objectives:

■ After completing the exercise, the reader should have a clearer understanding of each ethical theory and be able to make comparisons with other theories in the same or different quadrants of the Moral Compass.
■ After collating personal scores with the different ethical theories (see the Appendix), the reader should be able to use ethical analysis more effectively in evaluating the moral problems described in the various case studies at the end of each chapter in the book.
■ Finally, the reader should be better prepared to cope with ethical issues as these arise during work-placement experiences or in the course of carrying out managerial or other responsibilities during full-time employment.

## The simple 8-point Moral Compass

### Individual deontological (means) theories

The following normative theory is included in the individual quadrant of the simple Moral Compass shown in Figure 4.3.

**Idealism**

Idealism[6,7] is the major form of deontological ethics. Based on the application of moral laws to human behaviour proposed by Plato (*c.* 428 BCE–348/347 BCE), it provides a logic for evaluating behaviour according to formal rules of moral behaviour. These state that moral decisions should stress first principles in defining appropriate behaviour, rather than consider the consequences of actions. Idealists regard moral values as unchanging and timeless realities, which link the unique experiences of the individual with the good harmonious life. The ethics of human behaviour are governed by universal moral laws binding on everyone which become known through the exercise of reason. This view is based on the assumption that the moral value of any human life is governed by that person's obligation to form a rational, ethical personality. Idealist ethics originate in the concepts (or ideal form) of goodness (or the 'good'), justice, knowledge and virtue. The moral or just society described in Plato's *The Republic* is an idealised, hierarchical state based on a 'division of labour' involving the rulers, guardians (who enforce the rulers' decisions), providers of food, and crafts-specialists, who coexist by practising the four cardinal virtues of wisdom, courage, temperance and justice. Harmony is achieved by each contributing to society according to the predetermined limits of his/her function. Although this occurs within society, idealists claim that the development of ethical behaviour is through cognitive deliberation 'internalised' by the individual. Kant[8] (1724–1804) extended Plato's ideas by emphasising the need for conformity of ethical behaviour to a priori, or first principles of the mind and his categorical imperative is summarised in Chapter 2.

**Criticism**

Since the late nineteenth century, idealist ethics have been on the defensive due to the rise of science. Bertrand Russell (1872–1970) argued that idealism fails to distinguish between a person's perception of, and the separately existing content of, an act which is its *sense datum*. For him, 'What science cannot discover, mankind cannot know.' Therefore, idealistic ethical values are totally subjective and unknowable. Despite this and other criticism of the role of the ideal, or the spiritual in determining ethical behaviour, the assumptions of Plato and Kant that a normative, prescriptive, intelligible, or spiritual reality exists independently of the sensory world, are still widely accepted as a major source of ethical values.

**Impact on social sciences, organisational behaviour and management**

The notion of a moral or just society based on an idealised, hierarchical state, committed to a 'division of labour' comprised of ' rulers', 'guardians' and the 'ruled' living in harmonious coexistence, has influenced economists, sociologists, organisational behaviour and management writers as diverse as Adam Smith, Max Weber, F.W. Taylor, Henri Fayol and Henry Minzberg (see Mullins[1]).

## Group/organisational deontological (means) theories

The following relevant theory is included in the group/organisational quadrant of the simple Moral Compass shown in Figure 4.3.

**Natural law ethics**[9,10]
A widely held theory inherited from classical Greece is that the rightness of actions is determined by laws of human nature rather than the customs or laws of society. Aristotle (384–322 BCE) stated that each human being has a fixed human nature. This specific 'function' provides a capacity for rational thought, which means that moral actions result from fulfilling one's nature as a rational human being. Before this, 'particular' laws have to be separated from those that function 'according to nature', which Aristotle described as the 'common law' that is 'natural' to all humanity. The Roman philosopher Cicero (106–43 BCE) also recognised an eternal, unchanging law that prevails for all people and is grounded in human nature as: 'the highest reason, implanted in Nature, which commands what ought to be done and forbids the opposite'. His emphasis on the equality of all persons before this law of nature led to the wide acceptance of Roman Law in Western society.

Natural law ethics is mostly associated with St Thomas Aquinas (c. 1225–1274), who based his analysis on Aristotle's ideas. His *Summa Theologica* (1266–1273) summarises the principles of natural law morality in 'The Treatise on Law' section, which influenced Western moral and political philosophy through the spread of Roman Catholicism. He identifies the 'eternal law' as the law by which God directs everything towards fulfilment. Natural law enables human beings to participate in this eternal law by striving towards the goal of developing their vast potential. The primary moral obligation on each human is self-fulfilment of his/her nature in the most fully human way possible. Human nature is directed towards its own fulfilment through the first principle of morality which is to ensure that: 'Good is to be done and promoted and evil is to be avoided.'

Here, the word 'good' refers to the 'end' of self-realisation or self-fulfilment. All aspects of the natural law are based on the principle that each person follows his/her 'natural inclinations'. These inclinations are innate and justify the general principle to 'do good' when applied to human nature. However, they exist on both the animal and rational level. The former includes self-preservation, and the preservation of life and avoidance of death is part of the natural law. Human beings also need food, shelter and security to reproduce the species. They also naturally incline towards a life of reason and acquire knowledge, friendship and a social life, as part of their eventual self-fulfilment. A full list of natural inclinations is not included in Aquinas' account of the natural law.

The essential point is made, however, that only by following one's natural inclinations are self-fulfilment and happiness attained, providing reasonable steps are taken not to oppose one's own nature. These principles are unchanging because they emanate from the fixed, common nature shared by human beings. Natural laws are universal and provide a firm basis for all morality and law. Laws exist in an explicit hierarchy since the natural law is derived from the eternal law, whereas human law is subordinated to the natural law. This should be the ultimate guide and 'moral compass' for all legislators and leaders. However, differences occur between human law and the natural law due to historical variations in applying the natural law in communities, which arise because some people are unwilling to follow their own natural aptitude for virtue as indicated in natural law ethics.

**Modern application**

The long history of natural law ethics from classical to modern times has had a profound influence on public figures such as Martin Luther King, Jr[11] who refers to the defence of the natural law in St Augustine's argument that only human laws derived from the eternal and immutable law of God are valid. This means that all other laws are simply unjust and lack moral authority. King states that this lucid argument led him to break the law through civil disobedience in opposition to the unjust discriminatory laws enforced by some US states in the early 1960s. For him, a law was unjust and not really a law if it ignored the principle that all persons are equal before a higher 'natural law'. His moral stance against a long-standing injustice raises the vexed question for critics of natural law ethics of how civil laws can be justified without reference to an alternative, equivalent to the higher standard cited by Aristotle, Cicero and Aquinas.

**Criticism**

Natural law morality is criticised for not being more systematic and including only a few primary precepts to explain the content of a huge subject. For example, the description of natural inclinations in the list of specific and definable duties describing the natural law is incomplete. The purported unchangeability ('immutability') of human nature which gives natural law ethics its unique stability is also overemphasised, at the cost of neglecting the evolution of possible alternative aspects of human fulfilment.

Critics add that an unjust law is still a law, even if natural law supporters might wish it otherwise, and references to what ought to be do not change that reality. Some critics also argue that natural law ethics depends on the assumption that the universe is organised to ensure most human beings are destined to achieve the 'end' of self-realisation. This appears to be contrary to current scientific views about the origins of the cosmos. However, natural law supporters respond that, although modern science and reason do not support their assumptions, it is possible to amend the natural law ethics framework without sacrificing logical coherency.

**Impact on social sciences, organisational behaviour and management**

Natural law ethics have had a profound effect on political science, organisational behaviour and management. Modern theories of bureaucracy, commercial law, management hierarchy, human motivation and personal development are all influenced by these ideas. The close link between Aquinas' theory of natural law morality, with its theological unscientific base, and Maslow's Hierarchy of Needs Theory perhaps explains why researchers have reported difficulties in verifying the latter theory (see Mullins[1], pp. 415–26). Not to single Maslow out for criticism, however, the same argument applies to other theories of motivation which pursue objectivity but overlook their origins in natural law ethics.

## Individual teleological (ends) theories

The following relevant theory is included in the individual quadrant of the simple Moral Compass shown in Figure 4.3.

**Hedonism**

The view derived from the classical Greek Epicureans by Jeremy Bentham[12] (1748–1832) and others is that hedonism (from the Greek *hedone*, meaning 'pleasure') is the highest good and therefore desirable. Some supporters rely on psychological hedonism to argue that hedonism is compatible with the theory that all human beings are motivated by pleasure, or avoidance of pain. Others reject this link which purports to describe how things *are*, whereas ethical hedonism states how things *ought to be*. They claim that hedonism is true by definition following John Locke[13], who defined 'good' as that which 'is apt to cause or increase pleasure'.

Bentham proposed a quantitative hedonism of sensual pleasures that could be compared using a 'hedonistic calculus'. This allowed specific values of pleasures to be compared for their intensity, duration, certainty (probability of happening), propinquity (nearness or remoteness), fecundity (likelihood of leading to more pleasures), purity (probability of not being followed by pain), and extent (number of persons affected by them). John Stuart Mill[14] (1806–1873) rejected quantitative hedonism in favour of a qualitative version as pleasures differed in kind as well as in quantity, arguing: 'Better to be a human being dissatisfied than a pig satisfied; better to be a Socrates dissatisfied than a fool satisfied . . . if the fool, or the pig, are of a different opinion, it is because they only know their own side of the question. The other party to the comparison knows both sides.' Both quantitative and qualitative forms of hedonism probably survive today because of their appeal to common sense when ethical and psychological questions are raised about what is valuable or good about human existence.

Criticism

The definitional approach to hedonism is criticised for overlooking things that do not involve pleasure (e.g. vaccination or childbirth), but are regarded as intrinsically good, whereas other pleasurable things (e.g. smoking and alcohol) are regarded as intrinsically bad. Attempts to define 'good' also fail for trying to define the indefinable, especially when the 'good' is expressed in natural terms as 'pleasure'. This is known as the 'naturalistic fallacy'. Efforts to equate ethical and psychological hedonism are also rejected because individuals often fail in their deliberate search for pleasure yet find it unexpectedly when pursuing other things as an end. This is known as the 'hedonistic paradox'. Difficulties occur in linking ethical and psychological hedonism since, if the latter is true and all human actions are motivated by a desire for pleasure, then the hedonist's view that people ought to seek pleasure is redundant. Finally, the qualitative version of hedonism has been criticised because those who seek to make 'more satisfied than a pig' judgements require a criterion other than pleasure to identify what they claim to be intrinsically good.

Impact on social sciences, organisational behaviour and management

The study of hedonism is important in motivation and job satisfaction research in organisational behaviour; and also in the study of gratification of impulse buying, etc., in marketing and advertising (see Mullins[1], chs 12 and 18; Fill[15], chs 10 and 13).

## Group/organisational teleological (ends) theories

The following relevant theory is included in the group/organisational quadrant of the simple Moral Compass shown in Figure 4.3.

**Utilitarianism**       Associated mainly with Jeremy Bentham and John Stuart Mill during the eighteenth and nineteenth centuries, utilitarianism[16,17] is a decision procedure intended to promote the general welfare of society by providing the greatest happiness for the greatest number of people. Bentham[18] devised a hedonistic theory of value, arguing: 'It is the greatest happiness of the greatest number that is the measure of right and wrong'. Since happiness (as pleasure or the absence of pain) is the only intrinsic good, other things are valuable only if moral action occurs whenever the balance of pleasure over pain is maximised. A moral system also has to be objective and scientific and the principle of utility was valid because it was empirically possible to ascertain the results of people's actions, whereas their intentions could only be guessed at. However, this utility principle is not open to direct proof because it is a universal principle used to prove everything else.

**Criticism**        Supporters argue that utilitarian ethics are universal rather than egoistic and the good of all should be maximised, rather than any individual pleasure gained at the expense of others. Critics note, however, that this means that two forms of utilitarianism are necessary since a distinction has to be made between *act* and *rule* utilitarianism which leads to confusion and potential conflicts when the good of the individual clashes with that of the rest of society. Those supporting the rule version argue that the outcomes should be collective and egalitarian since the happiness of each individual is of equal value. Supporters of the act version reject rule utilitarianism because it tends to penalise an able or efficient individual for the benefit of the less capable majority.

**Impact on social sciences, organisational behaviour and management**        It would be difficult to overestimate the importance of utilitarianism since World War II on public policy in Britain and elsewhere in Europe, as it has underpinned major political agendas such as the welfare state, the National Health Service, comprehensive education and social security payments, etc. In the more specialised field of business administration and management, changes in post-World War II personnel practices which extended private health insurance, increased leave entitlement, superannuation schemes, etc., to most employees, may also be regarded as utilitarian in terms of organisational aims and objectives.

## Intervening theories at vertical points in the Moral Compass

The following two theories are indicated at the top and bottom vertical points of the simple Moral Compass model shown in Figure 4.3:

- ethical relativism;
- moral pluralism.

**Ethical relativism**     Ethical relativism[19,20] supports the proposition that different moral judgements made by more than one set of individuals, or culture, may all have right on their side. This implies that moral judgements are ultimately statements of opinion, or feelings, and moral evaluations of right or wrong are culturally determined. Ethical relativism rejects the notion that there are any objective or universal moral standards by proposing that what is morally right or wrong is relative to an individual, group or culture.

Instead, it seeks to adopt the sceptical position that the human mind is incapable of attaining any genuine or objective truth. Therefore, any acquired knowledge is always subjective and 'relative' to that individual. Ethical relativism is usually divided into individualistic and cultural versions. Individualistic relativism assumes that ethical values or norms differ among human beings within a society or culture because moral judgements are purely subjective and simply a matter of personal taste for the individual's conscience.

Cultural relativism avoids this dilemma by proposing that differences in moral values occur across societies or cultures. As a result, values considered to be essential in one society might be rejected in another culture, and vice versa. More formally, cultural relativism takes the ethical stance that no transcultural, universal moral norms exist, and that prevailing moral judgements in different cultures are equally valid. This means that a cultural relativist can accept there are no fixed standards that serve as an ultimate moral guide for a society, since all moral values are regarded as conditional and totally dependent on time, place and circumstances. At first glance, cultural relativism seems to be plausible, especially since it is clear that there are various societies with different moral codes, but this position has also been roundly criticised.

**Criticism**

Critics of individualistic relativism have questioned whether ethical judgements can ever be consistent with one another if individuals are unable to agree over any moral issue. Cultural relativism is also criticised, even when individual members of a society are in agreement over specific moral issues, because this does not exclude the possibility that a society may pass favourable judgements on the moral actions of its own members as a way of denouncing those of another. Alternatively, a society may conclude that disagreements on moral issues are neither right nor wrong as there is no acceptable way of deciding their validity. This version of cultural relativism is open to the further criticism that, without an agreed standard for evaluating moral codes, it becomes impossible to criticise one's own or other cultures. In addition, the notion of moral change becomes meaningless because, if change implies improvement or development, then independent transcultural standard(s) are necessary to judge how a nation or culture can achieve this moral development. Possible solutions to these problems may lie in moral pluralism, which is discussed below.

**Impact on social sciences, organisational behaviour and management**

Ethical relativism is generally shunned in the social sciences in favour of a moral pluralism perspective, for the same reasons that Social Darwinism (see below) is rejected. In short, it can lead to stereotyping, discrimination and elitism, by ignoring the specialised capabilities or accomplishments of those from other cultures, which may lead to low morale, racism or related conflicts in the work environment.

**Moral pluralism**

The rise of moral pluralism[21,22] coincides with a re-evaluation of the world as a global 'village', made up of international markets linked by new technology. Pluralism is the product of modern Western society, which is depicted as increasingly dynamic and culturally diverse, comprising different ethnic groups and traditions. At the same time, people are perplexed not just by how different the rest of the world is, both culturally and in terms of moral values, but also by how rapidly the West is changing in response to these other cultures and traditions. Moral pluralism attempts to address these issues by maintaining that values, obligations, virtues, beliefs and moral principles are essentially diverse and cannot be reconciled into one comprehensive scheme of morality.

De George[20] (p. 40) explicates moral pluralism on four levels: radical moral pluralism, moral principles, moral practices and self-realisation. It should be stressed that moral pluralism is not equivalent to moral relativism. In particular, it rejects the view that values are subjective, expressions of personal taste or cultural beliefs. Instead, moral pluralism supports the empirical position that values are objective but also may be incompatible. Radical moral pluralism contradicts the notion of a society by observing that mutually irreconcilable views about morality are held by people who reject common meanings of right and wrong and also which actions are right or wrong. A plurality of moral principles defends diversity in society by arguing that ethical principles are associated with major differences in the morality of social behaviour. For example, arson is universally regarded as wrong but often for different reasons. Some people regard it as contrary to God's law; others insist that it offends human dignity; others deplore it because the destruction of property threatens society as a whole. The relevant point is not that different moral principles are involved, but that these coalesce in a single moral judgement that condemns the act of arson. This approach differs from a pluralism of moral practices which states that moral judgements are influenced by the different ways people perceive facts or circumstances, or evaluate relevant values on a particular issue. For example, Western society generally opposes the use of narcotics but people with more lenient beliefs may not condemn 'soft' drugs in the belief that their use leads to less crime than 'hard' drugs, which should be prohibited. This view is not shared by those who condemn the use of all drugs whatsoever.

A pluralism of self-realisation, the most widespread form of pluralism in Western society, is based on tolerance and the notion that, if people conform to a set of minimum rules, norms or beliefs (see the section on Liberalism in Chapter 3), as members of a diverse and plural society, they should be free to choose their own moral values and lifestyles. Implicit in this ethical framework is a belief in tolerance as part of a diverse, possibly fragmented, value-system that would be rejected in a more cohesive society committed to moral absolutism.

## Criticism

Pluralism, like ethical relativism, has been criticised for either being 'all things to all persons' or for condoning various forms of deontological and teleological ethics on the grounds that these value-systems are practised in different cultures around the world, which should all be recognised and treated with respect. The pluralist reply is that a valid starting point of descriptive ethics should be the findings of social scientists about the moral codes and other belief-systems of different cultures; and the primary analysis thereafter should not be to criticise or devalue a particular culture by imposing, for example, a 'cultural imperialist' perspective. Rather, the task should focus on identifying common principles between different moral codes and belief-systems, as in the Golden Rule/Mean example in Chapter 3.

## Impact on social sciences, organisational behaviour and management

Moral pluralism has made a major impact on social anthropology, social psychology and sociology. However, its importance has also gained increasing recognition in the study of organisational culture, following the research of Hofstede and Trompenaars (see R. French in Mullins[1], pp. 31–3).

## Intervening theories at horizontal points in the Moral Compass

The following two theories are indicated at the left and right horizontal points of the simple Moral Compass model shown in Figure 4.3:

- social contract;
- pragmatism.

**Social contract**

Social contract theory assumes that civil society started when individuals entered into a 'social contract' by giving up some personal power and freedom to live in cooperation with others who had also sacrificed similar powers and freedom. Social contract theory, which provides a basis for analysing the organisation of human society, dates back to Thomas Hobbes, John Locke and Jean-Jacques Rousseau whose main assumptions are that people are autonomous rational agents who use individual free will as the source of all morality.

**Thomas Hobbes**

According to Hobbes[23], people naturally favour the society of others but cannot exist without a sovereign to protect individuals from other persons. People must otherwise live in a state of nature, where the basic right of self-preservation prevails together with the right to take anything that is within one's power. War is an inevitable outcome against everyone else if people seek to impose their rights, with each person living under the constant threat of personal violence and loss of property. To obtain their rights, people will act in anticipation of withdrawal by killing other persons perceived to be potential threats. Life in this state of nature is therefore 'solitary, poor, nasty, brutish, and short', unless reason leads people to reject this situation as intolerable. As rational autonomous individuals, they will agree to form a contract, sacrificing some of their power to a sovereign, in return for protection that binds them absolutely by the sovereign's laws, in a social contract based on self-interest.

**John Locke**

Locke's[24] description of this state of nature is more benign yet reaches similar conclusions. His state of nature is one of plenty, allowing people to fulfil their needs. Each has a right to all that can be used providing enough is left for others. The only limit on personal consumption is that unused goods will quickly spoil. The introduction of money, as a non-perishable unit of exchange, removes this limit but encourages hoarding and competition. A chaotic state based on the unbounded right to property would follow except that each person possesses reason. This leads to a state where people seek a peace that respects their natural rights of life, liberty and property. Judgements will still need to deal with any threats to the natural rights of each individual. This is because of the danger that people will misjudge their own safety needs, or those of others, and become so preoccupied with security, that they will seek to prevent personal injury by threatening the security of others. The absence of a common judge leads to a state of nature plagued by uncertainty and disharmony. To avert such misjudgements, people will enter into a social contract by forming a government that holds the power of the people in trust, and acts as a judge in a civil society to preserve each person's security.

**Jean-Jacques Rousseau**

Rousseau's[25] alternative ideal state describes pure and innocent people in a state of nature, typified by the noble savage. However, civil society has corrupted people and created strife whereby their wants and needs are no longer simple and easily satisfied. Since nature is good, what has gone wrong must be due to wrong actions by human society. The aim should therefore be to create a state in which people can retain their original freedom, without dependence on the opinion or will of others, or acquire power beyond their own needs, or at another's expense. There is a general will that requires each person to be free from these dependencies by being free from influence or obligation. Each individual has a duty to act in accordance with the general well-being and to ensure that others do the same. There is no greater sense of social obligation than to show individuals that, ultimately, there is no difference among people. If they are of equal vulnerability, then rationality and sentiment will direct them to form a community that addresses the interests of all. Provided these sentiments are cultivated, reason will lead to a general will that binds all individuals by their own will without any enslavement.

| | |
|---|---|
| Criticism | Critics of the social contract tradition doubt that it is possible for free, autonomous, rational people to agree to a social contract. This is because no one is free from pressure or coercion and it is impossible to tell if, and for whom, a contract is valid. Another problem in modern society is the role of women in the social contract (see Pateman[26]), which proposes free, autonomous males as the principal parties to the contract, although it is assumed that women, children and slaves are somehow bound by its conditions. |
| Impact on social sciences, organisational behaviour and management | The social contract has been hugely influential at the macro-political, organisational and micro-levels in society. At the politico-economic level, it forms the basis of the UK and European laws at transnational (e.g. the EU Environmental Impact Assessment Directive) and intra-national levels (e.g. the Company Securities (Insider Dealings) Act 1985). It has also influenced the US Constitution and Bill of Rights, the United Nations Charter of Human Rights, the World Court, the North Atlantic Treaty Organisation (NATO), the World Trade Organisation, UNESCO, the International Labour Organisation, and so forth. At the organisational level, employee relations agreements between employer and trade unions or other employee organisations; and contractual arrangements involving employers and individual employees at the micro-level are all based on ethical and socioeconomic principles derived from the social contract. The male-dominated interpretation of the social contract has been re-evaluated in Western society, yet the large discrepancies in remuneration and other benefits for like employment indicate that the original inequity between men and women still persists in the modern working environment. |
| **Pragmatism**[27,28] | This is a theory of ethics with classical Greek origins first presented in the USA near the start of the twentieth century and associated with C.S. Peirce (1838–1914), William James (1842–1910), John Dewey (1859–1952) and G.H. Mead (1863–1931) who, as pragmatists, challenged all formal, absolute and egoist-based principles of moral values on the principle that different ideas with similar consequences are really the same idea expressed in different words. This led to the view that an idea's meaning is determined by its effects on the person who accepts/believes it. Pragmatists accepted Darwinism and the principle that the future can be changed by human thought and action. Pragmatism's considerable influence on American culture is apparent in the |

emphasis on optimistic action supported by 'positive thinking' about the future, rather than the past. This resulted in greater stress on education, communication, cognitive development of personal perceptions, attitudes and goals, social interaction, and democracy, in understanding, evaluating and seeking to control a world of changing objects, ideas and events. Pragmatists view thought as a process influencing the whole life-activity. It occurs when any activity is disturbed by a belief that seeks to guide future action more positively or successfully. Beliefs are changing dispositions or habits that lead to a general 'pragmatic' theory of meaning as individuals respond to the environment through intelligent inquiry ('instrumentality'). This leads to 'feedback' based on personal experience and that of others, before acceptability occurs based on the overall 'workability' of beliefs in social interaction.

Since ethics deals with all human activity, individuals acquire reliable information through communication skills, experience, cooperation and deliberation in educational, political and other organisational contexts in creating new values and ideals. Ultimately, ethics means ensuring human existence becomes more meaningful and fulfilling. This does not require ethical problems to be handed over to some elite, but occurs by adopting the cooperative, experimental attitude of science, and proposing practical, democratic solutions to social problems that would otherwise leave many human lives devoid of hope or meaning. When moral issues are explored in this way, rather than as formal principles of ethical judgement, pragmatists argue that it should be possible to improve the human condition. They add that introducing such behaviour into society provides the most secure foundation for democracy, by incorporating every acceptable means to achieve conditions that enable people to lead more meaningful individual and socially significant lives.

## Criticism

Pragmatism has been criticised for inconsistency in wanting things all ways. It purports to be committed neither to deontological nor teleological ethics, but focuses on consequences without identifying real knowledge. Numerous outcomes are recognised yet the notion that all ends should be accepted indiscriminately is rejected, as is the hedonistic view that satisfaction should be maximised. Pragmatists reject the notion that aims should be pursued to their rational (or moral) outcome, yet accept the importance of rules and obligations in public life, which are then evaluated for their general effectiveness. The obvious pitfall is that the process can proceed indefinitely without ever reaching the point where 'workability' actually occurs.

## Impact on social sciences, organisational behaviour and management

Accountants and other management decision makers may see advantages in using William James' concept of 'cash value' (Popkin and Stroll[29]) as a way of evaluating moral issues in business. James argues that before any moral claim is accepted as true, its 'cash value' should be determined. This means establishing what function it has and what difference its being true or false would make. For example, if a claim has no cash value, it would make no difference whether one believed it true or false and therefore it should not affect one's action. If a theory is believed to be true, it must have a cash value which will depend on the use it is put to, its likely consequences and expected impact on others. It should be possible to list these moral issues and attempt to evaluate them without using quantitative measures initially, although this may become necessary in decision making based on cost–benefit analysis techniques.

## Detailed 16-point Moral Compass

### Individual deontological (means) theories

The following two relevant theories are included in the individual quadrant of the 16-point detailed Moral Compass shown in Figure 4.4:

- individualism;
- ethical egoism.

**Individualism**

The philosophical claims of individualism[30,31] were proposed by Thomas Hobbes[23] (1588–1679) and John Locke[24] (1632–1704) before Adam Smith explored the economic and political implications in *The Wealth of Nations* (1776). However, Alexis de Tocqueville is credited with introducing the term 'individualism' in *Democracy in America* (vol. 1, 1835–9). The theory regards individual human beings as fundamental units of reality and value. They are therefore the foundation of all ethical and social principles. Collectivism is rejected because individuals are assumed to control their own thoughts and actions. They also form their own characters unaided by anyone else. Individual value and potential is assumed to develop through self-reliance, independence, initiative, pride and courage, often in the face of disapproval. *Laissez-faire* policies are advocated in economics and politics because these leave the individual free to pursue his/her own ends through free enterprise and minimum government intervention.

The notion that individuals are subordinate to any social group is also rejected, as is the view that social groupings are more important than their members, or that individuals should defer to wishes of a group along class, racial, tribal, family, or national lines. Cooperation with others is not rejected, provided individuals are the sole beneficiaries of any participation in group activities. In the economic field, independence of thought and action do not require individuals to live alone, and the specialised division of labour in groups is encouraged, providing that it allows individuals to prosper from first accumulating their own financial needs before any surplus is traded with others for mutual benefit.

**Criticism**

Collectivists challenge individualism's notions that only individuals exist, and groups are merely aggregates of individuals. For them, social groups are organic wholes of which individuals are dependent members, and human behaviour is ultimately formed in the social groups to which most individuals belong.

**Impact on social sciences, organisational behaviour and management**

The individual/group relationship offers huge potential for unique creativity or conflict, on the one hand, and considerable benefits of collective cooperation or the narrow drawbacks of 'groupthink', on the other. These issues provide major themes which attracted specialists in psychology, sociology and organisational behaviour during the nineteenth and twentieth centuries. Further details on some of these contributions in organisational behaviour and management are included in Mullins[1] (chs 2, 3, 6, 7, 8, 13 and 14).

**Ethical egoism**[32,33]

This is a belief inherited from the Ancient Greeks that individuals should maximise their own self-interest, even when this is at the expense of a concern for others. The two main versions are individualism, discussed above, and the more common act egoism, which does not condemn selfishness and greed, because one has no basic or unconditional obligations to any other person. Egoists maintain that self-interest should be maximised because rationality and moral rightness are equivalent, therefore ethical egoism endorses moral rightness. Conversely, when conflict occurs between the two, ethical egoism emerges as a non-moral theory of rational action by raising the awkward question 'Why be moral, if it is irrational?'

Ethical egoists justify self-interest in different ways. Some maintain that personal pleasure should be enjoyed for its own sake but most insist that, when power over others is at stake, self-interest is preferable to sacrifice, if only to prevent the abuse of power by others. Other egoists argue that personal obligations and decisions should be based on a longer-term enlightened self-interest and not on immediate gratification of pleasure and desire. For these, character is intrinsically good and not achieved through self-sacrifice because self-interest is morally equivalent to happiness or well-being. They also argue that there is no unconditional obligation to serve another's interests, unless helping others, or restraining from harming them, enhances one's self-interests. That said, ethical egoists remain morally obliged to keep promises, be truthful, co-operative, and to treat others equitably, as long as it furthers their own self-interest. Otherwise, no ethical or rational reasons exist for limiting self-interested behaviour even if it might harm others.

Criticism

Three main criticisms are raised against ethical egoism. First, it is logically inconsistent when conflicts of interest arise, since egoists argue in favour of everyone coming out on top, which is impossible. However, egoists dismiss this criticism, pointing out that the aim is for each person to maximise his or her self-interest. Conflicts can be resolved by adopting rules which support one's self-interest as long as others prosper. Secondly, critics argue that it would be against one's self-interest to defend ethical egoism in professions such as teaching, medicine and counselling, when moral or professional commitment to others is essential. Ethical egoists insist that where no conflicts arise, these tasks can be performed professionally, and where they do occur, egoists can always stay silent. Finally, ethical egoism is dismissed as immoral for maintaining that any act is acceptable that promotes self-interest, which implies that lying, theft, blackmail and murder are justifiable. Defenders of ethical egoism deny that such acts are permissible, and even if they could be justified, such immoral acts would never promote one's self-interest in practice.

Impact on social sciences, organisational behaviour and management

Interest in ethical egoism revived during the 1980s and 1990s in the UK and USA particularly, following Milton Friedman's contributions to economics (see Chapter 1), and the renewed interest in small business development and entrepreneurship. Although the subject is not mentioned directly, psychological and organisational behaviour aspects of ethical egoism are explored in Mullins[1] (chs 9, 10, 18 and 19).

## Group/organisational deontological (means) theories

The following two relevant theories are included in the group/organisational quadrant of the 16-point detailed Moral Compass shown in Figure 4.4:

- libertarianism;
- Social Darwinism.

**Libertarianism**    This subject is introduced in Chapter 3 as a theory of ethics that advocates free enterprise and individualism, based on the principle that the defence of liberty requires a minimum form of government. Libertarianism holds that personal autonomy is the fundamental ethical principle. Followers adopt the view that any social or political institution is wrong if it interferes with the individual's control over his/her own life. Libertarians defend personal property rights, the free market economy and a wide range of civil freedoms.

Criticism    Critics raise similar objections to those made against individualism above, with the main difference that they are applied here to organisations or, more specifically, to managers who act as agents on behalf of institutions or companies. In practice, unless managers own controlling interests in profit-seeking firms, they are unlikely to be applying strict libertarian principles. What is more likely is that libertarian managers might carry out their responsibilities according to arguments advanced by writers such as Friedman[34] and Sternberg[35], who both argue that only those libertarian values that do not contravene the law should be adopted.

Impact on social sciences, organisational behaviour and management    In economics, libertarianism has drawn inspiration from the Austrian and Chicago 'schools of economics', notably from the work of von Hayek[36] and Friedman[34]. The impact of libertarianism on organisational behaviour and management theory is hard to assess, although more attention is probably focused on individual development in the USA than in the UK, where the preference for individual rather than group development appears less pronounced. For an even-handed discussion of idiographic and nomothetic theories of personality, see L. Hicks in Mullins[1] (ch. 9, pp. 299–307).

**Social Darwinism**    A misapplication of Charles Darwin's theory of biological evolution by natural selection led to the rise of Social Darwinism[37] in the UK and USA during the nineteenth century. Associated with Herbert Spencer (1820–1903), this ideology focused on the development of society and human social behaviour and was supported by early capitalists after the Industrial Revolution before it was adopted by Western colonialists in the late nineteenth century. Spencer developed his views on social evolution before Darwin's *On the Origin of Species* was published in 1859. He modified Darwin's ideas before concluding that the 'struggle for existence' and 'survival of the fittest' explained the unequal distribution of wealth in a changing capitalist environment. Regrettably, the latter slogan appeared in the fifth edition of Darwin's book in 1869, by when his ideas on natural selection had been misconstrued by Social Darwinists to account for biological evolution. The latter phenomenon supposedly justified both the mistreatment of non-Western peoples and the lower classes in Europe and the USA. Otherwise, Western colonialism and imperialism would have found it very difficult to reject the principle that all people should have benefited from the wealth produced by the Industrial Revolution since the late eighteenth century. Disparity in access to resources, wealth and social status was already well established (see Capitalism in Chapter 3), but far more non-Western peoples and their natural resources, situated in what are now called 'Third World' countries, were exploited by Western nations. Social Darwinism provided a rationale for this behaviour. It allowed Western governments to justify expansion of their political and economic power and influence, entrepreneurs to increase their fortunes at home and overseas, and Western missionaries to compete in spreading their rival versions of the Christian gospels.

Darwin had demonstrated that evolution was due to the slow impact of variation, inheritance and natural selection over time. Less accurate, were his beliefs that the environment explained variation and that biological success was measurable by the frequency of reproduction. However, the moral and value judgements introduced by Social Darwinists suggested that the struggle for existence within and between societies was a natural condition of cultural evolution. Human societies were compared with biological organisms as slowly evolving from the simple to the complex through competition for resources. Since competition was natural and predictable for Social Darwinists, they argued that individuals, organisations and other institutions that achieved the greatest political and economic power were the 'fittest' compared with those that fell behind.

In the USA, Social Darwinism was linked with leading supporters of *laissez-faire* capitalism during the nineteenth century, who insisted that people were not born equal and that millionaires were a product of natural selection. Two such entrepreneurs were Andrew Carnegie and John D. Rockefeller, Sr (see the case study in Chapter 3). Hofstadter[38] quotes the latter as stating: 'The growth of a large business is merely a survival of the fittest . . . it is merely the working-out of a law of nature and a law of God.' Rockefeller's views echoed those of less prominent Social Darwinists, who opposed social and economic planning on the grounds that such interventions by governments distorted the normal workings of the marketplace and the natural process of social evolution. Social Darwinists defended individual competition, arguing that customs and morals are instinctive responses to fear, sex, and hunger drives, which merely led to more exploitation of the poor by the rich in society.

Criticism

Social Darwinism has been widely criticised for supporting Western ethnocentrism, racism and the pseudo-science of eugenics during the nineteenth century by claiming that social progress demanded a competitive struggle between nations and races. What could not be foreseen was that these ideas would find expression 40–50 years later from other European sources in the rise of Nazi extremism in Germany, ending in World War II. It was the widespread revulsion against Nazism (and, later, apartheid in South Africa) that halted the spread of Social Darwinism, although only a dedicated optimist would insist that another version will not appear in the future.

Impact on social sciences, organisational behaviour and management

Social Darwinism is so incompatible with post-World War II socioeconomic and political developments in Western society that reputable texts defending these views are not published. That aside, Hofstadter's study of the rise and fall of Social Darwinism in the USA received justifiable critial acclaim and should be regarded as essential reading by aspiring managers in the global economy.

## Individual teleological (ends) theories

The following two teleological (ends) theories are included in the individual quadrant of the 16-point detailed Moral Compass shown in Figure 4.4:

- Machiavellianism;
- virtue ethics.

**Machiavellian-ism**[39,40]

The name is taken from an amoral view of ethics and politics developed by the Italian Renaissance writer and diplomat, Niccolò Machiavelli (1469–1527), which condoned questionable policies for obtaining and holding on to political power. In *The Prince* (1513)[41], political and military affairs received priority by being separated from religious, moral or social issues, except when the latter were politically expedient. Whether a policy was brutal or treacherous in the pursuit of power was immaterial, unless this affected the success of the policy, which was more likely to occur if the policy was regarded as honourable and fair. In short, Machiavelli never advocated mindless cruelty, but analysed its political uses objectively.

His ideas on human nature, power, the nature of the state and the role of popular government were based on the pessimistic assumption that the primary human motivations are greed and egoism. Successful government thrives on human weakness, control of the conflict that grows out of human self-interest, and the state's capacity to counteract the natural aggression of its citizens. Machiavelli emphasised the role of the ruler as lawgiver. Moral and civic virtues grow out of law and government because they are not inherent in human nature. The ruler must exercise *virtu*, an amoral dualism that included the strength and vision to maintain stability, complemented by the flexibility to adapt to an unpredictable future. Since the goal of the state was to preserve its reputation, property and assets, it could not survive without popular support. A ruler should therefore strive to be both loved and feared, although Machiavelli admitted it was difficult to have things both ways. If one could not be both loved and feared, it was better to be feared than loved.

Machiavelli defined the state through identification with its citizens, who were easier to control than the nobility, therefore government should be popular whenever practical. Because the nobility were divisive and pursued interests that often clashed with those of the state, the law and prevailing morality should be used against all opponents, providing the ruler remained above morality and practised *virtu* by acting out the contrasting roles of 'lion and fox'. In the former role, brute force should be used to crush dangerous opposition whenever necessary. Otherwise, a ruler should adopt the fox's role, concealing the real intent of his policy by controlling outward appearances to confound any opposition discreetly through an effective 'divide and rule' policy. Machiavelli was a sceptical realist, whose ethics of expediency made power the primary goal of politics, while moral, economic and social considerations were mere factors to be controlled by the effective ruler. The purpose of the state is to preserve power, and because the one criterion of evaluation is success, failure should never be risked because of moral considerations.

Criticism

The amoral objectivity of Machiavelli's ideas make him an obvious target for all shades of religious, libertarian, idealist and collectivist criticism, not all of which is accurate. He undoubtedly exaggerated the importance of power by confusing the objectives of politics with the actual political process, and undervalued the importance of socioeconomic and ethical issues in society. Criticism of his ethics of expediency, which led to Machiavelli being associated with the darker side of politics, is also valid. That said, he was unfairly criticised in France at a time when most Italian ideas were rejected, which prompted the inaccurate charge that he advocated unrestrained treachery and evil in government. There is also little evidence that he acted as a sinister influence who advised leaders to employ force and cruelty in retaining power. This view undervalues his original contribution to political science and the philosophy of history. It also ignores his systematic analysis of the complex ambiguities of power and his rational defence of prudence in politics, which sanctioned expediency only as a last resort when popular government broke down. Machiavelli was probably responsible for cultivating his reputation for amoral cynicism, as he was regarded as a good parent and an upright, patriotic citizen by his contemporaries.

**Impact on social sciences, organisational behaviour and management**

Even Machiavelli's sternest critic might concede that to exclude Machiavelli's massive contribution on the analysis of power in organisational behaviour and management would be like watching a film of Robin Hood without a Sheriff of Nottingham. Now that corporate governance statements are a requirement of companies seeking inclusion in the FT/SE Index, a detailed discussion of Machiavelli's analysis of the use/abuse of personal and institutional power in management education appears long overdue. However, with a few exceptions, studies of formal and informal power in organisations are found in the related fields of sociology, political science and organisational communication.

**Virtue ethics**

Virtue ethics[42,43,44] emerged in the 1950s as an ethical approach to the understanding and practice of the 'good' life. Virtue is defined as action shaped by moral judgement and discipline, rather than by moral rules, principles, obligation and consequences. Virtue ethics declares its task as focusing on what is important to the individual and society in contemporary life, which occurs in patterns of interaction. Its central principle is that people are good and perform right actions, less as individual acts of moral reasoning, than as a consequence of inherited patterns of right and wrong. A meaningful ethical life develops by taking responsibility for inherited patterns of behaviour rather than through abstract discussion. In discussing new ethical challenges, the importance of character, values and virtues in everyday life should not be neglected. A 'good' character is as important as any point of view expressed in thoughts, actions and values, etc., and emerges as virtuous behaviour through self-discipline and reflection. However, the ethical life is not isolated from society, but is influenced by others since virtues are often inherited from parents, peers and significant others. These virtues are sustained as a pattern of action over time through encouragement and positive reinforcement (see 'Operant Conditioning' in Mullins[1], pp. 357–60).

Because it focuses on the whole person, virtue ethics is concerned with the emotions and the psychology of ethics, including the influence of cultural factors on the formation of a virtuous character. How a person becomes a fulfilled human being, and whether criteria vary according to gender, race, ethnicity and socioeconomic status are therefore important questions in virtue ethics. Many of the essential virtues were discussed in classical Greece and are still vitally important today. These include justice, courage, generosity, temperance, gentleness and wisdom. However, defenders of virtue ethics recognise that people can mislead themselves by searching for the good and they prefer to focus on human development towards personal goodness instead, rather than dwell on the presence of the good, or its absence in evil.

Criticism

Since the emotions play an important role in virtue ethics, critics have enquired how consistency is achieved in an ethical life that is prone to transient feelings. However, defenders of virtue ethics turn this problem on its head by pointing out that one reason for the interest in their approach is precisely because 'rules and consequences ethics' ignores this essential part of human experience. They insist that any valid ethical theory must deal with the whole person, including personality and feelings, not just the rules and consequences of means/ends analysis. Other critics are sceptical of the notion that virtue ethics can attract individuals towards a personally perceived good, since human beings appear to find the bad more attractive than the good. They also query the proposition that one will be good at some future date, but not today, since once a duty is recognised, there is an obligation to carry it out without undue delay. Supporters of virtue ethics acknowledge that setbacks will occur, but maintain that vice will always be part of any journey towards improvement. They add that virtue usually emerges from dealing with vices once it is acknowledged that virtuous behaviour is better than vice. Finally, others note that some conflicts between virtues such as gentleness and courage, for example, cannot be easily reconciled. However, defenders point out that only virtue ethics allow individuals to evaluate such conflicts in a mature manner which, in turn, helps to develop their moral characters.

Impact on social sciences, organisational behaviour and management

Virtue ethics has only had an indirect influence on the social sciences, organisational behaviour and management, but its impact is subsumed in the study of transactional analysis, body language, group cohesiveness, development and maturity, training, job enrichment and satisfaction, empowerment, appraisal and employee relations (see Mullins[1], chs 11, 13, 18 and 19).

## Group/organisational teleological (ends) theories

The following two teleological (ends) theories are included in the group/organisational quadrant of the 16-point detailed Moral Compass shown in Figure 4.4:

- socialism;
- communitarianism.

**Socialism**

Socialism is analysed as a political and economic ideology in Chapter 3, and is discussed here from an ethical standpoint as a system that identifies social equality as the basis for human freedom. Although, as Vincent[45] notes, Marx neither wrote any specific works on ethics nor saw himself as a moral philospher. Nevertheless, socialism[46,47] is regarded by others as providing a broad framework of ethics within which social justice and material equality are jointly pursued as a means of eliminating capitalistic exploitation. The ultimate aim is to enable all members of society to satisfy their needs through freedom of association leading to the eradication of inequality through the cooperative efforts of the larger community. This should allow unused human potential to flourish by eradicating exploitative social relations derived from the capitalist version of the Protestant work ethic. The main elements of socialism, which became unified in the early nineteenth century as utopian socialism, rest on three ethical principles. First, early industrial capitalism, which promoted human greed to exploit labour and the environment, was morally bankrupt and should not continue. Secondly, the majority of human beings should live in a more equal, communal society in which the ethic of cooperation prevailed over the ethic of personal greed. Thirdly, violence was rejected as a means of creating this new society in favour of mass education because of the belief that an alternative socialist world would ultimately be achieved through enlightened choice.

Marx and Engels' revolutionary alternative has already been discussed in Chapter 3. They criticised utopian socialism for lacking a strategy, but used part of its moral critique in their attack on capitalism. First, moral priority was attributed solely to the historically exploited working class, which they assumed would be sufficiently motivated to participate in the forthcoming socialist revolution. Secondly, an amoral version of 'The ends justifies the means' argument was introduced to support the argument that the larger working class should overthrow the smaller capitalist class, since revolutionary socialism was based on the practical task of ending class exploitation. Thirdly, this proposal was justified by the argument that revolutionary socialism viewed all systems of morality as dynamically situated in history. In short, morality supposedly changes over time in reaction to the continuing struggle between the social classes. Morality is therefore depicted as contradictory in nature since what is regarded as ethical at one period of history becomes obsolete later as social relations change. Engels, who survived Marx, was evidently uneasy with this argument as he subsequently asserted that the moral basis of the revolutionary struggle itself would disappear once all social inequalities were eradicated.

**Criticism**

Critics of utopian and revolutionary socialism often adopt a liberal or libertarian standpoint to condemn the denial of individual autonomy and the rational pursuit of self-fulfilment. Critics have history on their side, since the systematic attempt to deny individual wants in favour of collective needs has led to repressive forms of centralised communist governments, which have also failed to match the socioeconomic achievements of Western governments. The struggle between the competing systems of capitalism and socialism during the twentieth century appears to have ended with the collapse of the Soviet Union in the early 1990s, although revolutionary socialism still prevails in China and Cuba.

**Impact on social sciences, organisational behaviour and management**

The study of both forms of socialism falls more within the fields of political scientists, economists and sociologists than within the scope of organisational behaviour and management (but see Mullins[1], pp. 635, 816) . It seems likely that organisational behaviour and management practitioners will need to address these issues more closely as the spread of global capitalism continues during the twenty-first century, because socialism's powerful moral critique of capitalism for sustaining working class, gender-based, racial and 'Third World' exploitation, remains valid in China, for example, as it was elsewhere in Europe during the last century.

**Communitarianism** Communitarianism[48,49,50] is a theory of ethics with roots in classical liberalism (see Chapter 3), which re-emerged in the USA during the 1980s, challenging Western society's emphasis on individual rights by seeking to balance these with greater responsibilities to the community. Communitarianists claim that the interests of the community should never be subordinated to those of the individual. The theory arose because of a perceived sense of urgency that the social fabric of urban society has deteriorated, making moral behaviour almost impossible. Communities, institutions and social relationships have become fragmented because of excessive individualism and the social costs are most apparent in poverty-stricken urban areas, but are spreading throughout society. Social institutions such as families, places of worship, community groups, towns and cities have become weakened in a society of alienated individuals with only self-interest, immediate gratification of wants, and a fear of death in common.

Communitarianists argue that moral discourse in the West has become meaningless since the Enlightenment, which developed a flawed morality based on individuality and reason. This failed because morality depends equally on community and tradition. Systematic neglect or indifference by government and the business community has led some communitarianists to adopt a pessimistic view of the future. Other studies of individualism and commitment in American life are more positive, concluding that, although many forms of community are being undermined, numerous voluntary associations and non-profit institutions have survived as religious, voluntary service, youth organisations and charitable forms of community (NB political parties were excluded from the survey). This 'third sector' of American society is distinguishable from the public and private business sectors but needs support if democracy and social cohesion are to flourish.

Communitarianists seek to foster such 'third sector' communities by nourishing social activities based on an ethic that condemns both modern libertarianism (see above and Chapter 3) and the spread of uncaring capitalist values since the 1980s. They also question political beliefs that promote personal property and wealth at the expense of community. A new 'culture of coherence' should be encouraged that acknowledges the roles of personal income and welfare in individual lives, but acknowledges the individual's inability to sustain economic activity which supports human communities and relationships. Undue stress on the abstract 'rights' of individual children and parents is regarded as secondary to improving the human ecology of the family, especially by discouraging divorce. Maximising women's freedom is also less critical than advancing the well-being of women in the context of community and their relationships with men and children. Racial diversity and multiculturalism are supported in communities whereas any policy that divides society into cultural ghettos is rejected. Scepticism towards animal or species 'rights' in environmental matters is balanced by interest in sustaining the essential yet dangerous role of human beings in the community of nature. Comunitarianism also supports a public role for religion in society.

## Criticism

Communitarianism is criticised for either its nostalgic allusions to a past that never existed or for describing the past as the breeding ground of terrible wrongs against society. If civilised people castigate communities that embody racist and sexist practices as morally outrageous, then communitarianists are open to the same criticism for ignoring the considerable achievements of the Enlightenment. After all, which other movement encouraged science and technology, abolished slavery, recognised civil liberties, introduced press freedom, and widened political enfranchisement, introducing religious tolerance and human rights nationally and extending these to other continents? Critics note the communitarianist concern about American society which neglects advances in social welfare achieved in EU countries and South East Asia. They reject both this lack of an inclusive perspective and a coherent set of moral values which reflects the need for a more pluralist response to the emergence of an information-based society.

**Impact on social sciences, organisational behaviour and management**

Communitarianism is included in the social sciences syllabi at numerous US and UK higher education institutions, and is also discussed in tutorials on corporate philanthropy and organisational culture in the equivalent organisational behaviour and management courses.

## Synopsis

- Means (deontology) / ends (teleology) analysis is concerned with the comparative evaluation of the moral value of human activity. Deontology regards duty as the fundamental moral objective of an individual's actions. Teleology regards outcomes or consequences as the moral goal of human activity.
- These two concepts of ethics have also been identified as the right (which places an obligation on the individual to act in a certain way) and the good (which is the value individuals place on things or on human actions.) Deontological theories give priority to the right over the good. Teleological theories give priority to the good over the right.
- Ethics is also classified as descriptive or analytical. Descriptive ethics is concerned with studying the development of moral behaviour in applied fields such as medical, legal or business ethics. Analytical ethics seeks to make rational statements about new developments in descriptive ethics (e.g. the ethics of growing genetically modified foods to feed people in the Third World).
- Various deontological (means) and teleological (ends) theories are summarised for evaluation by the reader in an original Moral Compass exercise, using the Lickert scale which is included at the end of Part I and the other parts of the book.
- The objectives of the Moral Compass exercise are:
  - to provide an understanding of each ethical theory so that the reader can compare personal evaluations of each theory;
  - to enable these evaluations to be recorded as indicated and overall evaluations carried forward for possible discussion with fellow students or colleagues;
  - to provide an opportunity for the reader to develop skills in using descriptive and analytical ethical techniques to evaluate moral issues raised in the different case studies presented in the book;
  - to enhance the reader's skills in recognising, understanding and evaluating different ethical positions that may arise as real issues either at home, at work or in the community.

## Review and discussion questions

**1** Explain what is meant by a deontological approach to ethical reasoning and how it differs from a teleological approach.

**2** What is meant by descriptive and analytical ethics and why are these approaches important in areas of applied ethics, such as medical or business ethics?

**3** Explain why idealism is regarded as a deontological theory of ethics in contrast to hedonism, which is classified as a teleological theory of ethics.

**4** What is the relevance of the natural law and utilitarian theories of ethics in subjects such as organisational behaviour and management, and how would you criticise either one of these ethical theories?

**5** What are the main differences between ethical relativism and moral pluralism and why are both ethical theories likely to be increasingly discussed by managers in the future?

## Case study
## The US tobacco industry v. the American people[51,52,53]

**Introduction**

After months of secret negotiations, the legal representatives of the six largest US tobacco corporations met their state attorney counterparts at a Washington press conference in June 1997 to announce a unique $368.5 billion settlement. Not only was it the largest legal settlement in US history, but it followed a long record of failed law suits against US tobacco companies; the latest of which had occurred only six weeks before the press conference. The other reason why the media travelled to Washington was that a special White House attorney had previously been assigned to the case by President Bill Clinton, who wanted it known that he had taken a special interest in the case against the US tobacco corporations.

**Questions about the settlement**

No matter how much White House involvement had occurred, it could not explain the huge international coverage by the media, which wanted answers to four major questions. What had suddenly caused the massive, hard-nosed US tobacco industry to lose its nerve after years of successfully defending itself in open court against numerous charges of endangering public health? Secondly, why were the US state attorneys able to clinch such a large settlement when so many previous law suits had ended in failure? Thirdly, how would the agreed billions be raised without bankrupting the industry? Finally, would the settlement arrangements be implemented before a new president was elected in November 2000? These and other related issues are discussed in this case study.

**The six tobacco corporations**

In order of size, the six corporations involved in the settlement were Philip Morris Inc., RJR Nabisco Holdings, British American Tobacco Ltd (BAT), Loews Corporation,

Brooke Group Ltd and UST Inc. Of these, Philip Morris held 48 per cent of the US cigarette market, with Marlboro as its main brand. Total sales of $68.9 billion and profits exceeding $12 billion were reported in 1997. Like its main US tobacco rivals, Philip Morris had diversified over a decade earlier by purchasing the two largest food companies and the second largest brewer and distributor in the USA. These and similar diversified purchases meant that about two-thirds of Philip Morris profits were from non-tobacco products in 1997.

Of the remaining tobacco corporations RJR Nabisco Holdings held over 25 per cent market share with sales and profits of almost $9 billion and $900 million, respectively, in 1997. Its diversification strategy had achieved notoriety when it acquired 80 per cent of Nabisco Corp., the largest US cookies and crackers manufacturer, after a hostile takeover battle in 1985. The acrimonious background to the acquisition led to a best-selling book and film *Barbarians at the Gate* in 1987. Loew Corporation and Brooke Group had 7.9 and 1.6 per cent market share respectively. Loew's sales exceeded $20 billion with profits of over $1 billion, compared with $450 million and a loss of almost $63 million by Brooke between 1996 and 1997. Loew had also diversified into hotels, insurance and offshore oilwells whereas Brooke Group had entered the US real estate business. The remaining US company, UST Inc., dominated the smokeless tobacco products market with sales of $1.4 billion and profits of $464 million mostly from snuff, pipe products and the growing of grapes and distribution of wine.

The third largest cigarette company was a new arrival and the only non-American manufacturer in the industry. BAT is based in London with over 16 per cent of the US market since purchasing American Tobacco Corp. in 1994, a sale which was a major factor in achieving the record settlement in Washington three years later. Before that, the UK-based multinational company was not required to publish its global sales in the USA, although its total profits exceeded $4 billion in 1996. It had also diversified successfully into insurance and financial services (Allied Dunbar and Eagle Star Insurance) and employed 440,000 worldwide, second only to Philip Morris, in 1996.

**The representatives of the people**

Opposing the six tobacco corporations were six different federal agencies and legal advisers, representing the American people. These included the attorney-generals of six US federal states; five attorneys from the 'Castrano Group', discussed below; the US Center for Tobacco-Free Kids (CT-FK); the US Food and Drug Administration (USFDA); the former US Surgeon General; and legal aides of President Clinton, Vice-President Gore, and senators and state governors from both political parties. The six attorney-generals also represented 33 other US federal states who had agreed to this arrangement so that the settlement negotiations would not be delayed.

The five 'Castrano' attorneys involved in the settlement negotiations were also representing 65 US lawyers who, in turn, were acting for over 50 million smokers in the first federal class action suit in US history. This case was filed for millions of clients after a previous lawsuit on behalf of a Mr Castrano had been rejected by the US Supreme Court of Appeals in 1996 for being too unwieldy, complicated and involving the separate laws of too many US federal states. This led to a decision by the Castrano lawyers to circumvent the judgment by launching multiple cases on behalf of their clients in as many states as possible, hence the large number of lawyers involved.

**Key individuals in the settlement actions**

In addition to the direct and indirect action of a sizeable portion of the US population, settlement was ultimately possible because of the independent contributions of the four key people mentioned below.

*Merrell Williams* was a former US drama teacher, pub owner in England and car salesman who obtained a job sorting legal papers for lawyers representing a subsidiary of American Tobacco Corporation. During his employment, he systematically stole 4,000 pages of confidential documents linking cigarette smoking with serious public health problems in the USA between 1988 and 1992. However, his attempts to publish these privately failed because he was unable to agree terms with interested anti-smoking academics and journalists. Williams next attempted to sell the documents back to his former employers for $2.5 million, but they refused and sued him for breach of his confidentiality contract in September 1993. He next contacted the law firm that eventually represented the State of Mississippi in its legal action against American Tobacco Corporation and agreed to hand over all the documents in return for $3,000 cash, a job with another law firm for a $3,000 per month salary, a house worth $109,000, loans to buy a 30 ft sailboat, a Ford Mustang for his personal use and a smaller car for his daughter. This expenditure was met by the law firm which included it as expenses in its share of the final settlement. Once rumours circulated that the state attorneys might have access to incriminating evidence, American Tobacco Corp. evaluated the cost–benefit effects of winning or losing a law suit before deciding to sell its US cigarette interests to the UK-based BAT conglomerate. Both tobacco corporations counted on being able to minimise any possible heavy settlement costs, as the past owner and recent overseas-based buyer, from any future legal action.

*Professor Stanton Glantz.* Since the 4,000 pages of documents were known stolen documents, no reputable US law firm could do anything with them, until an ingenious solution was found. This entailed photocopying the papers and distributing them anonymously to leading politicians and the media across the USA. The contents impressed the prestigious *New York Times* enough to include feature articles based on the material several days before the State of Mississippi's case against the cigarette companies came to court. Yet the most damaging blow occurred when Professor Stanton Glantz of the University of California, a prominent critic of the industry, received an anonymous set of the stolen papers with the compliments of a 'Mr Butts'. Glantz duly published them on the Internet for all the world to read. From then on, no amount of 'fire fighting' by the tobacco corporations could extinguish the blaze of bad publicity that broke out after these revelations were published in 1994.

*Dr Jeffrey Wiggand.* Six months after Professor Glantz published the stolen papers on the Internet, Dr Jeffrey Wiggand, a former American Tobacco Corp. research scientist, acted as a whistleblower by providing confidential information on the CBS *Sixty Minutes* nationally broadcast programme that the tobacco industry had deliberately manipulated nicotine levels for years to increase addiction. The industry took prompt legal action to silence Wiggand, who lost his well-paid position and had to take a low-paid post as a high school science teacher, when the legal 'gag' on his making further statements about the tobacco industry was enforced.

*Judge William Osteen Sr* Between August 1995 and April 1997, the leading tobacco corporations sued the USFDA in the small town of Greensboro, North Carolina, for claiming the right to rule whether the nicotine in cigarettes should be classed as a drug so that control over its use would fall within the control of the US government agency. One of the strengths of American democracy is that long and costly disputes between 'Big Business' and 'Big Government' are often settled by the decision of one independent-minded person. In this case, it was the unknown district court judge William Osteen Sr whose lucid ruling stated that the US Congress had never expressly excluded the USFDA from controlling the amount of nicotine in cigarettes and, since cigarettes deliver nicotine into the user's metabolism, they could be regarded as a drug-delivery device and something the USFDA was empowered to regulate with full US legislative authority. Judge Osteen's ruling also authorised the USFDA control over the tobacco industry in ways that were previously unavailable.

**The State of Mississippi v. the US tobacco industry**

In May 1994, the attorney-general of the State of Mississippi filed a law suit in the Chancery Court of Jackson County against the 13 most prominent tobacco companies, wholesalers, trade associations and their public relations consultants in the USA for $940 million damages. Rather unwisely, the tobacco industry was not legally represented in court. However, a public relations spokesperson informed the *New York Times* that the state would have the same burden of proof as an individual, adding that no jury had ever concluded that illnesses were directly caused by smoking. The attorney-general immediately informed the court that the State of Mississippi had never smoked a cigarette. Their case was based on the single premise that the tobacco industry had caused a health crisis in the USA and the time had come for these hugely profitable tobacco companies to reimburse the Mississippi taxpayers for the high cost of providing medical care for the thousands of people who had suffered ill health attributable to smoking. The terms of King James' legacy to the USA were about to be legally contested.

**King James of England's legacy to the US tobacco industry and government**

On landing in America in 1492, Columbus observed native Indians chewing and smoking tobacco leaves. Through him, the habit reputedly spread to Europe, via Portugal, becoming fashionable in France and England during the sixteenth century. An observant diplomat of the day was Count Nicot, French ambassador to Portugal, who reported the habit to Paris only for his name to be permanently associated with the narcotic effects of smoking or chewing tobacco. An important consequence of the fashion was the decision by King James I of England, who hated tobacco, to increase state revenues by imposing a tax of over 4,000 per cent on tobacco imports in 1604. The King immediately placed himself in the win–win position of being able to condemn an increasingly popular habit at the same time as benefiting from the massive customs and excise duty. The lesson of King James of England's legacy was inherited by modern governments which support restrictions on tobacco products for health reasons, but not to the point of banning their use, as high duties are imposed to subsidise other state expenditure.

**The US government's understanding with the tobacco industry**

After years of implementing a mutually beneficial version of King James of England's legacy in the USA, it was clear by the 1990s that the US government was increasingly uneasy about its relationship with the tobacco industry. Most tobacco companies were very profitable, yet it was smokers who paid the major portion of taxation as duty on every purchase. This situation was unlikely to change as the industry allegedly possessed unpublished research that only one in eight regular smokers ever succeeded in breaking the habit. More serious, increased profits seemed assured as some 6,000 US teenagers started smoking every week. Moreover, the industry had yet to lose a court case brought by dependants of heavy smokers who had died from lung cancer and related illnesses.

**The tobacco industry's secret defensive strategy**

The industry responded to attacks that its products damaged the nation's health by implementing a six-pronged strategy, as follows:

1 They would always inform the court that every US citizen was an independent free agent, some of whom had exercised their inviolable right to freedom of choice by deciding to smoke cigarettes. No coercion had occurred and therefore no liability could be accepted by the tobacco companies.

2 The companies also resolutely rejected the argument that the nicotine in cigarettes was addictive, saying this was both untrue and unproven.

3 Even those who insisted that nicotine was addictive could provide no evidence that anyone so 'addicted', but now deceased, had made a sustained or successful effort to stop smoking.

4 It could therefore be reasonably assumed that the deceased in question had actually enjoyed smoking.

5 Similar arguments were employed by each tobacco corporation which generally used the same legal advisers.

6 They also funded the Tobacco Research Committee which published a national two-page declaration as 'A Frank Statement', which stated that the cigarette corporations had seen no evidence to make them change their belief that cigarettes were not injurious to health.

**The strategy begins to fall apart**

Once the stolen American Tobacco Corp. papers were released into the public domain, this defensive strategy was unsustainable. For example, they included a memo written in the early 1960s by a senior legal adviser stating that: 'We are . . . in the business of selling nicotine, an addictive drug.' In fact, this merely confirmed the findings of the German scientists who identified nicotine as a dangerous drug some 170 years earlier in 1828. However, arguments about the harmful effects of cigarette smoking remained inconclusive until 1941 when the eminent medical scientist, Michael Debakey, published detailed research showing a clear correlation between increased tobacco sales and the incidence of lung cancer in the USA. These findings were confirmed by additional US and European research which concluded that over 95 per cent of lung cancer cases were diagnosed in moderate to heavy smokers. Around the world, compromises were reached between governments and powerful tobacco lobbies which generally banned TV and radio advertising of tobacco products, but allowed these in cinemas, newspapers, magazines and on billboards. Sponsorship of major sporting events was also permitted. However, smoking was increasingly banned in government buildings, sports arenas, auditoriums, airports and on public transport. Yet the public perception was that restrictions were mostly aimed at reducing fire hazards rather than due to any increased concern about public health, although warnings about the latter were printed on every pack containing a tobacco product.

**Breaking ranks with the tobacco industry**

It came as no surprise that during the same month that the sale of American Tobacco Corp. to the BAT conglomerate was finalised in April 1994, executives from the seven leading tobacco corporations testified before the US Congress on national TV that they believed nicotine to be non-addictive. One month later, documents showing that American Tobacco Corp. executives had known of the risks for years were published in the *New York Times*. The defining moment in the collapse of the tobacco industry's defensive strategy occurred in March 1996 when the smallest cigarette manufacturer, the loss-making Brooke Group Ltd, announced that after secret negotiations it had reached an out-of-court settlement with five state attorneys and 65 Castrano lawyers in order to avert imminent bankruptcy. That a smaller firm had broken ranks infuriated the rest of the US tobacco industry, especially their latest member, BAT, for reasons discussed below. Yet the industry failed to stop Brooke Group's agreement going ahead as the first independent legal settlement of its kind in 40 years.

**Fighting on too many fronts**

Five months later, a Jacksonville court also broke new ground by awarding the dependants of a deceased heavy smoker $750,000 against a former American Tobacco Corp. subsidiary. The US stock market responded by wiping $12 billion off the value of Philip Morris shares within the hour. President Clinton later announced that the reduction of teenage smoking would be a major political initiative in his second term of office. Soon afterwards, Judge Osteen delivered his ground-breaking judgment in favour of the USFDA against the tobacco industry. These related events were greeted with a major public announcement by Geoffrey Bible, the Philip Morris CEO, who concluded that the industry was 'fighting on too many fronts'. His response was to persuade other companies to appoint legal advisers to arrange secret negotiations with the federal state attorneys and other interested parties so that an acceptable out-of-court settlement could be reached.

**The secret negotiations and settlement**

Secret negotiations had already begun in December 1996 when the industry's lawyers began lobbying the White House with the aim of meeting the Mississippi state attorney before the pending law suit came to trial. The White House responded by appointing a special counsel to liaise between the industry and the 39 federal states and the larger Castrano group of lawyers and other interested parties, who all planned to launch separate law suits against the tobacco corporations. As mentioned in the Introduction, agreement was reached which led to the two largest groups selecting up to six representatives for secret negotiations with the tobacco industry's lawyers. These began in earnest in April 1997 and the final settlement was agreed in June 1997 which included the following resolutions:

- The industry will pay the 39 federal states $368.5 billion over the next 25 years.
- $308 billion will be used in compensatory law suits to recover medical expenses and 17 separate class action suits.
- $60 billion in punitive damages. Of that $25 billion will be placed in a public health trust and the rest will fund healthcare for uninsured children as dependants involved in law suits.
- $500 million will be used annually for financing anti-smoking advertising campaigns.
- The industry will fund programmes to help smokers to stop the habit and reduce adolescent smoking by 50 per cent over the next seven years, with an annual penalty of $80 million for each per cent that the industry falls below target.

- Payments will start with an immediate $10 billion and subsequent payments of $8.5 billion rising annually to $15 billion in perpetuity.
- Full regulatory control over tobacco would be conceded to the USFDA who announced their intention to label cigarette packs as a 'Nicotine Delivery Device'.
- The USFDA will control the amount of nicotine in cigarettes and announced its intention to lower the amount gradually over the next 12 years.
- The USFDA's additional powers will allow it to enforce the appearance of bigger warning labels on cigarette packs with more direct messages such as 'Smoking Can Kill You' and 'Cigarettes Cause Cancer'.
- Manufacturers also conceded that they could not use advertisements showing humans or cartoon characters, or advertise on billboards, in stadiums, outdoor sites, on the Internet, or in cinemas or theatres. Cigarette vending machines will also be banned.
- The tobacco companies will receive immunity from future class action suits from, for example, federal states or by legal partnerships like the Castrano group.
- Individuals will still be able to sue tobacco companies and, even if they have yet to win a case, compensation will not exceed $5 million.
- The legal gagging of Dr Jeffrey Wiggand to be withdrawn and legislation protecting the rights of whistleblowers would also be introduced.

**How the tobacco corporations will pay**

To pay for the huge cost of the agreement, the industry will be allowed to raise the price of cigarettes progressively by 50c to $1 per pack, although this is predicted to lead to a 15 per cent fall in consumption. Profit margins average 34 per cent and the companies are expected to recover settlement costs through price increases and implementing the mandatory reduction in advertising costs and legal expenses in opposing claims from consumers. Perhaps the key factor is that the agreement is only applicable in the USA, where overall sales are falling, whereas over half of the industry's sales occur abroad, where sales are increasing 3–5 per cent annually. Put another way, the cost of the settlement can be paid without difficulty from overseas profits.

**Political aftermath of the settlement**

The settlement, approved by President Clinton, failed to become law in 1999 mainly because the Republican Party used its majority in the US Congress to challenge payment arrangements, especially an allocation of $3.5 billion to the trial lawyers which was regarded as excessive. The block on attempts to codify the agreement in law were unlikely to be lifted until the election of a new president in November 2000. Four unresolved issues appeared to be holding up the agreement's progress into law. First, the tobacco industry is known to be a major contributor to Republican Party funds. Second, there is no mention of compensation for US tobacco growers in the agreement. Third, provisions for the 2.3 million people directly or indirectly employed in the tobacco industry are also excluded. Fourth, the prospect of the settlement being funded by profits from smokers outside the USA is a concern for far-sighted US legislators.

**When partners fall out!**

If Brooke Group expected to escape further penalties by breaking rank to agree their secret out-of-court settlement, then they were quickly disappointed. It was later reported that a condition of the settlement by the tobacco companies required costs to be apportioned proportionately across the industry, including Brooke Group Ltd. The company most insistent on this condition was BAT which was no doubt unhappy at having to pay massive 'costs of entry' to diversify in the USA. More worrying to this conglomerate, however, was the distinct probability that questions about the terms of the US agreement would ultimately be raised by the British government where its head office was located, and by the Commission of the European Union, where it had developed various profitable markets.

**Questions**

**1** How would you evaluate the morality of the financial arrangements agreed between the Mississippi State's lawyers and Merrell Williams in exchange for the stolen papers belonging to a major US tobacco corporation?

**2** What are the moral arguments for and against the 'ends justify the means' decision to place incriminating stolen materials belonging to a US tobacco firm on the Internet?

**3** Assuming the medical facts about nicotine had not been suppressed by the US tobacco industry, what moral arguments would you raise to support or oppose the individual's right to decide whether or not to smoke cigarettes?

**4** Evaluate the moral validity of the policy of Western governments which condemn cigarette smoking on health grounds, yet obtain large duty revenues from cigarette sales and allow the tobacco industry to advertise their products and sponsor major sporting events.

## Notes and references

1. Mullins, L.J., *Management and Organisational Behaviour*, 5th edn, London, Financial Times Pitman Publishing, 1999.
2. Aristotle, *The Nichomachean Ethics*, trans. W. David Ross, New York, Oxford University Press, 1980, Bk 1, 1094, 1–3.
3. Frankena, William, *Ethics*, Englewood Cliffs, NJ, Prentice Hall, 1963.
4. Rawls, John, *A Theory of Justice*, Cambridge, Mass., Belknap Press of Harvard University Press, 1971.
5. De George, R.T., *Moral Issues in Business*, 3rd edn , New York, Macmillan, 1990.
6. Foster, John, *The Case for Idealism*, Boston, Routledge & Kegan Paul, 1982, x.
7. Vesey, Godfrey, ed., *Idealism, Past and Present*, New York, Cambridge University Press, 1982.
8. Kant, Immanuel, *Lectures on Ethics*, trans. Louis Infield, Indianapolis, Hackett, 1980.
9. Thomas Aquinas, *On Law, Morality and Politics*, ed. William P. Baumgarth and Richard J. Regan, Indianapolis, Hackett, 1988.
10. Finnis, John, *Natural Law and Natural Rights*, New York, Oxford University Press, 1980.
11. King, Martin Luther, Jr, Letter from Birmingham Jail, in *Why We Can't Wait*, New York, New American Library, 1968.
12. Bentham, Jeremy, *An Introduction to the Principles of Morals and Legislation*, Oxford, Clarendon Press, 1879.
13. Locke, J. *Essay Concerning Human Understanding*, Bk 2, ch. 21.
14. Mill, John Stuart, *Utilitarianism*, ed. Samuel Gorovitz, New York, Bobbs-Merrill, 1971, 221.
15. Fill, C., *Marketing Communications: Contexts, contents and strategies*, 2nd edn, London, Prentice Hall, 1999.
16. Habibi, D.A., Utilitarianism, *International Encyclopaedia of Ethics*, ed. J.K. Roth, London, Fitzroy-Dearborn, 1995, 894–5.
17. Mill, John Stuart, *Utilitarianism*, ed. George Sher, Indianapolis, Hackett, 1979.
18. Bentham, Jeremy, *Collected Works*, ed. J. Bowring, vol. 10, 142.

19. Spinello, R.A., Relativism, *International Encyclopaedia of Ethics*, ed. J.K. Roth, London, Fitzroy-Dearborn, 1995, 733–4.

20. De George, R.T, *Moral Issues in Business*, 3rd edn, New York, Macmillan, 1990, 32–6.

21. Mackie, John, *Ethics: Inventing right and wrong*, Harmondsworth, Penguin, 1977.

22. Ladd, John, *Ethical Relativism*, Belmont, Calif., Wadsworth, 1973.

23. Hobbes, Thomas, *Leviathan*, 1651.

24. Locke, John, *Two Treatises of Government*, ed. and intro. Peter Laslett, Cambridge, Cambridge University Press, 1988.

25. Rousseau, J.J., *The Social Contract*, 1797.

26. Pateman, Carole, *The Sexual Contract*, Stanford, Calif., Stanford University Press, 1988.

27. Holliger, R., Pragmatism, *Encarta 98 Encyclopedia*, New York, Microsoft, 1998.

28. Dewey, John, Philosophies of Freedom, in *The Collected Works: The later works*, vol. 3, ed. Jo Ann Boydston, Carbondale, Southern Illinois University Press, 1984.

29. Popkin, R.H. and Stroll, A., *Philosophy Made Simple*, London, W.H. Allen, 1972, 265–6.

30. Campbell, M.B., Individualism: True and False, in *Individualism and Economic Order*, University of Chicago Press, 1948.

31. Machan, T.R., *Individuals and Their Rights*, La Salle, Ill., Open Court, 1989.

32. Regis, Edward, Jr, What is Ethical Egoism? *Ethics 91*, October, 1980, 50–62.

33. Williams, Bernard, Egoism and Altruism, in *Problems of the Self*, Cambridge, Cambridge University Press, 1973.

34. Friedman, M., The Social Responsibility of Business is to Increase its Profits, *New York Times Magazine*, 13 September 1970.

35. Sternberg, E., *Just Business*, London, Warner, 1994.

36. Von Hayek, F.A., *The Road to Serfdom*, New York, Macmillan, 1944, 36, 41, 105–7, 221–2.

37. Murad, T.A., Social Darwinism, *International Encyclopaedia of Ethics*, ed. J.K. Roth, London, Fitzroy-Dearborn, 1995, 817–18.

38. Hofstadter, Richard, *Social Darwinism in American Thought*, New York, George Braziller, 1959, 45.

39. Brunello, A.R., Machiavellian Ethics, *International Encyclopaedia of Ethics*, ed. J.K. Roth, London, Fitzroy-Dearborn, 1995, 518–19.

40. Berlin, I., The Question of Machiavelli, *New York Review of Books*, 17, 4 November 1971, 20–37.

41. Machiavelli, Niccolò, *The Prince*, ed. and trans. Thomas G. Bergin, Arlington Heights, Ill., AHM, 1947.

42. Kruschwitz, R.B. and Roberts, R.C., *The Virtues: Contemporary essays on moral character*, Belmont, Calif., Wadsworth, 1987.

43. MacIntyre, A., *After Virtue*, Notre Dame, Ind., University of Notre Dame Press, 1981.

44. Carr, David, *Educating the Virtues: An essay on the philosophical psychology of moral development and education*, New York, Routledge, 1991.

45. Vincent, A., Marx and Ethics, *Encyclopedia of Applied Ethics*, 3, New York, Academic Press, 1998, 115–27.

46. Berki, R.N., *Socialism*, New York, St Martin's Press, 1975.

47. Bottomore, T.B. and Maximilien, R., eds, *Karl Marx: Selected writings in sociology and social philosophy*, New York, McGraw-Hill, 1964.

48. Paul, G.E., Communitarianism, *International Encyclopaedia of Ethics*, ed. J.K. Roth, London, Fitzroy-Dearborn, 1995, 172–3.

49. Etzioni, A., Communitarian Solutions/What Communitarians Think, *Journal of State Government*, 65, January/March 1992, 9–11.

50. Etzioni, A., *The Spirit of Community: Rights, responsibilities, and the communitarian agenda*, New York, Crown, 1993.

51. The Tobacco Settlement: Tobacco's can of worms, *Fortune*, 21 July 1997, 30–1, 34–7.

52. 'Sorry Pardner' and 'Is it really a Good Deal?' *Time*, 30 June 1997, 21–32.

53. Mollenkamp, Carrick *et al.*, *The People v Big Tobacco: How the States took on the tobacco giants*, Princeton, NJ, Bloomberg, 1998.

# Moral Compass exercise

The Moral Compass instruments below are divided into two questionnaires, which should be evaluated using the 7-point Lickert scale shown in Box A. The simple Moral Compass contains the eight statements shown in Box B. The detailed Moral Compass includes the additional eight statements shown in Box C. Each statement corresponds with one of the ethical theories summarised in Chapter 4.

## Instructions

1 Decide whether you wish to complete the simple or the detailed Moral Compass instrument.

2 Read each statement carefully before recording your response, using the 7-point Lickert scale shown in Box A below.

3 Record your scores for each part of the instruments in the Moral Compass section in the Appendix at the end of the book, where the corresponding ethical theories are shown.

**Box A**

| Strongly disagree | Disagree | Slightly disagree | Neither agree nor disagree | Slightly agree | Agree | Strongly agree |
|---|---|---|---|---|---|---|
| 1 | 2 | 3 | 4 | 5 | 6 | 7 |

## Box B

| | | |
|---|---|---|
| **S.1** | The manager of a global company can have loyalty to no one country. | 1 2 3 4 5 6 7 |
| **S.2** | Money is the most important thing in the world. It signifies health, strength, honour, generosity and beauty. | 1 2 3 4 5 6 7 |
| **S.3** | No one would remember the Good Samaritan if he'd only had good intentions . . . he also had money. | 1 2 3 4 5 6 7 |
| **S.4** | Justice and leadership are necessary for harmony at work as leadership without justice is tyrannical. | 1 2 3 4 5 6 7 |
| **S.5** | A sufficient moral rule is to follow your own instincts controlled by the moral standards of the society in which you live. | 1 2 3 4 5 6 7 |
| **S.6** | The test of progress is not whether we add to the wealth of those who have so much, but whether we provide enough for those who have little. | 1 2 3 4 5 6 7 |
| **S.7** | The primary responsibility of a manager is not to direct people at work, but to maintain harmonious relations within the group/organisation. | 1 2 3 4 5 6 7 |
| **S.8** | Honesty is incompatible with the amassing of a large fortune. | 1 2 3 4 5 6 7 |

## Box C

| | | |
|---|---|---|
| **S.9** | The easiest way to block a new idea is to split the ranks by appealing to a principle. | 1 2 3 4 5 6 7 |
| **S.10** | There are some people whose support cannot be won over either with gifts, honours, money or promotion. | 1 2 3 4 5 6 7 |
| **S.11** | Human survival will require global business to become more transparent and be brought increasingly under public control in the future. | 1 2 3 4 5 6 7 |
| **S.12** | We have to use technology to create more rewarding tasks in the workplace that are worthy of human beings. | 1 2 3 4 5 6 7 |
| **S.13** | Throughout business history there has been a ceaseless devouring of weak companies by the strong. | 1 2 3 4 5 6 7 |
| **S.14** | The pursuit of private gain is the only way to provide for the needs of others whom we do not know. | 1 2 3 4 5 6 7 |
| **S.15** | I've never been an idealist: that implies you aren't going to achieve anything. | 1 2 3 4 5 6 7 |
| **S.16** | If I see something I admire, I buy it . . . then I sell it. | 1 2 3 4 5 6 7 |

# PART II

# The internal environment

The world

# Individual morality in organisations

*Whenever management talks about tackling 'Them and Us' problems here, I think of how keen to please these workers were when they started as raw kids years ago; and I know we're to blame . . . although Head Office would never admit it . . . for letting all that fresh talent go to waste like rotting apples.*

UK car factory foreman, and gardening enthusiast, 1979

## Learning objectives

After reading this chapter you should be able to:

■ consider the common duty of employers and employees towards other members of organisations;

■ explore the main findings of character education programmes and their relevance to employee training in organisations, in terms of the basic values shared by all the major cultures and world religions;

■ investigate the key characteristics of personal integrity, and their importance for professional managers, in view of the growing absence of civil liberties in organisations;

■ identify the major negative and positive human rights and their relevance to the main forms of justice likely to arise in an organisational context;

■ evaluate the importance of additional human rights on the behaviour of managers and employees in organisations.

## Introduction

A common reason why some individuals fail to obtain positive and rewarding experiences from their employment is because they have different values from those responsible for managing the organisations in which they work. These differences either developed after employment started or, if apparent, were not seen as important during the selection process, otherwise the offer of employment would probably not have been made or accepted. A reader wishing to understand why the joint expectations of employees and their employers may fail to materialise can find well-researched explanations in reputable social science and personnel management textbooks. What is less often discussed is why commitment to an organisation may be withdrawn because of the individual's perception that his/her civil liberties and moral right to justice have been abused by co-workers, supervisors or managers.

## Duty, rights and justice in employment

The moral duty and rights of individuals are examined below in terms of the different forms of justice that may arise during their employment in an organisational context. It will be recalled from Chapters 3 and 4 that those whose behaviour is guided by deontological ethics, such as Kant's categorical imperative, believe that their individual rights are not open to any utilitarian evaluation because the former do not depend on any calculation of the consequences of the activity in question. In terms of employment, this means that the individual is required to carry out his/her duties and responsibilities, as agreed with an employer or the manager as the latter's agent.

This also means that the individual employer or manager is duty bound to ensure that employees receive what they are entitled to, even if this results in an inefficient use of resources such as time, money and 'opportunity costs' in an organisational context. The prospect of an overall loss does not reduce the right of others to what they deserve, and the likelihood of waste would not make it any more just to offer them less than their full entitlement. Underlying this deontological position is the belief that any tendency towards moral behaviour by an employee, on the one hand, or an employer or manager, on the other, should not be exploited by another person within an organisation.

## Deontological aspects of employment

This chapter is more concerned with moral aspects of individual freedom in a working environment than with aspects of employment law. After all, the latter is subject to periodic political and social change which requires experienced legal and personnel specialists to ensure that new developments are correctly interpreted and implemented.

### Assumptions about the employer

For the sake of analysis, it will be assumed that Organisation X is a reputable and profitable company and that its latest appointee, Y, has emerged successfully from a battery of selection procedures, interviews, seven-point recruitment plan criteria, group exercises, psychometric tests and questionnaires, and is seated in the company's reception centre waiting to start on the first day in her new job. It will be further assumed that the Organisation X is a legal entity and is operating according to the legal rules and regulations of the country where its head office is registered (i.e. the UK, in this example).

Secondly, all relevant employment legislation and codes of practice have been included in the formal contract of employment. This is a job description, stating the location of the job, starting date and salary, hours of work, the name of the line manager, notice period, induction training and staff development provisions, appraisal arrangements, remuneration reviews, sickness and annual leave entitlements, opportunities for promotion, disciplinary, grievance and appeal procedures, and termination and dismissal arrangements. This has been communicated in writing and agreed to by Employee Y, who possesses the required qualifications and experience for the position.

## Assumptions about the employee

Given the above comprehensive provisions, the question that arises from a deontological perspective concerns the moral attributes of the employee, which will affect her capacity to carry out agreed duties and responsibilities in the employment contract which, it is assumed, refer to a job that she is keen on having and carrying out effectively to the best of her capabilities. The outstanding enquiry here, therefore, is how, when and where did Employee Y acquire the desired standards of moral behaviour in the pre-employment period? Of equal importance – since there are two parties to the employment contract – is the obligation of the employer to protect the civil liberties and moral right to justice of the employee, which raises a further query about how this knowledge and skill is acquired by managers and supervisors.

## Moral attributes of individuals

Implicit in an employment contract is the assumption that the employee enters an organisation with a *mens sibi conscia recti* (a mind conscious of its own rectitude), rather than a *mens rea* (or a guilty mind intent on criminal action) condition. Otherwise, the judgement of the manager(s) responsible for approving the appointment could automatically be called into question. The desirability of 'good' moral attributes in individuals, such as new employees, was referred to briefly in the section on virtue ethics in Chapter 4. Common sense insists that virtuous behaviour such as honesty is essential, otherwise, how could it be assumed that the employee will perform her duties and responsibilities in a mature manner? That said, long-standing research in the USA discussed below concluded that the development of a 'good' character, based on values of integrity and goodness, cannot be assumed and is more difficult to achieve than might be hoped for.

### Character

Clouse[1], defines character as 'a person's pattern of behaviour related to the moral qualities of self-discipline and social responsibility'. This is normally enacted in a system or code of ethics (not always 'good' in the law-abiding sense; after all about 3 million people in the UK have criminal records), which the individual practises in his/her daily life. In short, a 'character', unlike a 'personality' (i.e. from the Latin for a 'mask') is associated with more permanent behavioural and attitudinal characteristics that are consistent with the ethical standards of the community. For example, the research of Kohlberg and Gilligan discussed in Chapter 3 indicates that a moral character begins to form in early childhood and develops throughout adulthood.

**Research into the character of individuals**

The assumption that a moral character is formed early in life is supported in earlier character education programme research by Hartshorne and May[2], which explored the effects of character education programmes on the ethical behaviour of children over a five-year period. Nearly 11,000 children of between 11 and 16 years of age, from both private and state-funded schools, participated in tests of different behaviours that fell into the category of 'character'. For example, participants were provided with opportunities to cheat by copying correct answers, or lie to questions such as 'I always obey my parents cheerfully' and 'I always smile when things go wrong'. They were also able to steal from money boxes left around on desks. Participants were not asked to justify their behaviour since the purpose was to determine the variables which correlated with good character for the group as a whole. Of more than 17,000 tests given, it was found that almost all children were dishonest under some circumstances but not under others.

Moral behaviour tended to be specific to the situation. Age and gender were not relevant. Furthermore, children who had received either some religious education or participated in character development training were found to be no more honest than children without these experiences. What made a difference, however, was that more intelligent children were less likely to lie, cheat or steal, as were those from socioeconomically better off homes. Siblings also tended to display similar behaviour, confirming the importance of family influences. The researchers concluded that a private sense of 'shame' or 'loss of face' was probably considered to be too high a 'cost' for these participants compared with the 'benefits' of lying, stealing or cheating, even though none of these anti-social behaviours were censured during the studies.

Subsequent research included a worldwide study of value-systems which attempted to identify the basic values that are 'shared by all major cultures and world religions'. The 15 values identified were: courage, conviction, generosity, kindness, helpfulness, honesty, honour, justice, tolerance, freedom of choice, freedom of speech, good citizenship, effective use of personal time and talents, the right to be an individual, and the right of equal opportunity.

**Boston and Pittsburgh character education research**

Clouse[1] also reports that similarities were identified with the independent University of Boston's character education research programme when student participants revealed the basic virtues of honesty, courage, persistence, loyalty and kindness in practical exercises based on personal evaluations of historical and literary texts. A further study in Pittsburgh state-funded schools identified seven universal values which children entering elementary grades are encouraged to develop. These are personal courage, loyalty, justice, respect, hope, honesty and love. These are learned through stories, songs and art. Pupils also learn to say these seven words in the language of another ethnic group in the local community. The aim of the project is to create an awareness of what civil society expects of its members and a motivation to include these expectations into one's daily life.

**Integrated character development**

Studies by Lickona[3] concluded that a good character consists of knowing the good, desiring the good, and doing the good, which he likens to habits of the mind, habits of the heart, and habits of action. His integrated approach to character development also included 15 character traits grouped into the following categories:

- moral knowing, including self-awareness, personal values, perspective taking, reasoning, decision making, and self-knowledge;
- moral feeling, including conscience, self-esteem, empathy, loving the good, self-control, and humility;
- moral action, including competence, will, and habit.

## Integrity

Forrest[4], defines integrity as 'a consistent adherence to moral, intellectual, professional, or artistic principles despite temptations to abandon them'. Integrity has always been valued since pre-classical times as an important personal characteristic in ethical systems based on virtue and moral character. This is apparent from its origins in the Latin word *integritas*, meaning a 'sound, healthy unimpaired condition', which is related to the word integral, meaning 'necessary for completeness' and 'made up of parts forming a whole'.

Personal integrity refers to a willingness to adhere to and defend one's principles, which may be intellectual, artistic or professional, and are regarded as such deeply held beliefs and moral commitments that they prevent an individual from behaving in a contrary manner even under extreme circumstances. For example, in a case known personally to the author a graduate with a first-class honours degree in biochemistry from a leading UK university decided to start afresh on a nursing career, rather than enrol on a postgraduate degree, because of reservations about the direction of the proposed research programme.

Hypothetical examples include the 'romantic' view of the artist as an individual whose personal identity and principles are so inseparable from his art that any alternative way of life is rejected, even if this results in a life of dire poverty. Possibly more common, are examples of professional integrity displayed by public officials or professional accountants who reject the temptation to compromise their professional principles by turning a blind eye to some wrongdoing, in the interests of protecting both their personal reputation and that of their organisation.

Forrest notes that integrity is a characteristic for which one bears an individual responsibility and refers to Alexander Solzhenitsyn's Nobel Prize acceptance speech in which he identifies integrity as: 'the simple step of a simple courageous man . . . not to take part in the lie, not to support deceit. Let the lie come into the world, even dominate the world, but not through me.'[5] Integrity is a characteristic of the good, which means that which one ought to do as a substantive answer to the question: 'what ought one to do?' since the way in which one approaches the good shapes the nature of one's entire ethical thought. All of which begs the question: how and when are these desirable moral attributes to be acquired if they are not included in the new employee's induction and training programme?

## Character and integrity as recurring features of human behaviour?

Before concluding this section, similarities between information provided above and in previous chapters may have been noted. For example, to what extent do Hartshorne and May's[2] worldwide study findings confirm the general principles of the Golden Mean summarised in Chapter 3? Secondly, how closely does Alexander Solzhenitsyn's Nobel Prize acceptance speech resemble Kant's categorical imperative in Chapter 2? What significance, if any, should be attached to any similarities is obviously a matter for the reader to evaluate. Hence, the inclusion of the question mark at the end of the heading of this paragraph. Whether or not character and integrity are recurring features of human behaviour, a more pertinent question is what justification can there be for people behaving 'out of character' as employees of profit-seeking or public sector organisations?

## Moral rights of individuals in organisations

Deontologists maintain that valid moral judgements are based on a recognition that, although individuals are obliged to respect certain moral rules or duties, failure to do so does not alter the fundamental principle that every individual possesses an intrinsic set of 'moral rights'. Green[6] divides the latter into negative and positive human rights. To recap, negative rights are so called because they impose restraints on individuals in their behaviour towards others. For example, the principal negative right is the 'right to life' which puts a burden of duty on the behaviour of one individual not to act in a way that endangers the existence of another. Positive rights are so called because they cannot be achieved without the direct efforts of individuals or similar collective behaviour. For example, the 'right to employment' is regarded as a positive right. A fuller list of negative and positive rights is presented in Table 5.1.

### Negative rights

In terms of Green's list below, the right to life and physical security are included in the prevailing health and safety regulations which are legally binding on the organisation and all of its members. The right to personal freedom is also covered in the common law 'at will' provision in employment contracts which would, if need be, support Employee Y's freedom to terminate her employment with Organisation X subject to mutually acceptable notice provisions. That said, there are limits on her personal freedom to act within the organisation as she, rather than her employer or its managers, might wish, which should be set out in the terms and conditions of employment.

For example, the right to free speech is also normally subject to a 'loyalty to her employer' provision which is discussed below. As mentioned in Chapter 3, the right to freedom of conscience is also guaranteed subject to the provision that the

**Table 5.1 Basic negative and positive human rights**

| Negative rights | Positive rights |
| --- | --- |
| The right to life. | The right to food and drink. |
| The right to physical security. | The right to shelter. |
| The right to personal freedom. | The right to work. |
| The right to free speech. | The right to basic education. |
| The right to freedom of conscience. | The right to healthcare. |
| The right to due process and a fair trial. | The right to legal advice and representation. |
| The right to property. | The right to a safe environment. |
| The right to informed consent. | |
| The right to free association with others. | |

*Source*: Based on R.M. Green, *The Ethical Manager: A new method for business ethics*, New York, Macmillan, 1994, p. 69.

management of Organisation X will wish to be satisfied that Employee Y will not use her place of work as a platform for airing her religious or political views in a way that threatens the freedom of conscience of other members of the organisation. The right to due process becomes relevant should a disciplinary matter occur when Employee Y would be entitled to have her case investigated and resolved internally within a reasonable period, rather than having it drag on for perhaps weeks or months without reaching a fair conclusion, which could be offset by bringing her grievance before an independent tribunal.

The right to property is covered under the prevailing security arrangements in place at Organisation X which would normally ensure that personal property such as a motor vehicle is not damaged or stolen during working hours on Organisation X's property. To ensure an effective security system, Employee Y may have to agree to a supervised random body search as an employment condition. The right to informed consent means that in matters where Employee Y's expertise is pertinent, it would only be reasonable of Organisation X to utilise its investment in her skills by seeking her views, rather than have someone else express an opinion or judgement on her behalf. Finally, freedom of association means that, subject to prevailing legislation and the declared policy of Organisation X, Employee Y has the right to be represented by a recognised trade union or professional body without interference by Organisation X.

## Positive rights

Most of the positive rights in Green's list are usually assumed to be indirect outcomes or benefits of the contract of employment. For example, in a country such as Britain, the rights to food, drink, shelter, basic education and healthcare would be the personal responsibility of Employee Y or, in a case of unemployment or long-term illness, the appropriate government agency. That said, most reputable organisations provide these benefits as part of the total employment package. The right to employment, subject to the terms and conditions of the employment contract, has already been provided. The right to legal representation would normally be expected on a 'needs must' basis, subject to the circumstances in which professional assistance is required. Finally, the right to a safe environment would usually be included under mandatory health and safety at work regulations which are discussed in Chapter 8. Additional rights not included in Green's list above include:

- the right to privacy;
- the right to confidentiality;
- the right to information;
- the right to intellectual property;
- the right to justice.

## Civil liberties in organisations

Before discussing the above rights, attention is drawn to Ewing's[7] critique of what he describes as the corporate intrusion on employees' civil liberties. The former editor of the *Harvard Business Review* condemns this behaviour as 'rampant . . . in most . . . organisations, during working hours, civil liberties are a will-o'-the-wisp. The . . . rights that employees have grown accustomed to in family, school . . . must generally be left outdoors, like cars in the parking lot' (pp. 139–40). He notes that the absence of civil liberties and the rise of authoritarianism in the working environment can be attributed to two historical factors.

First, there was the rise of professional management, called 'personnel engineering', at the start of the twentieth century. This followed the emergence of large corporations, as noted by Burnham and Chandler (see Chapters 2 and 3), and led F.W. Taylor, the founder of 'scientific management', to proclaim: 'In the past the man has been first. In the future, the system must be first' (Shaw and Barry[8], p. 250). The second historical factor is the continuing reluctance of the courts to intervene in the hiring and firing of employees by employers, although this is more prevalent in the USA than in EU countries.

The implications of Ewing's criticism are that the moral attributes and rights of individuals are unlikely to be discussed during, say, confidential management meetings about redundancies, and perhaps not even in face-to-face appraisal interviews with employees. Still less, during disciplinary proceedings involving line managers or team leaders when 'battle-lines' are often drawn with the employee on the other side during meetings. If the employee is accompanied by a trade union or another representative, 'groupthink' behaviour (see Chapter 2) might occur which would make consensus difficult to achieve.

The deontological position cannot easily be dismissed since arguments based on any criterion other than duty ignore the fact that failure to consider individual rights at the start of any discussion increases the possibility of injustice, recriminations and other inefficiencies from any conflicts occurring afterwards. In short, this raises the 'moral hindsight' question that was discussed in Chapter 2 which, in turn, may raise questions protecting the employee's moral rights, and the provision of justice, as a moral responsibility of employers or their agents in organisations.

## The right to privacy

Jacobs[9] notes that the right to privacy as a civil right implies that there is a zone of individual autonomy in which people ought to be free to behave as they wish, although he adds that the dimensions of this zone are among the most controversial issues in philosophy and law, which is discussed below in the section on the invasion of privacy. Ordinarily, the right of privacy protects the individual from unwarranted government interference in intimate personal relationships or activities, although this interpretation has been extended to include employment arrangements with individuals in organisations.

The starting point of most discussions on the right to privacy in Western countries is usually John Stuart Mill's *On Liberty*[10] (1859), which states:

> There is a sphere of action in which society, as distinguished from the individual, has, if any, an indirect interest; comprehending all that portion of a person's life and conduct which affects only himself, or if it also affects others, only with their free, voluntary and undeceived consent and participation.

Not everyone agrees with Mill's assertion that there is a 'sphere of action' in which society has only an indirect interest. Stephens and Schab[11] describe the controversy over the right of privacy as

> ultimately, a debate between . . . the libertarian view, [that] the law exists to protect individuals from one another [in which] morality is not [regarded as] a legitimate basis for law; and the classical conservative view that . . . sees law and morality as inseparable and . . . the maintenance of societal morality (as) one of the essential functions of the legal system.

## Invasion of privacy

This occurs as a result of breaches of the civil right to privacy. The public is generally more aware of cases where exposure of the private life of public figures by the media occurs, rather than more mundane examples of the right to privacy of an individual being invaded by an employer. However, once privacy is acknowledged as a moral and legal right, then intrusion by another party, including the media or an employer, is secondary alongside displaying respect for the more private areas in a person's life. Jacobs[9] lists the following three ways in which invasion of an individual's privacy may occur:

- by appropriation, where another's name or likeness is used for commercial purposes without that person's consent;
- by intrusion upon another person's seclusion with the aim of placing that person in a false light;
- by publication of private information about a person.

Common sense suggests that the more reputable the organisation, the less likely will be the occurrence of these different ways of intruding on an individual's privacy, yet situations may arise where some invasion of an employee's privacy is unavoidable. Green[6] proposes two moral rules for dealing with these situations which are set out in Box 5.1.

---

**Box 5.1**   **Moral rules for dealing with invasions of privacy**

**First proposed moral rule:**
When an employee is absent and unable to give permission for urgently required materials in her desk or files to be obtained for organisational purposes, a supervisor (with a fellow employee as a witness) may conduct a search for the materials providing a record is kept of what material was removed during the operation.

**Second proposed moral rule:**
Whenever a manager suspects an employee of a serious breach of organisational procedures, including violation of the right to privacy of another employee, the manager may (with a fellow employee as a witness) conduct a search of the employee's desk or personal files with the employee's permission or some other authorisation, so that the existence of relevant materials can be confirmed or rejected.

*Source: Green, R.M., The Ethical Manager.*

---

## The right to confidentiality

For Swenson[12], confidentiality is the state or quality of communications being kept secret, in the expectation that disclosures in certain relationships should remain private. Confidentiality becomes important within the context of employment when an individual reveals sensitive information on trust; that is, in the belief that the disclosed information will remain private. This is why many professions have strict ethical rules that prevent practitioners from disclosing confidential information about a client to a third party unless exceptional circumstances make such a revelation essential.

A point that is sometimes overlooked is that the moral commitment to confidentiality, undertaken automatically by members of professions such as medicine, law and religion, is just as relevant in organisations. Here, information that is revealed by an employee in confidence may be disclosed to a manager or supervisor in the reasonable expectation that it will remain private. Anything disclosed within the hearing of other people is therefore not confidential. Ethical considerations do not apply therefore to general gossip but include any secrets revealed by individuals to managers in organisations.

## The right to information

The individual's right to personal information stored on computers is guaranteed by law in most industrialised countries. The need to protect this data and limit access to it becomes apparent from the extent to which computers are increasingly used to gather, store and exchange information about individuals, especially if access to such information raises the possibility of conflict with the individual's right to privacy. The capacity to store and exchange computerised data on individuals also raises ethical questions about who should have access to this personal information. At what point do the 'need to know' demands of government, another institution or organisation, take precedence over an individual's right to privacy? What kind of information should be held as eligible for distribution, or not kept or shared? What steps need to be taken to ensure that information obtained from a computer is entirely accurate? Is there any information relating to themselves that individuals should not have a right to examine? The moral implications of these questions are discussed in more detail in Chapter 7.

## The right to intellectual property

As Francischetti[13] observes, this refers to the lawful right of inventors, authors and other creative people to restrict the use of their ideas or creations, and recognises that creative individuals and others in society share an interest in the products of creative activity. Society has a vested interest in encouraging useful inventions and artistic creations and treats the ideas, designs, texts, images or musical compositions of creative persons as their private intangible property, usually by allowing them to restrict the use of this intellectual property for a specified period.

Four types of intellectual property are identified as trade secrets, patents, copyrights and trademarks. Inventors are allowed the legal right to keep their invention as trade secrets, if this is practicable, in return for disclosing their inventions and obtaining exclusive rights protected by a patent to exploit their inventions for a fixed period. Similarly, authors, artists and composers may generally claim a copyright for their work, which is intended to prevent others from using, reproducing or performing these creative works without permission, unless a fee or royalty is paid. A trademark is a word or symbol used by a manufacturer to distinguish products from those of competitors, which allows the firm to profit from its (intangible) reputation for quality or reliability. Unauthorised use of intellectual property is called infringement as distinct from plagiarism, which is the intentional presentation of another's idea or creation as one's own, although both are regarded as serious contraventions of ethical behaviour. Underlying the legal concept of intellectual property is the ethical principle that an individual is entitled to compensation for the products of his/her own labour; and to ignore this is to contravene the inventor's right to privacy.

By applying for a patent, however, the inventor effectively enters into a contract with society in which secrecy is sacrificed in return for the exclusive right to control the use of the process over an agreed number of years. The question of balancing the individual's right to his/her own intellectual property with the interests of an employer may become legally complicated, but the important ethical point is that the individual's rights should not be abused on the grounds of 'might is right' by an economically more powerful employer.

## The right to justice

This broad concept is defined as 'just conduct, fairness, exercise of authority in maintenance of right' (*Concise OED*); and as 'giving each person her due, treating equals equally and unequals unequally' (De George[14], p. 78). Neither definition is exhaustive and various forms of justice are discussed in business ethics as relevant to organisational activities:

- compensatory justice;
- retributive justice;
- procedural justice;
- distributive justice, which is discussed in Chapter 12.

Compensatory justice occurs when an individual is compensated for a previous injustice or injury, as in the case of an employee who receives a financial settlement after being injured as a result of carelessness by another employee while carrying out his/her duties on the company's premises. Retributive justice occurs when a person is punished in some way for breaking the law, as in the case of a fork-lift truck driver who breaks health and safety regulations, causing damage to company property, who is demoted to a lower paid job for a stated period.

Procedural justice is so common in organisations that it often goes unnoticed until things go wrong and problems occur, not unlike the examples of compensatory and retributive justice discussed above. In short, procedural justice occurs whenever equitable decisions, fair procedures and agreements are put in place and implemented by members of an organisation. Applications of procedural justice in organisations are so numerous that all the essential activities of business and organisational life would probably collapse without it. Certainly, effective human resource management and efficient bureaucracy, if not based on sound procedural justice, would not be possible in a formal organisational structure. However, even when the latter arrangements are in place, ethical aspects of the civil rights of individual members of an organisation may still be overlooked, as indicated below.

## Commonly accepted employee rights

A comprehensive list of commonly held employee rights based on proposals by Smith[15] is presented in Box 5.2.

---

**Box 5.2** | **Commonly accepted employee rights**

- The right to a fair and non-discriminatory selection process;
- The right to an equitable remuneration and benefits from employment;
- The right to a safe and healthy working environment;
- The right to information relating to job security and safety;
- The right to privacy and freedom from interference;
- The right to freedom of expression;
- The right to freedom from undue stress;
- The right to freedom from sexual harassment;
- The right to personal freedom outside normal working hours;
- The right to freedom from political or religious propaganda, etc.;
- The right to reasonable job security;
- The right to participate in decisions relating to future employment;
- The right of association including membership of a trade union, etc.;
- The right to equitable promotion, disciplinary or redundancy treatment.

*Source*: R.E. Smith, *Workrights*, New York, Dutton, 1983.

---

## Whistleblowing

The practice of whistleblowing occurs when an individual exercises his/her right to act as an independent agent by informing the public, or a government agency, of some activity carried out in an organisation that:

- causes unnecessary harm to customers;
- violates human rights;
- is illegal;
- contravenes the stated purpose of the organisation;
- is otherwise considered to be immoral.

The ethical dilemma for the individual is in deciding whether and under what circumstances whistleblowing is acceptable or even morally required behaviour. In resolving this dilemma, the individual will need to address the following two issues which generally arise in all cases of whistleblowing:

- the moral basis of the presumed obligation of loyalty to an employer;
- the moral basis of the presumed overriding obligation to the public.

## The presumed obligation of loyalty to an employer

Although it is widely accepted in business ethics that an individual entering into an 'at will' contract of employment with an organisation has an obligation of loyalty to his/her employer, it should be stressed that the moral boundaries of this loyalty cannot be presumed because they can never be fully known in advance, and therefore need to be specified in terms of individual responsibilities and reporting procedures in the employment contract. For example, it is unusual for any individual to work entirely alone in an organisation and the notion of membership of a team, group or section is implicit in a contract of employment. Using team games as an example, a good deal of management theory is devoted to developing concepts of team spirit in organisations (see Mullins[16]), therefore for an individual to detach him/herself from the team by assuming the role of judge or referee, often without notice, to 'blow the whistle' on other members of the group, is likely to be seen as an act of disloyalty which may result in a hostile reception when details become known.

Attention has already been drawn in Box 5.2 to the recognised employment rights of privacy and freedom from interference, and also of freedom of expression, which every individual may reasonably be expected to enjoy from their employment. If these rights are given, it may therefore be assumed that a more urgent countervailing obligation to the general public would be the only moral justification for overriding the personal obligation to the team, group or organisation.

## The presumed obligation to the general public

The moral justification for whistleblowing can be approached from either a deontological or a teleological standpoint. For example, in deontological terms, the individual must first ascertain that s(he) is acting out of a clear sense of duty, without regard to the consequences, in keeping with the Kantian categorical imperative principle discussed in Chapter 2. If there is any doubt on this issue, then a more pragmatic approach would be to evaluate the 'cash value' of the rival costs and benefits of loyalty to the organisation, on the one hand, against any presumed obligation to the general public, on the other. This sort of moral evaluation is, of course, based on the utilitarian principle that precedence should be given to maximising the good of the greatest number of people unless there are clear reasons for acting to the contrary. This obligation of acting in the public good is based on the following principles:

- The whistleblowing has the sole purpose of exposing avoidable harm, violation of human rights, illegal activity, or behaviour contrary to the legal purpose of the organisation.
- The purpose must have a moral motive and should not be based on the prospect of gaining personal advantage, or 'settling scores', etc.
- The act of whistleblowing should be 'impersonal' in the sense that it is provoked by the behaviour of the organisation rather than by any personal motives.
- The individual should be certain that his/her complaint(s) are based on first-hand knowledge of inappropriate behaviour by the organisation that would satisfy an impartial third party that an improper act had occurred.
- In assessing the moral 'cash value' of a complaint before bringing it to public attention, the individual would be expected to evaluate its seriousness, by giving

priority to a major rather than to a minor issue, its immediate relevance in terms of whether there is still time to prevent the action from happening, and whether it is a specific rather than a general complaint that can be more easily identified.

■ The whistleblower should ordinarily have explored all internal procedures before deciding to go public, thereby giving members of the organisation the opportunity to respond internally to the complaint, and preferably through the recognised upward channels of communication. Circumstances may arise where the individual decides to leap-frog over upper layers of supervision and communicate directly with senior management because of fear of reprisals. However, before taking this step, the individual should weigh up the chances of success and consider the risks incurred which may result in personal stress, loss of employment and hardship for other members of his/her family, etc.

There is some protection for employees in the UK, USA and the European continent who become concerned enough about malpractices at work that they decide to disclose information about their employer's activities in public. Ordinarily, the information disclosed must relate to a possible criminal offence, failure to comply with a legal obligation, contravention of a health and safety issue, damage to the environment or an attempt to conceal any of these malpractices. For example, in the UK, the organisation Public Concern at Work provides confidential advice to individuals on how to proceed with complaints in which whistleblowing may be necessary.

Marlene Winfield founded Public Concern at Work in 1990 after her research showed that:

> although 75 per cent of companies surveyed recognised circumstances in which whistleblowers would be justified in going public, few companies had a procedure that protected them from punishment for breach of confidence, or assured them their concerns would be addressed.[17]

Commenting on in the UK social services, Dr Geoffrey Hunt[18], Director of the European Centre for Professional Ethics, observes that: 'The whistleblower is caught in the middle – a hero to the public, and a troublemaker, even a deviant, to the organisation, and that takes its toll on their mental and physical health.' He adds that a large proportion of the 200 whistleblowers who have contacted the Centre have suffered ill-health as a consequence of their actions, and that

> We now have plenty of evidence that whistleblowing affects health . . . severe depression is pretty common . . . people lose weight, have panic attacks, and suffer with insomnia. We know, too, that the very high stress levels they experience are predictors of physical disease.

Etorre[19] advises would-be whistleblowers to take the following precautions:

■ Talk things over with family and trusted friends outside work.
■ Try to work within the organisational system first before going outside, bearing in mind that raising the subject may provoke a cover-up.
■ Keep a detailed factual record of critical events and any related harassment.
■ Prepare a signed and dated summary of the key points in the record; and have it witnessed if possible.
■ If you expect your word to be challenged, adopt the 'poor person's copyright' procedure of mailing a copy to yourself at your home address in a sealed envelope, signed and dated preferably across the back seal, which should be stored safely and left unopened until it may be needed.

- Identify and copy key written records of critical events/incidents and include these with your 'poor person's copyright' document, as you will probably be denied access to any records once your concerns become public.
- Seek the confidential advice of specialist organisations, citizens' advice bureaux, or the local library about how to proceed, particularly in making contact with constituencies outside the organisation that would be interested in your findings and allegations.

Overall, the basis for any contract of employment is to be found in common law which contains two important principles. First, an employee is required to be loyal to an employer, to act solely in the latter's interests and not to act or speak disloyally in all matters related to employment. Secondly, without a specific contractual provision, every employment is 'at will' and either side may terminate arrangements without additional notice to that already agreed. The contract should otherwise protect the moral rights of the employee in return for his/her displaying the requisite moral attributes in carrying out agreed duties and responsibilities on the basis of 'a fair wage for an honest day's work'.

## Synopsis

- The notion of individual morality in organisations ultimately depends on the deontological belief that any tendency towards moral behaviour by the individual, on the one hand, or an employer or manager, on the other, should not be exploited by any other person. In employment terms, this means that the individual has a duty to carry out his/her responsibilities in a loyal way as agreed with his/her employer, and vice versa.
- This arrangement is dependent on the assumption that both parties will display a 'good' character towards each other, although the development of a 'good' character, based upon the values of integrity and goodness, cannot be taken for granted and is probably not inherited but forms in early childhood and develops throughout adulthood.
- Moral behaviour is also not dependent on gender, previous religious education or participation in character development programmes, although more intelligent children are less likely to lie, cheat or steal, as are those who have socioeconomic advantages.
- Probably because of fears about individual integrity, the intrusion on employees' civil liberties during working hours has been criticised as rampant in most organisations, where the rights that employees are accustomed to outside of work are often neglected.
- However, valid moral judgements are based on the assumption that members of organisations will carry out agreed moral rules or duties providing their individual 'moral rights' are respected. These rights may be divided into negative and positive human rights. Negative rights impose restraints on individuals in their behaviour towards others. Positive rights cannot be achieved without the direct intervention of others.
- Of additional importance to individuals in organisations are the rights of privacy; confidentiality; information; intellectual property; and justice.

- Various forms of justice relevant to organisational activities include compensatory justice; retributive justice; procedural justice; and distributive justice discussed in Chapter 12.
- The right of an individual to act as an independent agent by 'whistleblowing' when the actions of other members of an organisation are either illegal, or likely to damage the interests of consumers or the general public, is upheld in most industrialised nations; however, the costs may be high in terms of personal stress, illness and rejection by others.

## Review and discussion questions

**1** What is the common duty of both an employer and employees towards another individual member of an organisation?

**2** What were the main findings of the US research into character education programmes, and what are the implications for employee training in organisations?

**3** What are the basic values shared by all the major cultures and world religions?

**4** What are the key characteristics of personal integrity, and what is their relevance for professional managers employed in organisations?

**5** According to Ewing, what two historical reasons account for the absence of civil liberties in most organisations?

**6** What are the major negative and positive human rights proposed by Green?

**7** What are the main forms of justice likely to arise in an organisational context?

**8** What are the additional human rights proposed by Smith, and why are these of importance to both managers and employees in organisations?

## Case study
## Battling with dinosaurs

Mary Schiavo was Assistant Secretary of Labor under Elizabeth Dole until August 1990, when she was appointed Inspector-General of the US Department of Transportation. Shiavo held the latter post for over five years but resigned following her appearance on the ABC TV network *Nightline* programme on 12 May 1996, to denounce the safety record of ValuJet Airlines after its Flight 592 had crashed in the Florida Everglades on the previous day with the loss of 110 passengers and crew. This case study explores the reasons why a successful career public official decided to act as a 'whistleblower' by, first, denouncing ValuJet Airlines on a nationwide TV network and then the operational policy of the US Federal Aviation Administration (FAA) in her book, *Flying Blind, Flying Safe*[20], published in 1997.

*Time Magazine*[21] reported that news of the crash of the ValuJet Flight 592 had made Mary Schiavo feel 'queasy and sick' because it was the realisation of a nightmare she had long feared. A fire had broken out in the cargo hold of the jet, an old DC-9, *en route* to Atlanta from Miami. The cabin became filled with smoke and almost certainly asphyxiated the passengers and crew before the plane crashed into a Florida swamp. What disturbed Schiavo more than most was not just the scale of the tragedy, but the belief that it could have been averted had her warning about ValuJet's unacceptable safety record, which had been reported to the FAA three months before the fatal accident, been acted on more promptly.

Although Mary Schiavo's TV criticism of the airline company may have seemed like that of a whistleblower being wise after the event, it was actually the culmination of a personal campaign to make the FAA accept more responsibility for airline passenger safety on internal flights in the USA. For her, the FAA was too sympathetic to the demands of the airline companies, which was the reason why she resigned so that she could have her side of the story published. Otherwise, as a government official, she could not disclose her experiences at the Department of Transport in public and remain in post. She resigned 'dismayed, disillusioned and afraid for the flying public' whereas the FAA claimed that all US airlines were safe, despite Mary Schiavo's declaration that: 'I would not fly ValuJet.' She had already warned the FAA about ValuJet's alarming safety record; however, the airline carrier was allowed to continue with its passenger services despite her concern and the off-the-record recommendations of some of the FAA's own inspectors that ValuJet Airlines should be closed down.

Following the disaster, the airline carrier was forced to withdraw its services for over three months and has since reintroduced a reduced number of passenger flights. ValuJet Airlines is an Atlanta-based carrier which was founded in 1993 with two aircraft that operated eight routes between Atlanta and three cities in neighbouring southern states. It quickly became probably the most successful internal airline carrier in the USA with 51 planes operating 320 routes and a turnover exceeding $368 million in 1995. However, Mary Schiavo considered it was only a matter of time before ValuJet was involved in a major crash because its unacceptable safety standards were linked to a slipshod maintenance record. Along with several other FAA inspectors, she had concluded that the airline's managers were out of their depth which is why the inspectors had pressed for it to be shut down months before the Everglades crash had occurred. Although the FAA senior management may have refused to listen, the US Defense Department was far more attentive when ValuJet submitted a bid for a contract to fly military personnel on internal US flights in 1995. The Pentagon team of inspectors raised serious complaints about virtually every aspect of the ValuJet operations before refusing to award a military contract to the airline.

So used are people from abroad to thinking of the technological developments, quality assurance standards and commitment of the US public to open government as beyond reproach, that it is hard to believe that an airline carrier with ValuJet's poor safety record was ever allowed to carry on business. Perhaps the sober truth, as Mary Schiavo concluded, was that 'Only with people dead and sobbing survivors filling television screens does the FAA make changes.' What is indisputable, however, is that the airline's safety record had deteriorated almost in direct proportion to its record growth. For example, ValuJet pilots made a worrying 15 emergency landings in 1994, which increased to 57 (i.e. more than one a week) in 1995 and, as the Flight 592 inquiry revealed, this grew to 59 emergency landings between February and May 1996 when the disaster occurred, or one unscheduled landing every other day.

Nearly 5,000 FAA inspections of ValuJet's planes had occurred in the three years since the company had started, yet no significant problems or concerns were formally reported to the company by the FAA executive up to three months before the Everglades air crash. Mary Schiavo and her deputy assistant inspector-general, Larry Weintraub, were sufficiently concerned to contact the FAA inspectorate at Atlanta who refused to acknowledge that ValuJet had an unacceptable safety record. Weintraub and his team provided details of the spate of accidents ValuJet Airlines had recorded during its short existence. Its planes had repeatedly overshot runways, stalled under collapsed landing gears, and taken off in poor weather when other airlines had cancelled flights. Engines had exploded, fires had broken out in flight and in one very dangerous incident the exploding engine had showered shrapnel into the fuselage of a plane, piercing the metal and resulting in injuries to seven passengers. The Atlanta FAA inspectorate advised Weintraub that the number of accidents and incidents was not 'disproportionate' and there were not enough links between them for the FAA to consider closing down ValuJet.

If only to justify this position after the fatal crash, the Department of Transportation Secretary, Federico Pena, insisted: 'I have flown ValuJet. ValuJet is a safe airline, as is our entire aviation system. If ValuJet was unsafe, we would have grounded it.' In addition, the FAA chief administrator, David Hinson, was on record since the crash as stating that ValuJet is 'safe to fly. I would fly it myself.' A separate statement by an FAA spokesperson indicated that there was a reluctance to take formal action against the Atlanta-based ValuJet because it might have a disastrous impact on the Olympic Games which were due to be held in Atlanta later in 1996. Mary Schiavo maintained that the FAA was protecting the airline in the same way that government officials had defended the airline industry for decades, by insisting that an FAA report showed the smaller carriers to be as safe as the major international airlines. However, this report was skewed because one airline, Southwest, had an almost perfect safety record. This data raised the average for the industry, including ValuJet, which had recorded 14 times more safety violations than any other US carrier. The FAA administrator, David Hinson, was also a former McDonnell Douglas executive who knew that the crashed Douglas DC-9 plane had been plagued with defective equipment which had led to repeated emergency landings since January 1996.

In Mary Schiavo's opinion, Hinson and his FAA associates were lying to the public about ValuJet Airlines' safety record. The 'damage limitation' exercise by the FAA executive might have continued had not Mary Schiavo received a telephone call at her home a week after the crash from an unidentified FAA inspector who informed her that, following Weintraub's visit to Atlanta, the local inspectorate had revisited ValuJet and written an eight-page memo to the FAA head office in February, expressing similar concerns to the Inspector-General's team, which concluded with a recommendation that the airline's planes should be grounded. However, no action had been taken against the airline and the FAA had filed the memo away without contacting ValuJet three months before Flight 592 crashed in the Everglades. The anonymous caller added that he had just left a meeting at FAA headquarters where the secret Atlanta memo was being discussed, which he claimed was in his hand during the telephone call.

Mary Schiavo acted promptly by having a subpoena served on the FAA executive to hand over the memo to the Inspector-General's office. However, the court official arrived at the FAA headquarters after the meeting had ended and was informed that those present knew nothing about the secret memo from Atlanta. The anonymous caller was not to be put off so easily and when a large pile of ValuJet documents was released at a press conference the next day, buried in the middle was the eight-page memo from the Atlanta inspectorate. Its main conclusion, written in official FAA jargon, was that 'Consideration should be given to an immediate FAR 121 recertification of this airline' and recommended, in plain words, that the ValuJet airline fleet should be grounded immediately.

Once the contents of the memo became public, the FAA's position altered immediately. The ValuJet planes were grounded within weeks as the FAA published 34 safety violations going back three years. ValuJet agreed not to challenge the FAA decision in the courts and paid $2 million towards the cost of the FAA inspecting its fleet of planes. This was not a penalty because a separate agreement was reached with ValuJet Airlines, under which the FAA stated that 'it will not pursue a civil penalty for any violation of the regulations known by the FAA as of the date and time of this agreement'. Why had the FAA backed away from prosecuting ValuJet? According to Mary Schiavo, the reason was obvious; the FAA could hardly prosecute the airline for safety violations without admitting that it was to blame for having missed or ignored them, if not over three years, then certainly during the three months immediately prior to the crash. To make matters worse, the ValuJet experience was not an isolated case and Mary Schiavo had spent four years as Inspector-General compiling evidence of FAA malpractice.

The Federal Aviation Administration is responsible for certifying and examining aircraft design and airline operations and monitoring the performance of aeroplanes, pilots, mechanics, repair hangars and aircraft parts at every stage of the US commercial aviation industry. The FAA's most effective weapon is unannounced inspections by nearly 3,000 inspectors, who form a crucial link between the regulatory arm of government and the airlines, to ensure that all carriers operate within the stringent US aviation law. The FAA inspectors are paid between $40,000 and $70,000 (£25,000–£45,000) per year to carry out their detailed inspections diligently and, above all, with impartiality. However, in the considered opinion of the Inspector-General's Office (IGO), the FAA was too responsive to the needs of the aviation industry at the expense of adopting a complacent attitude towards passenger safety.

Starting in 1992, the IGO investigated seven FAA regions and found that the inspectors did an abysmal job of examining US airline companies. This led Mary Schiavo to authorise a survey of all inspections carried out from 1988 up to her appointment in 1990. Findings revealed that out of 833,000 inspections nationwide, only 4,000 (less than 0.5 per cent) violations were reported, or just over one per FAA inspector every two years. Landing gear, oxygen supplies and engine controls were checked less than half of the time, whereas engines were inspected on just over half of the total visits. In the case of Delta Airlines, nearly 13,000 inspections were carried out in 1996 but only seven violation orders were issued. More worrying, follow-up reports on the few problems discovered were rarely completed by FAA inspectors.

Ten critical reports on FAA activities were issued by the IGO between 1990 and 1996 which included 70 recommendations calling for more improved FAA inspections on aircraft operators, parts manufacturers, repair units, and the designated mechanics examination system. The FAA response to IGO criticism was seen as slow or evasive, particularly on findings about aircraft spare parts.

The FAA received only a few hundred reports of bogus spare parts in 1991, although each report referred to consignments of thousands of parts. The trouble was that nobody knew exactly how many brokers were trading as middlemen, supplying spare parts to the industry, which included items manufactured in the USA and also in numerous known and unknown countries abroad. In response to an IGO enquiry, the FAA indicated between 2,000 and 5,000 brokers, whereas some aviation industry experts put the figure at closer to 20,000. The uncertainty arose because brokers are unlicensed and unqualified and did not have to register in the USA so they were not subject to FAA regulations. Bogus parts were impounded by the IGO for every type of aircraft and helicopter in service. These even included parts ordered for the US President's official helicopter and spare parts for the oxygen and fire-extinguishing systems on the Air Force One and Two presidential aircraft.

Overall, the IGO believed that at least two plane crashes, one in 1988 that killed 12 people and another in 1990 involving a Pan Am Express plane, could have been prevented had more effective FAA checks on airlines, pilots and spare parts been in place. Five years of inspections across the USA and overseas led to the Inspector-General's evidence rooms being filled with crates of reworked scrap and other counterfeit parts. This evidence was classified as 'suspected unapproved parts' by the FAA due to paperwork problems. However, the IGO survey of repair station parts bins found that 43 per cent of items bought from manufacturers were bogus and a bewildering 95 per cent supplied by parts brokers were also fraudulent. Perhaps the clearest sign that the FAA could not even keep its own house in order was that a IGO audit of the former's Logistics Center found that 39 per cent of its spare parts were suspect. The FAA refuted the findings indignantly only to find that its own audit revealed an even higher total of bogus parts than the original IGO audit.

Mary Schiavo found that dealing with the FAA and the US air traffic control (ATC) system was increasingly like battling with dinosaurs. The FAA had announced a plan in 1981 to replace the entire ATC system; however, little had been done four years later when a leading congressman stated it was because 'the air traffic system is overloaded'. Thirteen years after the plan was introduced, the FAA announced in 1994 that the programme was a failure after $1 billion government funding had been expended.

Following her resignation, Mary Schiavo's outgoing report on the FAA to the Secretary of Transportation was shelved until after the Olympic Games and the Democratic National Convention had passed off successfully. When the report was finally released later in 1996, all incriminating references to the FAA, including aircraft safety failure rates and responses to IGO criticism, were deleted. Nevertheless, FAA administrator Hinson resigned in November 1996 and Secretary of Transportation Pena was subsequently transferred and appointed as Energy Secretary. A Congressional Committee recommended that the FAA terms of reference should be changed to give priority to passenger safety. Nevertheless, the vacant post of Inspector-General remained unfilled for over eight months and the new appointee was advised in 1997 to keep a lower profile. In future, the IGO would no longer get involved in FAA or Department of Transportation policy issues, even though this is still a stated requirement under US Inspector-General legislation. Safety issues would no longer fall under the jurisdiction of the IGO, whose staff could no longer make public statements to the media. An FAA spokesperson indicated that her organisation wanted peace with the IGO whose inspectors would continue to carry out their jobs satisfactorily. After all, no planes were crashing or falling out of the sky.

**1** If you had been in Mary Schiavo's post as Inspector-General, (a) what reasons would you have given to justify acting as a whistleblower by criticising the FAA publicly on a national TV programme, or (b) in what ways would you have acted differently to ensure that passenger safety was improved on US airlines?

**2** What arguments would you give in support of (a) the Department of Transportation's decision to suppress the critical IGO report of the FAA until after the 1996 Olympic Games in Atlanta and the 1996 Democratic National Convention; and (b) deleting critical references to the FAA when the report was eventually published?

**Questions**

**3** How would you justify (a) the actions taken by the US Congress Committee in response to Mary Schiavo's critical whistleblowing actions; and (b) the reaction of the FAA spokesperson that this inspection service was satisfactory since no planes were crashing or falling out of the sky?

## Notes and references

1. Clouse, B., Character, *International Encyclopaedia of Ethics*, ed. J.K. Roth, London, Fitzroy-Dearborn, 1995, 127–8.
2. Hartshorne, H. and May, M.A., *Studies in Deceit*, vol. I, *Studies in the Nature of Character*, New York, Macmillan, 1928–30.
3. Lickona, T., *Educating for Character: Our schools can teach respect*, New York, Bantam Books, 1992.
4. Forrest, B., Integrity, *International Encyclopaedia of Ethics*, ed. J.K. Roth, London, Fitzroy-Dearborn, 1995, 441–2.
5. Solzhenitsyn, A., Nobel Prize Speech, quoted in Forrest, ibid.
6. Green, R.M., *The Ethical Manager: A new method for business ethics*, New York, Macmillan, 1994, 69.
7. Ewing, D., An Employee Bill of Rights, in *Freedom Inside the Organization*, New York, Dutton, 1972.
8. Shaw, W.H. and Barry, V., *Moral Issues in Business*, 7th edn, Belmont, Calif., Wadsworth, 1998, 250.
9. Jacobs, R., Privacy, *International Encyclopaedia of Ethics*, ed. J.K. Roth, London, Fitzroy-Dearborn, 1995, 697–8.
10. Mill, J.S., *On Liberty*, London, Macmillan, 1938.
11. Stephens, O.H. and Schab, J.M. II, Privacy, in *American Constitutional Law*, Minneapolis, West, 1993.
12. Swenson, L.C., Confidentiality, *International Encyclopaedia of Ethics*, ed. J.K. Roth, London, Fitzroy-Dearborn, 1995, 180–1.
13. Francischetti, D.R., Intellectual Property, *International Encyclopaedia of Ethics*, ed. J.K. Roth, London, Fitzroy-Dearborn, 1995, 441–3.
14. De George, R.T., *Moral Reasoning in Business*, New York, Macmillan, 1990.

15. Smith, R.E., *Work rights*, New York, Dutton, 1983.
16. Mullins, L.J., *Management and Organisational Behaviour*, 5th edn., London, Financial Times Pitman Publishing, 1999.
17. Winfield, M., *Minding Your Own Business*, 1990, in Safe Haven for Workers to Blow the Whistle, *The Independent*, 15 October 1993.
18. See: Hunt, G., Whistleblower Wins Unfair Dismissal Case, *The Independent*, 3 June 1995; and also Whistle-Blowing, *Encyclopaedia of Applied Ethics*, vol. 4, New York, Academic Press, 1998, 525–35.
19. Ettorre, B., Whistleblowers: Who's the real bad guy? *Management Review*, 1994, 18–23.
20. Schiavo, M. and Chartrand, S., *Flying Blind, Flying Safe*, New York, Avon Books, 1997.
21. *Time Magazine*, Dangerous Skies, 31 March 1997, 34–44.

# Unethical behaviour by individuals in organisations

### Learning objectives

After reading this chapter you should be able to:

■ examine what is meant by dysfunctional behaviour in terms of 'sociopathic' and unethical behaviour by individuals in organisations;

■ explore the main forms of dysfunctional behaviour including lying, greed, free-riding, white collar and other employee crime, embezzlement and fraud, and bribery;

■ discuss the need for adequate training, supervision and appraisal of individuals as ways of eradicating dysfunctional behaviour in organisations;

■ explore the origins of the professions and what is entailed in the establishment of management as a professional activity.

## Introduction

Unethical behaviour tends to occur in organisations for a number of reasons depending on the perspective adopted. At the individual level, the cause may be employees failing to respect each other's unique personalities and ceasing to aspire towards personal achievement and happiness. Such dysfunctional behaviour towards others may also not be questioned by fellow employees, supervisors or managers and, if not addressed, may undermine an individual's self-belief, value-system and sense of general well-being as an effective member of a group or organisation. Alternatively, unethical behaviour may occur because managers act in an unprofessional manner towards their various constituents, or each other, putting their own self-interests before those of other members of the organisation and external stakeholders.

## Dysfunctional behaviour in organisations

Various psychological and socioeconomic factors may account for why individuals lose self-respect and personal motivation, or develop negative attitudes towards other members of an organisation. Sometimes this dysfunctional behaviour may be due to negative work experiences or else be deeply ingrained and hard to change. In discussing the latter phenomenon, Clouse[1] notes that there are persons in society who are so deficient in their moral makeup that they are said to have a 'character disorder'. Research shows them to be of average or above-average intelligence, neither neurotic nor psychotic, able to verbalise the rules of society, yet seemingly unable to understand or accept why they should obey these rules or conform to the expectations of others.

Clouse adds that they are sometimes called 'sociopaths' because of a tendency to project blame on to others and a refusal to accept responsibility for their own failures. They may also act impulsively, and display unconcern about the rights and privileges of others. Some may also be pathological liars, who are unable to form deep attachments to other persons, display poor judgement and planning, and lack emotional control. The outlook for such persons after psychological counselling and therapy is apparently poor, since they experience minimal anxiety or distress because of their social maladjustment, and are unwilling or unable to understand why they should change their behaviour. Clouse adds that there are also grounds for concluding that the ethical values of personal integrity and goodness, discussed in Chapter 5, are given low priority as life-goals by sociopathic individuals.

## The main forms of unethical behaviour by individuals

The main forms of unethical behaviour displayed by individual members of organisations include:

- lying;
- greed;
- free-riding;
- employee crime;
- white collar crime;
- embezzlement and fraud;
- bribery.

### Lying

Kagan[2] notes that lying is considered in philosophy, as in everyday life, to be the opposite of truth and is also condemned in all of the world's great religions; for example in Christianity, under the Commandment 'Thou shalt not bear false witness'. Lying is defined by Bok[3] as 'making a false statement to another person with the intention of misleading that person'. However, in ethics, lying may sometimes be permissible although it is generally unacceptable because it is regarded as eroding the self-respect of the individual and can lead to social institutions being undermined.

The great Humanist scholar, Hugo Grotius (1583–1645), argued that lying may be permissible when it it is directed towards children, the insane, thieves, and unrighteous persons, or when it is done for the public good. Immanuel Kant rejected any emotional or pragmatic justification for lying and argued that a lie always damages human society because it 'vitiates the source of law itself'. Kant's deontological view would not excuse lying in any form of lie, even if it was intended to alleviate a life-threatening situation. His 'categorical imperative' was discussed in Chapter 2.

Bok's detailed philosophical study of the ethics of lying explores the rationale of 'white lies', false excuses, inauthentic justifications, lies in a crisis, lies to liars, lies to enemies, lies for the public good, lies to protect peers and clients, deceptive social science research, lies to the sick and dying, and the moral effects of lying on both the liar and other people. Unlike Kant, Bok adopts a teleological position towards lying by emphasising the consequences which include the deceived person becoming distrustful of the liar and, by extension, this perception is accepted by a wider public, as the liar loses both self-respect and a sense of reality if he/she continues to remain involved in a system of transmitting lies to retain power or authority. From this point of view, lying harms not only the individual but also the community.

Bok shifts part of the responsibility for identifying and correcting the problems of lying from the individual to society. With profit-seeking organisations in mind, she enquires, how can an individual change the whole structure of a business system that values sales, bottom-line income, and success more than it does honesty? How can an individual change misleading advertising, deceptive marketing research, deceitful claims, and fallacious government reports and regulations? These fraudulent activities contribute to the destruction of moral values, the loss of respect for authority, and the proliferation of individual despair in the pursuit of justice. In short, if the system itself encourages deceit, on what grounds should individual dishonesty be condemned?

Again unlike Kant, Bok acknowledges that certain types of lying may be permissible. For example, lying to a terrorist or a criminal, or to minimise harm in life-threatening situations to protect the innocent, should not automatically be condemned. Certain 'white lies' are also conditionally acceptable, if they are intended to protect someone's feelings, or to avoid a painful situation, but only as a last resort. In short, lying must be morally evaluated in the overall societal or organisational context. The task of those responsible for managing organisations is to assess the significance of deceitful behaviour by themselves or other members when questions such as 'Will one white lie lead to others and result in increased distrust or other harm for those who are deceived?' need to be brought into the open and evaluated.

Bok also explores the impact of lying on personal relationships and warns against creating a culture in which the pressure to lie exceeds a commitment to truthfulness, especially in bureaucratic institutions or in professional legal, medical or business organisations. She advocates a discussion of ethical standards relating to lying in all institutions since, without the active or passive support of society and its institutions, the problem of lying will not be corrected and individuals will see no need to overcome the temptation to tell lies.

## Greed

According to Miller[4], greed is a defect of character or will in which a person, corporate entity or government is unwilling to restrain itself from taking more than is its due, or may be prudent. As with lying, greed is regarded as immoral behaviour in all of the world's great religions either because it results in evil behaviour, and alienation from God, or because it has possibly ruinous and destructive effects on other people. Despite its universal condemnation, greed is regarded as pervasive in society and occurs at all levels of human activity from the individual, the group, to the institutional.

Worster[5] has documented the effects of greed at the institutional level and criticises the 'greed is good' mentality of the US agricultural industry, which pursued unrealistic short-term profits by promoting a 'slash-and-burn' policy of economic development that resulted in environmental destruction and created long-term soil erosion, water shortage, dust bowl conditions, and the extinction of wildlife. Worster concluded that it will take future generations decades to reverse the effects of this short-term strategy based on greed. Lekachman[6] also analysed the impact of greed as a central aim of government policy on the rest of society by citing the case of US president Ronald Reagan's administration's purportedly enthusiastic and massive redistribution of wealth and power during the early 1980s. This only further benefited those already rich at the expense of the working poor, minorities, and families on social security.

In studying the origins of greed, Fromm[7] sets aside its religious associations with sin and explores the way parents educate their children to comply with society's values. Fromm regards Western society as passing through stages, one of which is characterised by 'hoarding behaviour' which is preoccupied with accumulating, and retaining objects valued by the rest of society. He also claims that social ills associated with greed can be linked with the basic right to own property and dispose of it as one wants, thereby acting according to self-interest.

This view has resulted in animals and plants being subordinated to human use, in compliance with the Protestant work ethic which advocated that control and exploitation of nature for profit was justifiable. Finally, economics also encouraged the belief that the source of value was human labour and that nature lacked any intrinsic value unless it was exploited for the purpose of increasing wealth which, in turn, led to a popular belief in a 'greed is good' mentality. This is condemned by the Golden Rule/Mean (see Slomski)[8] as potentially destructive to the individual and to society because it describes extreme social behaviour far removed from moderation.

## Free-riding

Free-riding refers to behaviour that allows an individual to enjoy a benefit produced by the effort of others without contributing a fair share and it is regarded as unethical because it threatens the success of cooperative endeavours among people. As the term suggests, free-riding involves gaining a benefit at no cost to the person who enjoys the benefit. Morelli[9] notes that free-riding is seen as unfair in situations where the provision of the benefit involves costs borne by others and there is an expectation that those enjoying the benefit will share in the cost. Two common forms of free-riding occur in organisations when individuals are unwilling to participate in group activities, yet draw benefits from this collective effort, or when an individual exercises his/her right not to join a trade union or staff association, but is content to obtain the benefits of union membership as a result of negotiations with management. As a result, free-riding usually receives moral condemnation as unfair.

That said, certain types of goods or benefits in organisations are the product of cooperative activities and become available to all. They may also not be easily divisible so it becomes difficult or impossible for management to exclude non-contributors from sharing these benefits. It may therefore seem only rational for an independent-minded person to play a free-riding role since benefits may be obtained at no personal cost. This may, of course, cause morale problems among the group involved if other members refuse to cooperate with the free-riding individual. In the trade union or staff association membership example, closed-shop agreements may be negotiated with management as a way of excluding free-riding individuals from particular occupations.

From the view of the individual intent on maximising personal satisfaction, free-riding seems like a rational course of action, so long as enough others cooperate to ensure that a cooperative venture is successful, and do not object to the individual withdrawing his/her participation. From the group's standpoint, however, if co-operation with each other offers mutual benefits, it may seem equally rational that each individual should cooperate so that free-riding is eliminated. If a group activity is in operation, management's task will be to ensure that any free-riding activity does not undermine cooperation between group members in an organisation.

Morelli (ibid) introduces the example of a lighthouse to illuminate the problem facing managers when free-riding occurs in an organisation. Employees who choose to cooperate are comparable with shipowners who find it beneficial to build and maintain a lighthouse to safeguard their vessels, even though other ships may also benefit from the lighthouse. The other free-riding shipowners will benefit without paying their share of the cost of building, manning or maintaining the lighthouse. If management decides not to act against free-riding employees, those who may be compared with the builders of the lighthouse may have to re-evaluate the benefits of cooperation.

## Employee crime

Gray[10] notes that, in addition to the conventional concerns of running a successful small business, one of the most serious problems is the rise in employee crime, which is estimated to exceed annual losses due to fire damage in the USA. Examples of employee crime recorded since the 1980s include:

- an increase in incidents of managers establishing their own businesses in company time by making use of their employer's resources;
- bank officials who kept deposits to pay off outstanding debts and wrote off the losses against the banks;
- store managers who stole items from incoming shipments and sold the goods which were made up by the company whenever customers complained of short orders;
- a machinery manufacturer's trusted employees selling equipment illegally and pocketing the proceeds.

Research cited by Gray notes that in the USA the costliest offences of employee crime occurred in small companies with less than 100 staff. Its estimated cost exceeded $400 billion annually, or $9 per day per employee. Male employees made up 54 per cent of the workforce yet were responsible for over 75 per cent of the crime. Finally, business losses due to thefts by managers were over four times more costly to the company than those involving blue collar or administrative staff.

## White collar crime

White collar crime was legally recognised first in the USA and later in other Western countries in the 1970s as criminal activity in the corporate, commercial, professional and political arenas. White collar crimes are distinguished from other criminal activity by taking place mostly at the workplace and involving activities related to otherwise legitimate occupations, which also rarely involve the use of violence. At the most basic level and easiest to identify and prosecute, is theft by white collar employees which ranges from taking office supplies for use outside work to the theft of products intended for sale. At the highest level, white collar crime typically involves manipulation of accounting records or legal documents for personal gain. These latter crimes are increasingly more difficult to trace as more records are kept in electronic form, leaving fewer 'paper trails' to identify wrongdoing. This topic is explored in more detail in Chapter 7.

A variation of white collar crime, involving manipulation of company records, includes alteration of the terms of a business contract with the aim of earning a profit not intended or agreed to by the other contracting parties. Another example is insider trading that allows dealers in shares or bonds, or commodity traders, to use information before other dealers to make an illicit profit from their trading activities. Insider trading provides an example of the difficulty of prosecuting some perpetrators of white collar crime, especially as it is difficult to identify illegally obtained information, since financial markets are intended to reward those who make early use of financial information.

## Embezzlement and fraud

Embezzlement and related fraud were first established in law in 1330 as intentional deception intended to give one some advantage in a financial transaction, although the moral condemnation of deception dates back earlier in the Judaeo-Christian tradition which has always denounced embezzlement and fraud. The English Statute of Frauds of 1677 was later adopted across the United States and established the principle of recording details of any contract 'in writing' before one party could sue another for the recovery of a specific monetary sum, or to enforce a contract beyond a pre-stated period of time. The purpose of the statute was to reduce the number of claims for alleged fraud by ensuring that important business matters were not left to disputed recollections of oral statements which pitted one person's word against that of another.

Embezzlement and fraud can be committed by either commission or omission. An act of commission involves lying or making some form of material misrepresentation, whereas an act of omission refers to any failure to disclose a significant fact that the law requires to be disclosed. Financial markets like the London Stock Exchange attempt to minimise this sort of malpractice by a dualistic approach which supports the principle of *caveat emptor* ('Let the buyer beware') on the one hand, in order to reduce the amount of bureaucracy that could interfere with the free market. On the other hand, however, the regulatory authorities also enforce the ethical principle that any withholding of required information may be regarded as fraud, or exploitation of innocent persons. Such acts are therefore prohibited so that occasions when key financial information is not disclosed through active deception or a lie are minimised.

Granelli[11] reports that the typical US organisation loses 6 per cent of its total annual turnover due to fraudulent malpractice by employees. These findings also confirm those of Gray[10] that, on a per capita basis, small firms with fewer than 100 employees incur the highest median losses of about $120,000 per annum. Blue collar and administrative staff committed 58 per cent of the proven fraud and embezzlement crimes; however, the cases perpetrated by managers, who had greater access to financial sources, were the most costly and resulted in median losses over three times higher than that of other employees. Apprehended employees who committed fraud on a regular basis confessed that they believed that they would not be caught, or at least would not be prosecuted.

Separate studies by the US White Collar Crime Center confirm that in over 90 per cent of the cases investigated by the Center the employer described the prosecuted person as a trusted employee right up to the time that the crime was discovered. White collar crime security experts stress the importance of screening employees during the hiring process and suggest the watchword that: 'There is only one way that people get into positions where they can steal from you: you appoint them there.' White collar fraud in the UK exceeded £4 billion in 1999 (*The Independent*, 16 August 2000). As in the USA, there is also a reluctance for companies to prosecute managers suspected of fraud, apparently because of fears of adverse publicity about inadequate management information systems should the incident be reported in the media. The usual practice is for charges to be dropped in return for information about how the fraud was perpetrated so that this flaw in the company's security system can be changed. A change of policy may be underway, however, as the UK financial services company, Allied Dunbar, is reportedly suing a former employee at one of its subsidiary banks for £1.77 million, which they allege went missing as a result of misappropriation of funds over a 10-year period. The person being prosecuted was described by the police as a 'respectable middle class woman with a family' (*The Independent*, 9 August 2000, p. 6).

## Bribery

O'Neill[12] notes that the word 'bribe' is found in Chaucer's *Canterbury Tales* and refers to illegal or improper favours obtained in exchange for the payment of money or something else of value. Bribery involves making such payments in return for someone violating an obligation or duty. In modern organisations, bribery is regarded as inconsistent with efficiency but is usually condemned as intrinsically immoral, a wrong in itself, because its aim is to manipulate people into neglecting duties they have willingly taken upon themselves in accepting a public or private position with inherent responsibilities.

Bribery is intrinsically wrong for two primary reasons: first, the person being bribed violates his/her duty, and secondly, harmful consequences may flow from the acceptance of the bribe. O'Neill quotes the example of a human resource manager who accepts a bribe to hire a particular candidate for a job with her organisation. Even if the candidate is suitably qualified, if the bribe means that a less-than-best candidate is selected by the manager, this makes the organisation marginally less competitive in the free market which, depending on the seniority of the position could have potentially damaging effects on its viability in terms of jobs and future profits, etc.

O'Neill adds that it is customary in many regions and countries for moderate payments to be made to public officials for performing tasks such as issuing permits, licences, visas, passage through customs, and so forth, when small 'bribes' may have to be paid to the appropriate officials. These practices are based on long-standing customs (even though technically illegal) and payments are regarded more as tips than as bribes by officials who receive low salaries. The offering of bribes, whether taken or not, is regarded as morally unacceptable in circumstances in which the taking of bribes would be blameworthy. In situations in which taking a bribe is regarded as normal custom and practice, making nominal payments to public servants is regarded as morally blameless.

The key point being made by O'Neill supports a moral pluralism perspective (see Chapter 4 ) on the offer and taking of bribes which appear to be part of the normal business culture in some countries yet generally condemned in Anglo-Saxon business cultures. For example, it is apparently an acceptable practice in some Mediterranean countries to offer a small percentage of a pay award to a line manager as a gratuity for support rendered. Yet the report that managers at the Rover car company took 'bribes' of approximately £2,500 to approve staff redundancy applications (*Financial Times*, 31 August 2000) is likely to end in, at least, the dismissal of these managers and, at worst, prosecution for accepting bribes.

## Dealing with dysfunctional behaviour in organisations

It would be unrealistic of management to expect that dysfunctional behaviour, such as that described above, could ever be completely eradicated from any organisation. At best, prompt identification of problems through the implementation of effective control systems should minimise the incidence of dysfunctional behaviour. Thereafter, management needs to ensure that established human resource management procedures, including adequate supervision and relevant training, regular appraisals and specific job satisfaction evaluations, aimed at obtaining a closer 'fit' between individual expectations and actual experiences, are carried out preferably by an employee's line manager or supervisor. As Mullins[13] observes, the aim of the latter interviews should be to carry out a thorough analysis of five ongoing 'contracts' that exist between a committed individual and the organisation, which cover the following critical personal development issues:

- the knowledge contract;
- the psychological contract;
- the efficiency contract;
- the ethical contract;
- the task structure contract.

The overall aim of these job satisfaction interviews is to improve communications and develop trust between the individual and his/her immediate supervisor, by reviewing the outcomes of any previous interviews and identifying any problem areas in a non-aggressive and constructive manner, so that agreement is reached on any outstanding training needs and when these will be provided and implemented. Here again, however, the underlying assumption is that managers are acting in a professional manner towards the employees in question.

## Professional ethics

### Differences between professional and occupational ethics

Airaksinen[14], Barker[15] and Brooks[16] note that professional ethics deals with the ethical obligations of those in professional occupations who, unlike their non-professional counterparts, are assumed to have special responsibilities towards their clients and the general public. Professional ethics is usually distinguished from the ethics of work which govern the practices, rights and duties of those in paid occupations. The latter are assumed to lack the autonomy and power of professionals. There is more than a suggestion of self-serving elitism about this distinction as every legal occupation has some characteristic ethical obligations that have emerged out of historical, legal and social contexts. The difference is that occupational ethics are mostly taken for granted by society.

People no more assume that butchers will cut cloth, or tailors carve beef, than they fear that bakers will intentionally poison their bread, or hairdressers deliberately electrocute their customers under the hair-dryer. In short, there are no major rational or moral reasons for excluding the ethics of work from the study of professional ethics as the two differ less in kind than by degree which is reflected in the higher remuneration society awards to professionals for carrying out their duties.

Supporters of professional ethics assert that the activities of professional people (e.g. doctors, lawyers, accountants) are different. The latter are said to possess distinctive characteristics, in terms of training, knowledge, experience and relationships with clients, that separate them from non-professional workers. The obligations and problems that fall within the domain of professional ethics are therefore concerned with how practitioners reach conclusions about how they ought to behave, rather than how they may actually conduct themselves in a professional context. Professional ethics is also concerned with the foundations of professional values and obligations. These question the nature of professional power and authority in a democratic society, as well as the nature of professional knowledge, and the impact of possible paternalistic practices on clients' rights.

### Characteristics of professional ethics

There is no single definition that covers the numerous uses of the word 'profession'. Airaksinen (ibid) suggests, however, that: 'a professional is a member of an exclusive group of individuals who possess a value-based service ideal, and an abstract knowledge of their own field.' He shares some of the doubts expressed above by noting that the concept of a profession is essentially a contested one, in the sense that it has no single meaning in the literature. A sociologist or an economist might add that a profession normally indicates a person's principal career, skilfully carried out to acquire an above average income, because the service provided is considered indispensable by society. An above average education and extensive training are therefore required before new entrants can practise a profession.

As a consequence, most professions are accorded a favourably high status in society. In return, explicit ethical standards are normally maintained by practitioners and entry to the professions is restricted by independent associations. These are legally required to regulate standards, if only because professionals often work alone as independent practitioners. The above characteristics, however, do not justify the claim that a distinct set of normative ethics should be attributed to professions, because these do not raise moral criteria that are sufficiently different from those required to carry out occupations (e.g. a barber or baker), which are classified as non-professional by the sociologist or economist.

## The moral basis of professional behaviour

The Latin word *professionem* means a public declaration and, up until the sixteenth century in England, the word 'profession' referred to the public act of taking a religious vow. It later described an occupation involving the application of specialist knowledge to the affairs of others and was restricted to the four fields of medicine, law, divinity or university teaching. The taking of an oath was retained for entry into these professions at medieval universities and students preparing for careers as physicians, lawyers, clerics or university 'dons' were required to take religious oaths in public at the conclusion of their studies. These oaths fulfilled the three purposes of affirming loyalty to Church doctrine, acknowledging the authority of the university, and publicly accepting the ethical standards of the learned profession they were 'called' to enter by eminent members of the same profession. Oaths were rarely taken lightly and, if only to avoid the threat of divine retribution or loss of recognition from a university and ostracism by fellow practitioners, entrants were required to respect the standards of service of their professions, which included different ethical obligations from those prevailing in other occupations.

## The modern conception of professional behaviour

As Western society became less influenced by religious values, the conception of a profession changed into a broad contractual relationship, with benefits on both sides, between professional practitioners and the public. Hence, a professional attitude towards work came to be regarded as a virtue which sociologists associated with the influence of the 'Protestant work ethic'. Many of the terms and conditions of the practitioner/client relationship became explicit, although aspects were often left unstated and taken for granted (e.g. addressing medical practitioners as 'Doctor' and specialists as 'Mr, Mrs, Ms or Miss'). In return for a professional's pledge to provide certain necessary services, society also permitted practitioners considerable control over their own activities.

Amongst these are the right of professionals to define their own standards of performance and organise their own disciplinary procedures for enforcing these standards, and the restricting of entry into the profession through examinations or other licensing requirements. These arrangements have the obvious benefit of ensuring that an acceptable minimum quality of service is provided to society and excludes outsiders, who may make unreliable judgements and lack expertise and discipline, from posing as professionals. Such privileges are not without costs to society, however, as the elimination of competition normally results in higher professional fees, and public confidence is damaged when a practitioner contravenes set standards, or if these are not rigorously enforced by a professional body.

## The study of values in professional ethics

Airaksinen proposes that the study of values in professional ethics should include four main approaches, as follows.

**The characteristic professional values approach**

On the assumption that professional ethics is more than a collection of values borrowed from law or medicine, a statement of the values that the profession promotes is necessary. Complex issues need to be simplified so that their logic is clear, but without losing sight of their 'real world' application. A simple method would be to list the characteristic values of different professions and compare these in the relevant codes of ethics.

**The quandary ethics approach**

Since professional practices are often controversial, professional ethics should include criticisms of professional malpractice. The quandary approach is diametrically opposed to the 'codes of ethics' approach mentioned above, the codes being criticised as idealistic documents. The quandary approach recognises that professionals often hide behind official declarations of values even when their practices are dubious. Quandary ethics seeks to reveal such problem areas but without losing evenhandedness between the practitioner and the public when examples of malpractice are exposed, often sensationally by the media.

**The standard approach**

Instead of exposing sensational problems in professional life, a standard professional ethics approach describes the features of professional practices before applying ethical concepts such as duties and rights. Supporters of this approach often claim there is no separate field of professional ethics, merely opportunities to apply ethics to everyday social relations in professional life. For example, a lecturer has obligations to students but also various rights, such as the right to evaluate the student's progress. In addition, a lecturer has the right to make decisions that promote his/her success professionally, both in and outside a college or university.

**The ethical norms of a profession**

Society obviously expects to receive a higher quality service from professionals and the elimination of self-interested exploitation of their expertise by practitioners. These expectations fall under three sets of ethical norms, as follows:

- *Responsibilities towards clients.* Of the three, the interests of the client are accorded the highest priority, and the professional's specialised skills are placed at the client's disposal for any reasonable and lawful purpose.
- *Responsibilities towards the profession itself.* Moral responsibilities towards the profession itself aim at enhancing its reputation through high personal standards and supporting its good name in the public domain.
- *Responsibilities towards society.* The responsibilities to society are also important, but less so when good relations already exist between a profession and the general public. Should relations deteriorate through professional misconduct by another practitioner, then professionals will tend to 'close ranks' by enforcing a rigorous implementation of standards and disciplinary procedures until public confidence is restored.

## Professional ethics in public and private organisations

As public and private organisations have grown in number, size and complexity in the West during the last century, a corresponding increase occurred in the numbers of 'technocrats' who provide professional services either as employees or consultants. In profit-seeking companies, for example, these include human resource managers; engineers; computing, statistical and management information specialists; economists; and marketing, financial and strategic planning experts. Depending on the type of organisation, professional specialists may be employed to advise on scientific matters; health and safety; consumer affairs; design; environmental protection; local government; quality assurance, purchasing and supply; public finance; security; trading standards; transport and distribution; and public relations and journalism. This list is by no means exhaustive.

The ethical responsibilities of these technocrats are less clear-cut than for other independent professionals such as architects, engineers or accountants (especially certified public accountants), who take on clients in 'private practice'. When the practitioner is an employee of a profit-making organisation, for example, the employer normally exercises considerable control over the way that work is carried out which reduces the professional independence of the practitioner. In the case of less scrupulous employers, considerable moral effort and corresponding personal stress by the practitioner may be necessary to maintain independence, by questioning or rejecting directives that are contrary to accepted professional practice. The support of outside professional institutions and associations is obviously vital in such situations.

## Professional institutions and associations

There is not enough space here to discuss the origins and objectives of the huge number of diverse professional institutions and associations established in Britain and around the world. Suffice it to say, with the UK in mind, that professional bodies exist in every recognised specialist area. In the field of business and commerce, Scottish institutions led the way and were established shortly after the Industrial Revolution in the late eighteenth century. The first association of commerce and management and first chamber of commerce and enterprise were established in Edinburgh in 1783 and 1786, respectively. The golden period for establishing professional bodies was from the mid-nineteenth into the early twentieth centuries when chartered institutes and associations were established in administration management (1915); British engineers (1928); chartered secretaries and administrators (1891); directors (1903); electrical engineers (1871); environmental health (1883); legal executives (1892); marketing (1911); mechanical engineers (1847); and practitioners in advertising (1927); as well as the Royal Statistical Society (1834); the Society of Engineers (1854); the Society for Promoting the Training of Women (1859); the Trading Standards Association (1887); and the Women's Engineering Society (1920). As new business-related professional disciplines emerged after World War II, new professional bodies were established for consultants (1965); corporate treasurers (1979); consulting scientists (1958); local authority chief executives and senior managers (1974); occupational safety and health (1946); public relations (1948); purchasing and supply

(1967); and women graduates (1957). More recent professional bodies have been launched in management services, and management (1992).

## Management and professional ethics

Mention was made at the end of the previous paragraph of the establishment of management as a profession in Britain. It should be apparent that professional ethics is not a unified field of study and suffers from both problems of definition and too wide a use of the term 'profession'. This has led to a fragmented approach which sacrifices consistency and clarity. Efforts to explore these issues by adopting sociological or economic definitions of a profession are self-defeating as these focus on technical or commercial considerations which tend to treat the moral rights and values of some clients or constituents in an inequitable manner. This raises particular problems for managers in profit-seeking organisations where professional ethics is often narrowly applied and who, following Friedman's dictum, may pursue shareholder interests exclusively.

Compared with medicine and law, management in profit-seeking organisations has yet to establish itself as a profession, simply because business is not an exclusive occupation. This is not to deny that managers must comply with standards imposed when they are simultaneously engaged in professions such as commercial law, accounting or engineering. That important proviso aside, however, it should be noted that anyone can start a business or apply for a job in a corporation or enterprise. In a free enterprise system, it is also ethically permissible for managers to pursue their own financial advantage as a primary goal, as long as they do not break the law.

This is in contrast to most professional practitioners, who have an ethical obligation not to pursue self-interest; and are also not supposed to be as single-minded in their profit-seeking as business managers or entrepreneurs. Medical and legal practitioners are legitimate exemplars for other professions because of their unambiguous ethical responsibility towards their patients or clients. Management can only begin to emulate this in profit-seeking organisations when shareholders are allocated the same sovereign rights as clients and patients. In addition, ethical relationships would have to be maintained with employees, consumers, suppliers, creditors, central government, local authorities, other quasi-government agencies, institutions such as trade unions and employers' associations, and local communities. A tall order, but not out of reach as the discussion on stakeholder theory in Chapter 14 attempts to show, providing fundamental questions about the rights of these various constituents in a democratic society are resolved. If it is contended that management should enter into equivalent doctor–patient or lawyer–client relationships with each of these constituents, several fundamental questions need to be addressed. First, from whom does management obtain its authority to deal with these various constituents? Secondly, if it is from the owners or shareholders, are their best interests being pursued by maximising profits if management also has to enter into binding agreements with other constituents? Finally, how are any one of these agreements with shareholders or other constituents to be evaluated morally if they are based on compromises or expedient behaviour by management?

## Synopsis

- Unethical behaviour by individuals in organisations occurs for several reasons when a person either fails to respect his/her own unique personality and aspirations towards achievement, and displays similar behaviour towards others, or else fellow workers and supervisors undermine his/her self-belief, value-system, or sense of general well-being as a member of an organisation. Alternatively, the individual may not receive adequate training, be regularly appraised or gain a clear understanding of his/her responsibilities.

- In a minority of cases, there are persons who are deficient in their moral makeup and have a 'character disorder'. They may be of average or above average intelligence, neither neurotic nor psychotic, be familiar with the rules of society, yet unable to understand or accept why they should obey these rules or conform to the expectations of others.

- The main forms of unethical behaviour by individuals in organisations are lying, greed, free-riding, employee and white collar crime, embezzlement and fraud, and bribery.

- Lying is making a false statement to another person with the intention of misleading that person, which is sometimes permissible in exceptional circumstances, but is generally seen as eroding individual self-respect as it can lead to social institutions being undermined.

- Greed is a defect of character or will in which a person, corporate entity, or government is unwilling to restrain itself from taking more than it is due, or is prudent. At the institutional level, the 'greed is good' ethics of the US agribusiness allegedly led to unrealistic short-term profits being pursued by 'slash-and-burn' economic development that resulted in long-term environmental destruction. The impact of greed on the rest of society is also claimed to have encouraged enthusiastic and massive redistribution of wealth and power during the early 1980s which only further benefited those already rich, at the expense of the working poor, minorities, and families on social security.

- Free-riding allows an individual to enjoy a benefit produced by another's effort without contributing a fair share, which is regarded as unethical because it threatens the success of cooperative behaviour among people. Two common forms of free-riding occur when individuals are unwilling to participate in group activities, yet draw benefits from this collective effort, such as a group bonus scheme, or when an individual exercises his/her right not to join a trade union or staff association, but is content to obtain the benefits of union membership as a result of negotiations with management.

- Employee crime is rapidly becoming one of the most serious problems facing otherwise successful small businesses with estimated costs exceeding annual losses due to fire damage. One form, known as white collar crime, occurs as criminal activity in the corporate, commercial, professional and political arenas of society. White collar crime differs from conventional crime by taking place mostly at work and involving activities related to legitimate occupations which rarely involve the use of violence.

- Embezzlement and fraud can be committed by either commission or omission. An act of commission involves lying or making other material misrepresentations, whereas an act of omission refers to any failure to disclose significant facts required by law. Financial markets try to minimise this sort of malpractice by employing the *caveat emptor* ('Let the buyer beware') principle, on the one hand, and also striving to reduce bureaucracy from interfering with the free market system.

■ Bribery refers to illegal or improper favours obtained usually in exchange for money or something else of value, and involves making payments in return for someone violating an obligation or duty. It is regarded as inefficient and usually condemned as immoral because it aims to manipulate people into neglecting duties they have willingly accepted in a public or private position carrying inherent responsibilities.

■ Managers must clearly act in a professional way to minimise the effects of dysfunctional behaviour in organisations, despite management having still to establish itself as a profession like medicine or law, because business is not an exclusive occupation.

■ This may place considerable strain on professional accountants, engineers and architects who have to reconcile standards set by their professional bodies with the profit-maximising objectives of their employers.

## Review and discussion questions

**1** Given that you accept the notion that there are a minority of 'sociopaths' in society, how do you think such people should be treated when they are employed by organisations?

**2** As a supervisor or manager, how would you deal with the problem of a free-riding member of a successful work group repeatedly drawing benefits from membership but without making a fair contribution to group productivity?

**3** Again, as a supervisor or manager, how would you deal with the situation where an individual was labelled by fellow employees as a free-rider for refusing to join a recognised trade union, yet informed you that he refused to join as a matter of principle?

**4** What action would you take if you became aware of a serious incident of white collar crime involving senior members of management in the place where you work and would prefer not to leave?

## Case study
## Barings Bank and rogue trading in Singapore[17,18]

**Introduction**

The history of the bank founded by the Baring brothers in London on Christmas Day 1762 matches much of that of modern capitalism. The first Baring, Johann, a devout Lutheran, arrived in England from Bremen, Germany, in 1717. One of his two sons, Francis, who founded the bank, was a friend and confidant of the eighteenth century utilitarian philosopher, Jeremy Bentham, and both were advisers to various prime ministers and foreign ministers between 1780 and 1800. By then, Baring Brothers and their great rivals, Rothschilds, were merchant bankers on an international scale, and Barings was able to arm the USA in its war with France at the same time as it supplied credit to the French Navy. Barings Bank was also active in the sale of French territory to the United States, known as the Louisiana Purchase, in 1803. As a result, for almost seventy years, Baring Brothers were the principal London financial bankers for the US government until 1871.

Barings' European interests also extended to France, Spain, Portugal and Russia during the nineteenth century. In 1818, Barings secured a Ffr315 million loan for France, causing its foreign minister, Cardinal Richelieu, to observe that, after Britain, France, Austria, Prussia and Russia, the sixth great power was Baring Brothers. This was borne out by huge annual profits of between £620,000 and £725,000 from 1810 to 1818, when Barings was recognised as the largest private bank in Europe. Throughout the nineteenth century the bank concentrated mainly on the overseas development of railways and shipping by financing foreign loans and government bonds mostly in the USA, Canada, Russia (where it was appointed as Imperial banker until the 1917 revolution) and South America.

**The first collapse of Barings Bank**

It was in South America that the first Baring Brothers crisis occurred in 1890 when the bank unofficially became bankrupt after successful financial ventures in Chile, Uruguay, Mexico, Venezuela and Peru. However, the bank decided to expand heavily into Argentina which, by 1889, accounted for almost half of Barings' overseas investments. A crisis developed in 1890 when Barings invested in the Buenos Aires water supply company but was unable to honour the last financial commitment. To avoid humiliation, rival banking families, including Hambro and Rothschilds, persuaded the Bank of England to intervene with a short-term loan to Barings, which was supported by a separate fund of £17 million raised by rival banks and City institutions. As a result, Baring Brothers & Company Limited was formed with £1 million share capital mainly owned by the Baring family and friends who took over the old banking house's activities. A sister company, Baring Estate Company Ltd, formed four years later, repaid the debts of the original business.

Almost every reputable London-based bank, City accounting practice and law firm was involved in bailing out Baring Brothers and a huge wave of litigation swamped the threatened bank between 1890 and 1894 when, thanks largely to Bank of England support, Barings was finally able to carry on with business as usual. For another hundred years it successfully financed the Russian Imperial government, London Transport, the Cunard Shipping company and the US Telephone & Telegraph Corporation. By the early 1990s, its financial management activities on behalf of clients in London (including HM The Queen), Boston, Tokyo, Hong Kong and Singapore exceeded £10.7 billion. So successful was the bank, that few could foresee that it would be brought down a second time by the unregulated dealings of a 'rogue trader' in Singapore in 1995.

**The final collapse of Barings Bank**

The 233-year history of Barings merchant bank came to a sudden end on 26 February 1995 when the Bank of England was unable to gain enough support from other London financial institutions to complete a satisfactory rescue package. The merchant bank was forced to apply for administration by the Bank of England following alleged illegal dealings, initially estimated at over £600 million, by a junior trader in

Barings' Singapore office. These dealings in unauthorised derivative contracts exposed Barings to the risk of unquantifiable further losses which the other London banks were not prepared to cover, although they had earlier informed the governor of the Bank of England of their willingness to recapitalise the merchant bank. What could not be predicted, however, was the size of the eventual loss when Far Eastern stock exchanges opened the next day as these markets were expected to expose the maximum financial liability on the outstanding derivative contracts.

This was confirmed in early trading on the Tokyo Stock Exchange when the Nikkei index fell over 500 points to below the 17,000 level for the first time in more than a year. The Bank of England, wishing to avoid any damage to the reputation of the London Stock Exchange, issued a statement confirming that the circumstances were 'unique to Barings, and should have no implications for other banks operating in London' before confirming that the leading accountancy firm, Ernst and Young, had been appointed as the administrator. Ernst and Young immediately confirmed that strong interest had already been shown by large US, German, Swiss and Dutch banks in purchasing parts of the Baring operations, including its assets in Far Eastern emerging markets and asset management operations, not at risk from the sudden collapse of the bank, which were thought to be worth over £30 billion. However, individual cash deposits by many of the world's 'great and good' companies and private individuals were far less secure. The jobs of 4,000 Barings' employees worldwide, 2,000 based in London, were also at risk, as was the immediate future of the Baring Foundation, a leading British charity, which had donated £13.5 million in 1994 from bank profits to good causes in the UK. The big question that most City officials were reluctant to discuss was raised by Alastair Darling, Labour opposition spokesman for financial affairs, who announced on 27 February that his party would be asking the government to state what control it exercised over the derivatives supervisory procedures in merchant banks, assuming that the collapse of Barings appeared to be due to a 'rogue trade'. He added: 'A rogue trader should never be in a position to ruin an entire bank.'

**Illegal trading in Singapore**

The illegal transactions carried out in Barings Bank's Singapore office by a 28-year-old junior dealer from Watford, Nick Leeson, were classified by the Bank of England as unauthorised speculations in high risk derivative securities which had obviously run out of control. What Leeson had attempted to do was bet against the future performance of the Japanese Nikkei index, apparently without the knowledge or approval of his immediate supervisor and manager at the Barings Head Office in London. Following the announcement that the bank had crashed, Barings' senior executives were unable to disclose the whereabouts of Leeson, nor were they able to explain how a junior dealer was able to accumulate high risk financial debts of such magnitude without these transactions being monitored by the bank's internal supervisory procedures, although it was suggested that unmonitored collusion by staff employed at their Singapore office may have been responsible for the illegal trading.

Inadequate supervision of Barings' Singapore office activities was probably the main cause of the bank's collapse; that, and the unexpected Kolbe earthquake in Japan in January 1995 which saw the Nikkei index plummet by over 1,000 points bringing to a sudden end the long run of profits recorded by Nick Leeson. Up to December 1994, Leeson could apparently not put a foot wrong in second-guessing the Japanese stock market; however, two weeks later he was allegedly inventing bogus names in a desperate attempt to cover up huge losses, while boasting at the same time that he had been taken out to lunch by a senior Barings executive who had approved his personal bonus worth almost £1 million as a reward for his recent performance. Leeson had become one of the bank's high-flyers and Barings had reputedly directed millions of pounds into their Singapore account to support his activities. His transactions were also allegedly cleared on a routine basis by an independent firm of accountants, Barings' Head Office in London and a senior executive of the Singapore International Monetary Exchange (SIMEX), responsible for regulating the Singapore Stock Exchange. Without informing any of these three independent bodies, however, Mr Leeson had operated a secret account on the backroom computer, known as Error Account 8888.

According to colleagues, Mr Leeson had invented fictitious customers and colleagues to cover transactions processed through the error account which gave the clear impression that all of his transactions had been hedged to minimise losses to Barings Bank. This secret fantasy world fell apart with the Kolbe earthquake on 15 January and the sudden fall in the Nikkei index. As the stock market fell, Leeson tried to recover his financial position by a technique known as the 'short straddle' which entailed making further investments on the supposition that the market would undergo a period of relative stability.

**An unsuccessful market-maker**

As the market continued to fall, Mr Leeson bought more longer-term future contracts which would only be profitable if share prices staged a rally. This failed to happen, forcing Mr Leeson to multiply his losses even further by buying yet more longer-term futures in the hope that his transactions would cause other dealers to follow his strategy, and bring about the market stability he so desperately sought. However, rival traders had already become suspicious of Leeson's efforts to 'buck the market' and began to invest against him reversing the post-Kolbe market swing. Not even Barings' coffers were deep enough to withstand what now amounted to reckless speculation and by the time of his sudden disappearance from Singapore, the bank's financial exposure due to Leeson's transactions exceeded $7 billion in equities and approximately $20 billion in EuroYen and Japanese bonds.

Many of these placements were eventually recovered, but the sheer size of these transactions led a rival British bank to conclude that Barings was dealing through Singapore on behalf of the Japanese government because the trades were so large. This rumour was promptly denied by the Japanese authorities and by late January, concern was being expressed privately in London and New York at the huge risk facing Barings Bank, which prompted a leading US securities firm to order its traders to reduce their exposure to Barings' transactions with immediate effect. The Singaporean authorities were also alarmed at the rumoured 'big problematic position' facing Barings and stated that local financial institutions would not be liable for any exposure incurred, which meant that all losses would be borne in London.

When details of the extent of Barings' losses were announced, the Singapore police promptly issued a warrant for the arrest of Nick Leeson, who was variously reported to have fled to Thailand and Malaysia. It also emerged that Leeson was such a major dealer on the Nikkei futures market that he was what is known as a 'market-maker', meaning that at the same time that he was buying future positions of the expected price level of the Nikkei index, he was also making deals with other local dealers by which they placed their contracts with him. These were at lower prices than those at which Leeson was buying his own future positions so theoretically he should have profited from any recovery of the Nikkei index; Barings Bank unfortunately lacked sufficient funds to cover the huge losses that accrued during the period of about three weeks when the Nikkei index refused to rally. As a result, SIMEX announced on 26 February 1995 that all positions taken by Leeson on behalf of Barings were immediately closed at a huge undisclosed loss to the London-based merchant bank; and that the SIMEX executive vice-president would be responsible for managing Barings' securities activities until further notice.

**The aftermath of the Barings collapse**

Two investigations were instigated, one in London, the other in Singapore, in March 1995 to probe into the causes of the collapse of Barings Bank. The London inquiry was by the Board of Banking Supervision (BBS), called by the Chancellor of the Exchequer and the Bank of England, and included six leading members of international banks under the chairmanship of the Governor of the Bank of England. City commentators were less than impressed and called for an independent inquiry similar to the recent inquiry into the collapse of the London-based BCCI bank under Lord Bingham. Critics were concerned about whether the BBS team would be sufficiently detached to carry out a detailed inquiry, as ex-officio members of the Bank of England were allegedly aware that Barings Bank was in an unsustainable position some weeks before the rest of the Western and Far Eastern markets. For example, the size and number of forward contract purchases on the Tokyo Stock Exchange by Leeson were published weekly in the Japanese financial press, yet the London, Singapore and Osaka regulators had apparently failed to note the magnitude of Barings' futures commitment, as had the Bank of England and the London Stock Exchange securities and futures regulatory authorities.

Furthermore, there was no evidence that Leeson had been adequately supervised from London or who at Barings had given him permission to control his own settlements, which was contrary to accepted good international banking practice. Finally, it was also unclear whether Barings Bank had been trading alongside Leeson, by putting up funds from London to support his purchases, in the hope that their intervention might revive the flagging Nikkei index, thereby helping to reduce their overall losses. In short, City commentators feared that the Bank of England's supervisory role of other banks' activities was, itself, under scrutiny and they were regarded as insufficiently neutral to act as judge and jury in their own cause.

**The takeover of Barings by ING bank**

Shortly after the London inquiry commenced, it was announced that the Netherlands ING banking group had agreed to take over the collapsed Barings' interests for the nominal amount of £1. By 15 March, ING announced that it had appointed four of its directors to replace the senior management team at the recently purchased merchant bank. In short, everyone employed in direct line management and supervisory positions in the London, Singapore and Tokyo future derivative markets was asked to resign. In particular, the chief executive officer of Barings Investments Bank and the manager of the futures trading section, to whom Leeson was responsible, were among the first to be asked to leave. A total of 21 senior banking officials were eventually dismissed and replaced by Dutch appointments. The new ING head of Barings

Bank explained that these changes were necessary for several crucial reasons. First, the Bank of England inquiry would almost certainly expect these managers to be removed or demoted. Secondly, a number of US security firms that were long-standing customers of Barings Bank had simply refused to extend their business until the people responsible for the Singapore crisis were withdrawn. Finally, there was an urgent need to restore the previously held 'highest regard' which the bank had enjoyed internationally before its recent collapse.

**The Bank of England inquiry's findings**

The London inquiry reported in July 1995 that senior Barings executives had known about Nick Leeson's secret derivatives trading over six weeks before these became public. Documentary evidence was available that SIMEX had asked the bank's senior management to comment on the size and status of Error Account 8888 as early as 11 January 1995, but without receiving a reply before the merchant bank's collapse. Nor was the inquiry able to find evidence that the existence of losses of almost £900 million in this account were discussed by either Barings' Risk Control Unit or its Asset and Liability Committee in London at their monthly meetings in January and February. Perusal of internal communications within the bank also revealed that its top executives unanimously denied all knowledge of this account between 11 January and the Bank of England's formal intervention on 24 February, even though independent auditing indicated that the merchant bank had been technically bankrupt in 1994 when uncovered forward options purchased by Nick Leeson exceeded $400 million.

Additional concerns included an estimated $80 million shortfall in Error Account 8888 which Barings Bank attempted to explain away by including internal expenses from the 'house trading account' into these calculations. The inquiry would have been more inclined to accept this explanation had the Barings management been able to explain why Leeson had traded in this secret account since mid-1992 and had been trading as his own customer without the apparent knowledge or supervision of Barings' senior management, even though broking fees and commissions earned from these fictitious customers were paid to Barings whose futures operations in Singapore had increased by over $40 million in 1994. Independent evidence also revealed that the numerous customer trades in Singapore were not monitored in London and that the computer software system that transmitted trading information daily between Singapore and London had also been adjusted to erase all references to Error Account 8888.

**Bank of England inquiry recommendations**

The main conclusion of the Bank of England inquiry was that the senior Barings executives were ultimately responsible for the bank's collapse. It recommended that clearly defined lines of responsibility and accountability covering all activities must be established by other merchant banks; and that all managers and employees had to be informed of the minimum reporting structure. A clear segregation of responsibilities between 'front' and 'back' office functions was also essential as the first line of defence in eliminating the risk of fraud or unauthorised activities. The failure of Barings' Head Office in London to justify unauthorised payments to its Singapore office was also criticised as imprudent, for lacking a 'robust system of verification and reconciliation of the settlements function' chiefly because it failed to distinguish between payments made on behalf of the merchant bank and those on behalf of clients. It was also recommended that the Bank of England should increase its understanding of financial services undertaken by banks over which it had responsibility for supervision; and also monitor how these banks interrelated with each other.

Measures to improve the Bank of England and other regulators were proposed along with the need for increased numbers and skills of on-site inspectors so that improved regulation of the future derivatives market occurred. Prior to the publication of the report, four senior Barings executives, including the chairman, his two deputies, the head of financial services and the regional manager for South-East Asia, resigned in anticipation of criticism which included not enquiring into how Mr Leeson could generate such high profits from risk-free transactions; not establishing effective controls or acting on numerous warning signs; failing to ensure that Mr Leeson had clearly laid down reporting lines; failure to implement internal auditing procedures; not checking on the Singapore trading activities in futures or its funding from London; nor monitoring Mr Leeson's 'back office' activities by ensuring that appropriate supervision and internal control measures were in place.

**The Frost interview with Leeson**

In September 1995, Nick Leeson disclosed in an interview with Sir David Frost that he had initiated Error Account 8888 in September 1992 to protect an inexperienced female dealer, employed as a part-timer by Barings, who had mistakenly incurred a loss of £20,000 on the Singapore Stock Exchange which he had decided to cover rather than report her to Head Office for disciplinary action. The account was approved by Barings and he had first used it in 1992 to hide such errors from the bank's regulators in London. Since then the error account had moved into credit due to other transactions he had made, and up to 20 of his colleagues in Singapore knew of the account's existence. No one else knew of his secret transactions, however, including his superiors in London. The account was audited monthly by the Barings subsidiary in Singapore so concealment was not difficult. As business increased, the size and quantity of 'errors' also increased so that a total loss of £208 million had occurred but this had not worried him excessively as there were days in 1995 when daily losses of £25–£30 million were followed by gains of £50 million. He stressed that he had never stolen from the error account but failed to indicate whether he had forged a document to conceal £50 million allegedly missing from the Barings' account.

By then, Mr Leeson was in gaol in Frankfurt awaiting extradition to face trial in Singapore. He had agreed to cooperate with the Singaporean authorities and, in return, the case against him was altered to include 12 charges of falsifying documents and deception. Prior to his trial, another inquiry in Singapore heavily criticised the activities of Mr Leeson's two superiors at Barings but an attempt to extradite both to stand trial in Singapore was unsuccessful. Through his wife in London, Mr Leeson appealed to the UK media to prevent him being 'thrown to the wolves' in Singapore but commentators all agreed that he received a fair trial and on being found guilty, was given a lenient gaol sentence which was reduced by approximately half to $6\frac{1}{2}$ years in total. He only served part of this sentence, however, and was released in 1998 when it was confirmed that he was suffering from cancer. A film about Nick Leeson's activities in Singapore, entitled *Rogue Trader*, later went on general distribution.

Judgements about the extent to which Nick Leeson was responsible for bringing down Barings Bank varied from those who saw him as a convenient 'scapegoat', the eldest son of a Watford plasterer and former school prefect who had left school with modest A-levels to work for Coutts Bank before joining Barings in 1990. In 1992, he had married his wife, Lisa, and she and his father-in-law remained loyal, portraying him as a sensible person who would eventually be found innocent. In Singapore, however, he was regarded as arrogant and flashy by fellow workers who regarded him as a miracle-worker, prone to take large risks, who thought he could not lose, and was convinced he could move markets. However, he played down this image during his interview with Sir David Frost, pointing out that his salary was £52,000 per year, with no mention of an alleged bonus of £1 million from Barings for his profitable activities in 1994, or of his expensive apartments and luxury yachts in Singapore.

**Questions**

1 In evaluating the collapse of Barings Bank from a deontological standpoint, how would you apportion moral responsibility between (a) Nick Leeson and (b) his line supervisors and managers in London?

2 If you were evaluating the collapse of Barings Bank from a teleological standpoint, how much moral responsibility for the financial consequences would you attribute to (a) Nick Leeson and (b) his supervisors and managers at the Head Office in London?

## Notes and references

1. Clouse, B., Character, *International Encyclopaedia of Ethics*, ed. J.K. Roth, London, Fitzroy-Dearborn, 1995, 127–8.
2. See: Kagan, R., Lying, *International Encyclopaedia of Ethics*, ed. J.K. Roth, London, Fitzroy-Dearborn, 1995, 514–15.
3. Bok, S., *Lying: Moral choice in public and private life*, New York, Vintage Books, 1979.
4. See: Miller, L., Greed, *International Encyclopaedia of Ethics*, ed. J.K. Roth, London, Fitzroy-Dearborn, 1995, 360–1.
5. Worster, D., *The Wealth of Nature: Environmental history and the ecological imagination*, New York, Oxford University Press, 1993.
6. See: Lekachman, R., *Greed is not Enough*, New York, Pantheon Books, 1982.
7. See: Fromm, E., *To Have or To Be?* New York, Harper & Row, 1976.
8. See: Slomski, G., The Golden Mean, *International Encyclopaedia of Ethics*, ed. J.K. Roth, London, Fitzroy-Dearborn, 1995, 353–4.
9. See: Morelli, M., Free Riding, *International Encyclopaedia of Ethics*, ed. J.K. Roth, London, Fitzroy-Dearborn, 1995, 321–2.
10. Gray, R.T., Clamping Down on Employee Crime, *Nation's Business*, US Chamber of Commerce 1997, April, 44–5.
11. Granelli, J.S., The Crime Within, *Los Angeles Times*, 19 October 1997, pp. D1, D12.
12. O'Neill, P., Bribery, *International Encyclopaedia of Ethics*, ed. J.K. Roth, London, Fitzroy-Dearborn, 1995, 103–4.
13. Mullins, L.J., *Job Satisfaction, Organisational Behaviour and Management*, 5th edn, London, Financial Times Prentice Hall, 1999, 661–3.
14. For a more comprehensive analysis see: Airaksinen, T., Professional Ethics, *Encyclopedia of Applied Ethics*, vol. 3. New York, Academic Press, 1998, 671–82.
15. See also: Barker, S.F., Professional Ethics, *International Encyclopaedia of Ethics*, ed. J.K. Roth, London, Fitzroy-Dearborn, 1995, 703–6.
16. For a Canadian perspective on the accounting profession see: Brooks, L.J., *Professional Ethics for Accountants*, Minneapolis, West, 1995.
17. *Financial Times*, Business Reports, CD Rom, January–July 1995.
18. *The Independent*, Business Reports, CD Rom, January–July 1995.

# 7

# The individual and computer/information ethics

*During my eighty-seven years I have witnessed a whole succession of technological revolutions. But none of them has done away with the need for character and honesty in the individual or the need to think.*

Bernard Baruch (1870–1965), Presidential Financial Adviser, *My Own Story*, 1957

## Learning objectives

After reading this chapter you should be able to:

- consider the rise of computer and information ethics in response to the recognition of the unique contribution of computers to modern society;
- explore the related issues of how to protect individual privacy and safeguard personal information stored on computers;
- examine the impact of computers on the disenfranchisement of employees due to the restructuring of work in organisations;
- evaluate the issue of the ownership of new software languages as intellectual property;
- consider problems arising from the misuse of computers and related computer crime;
- discuss the development of computer professionalism to enhance human values in the applications of new technology in organisations.

## Introduction

The unprecedented spread of computer technology and information systems in developed countries during the last 30–40 years has seen the emergence of computer and information ethics, which are both concerned with the impact of this technology on human values and behaviour. In recognising the impact of computer technology on modern society, some confusion remains about whether computer and information ethics raise new moral problems. Could it be that these ethical issues only appear to be different because of their context and the use of various coded languages which may result in users handing over responsibility for decisions that affect other people to computer technology?

## The rise of computer and information ethics

According to Rogerson[1], the need to treat computer technology and information processing as a separate field of applied ethics was identified by Parker[2] in the 1960s and led to the emergence of computer ethics in the mid-1970s. Johnson[3] defined computer ethics as 'the study of the way in which computers present new versions of standard moral problems and dilemmas, causing existing standard moral norms to be used in new and novel ways in an attempt to resolve these issues'. This recognises that as advances in computer technology occur, various pitfalls could undermine the benefits of the new resource for society. Examples quoted range from computer fraud to computer-generated disasters, caused by human error, in response to unforeseen problems related to the new technology.

The scope of computer ethics widened to include contributions from other disciplines and became known as 'information ethics' after Bynum[4] proposed the introduction of human values into computing technology so that future advances would protect, rather than damage, human values. As Rogerson[1] notes, this became necessary because computers have evolved into 'a range of forms including the stand-alone machine, embedded computer chips in appliances, and networked components of a larger, more powerful macro-machine' (p. 564). Similarly, a rapidly changing information industry has emerged which is characterised by increasing convergence of previously separate industries that specialised in computers, telecommunications, cable and satellite television, video and music, etc., alongside the exponential growth of use of the Internet by individuals and businesses.

## The uniqueness of computers

According to Maner[5], computers are unique because of their novel storage capacity, complexity, adaptability and versatility, processing speed, relative cheapness, limit-less exact reproduction capability, and dependence on multiple layers of codes. This uniqueness means that it has not been easy to find suitable non-computer analogies for evaluating computer-related ethical problems. Rogerson[1] observes that this raises 'distinct and special ethical considerations in response to the unique properties of computers which would not have arisen without their essential involvement' (p. 564). This view is shared by Maner, who identifies a need to discover new moral values, principles, policies and ways of thinking about the related distinct and special ethical considerations, particularly in the organisational context. However, Davis[6] and De George[7] argue that the majority of these ethical issues are possibly less unique than is widely accepted.

## Ethical issues relating to computer technology

In seeking to evaluate these ethical issues, a clear understanding is required of the social impact of computer technology on the following aspects of organisational policy:

■ protection of individual privacy;
■ safeguarding personal information;
■ disenfranchising employees and the restructuring of work;
■ the ownership of intellectual property;
■ the misuse of computers and computer crime;
■ developing computer professionalism to enhance human values.

## Protection of individual privacy

The use of computers was initially regarded as value-neutral but, as noted above, this view changed some forty years ago with the realisation that the massive amounts of information, much of it personal, stored on computers entitled individuals to protection against possible misuse of this data. This argument was strengthened by the rapid spread of computer networking systems across diverse communication channels, including ordinary telephone lines, which could be manipulated to gain electronic access to confidential information. The Watergate scandal not only brought down US President Nixon in 1974, by exposing the problem of political abuse of personal liberties, but it also revealed the huge potential for commercial exploitation and misuse of personal information through unauthorised invasions of individual privacy in most industrialised countries. De George[7] clearly had George Orwell's novel *1984* in mind when he described the growing concern about the invasion of privacy by computers as 'the Big Brother syndrome', although it is probably true that most people had not given much thought to the meaning of privacy.

**Privacy**

Kutper[8] states that privacy is essential in the development of 'an autonomous self concept . . . [as] a particular body whose thoughts, purposes, and actions are subject to one's control . . . [and] control over one's relation to others, including their access to us'. In practice, this implies that society recognises the individual's right to areas of privacy which are closed to intrusion by others, unless these pose a serious threat to other people. These areas of privacy include personal thoughts, beliefs and other intimate aspects of life which the individual is under no obligation to reveal information about to others. If privacy is regarded as a fundamental right, because of its essential part in individual self-determination, public concern about the capacity of government or other organisations to collect information about individuals and use it in a variety of ways is understandable and essential if civil liberties are to be maintained.

Yet the individual's right to total privacy cannot be absolute otherwise democratic, civil society would be impossible. It therefore follows that the rights and interests of different parties have to be balanced so that individual privacy is protected and balanced against the legitimate needs of government and business in a society that is increasingly dependent on technology. That said, the extent to which individuals must sacrifice some of their personal privacy so that some overall utilitarian benefit may be achieved is a moral issue that divides different writers on business ethics.

**The invasion of privacy**

De George[7] maintains that, it we accept the presence of records about us in different places, to regard the gathering of this data together on computers as an invasion of privacy is mistaken. He justifies this argument by asserting that facts about us are not always our property. In referring to those who possess facts about us, stored as data, which they own and have the right to sell or give away, he argues that: 'providing it does not harm or threaten to harm us, then collecting the data in one place does not violate our right to privacy' (p. 305). This is a contentious argument because it supports the view that the property rights of a collectivity, such as a government agency or a profit-seeking organisation, may take priority over the right to privacy of the individual.

This argument is not strengthened by Rogerson's[1] observation that computerised processing of personal information may occur without the consent or knowledge of the individuals affected. Nor will concerns about individual privacy disappear if advances in computer technology bring about more rapid growth of databases holding sensitive personal information in multiple formats including text, pictures and sound. Furthermore, the scale and type of data collected and the volume and speed of data transactions using computers have also increased. As a result, the capacity to breach people's privacy at greater speed, lower cost, and in intensive detail, has also grown exponentially. The rapid speed of these developments therefore raises two important issues about the rival moral rights of the holders of information and the individual whose privacy is open to intrusion:

- types of privacy;
- information as an all-inclusive concept.

**Types of privacy**

Spinello[9] identifies two major types of privacy: consumer privacy and employee privacy. Consumer privacy has already grown into such a large field of business ethics that it will be explored separately in Chapter 10. Employee privacy addresses the growing reliance on electronic monitoring and other technology to collate personal records, analyse work behaviour and measure employee productivity. Both Spinello and De George agree that employees have similar privacy rights to those discussed in Chapter 5, providing there is an additional right to control or limit access to personal information collected and stored electronically by an employer. For example, there are increasing opportunities to monitor employee activity in modern organisations and Rogerson[1] stresses the need to ensure that use of these facilities does not violate individual privacy rights in the following areas:

- e-mail systems and archives of generated messages that can be inspected by managers or technically capable specialists on their behalf;
- personal computer network programs that allow managers to inspect files, directories, and texts on individual computer screens without the knowledge of users;
- network systems that enable management to intercept and scrutinise communications, either internally between offices, or externally with more remote locations;
- electronic surveillance systems that permit managers to monitor and evaluate employees' work behaviour relating to productivity and 'down-time';
- close circuit television surveillance systems, equipped with computerised archiving and digital matching facilities, that managers may use for security purposes.

De George expresses similar concerns and notes that the rules for the handling of such data are often left unspecified and differ from company to company in the USA. There is common ground, however, that every company has the dual responsibility to ensure that its computerised systems containing confidential records are secure, and that employees with authorised access to these systems are both aware of, and fully trained in, relevant security procedures.

**Information as an all-inclusive concept**

Some confusion probably occurs because computer specialists increasingly describe their activities by using the concept of information in an all-inclusive way. De George notes that terms such as 'information processing', 'program' and 'information systems' are multi-faceted and their meanings and usage depend on the distinctions between 'facts', 'knowledge', 'understanding' and 'data' being clearly understood. Obviously, the concept 'fact' predates computers and its simplest meaning refers to any true statement about any phenomenon existing in the universe.

Because no one possesses total knowledge of the universe, facts are independent of any individual's knowledge about them, especially as one individual's knowledge of facts does not diminish that of another person, since facts and information may be shared indefinitely. Hence, the discovery, collection, analysis and storage of facts may take time and entail expense. This leads to the legally recognised claim that such facts are the property of the originators of this information, particularly if they happen to be profit-seeking organisations. Knowledge, however, is a more general concept that includes facts as verifiable information, in addition to all manner of beliefs, intuitions, musings, speculations and hypotheses, which may be untestable, but form part of the 'inner' spiritual and imaginative world of the individual.

Understanding occurs when knowledge is integrated and evaluated either by the individual or, collectively, by communication with others. Data refers to the ideas, words, numbers and letters entered into a computer in coded form for storage, collation, analysis, transformation, presentation, and possible transmission to other users. The immediate advantage of computers is that large volumes of data can be processed, manipulated and stored at high speed. Their main drawback is that they do not understand phenomena in the same way as human beings and therefore cannot distinguish between fact and fiction, unless these are carefully separated beforehand.

The relation between facts and data is not clear-cut because some facts are not widely known, such as the name of the gene that causes one person to be more prone than another to asthma attacks, whereas other facts are part of what is known as 'common or general' knowledge; for example, that there are 26 letters in the English alphabet. Because some facts are so new, original and important, their ownership and use can be legally protected by patents or copyright for a stated period. This is in contrast to other facts that form part of general knowledge (e.g. the height of Mount Everest), which cannot be similarly protected. Data, on the other hand, are different. Even when they include the analysis of facts that are general knowledge, they can still be owned and belong to the owner if the data are stored on a computer.

In terms of property rights, it is asserted that no one other than the owner has the right to view, manipulate, copy, or erase such data held on a computer without permission. That said, the copying of data held on a computer file or disk raises the issue of ownership in a novel way unique to computer technology, since this can be done without changing the data or interfering with their subsequent access or use by the owner. As De George[7] observes, however, in defending his argument above on the primacy of property rights over the individual's right to privacy, the act of copying violates the owner's exclusive use of this data and is therefore prohibited without prior permission being granted. Stripped of its non-essentials, this argument favours the private property rights (claimed by the owner of the data) over the right to privacy of the individual (about whom information is held as data using computer technology). Supporters of civil rights and freedom of information have always found this sort of reasoning to be unacceptable and their opposition has played its part in persuading governments in the USA, UK and other EU countries to introduce legislation which seeks to safeguard the individual's right to protection from unwarranted invasion of privacy by government agencies and other organisations.

## Safeguarding personal information

The two main aspects of safeguarding the storage of personal information considered below are:

- freedom of the individual to know what is being stored;
- protection of this information from unwarranted intrusion.

**Freedom of information**

As a response to the Watergate affair, US demands for the individual's right to know what information is being stored about them were enacted in law some time before similar legislation was adopted in principle by EU member-states. Weiss[10] notes that the US Freedom of Information Act, enacted in 1966, was amended several times prior to 1986. This was some years before similar legislation began to appear in Europe. The Act was passed in response to the movement towards 'open government', public access to records and information in the possession of US federal government agencies. It stipulates that every record possessed by federal agencies must be made available to the public upon request, with the exception of some records covered by the Act's nine exemptions or those excluded from its jurisdiction. The aim of the Act is to extend the public's right to know by reaffirming the view that an informed civil society is a crucial aspect of the democratic function in a country.

The Act[11] confers on all individuals an equal right of access to information by providing that 'any person (citizen, partnership, corporation, association, foreign or domestic government) may file a request for an agency record for any reason'. The purpose of the request has no bearing on its merits. The Act specifies only that requests must reasonably describe the documents sought by complying with the published procedural regulations of US federal agencies. The agency must provide the document unless it falls within one of the nine exemptions listed below. Failure to produce a requested record entitles the individual to go to court, where the agency must prove that the documents in question are exempt under the law and that its refusal to produce them is justified.

Two categories of information that must be disclosed under the Act are, first, publication of basic information regarding the transaction of federal agency business; and, second, descriptions of the organisation's functions, procedures, rules and policy statements. The second category requires the availability for inspection and copying of so-called 'reading room' materials including final adjudicatory opinions, specific policy statements, and administrative staff manuals. These materials must be indexed to allow immediate public access, help any citizen involved in a controversy with an agency, and guard against the development of internal agency secrets. Records not included under these provisions are subject to disclosure upon receipt by an agency of a request by any person. The nine categories of exemptions, which are discretionary rather than mandatory, are:

- national security and foreign policy matters;
- internal personnel rules and practices;
- exemptions specified by other federal statutes;
- privileged or confidential trade secrets;
- commercial or financial information;
- inter-agency or trans-agency memoranda;

- personnel or medical files constituting an unwarranted invasion of privacy;
- investigatory records compiled for law enforcement purposes;
- financial institution reports, and geological and geophysical information and data.

A less inclusive version of the US Freedom of Information Act was published as a White Paper in Britain in 1997 and became law in October 2000. Under the Human Rights Act, members of the public will be able to obtain more information about their personal medical treatment, and school and tertiary education records. Numerous private bodies, such as the British Board of Film Classification, the Jockey Club and private prisons, will also be subjected to this legislation. Whether it will lead to US-type 'open government' is contested by campaigners, who believe that the Act is biased in favour of maintaining government secrecy.

**Protection of information**

The need to strike an acceptable balance between accessibility and protection of information at a government level became apparent after 1982 when it was revealed that the US government computers contained more than 3.5 billion personal files, and the Federal Bureau of Investigation database had accumulated records on 25 million US citizens (or approximately 10 per cent of the population) – irrespective of whether or not their arrests resulted in convictions – since the FBI National Crime Information Center was opened in 1965 as a central repository of criminal arrest records. Weiss[10] notes that when the proposed centralising of government records of individual citizens in a National Data Center was strongly opposed in Congress, debate 'focussed national attention for the first time on the issue of invasion of privacy as people began to fear the prospect of an Orwellian all-seeing, all-knowing government becoming reality'.

But what of the private sector? Sutphen[12] notes that by the mid-1990s, personal information had become a very profitable commodity in the US. For example, it led to a huge industry in which the two largest credit companies maintained separate databases of over 150 million computer files, which were made available to banks, credit card companies and any other organisation willing to pay for the service. The Protection of the Fair Credit Reporting Act is seemingly unable to protect individuals from victimisation by false credit information, particularly after a 1991 Consumer Union study found inaccuracies in nearly half the consumer credit records it sampled.

Small businesses in the USA and EU countries were equally quick to specialise in providing demographic and consumer information to direct marketing firms. A small monthly fee provided customers with access to detailed information on millions of households, including addresses, telephone numbers, property details, estimated income and expenditure, credit ratings and legal records. Meanwhile, many small manufacturers routinely sell information, provided by consumers on product warranty registration forms, direct to marketing companies for use in identifying potential customers more accurately. All told, because access to personal information has permeated virtually every level of modern society, regulation by a single law or agency is now regarded as impossible in both the USA and the EU. Furthermore, the efforts of legal experts to incorporate the vexed issues of transparency versus privacy into appropriate legislation are not helped by charges of corruption against a former US president and, more recently, against the EU Commission. These incidences have led civil rights campaigners to question the capacity of Western governments to regulate themselves and their transnational agencies, let alone the private sector's increasing involvement in the global economy.

**Data protection legislation**

The UK Data Protection Act was introduced in 1984 but France[13] notes that its principles have since been modified to provide an EU Framework Directive (95/96) for protecting privacy. The aim is to develop a policy which ensures that the operation of information systems addresses public concerns about privacy. The modified principles are summarised as follows. Personal data shall:

- be processed fairly and lawfully;
- be collected for specified, explicit and legitimate purposes;
- not be further processed in a way incompatible with the purposes for which they are collected;
- be adequate, relevant, and not excessive in relation to the purposes for which they are collected or further processed;
- be accurate and, where necessary, kept up to date;
- not be kept longer than is necessary for the purposes for which they are collected and further processed.

In addition, an individual is entitled to be informed at reasonable intervals by any controller of the processing of personal data of which that individual is subject, including information relating to that processing. An individual is also entitled, without excessive delay or expense and under no duress, to access the personal data of which the individual is subject; entitled to any available information as to their source; and entitled to knowledge of the logic involved in any automatic processing of data concerning him or her involving certain automated decisions. Where appropriate, the individual is also entitled to have personal data rectified, erased or blocked; and to have details of any rectification, erasure or blocking made available to third parties to whom personal data have been disclosed.

Finally, the Framework Directive also requires that appropriate security measures are taken to prevent unauthorised access to, or alteration, disclosure, or destruction of, personal data and against the accidental or unlawful loss or destruction of personal data.

## Disenfranchising employees and the restructuring of work

**Disenfranchisement of workers**

The use of computer technology in both the rapid spread of the communications revolution, and to carry out dull, repetitive, complicated and hazardous tasks more rapidly and safely, has been widely promoted in most organisations of the developed world. Use of the same technology, however, to implement 'downsizing' strategies which replace employees, for the purpose of lowering costs by reducing payrolls, raises serious ethical questions about the equity and responsibility of companies to their employees. As noted above, the use of computers to monitor the activities of employees on computer terminals, intercept telephone calls and oversee electronic mail, without the individuals being aware of this surveillance, raises similar moral problems for the managers of organisations.

From a management standpoint, use of electronic surveillance techniques may be regarded as an updated version of ideas proposed by F.W. Taylor (1856–1917), as 'scientific management' almost 100 years ago (see Mullins[14]). Employers may seek to justify these modern methods by citing improvements in productivity and quality which can be shown to produce goods and services that satisfy customers and lead to increased business, enabling them to employ more staff, thereby making a direct social and economic contribution to the local community where the organisation is located. On the other hand, of what value is the social contribution to the local community if those laid off as part of the downsizing strategy are unable to find alternative employment? As to those who are employed in the new computer-based organisations, Davis[6] notes that awareness of electronic surveillance can produce stress and related health problems, so that 'employees who know that they are monitored feel that they are in an electronic straitjacket' (p. 179).

Improperly applied, electronic monitoring can be equated with eavesdropping on individuals' private lives. However, many managers may argue that every activity by an employee during working hours is a legitimate concern. Similarly, arguments that computer technology is necessary to create more dynamic organisational structures, in response to the demands of globalisation, are also morally suspect. This is not to deny that new, highly flexible, computer-based working practices, capable of responding rapidly to the environmental uncertainty of the marketplace, are here to stay. What is questionable, is the assumption that globalisation is a deterministic phenomenon beyond the control of transnational corporations, and other groups, which have actively promoted its expansion without having to bear the social costs of higher unemployment.

Much of the research that led to satellite communications and the Internet, on which globalisation depends, was funded by governments from the public purse. Astute managers of companies that have benefited, however indirectly, from the tax-payer, will therefore be cautious about taking the high moral ground with dubious claims about the social benefits provided by new employment opportunities for 'teleworkers' in the new twenty-first century version of scientific management. As Rogerson[1] notes, this involves employees working remotely via a computer link, 'from communal office desks and computers, and geographically dispersed virtual teams to reduce organizational operating costs' (p. 567). The effects are well known and can include possible destruction of supportive social groups in the workplace, and the disenfranchising of employees who lack the resources to participate in the financial benefits of globalisation. The relevance of Marx's criticism of nineteenth century mass-production methods (discussed in Chapter 2), may not be immediately apparent within the context of a global economy. Yet skilled labour in manufacturing firms is increasingly easy to replace with computer-aided technology monitored by unskilled operatives. Meanwhile, new teleworking firms offer mostly low-paid, unskilled, repetitive employment. Informed commentators have raised legitimate concerns about the reappearance of such meaningless work in the twenty-first century, leading to possible alienation, which have yet to be addressed by the senior managers of numerous manufacturing and service-sector companies.

The cautionary warning for management and other employees, noted by Mullins[14], is that Marx emphasised that the social organisation of work 'led to alienation for all persons involved irrespective of their position in the organisation' (p. 635). This revolutionary change in working practices will not end with teleworking, according to Rogerson[1], who identifies many activities that are open to reorganisation using flexible computer-enabled information systems, including:

- professional and management specialists such as accountants, design engineers, graphic designers, general managers and translators;
- professional support workers such as bookkeepers, proofreaders and researchers;
- field workers such as auditors, sales representatives, insurance brokers and service engineers;
- information technology specialists such as software programmers and systems engineers;
- clerical support workers such as data entry staff, telesales staff and word processor operators.

Peters[15], more optimistically, predicts that just as blue collar robots took the grunt work out of the factory, the same will happen to white collar work.

> The world is going through more fundamental change than it has in hundreds, perhaps thousands of years. . . . It's the biggest change since the caveman began bartering. Do you want to be a player, a full-time participant who embraces change? Here is the opportunity to participate in the lovely, messy playground called: 'Let's reinvent the world.'

The 'futurologist', Julie Rawe, is equally optimistic and lists among the 10 'hottest new jobs' of the twenty-first century: transplant tissue engineers, gene programmers, pharmers (of genetic proteins), data miners (extractors of relevant data on request) and knowledge engineers.[16]

## Software and intellectual property rights

The question of intellectual property rights (IPRs) raises complex issues which organisations have to address because, as Rogerson[1] notes, 'IPRs related to software and data are particularly difficult to assign and protect, and require careful deliberation before executive action occurs' (p. 566). Computer technology features more frequently in debates about intellectual property because of the difficulty in deciding between two rival arguments. The first is that the writing of software by a programmer is comparable with the creative processes of an artist painting a picture or an author writing a novel. The contrary argument is that programming is simply linking a series of instructions and algorithms that are in the public domain.

Supporters of the former view would conclude that programming is a creative activity and that programmers are entitled to regard the output as their own intellectual property, whereas opponents would claim that programming is not entirely original and creative, and that the end product cannot be regarded as someone's intellectual property. Rogerson supports the views of Johnson[3], who argues that software IPRs ownership issues are best resolved by recognising the continued creativity and development of software, which may be developed by a number of people who each make a contribution. However, as Sutphen[12] observes, those who take the view that software is intellectual property, must still tackle the question of ownership. For example, do programmers, as creators, own their software, or is it owned by the employer who pays them to create software? Are those who develop software, or pay others to develop it, entitled to be reimbursed by those who use it? How are the views of those who view software as their intellectual property to be reconciled with those who maintain that, once software is entered on a computer, it enters the public domain and cannot be regarded as the 'exclusive' intellectual property of any person or group? Rogerson adopts the view that if an organisation or group of individuals invests time, money and effort in creating software, they have an obvious moral right to own the product by virtue of this effort, and should be legally entitled to any economic reward from its use. In short, for the sake of fairness and equity, and to ensure initiative and application are rewarded, the creator or owner should have the right to retain control over the intellectual property and to sell or license the product. However, the extent of these rights is debatable. Parker *et al.*[17] argue that there is also a moral responsibility to distribute software that is fit for the purpose for which it was developed, so the owner does not have the right to distribute software that is known to be defective and that has not been thoroughly tested. Ample evidence exists of copyright owners who claim the financial rewards from successful software but are slow to accept responsibility when software fails to fulfil its stated purposes.

The critical point here is that users must be seen to benefit from the software if the claim to 'exclusive' copyright is to be recognised. For example, to insist on unrestricted rights may restrict the technological development and distribution of rival software, which will be to the disadvantage of consumers and, possibly, wider society. Rogerson[1] distinguishes between the broad agreement in Western countries which recognises the right of individuals or groups of individuals to possess intellectual property rights over software they have created. In the USA and most EU countries, the law acknowledges that computer software can be protected because of the creative process involved in its creation.

De George[7] notes that, unlike Japan, where both computer software and hardware are protected by patents, US law protects software with copyrights and hardware with patents. These differences arise because of differences in international law. Historically, copyright law in the West was formerly restricted to the written word. In extending it to cover some computer programs, the US courts have ruled that the contents must be intelligible to human beings as the end users, in the same way that applies to novels and plays. Programs written in machine language codes (e.g. as a series of zeros and ones) are ineligible, as these are ruled not to be intelligible to human beings. Similarly, computerised instructions to a machine and computer algorithms (i.e. mathematical equations and their underlying logic) are also ineligible. However, elsewhere, in non-EU and some Commonwealth countries, different legal practices apply and in the Far East, the use of minimum IPR safeguards is mainly due to a different legal philosophy that regards intellectual property as of less importance to society than the notion of communal or social property.

There is little doubt that ethical and legal disputes will increase, within and between countries, as computer technology and software developments become more sophisticated and their applications more widely available. The main ethical questions still to be more fully explored are whether computer programs should be treated as if they are the property of others, or as common property, unless they have been copyrighted.

Before this occurs, however, two important problems still to be resolved are those of computer misuse and how to improve the professionalism of computer programmers and information system managers.

## Computer misuse and computer crime

As computers have become more widely used, the likelihood of misuse and abuse has increased. For example, Rogerson[1] (p. 568) reports that in the UK, the number of computer abuse incidents reported tripled between 1990 and 1993. Virus infection, fraud and illicit software accounted for 40 per cent of the latter incidents. Rogerson lists the following different types of computer abuse:

- fraud (including unauthorised data input, alteration of data, destruction, suppression, or misappropriation of computerised data; and alteration or misuse of programs, excluding virus infections);
- theft of data or software;
- use of illicit, unlicensed or pirated software;
- using computers for unauthorised personal activities;
- invasion of privacy, resulting in disclosure of personal data, breaches of legislation and disclosure of licensed information;
- 'hacking' through deliberate, unauthorised access to computer systems, usually via telecommunication facilities;
- sabotage of computer processing by deliberate damage to the processing procedure or equipment;
- computer virus infections by distribution of programs that corrupt a computer process.

The ability to store and exchange computerised information about individuals inevitably raises ethical questions about who should have access to that information. For example, deciding what kinds of data should not be kept or shared may have a bearing on whether unauthorised people attempt to gain access to this information, especially if they are denied the right to examine information about themselves. The instances of computer crime noted above mostly involve breaches of well-defined ethical principles relating to theft of private property. What possibly complicates these issues is the unique nature of the computing process. It has already been noted that information held on computers is represented and exchanged as electronic signals which are not tangible objects. Therefore, the hypothetical question has been raised about whether the theft of a program or information from a computer can really be theft when what was removed remains in place after the act. Similarly, when illegal entry to a computer is detected, how can the traditional definition of trespassing be applied if the person is not physically present on the site where the computer is located; and may even be many miles away from the system which has been invaded?

De George[7] provides a clear evaluation of the main moral issues involved. For example, it is immoral to steal from others and whether this is done physically (e.g. by taking cash from a person's wallet), or electronically via a computer, makes no difference to the moral offence. Similarly, it is immoral to harm another person either physically, or by damaging another's reputation in writing or by word of mouth. Whether this is done by transmitting false information via a computer, or circulating accurate, but damaging information about the person from confidential records, makes no difference as both are instances of immoral behaviour. These are examples of one of three main types of computer crime which usually depend on surreptitious use of the technology, as follows:

■ unauthorised computer entry;
■ computer theft of funds;
■ theft of computer time.

**Unauthorised computer entry**

Unauthorised computer entry to gain access to the company database or trade secrets is immoral for the same reasons that it is illegal to break into another person's office, motor car, or other private property, without good cause or authorisation. Entry to a database without prior permission, as noted above, is also immoral because it violates the principle of exclusive use by the rightful owner. Similarly, unauthorised entry to confidential records breaches the owner's rights in three other possible ways:

■ Once entry has been detected, the owner normally incurs the cost of checking that the database has not been altered or compromised, which can be time-consuming.
■ Checks also have to be carried out to ensure that a virus has not been planted which might not be activated immediately after the original breach of privacy.
■ By its surreptitious nature, illegal access to a confidential database or trade secrets means that only the perpetrator knows what has been seen or unseen. The owner usually adopts a 'worst case scenario' and assumes that the whole database is compromised, which involves more time and expense in creating a replacement database, including extra safeguards to ensure it is more difficult to access illegally in future.

**Computer theft of funds**

This falls under the heading of white collar crime, as discussed in the last chapter. The main difference is that such theft by an outsider usually calls for considerable expertise to break into an organisation's computer system. Theft by an insider is probably more common because it often involves a person abusing a position of trust and compromising the system by inserting commands that divert funds from their rightful owner. According to De George[7], other reasons for the reluctance to act against perpetrators include the following:

■ The public make a distinction between white collar crime and, say, violent robbery. This is reflected in those found guilty of computer fraud in the USA receiving less punishment than those convicted of violent robbery.
■ Fewer white collar crimes appear in the media than crimes of violence. This is probably because white collar crime involves no violence, use of weapons, threats or physical harm to others.
■ White collar crimes are seen as 'intellectual' robberies and the most practical deterrent is to discover how they were perpetrated and, by a process of elimination, make them more difficult to repeat in future.

Ethically, however, white collar crimes are no less immoral than other forms of theft and De George adds that US insurance companies are increasingly refusing to meet claims unless the culprit, if discovered, is prosecuted. As noted in the Allied Dunbar example in Chapter 6 (p. 137), this practice may be spreading to the UK, although no evidence could be found that British authorities are also following the example of some US state authorities which have passed laws making it an offence not to report computer crimes leading to possible prosecutions.

**Theft of computer time**

This form of computer crime is the usual consequence of unauthorised entry, which can therefore also be carried out internally or externally. Yet the relationship between legal and ethical considerations is not entirely clear on matters concerning theft of computer time. Legally, computer time is normally bought or sold and the illegal use of that time is regarded as theft of that abstract commodity, i.e. computer time, which is an immoral act. Complications arise in the case of an organisation's employees, who have authorised entry, as to whether they are entitled to use computers in their own time when the technology is otherwise idle. After all, if the organisation has to pay for the computers whether they are used or not, and the employer does no harm to the technology nor attempts to enter unauthorised files, how does this activity differ ethically from other acceptable behaviour, such as writing ideas in a public place, before cleaning the black/white board afterwards? That said, most people would be unhappy if another person were to use a personal lap-top computer or drive their motor car without permission, even if no damage occurred.

As De George observes, there is no consensus on whether the use of computer time by employees when the technology is idle is entirely ethical. However, the pragmatist might argue that if company rules or guidelines exist, then people are ethically obliged to comply with these conditions. If no regulations exist, the instrumental 'cash value' approach of both employer and employee might be to evaluate the costs of prohibition against the possible benefits of improvements in the morale and computer skills of employees, which might enhance the formal activities of the organisation.

**Motivations for computer crime**

Sutphen[12] identifies three categories of motivations displayed by persons and groups who engage in computer abuse, as follows:

- personal gain of money, goods, services or valuable information;
- revenge against another person, company or institution, including political motivation against a government, or society at large;
- enhanced personal satisfaction, or impressing one's peers by demonstrating mastery over complex technology.

According to Parker[18] attention to security by programmers, systems managers, corporate management and government agencies is the single most effective method of computer crime prevention. This need increased almost exponentially once large mainframe computer systems were replaced by diverse micro networks of personal computers which provided much greater accessibility at the cost of sacrificing many of the security features that were possible with larger centralised systems.

## Developing computer professionalism

Rogerson and Bynum[19] draw attention to an emerging network of relationships involving computer professionals, employers, clients and society. Underlying tensions involving employers and representatives of different constituencies in the local community and wider society emphasise the importance of computer professionals developing the following skills so that professional duties are undertaken in an ethically sensitive manner, based on the ability to identify:

- likely ethical dilemmas in situations involving new uses of computer technology and information systems;
- the reasons for these dilemmas, and suggesting appropriate actions for resolving them by indicating the probable outcomes of each alternative action;
- a feasible action plan from these alternatives, including methods of implementation.

Action plans should include codes of conduct which indicate how computer professionals are discharging their duties ethically and how they intend to do so in the future. The code should provide a framework which indicates acceptable work practices and, following Collins *et al.*[20], identify the different obligations of computer professionals in their diverse roles in the following network of relations as:

- a supplier;
- a client;
- an end user;
- a member of the community.

**Supplier obligations**

As a supplier to a client, the computer specialist would be required to provide a reasonable warranty and be transparent about testing procedures and their limitations. In dealing with end users, the computer professional should also provide clear operating instructions as a supplier, ensuring that reasonable protection and requisite information are given so that abuse of the information system is avoided by offering reasonable technical support. Wider obligations to the community include ensuring reasonable protection against physical, psychological and economic damage from computer applications, and transparency about new developments and the limits of accuracy of the systems and technology provided.

**Client obligations**

As a client of a supplier, the computer professional should negotiate in good faith, and communicate requirements accurately, by learning enough about the new products and systems to make an informed decision. Obligations to the end user are to provide high quality solutions that meet needs within agreed budgetary constraints, by the prudent introduction of computing technology that protects the end users' interests with suppliers. Obligations to the community are to ensure that only products with reasonable public safety assurances are acquired and to ensure transparency in all discussions about product capabilities and limitations.

**End user obligations**

As an end user to the supplier, the computer professional is required to respect the latter's ownership of rights. Obligations to the client are to make reasonable requests for computing facilities, by communicating reasonable needs to the client effectively, and undertaking to use new equipment and systems in a responsible way. Obligations to the community should also ensure that any risk to the public is minimised; and that reasonable expectations about computing technology capabilities and its limitations are accepted.

**Community obligations**

As a community member, the computer professional should be aware of the limitation of computing technology, encourage effective economic and regulatory frameworks, support applications that benefit the community and oppose any potentially harmful applications.

**Managers of organisations**

The managers of organisations are responsible for ensuring that all computer systems used in pursuit of business objectives balance the different needs of individual members of the organisation with those of society. Senior management need to include computer usage in strategies which ensure that issues relating to individual privacy, ownership and information integrity, are fully integrated with effective human relations among employees, and the needs and expectations of the local community. Any additional training of computer professionals and managers should be provided to ensure that all are aware of the increasingly critical role of computer technology in the decision making process.

Everyone involved therefore needs to act in a socially responsible manner. The adoption of a broader systemic approach which addresses economic, technological, legal, societal and ethical concerns should ensure that a democratic, empowering approach is adopted towards the current and future use of new technology. Ethical objectives, in particular, will not be achieved unless problems relating to system design and responsibility are resolved.

**Poor system design**

A formidable obstacle to the ethical use of computers occurs when incompetent system designers, however well intentioned, develop information systems that do not accomplish the required tasks. This creates frustration among the system's users, which may well be aggravated if inaccurate information is generated. In terms of their overall costs to organisations, individual members and the wider community, poorly designed systems that fail to meet technological expectations probably create more ethical dilemmas than the risk of computer misuse and crime. This is because error-prone, inflexible and insensitive systems may raise persistent ethical issues that affect the well-being of numerous members at all levels of an organisation.

**Assigning responsibility**

As noted above, computers do not have values and cannot make independent decisions, or 'intentional' mistakes, because they can do no more than what they are programmed to carry out. The utilisation of computer technology is not a value-neutral activity as computer errors are created by faulty programs, invalid data or the lack of proper controls. It is therefore unethical for computer professionals and users to attribute the blame for their own errors to either the computer hardware or software as, ultimately, this involves a denial of personal responsibility and perhaps even lying. Finally, Rogerson and Bynum[19] also draw attention to the importance of applying ethical norms in situations in which computer technology is used, or misused, in actual acts of moral wrongdoing. For example, the use of a computer is an essential activity in gaining unauthorised access to a confidential database, and this is morally different from the act of stealing the computer equipment on which the database is stored.

Sutphen[12] suggests that appropriate levels of moral responsibility may be pursued by grouping individuals into three broad categories of development, implementation and maintenance of information systems in an organisation, so that the collection and input of data, and the output and dissemination of information are carried out as separate activities and responsibilities by computer specialists who should ideally be responsible to separate managers. Individual staff can then be properly briefed on their separate responsibilities to ensure that authentic and accurate best practice occurs in processing data and information. Staff should also be encouraged to undertake these responsibilities as part of the social responsibilities of the organisation.

**Information ethics**

Information ethics came into being as a result of computing specialists being drawn into the controversy over the individual right to privacy versus the right of government agencies and business corporations to acquire knowledge for sound utilitarian concerns relating to the public good, in the former case, and the free market pursuit of profits in the latter. Sutphen notes that some social scientists claim that the impact of computers on global communications has brought a change in values to modern society. As a result, the utilitarian benefits and convenience of increased access to information currently override any libertarian concern about the inviolate right to individual privacy. The radical response of some US libertarians is that, if personal information about individuals is now regarded as a commodity with increasing commercial value, they should receive a royalty whenever that information is sold.

## Synopsis

- Computer and information ethics have emerged to identify and evaluate the moral problems and dilemmas that have arisen as a result of the increasing use of computers and information technology in almost every aspect of society in developed nations.
- Moral issues may arise because computers offer unique ways of storing information as data which may intrude on individual privacy due to the rapid processing and transmission of data to others, using multiple versions of software codes to provide precise reproduction facilities over great distances at low cost.
- The protection of individual privacy is important because the ability to invade this aspect of a person's life at increasing speed, lower cost and in precise detail, by use of computers, raises ethical questions about the rival moral rights of those holding information and the persons whose privacy is open to intrusion.
- The moral evaluation of rival property and privacy rights requires detailed knowledge of the types of information stored, forms of privacy invasion possible, and the proposed uses of this information, particularly if it includes facts or data which are privately owned by profit-seeking companies rather than being regarded as common knowledge in the public domain.
- The privacy of employees is essential in any organisation and individuals must be entitled to obtain details of personal information held on computers, and also to a firm assurance from an employer about data protection measures to prevent this information becoming known by unauthorised persons, which is a statutory requirement in most developed countries.
- Without computer technology, the communications revolution and completion of repetitive, hazardous tasks, more rapidly and safely, would not have happened.

Yet moral concerns arise whenever technology is used to implement downsizing and employees are made redundant to reduce payroll costs and increase profits.

■ The monitoring of employees' activities at work, by intercepting their telephone calls and scrutinising electronic mail, without individuals being aware of this surveillance, also raises serious questions about the morality of illicit eavesdropping by managers of organisations.

■ The ownership of intellectual property divides claims that programming is a creative act from arguments that it is not an entirely original activity. The view that software is intellectual property has to address the issue of ownership and whether software is owned by the programmers, as creators, or employers who pay them to create software.

■ Equally important, is how to reconcile the notion of software as intellectual property with the view that, once it enters the public domain, it is no longer the exclusive intellectual property of any person or group, unless users are seen to benefit and other firms are able to develop alternative software.

■ The misuse of computers and computer crime include fraud; theft of data or software; use of unlicensed software, unauthorised personal activities such as 'hacking'; invasion of privacy to obtain private data or licensed information; sabotage of computer processing or equipment; and introducing virus infection programs to corrupt computing procedures.

■ The three main types of computer crime, resulting from surreptitious use of the technology, are unauthorised computer entry; computer theft of funds, also known as white collar crime; and theft of computer time.

■ Computer crimes may be motivated by the prospect of gaining money, or information; revenge against other persons, organisations, governments or society at large; or personal or peer satisfaction from manipulating complex new technology.

■ Developing computer professionalism to enhance human values in organisations is best achieved through approved codes of practice supported by training which enable employees to accept their different roles and responsibilities as suppliers, clients and users of the technology, in meeting the legitimate demands of consumers and the wider community.

## Review and discussion questions

1 What are the arguments for and against the need for computer and information ethics because of the unique impact of computer technology on modern society?

2 How might the use of computers in organisations violate the individual employee's right to privacy?

3 Summarise the case (a) for and (b) against the use of computer technology to monitor the output of employees and their electronic mail transmissions with other members of an organisation.

4 Identify the main differences between facts, data and information and explain why these distinctions are important in any discussion about intellectual property rights.

5 Indicate three common types of computer crime and suggest how these illicit practices might be eradicated in an organisation.

6 What ethical arguments would you raise (a) in favour or (b) against the white collar computer defrauding of £500,000 from an international bank being treated more severely by the courts than the armed robbery of £5,000 from your local fast-food restaurant?

7 Why should computer professionals be trained to view their activities in an organisation from the different standpoints of suppliers, clients, end users and members of the community?

## Case study
## Scientific management in British call centres

**Introduction**

Bertrand Russell's observation that the world of work is divided between those who get paid less for standing up than those who work sitting down is in danger of being made redundant by the rapid rise of teleworking* jobs in new call centres across the UK. Approximately 2,000 call centres are strategically located across Britain, many in or close to old industrial cities such as Newcastle, Liverpool, Glasgow, Leeds and Doncaster, where unemployment remains high. British and overseas companies have been encouraged by successive governments to locate call centres in areas where traditional manual work, mostly carried out by men, has disappeared due to falling international demand, so that alternative work is provided in the service sector for a predominantly female workforce.

Call centre employees, known as 'advisers', work in identical work-stations, equipped with a desk, a chair, a telephone and a personal computer. In addition to the low basic wage, employees criticise call centres for their biased selection procedures; the repetitive nature of the work; the vast open-plan layout of their working environment, but mostly for the aggressive work ethic imposed by management. This, advisers complain, contributes to burn-out within a six-month period of employment. Stanford and Salter[21], commenting on the organisational culture at one call centre, observe that 'they wouldn't shame a Victorian mill owner. Like other established service-sector industries, such as supermarket chains, call centres have adopted flexible working arrangements which require employees to work unsociable hours on shifts over weekends and public holidays.' Each of these criticisms is discussed below.

**A low basic wage**

At the time of writing reputable companies, like BT, pay advisers about £4.50 per hour for a 35-hour working week; however, many smaller firms offer their employees slightly more than the legal minimum wage of £3.60 per hour. Details on the financial performance of call centres are not easy to obtain since most are subsidiaries of larger British or American conglomerates; however, they are believed to be very profitable businesses with low set-up costs.

**Biased selection procedures**

Call centres employ a majority of female advisers. About 70 per cent of the workforce are women, rising to 98 per cent in Preston, in areas where predominantly male jobs have been lost in manufacturing industries. Nationally, there is a preference for employing advisers with Scottish, Welsh or Northern Ireland accents rather than applicants from Birmingham or Liverpool because customers are allegedly put off by their accents. Trade union membership is low and not encouraged by call centres so there is no way of establishing why female advisers are recruited except that they are a cheaper source of labour than males.

**Repetitive nature of the work**

Advisers either respond to telephone enquirers using the freephone '0800' service or 'cold call' potential customers selected randomly anywhere in Britain by a central computer. If the call is answered, advisers read from a pre-prepared script shown on their personal computer screen and, in the case of the BT call centre, use a politely assertive approach in attempting to persuade the unseen respondent into purchasing extras such as charge cards, extra lines or additional telephone services. A *Channel 4 News* report in February 2000 on a large call centre in Scotland, not owned by BT, stated that advisers were required to respond to two telephone enquiries every minute for over 55 minutes in every hour throughout their working day, or else risk dismissal.

**A vast unattractive open-plan working environment**

Stanford and Salter report that the BT call centre in Newcastle, opened in 1998 in an oversized warehouse,

> rocked me back on my heels. In the middle of downbeat estates . . . it is a place the size of three – maybe four – football fields, housing hundreds upon hundreds of people who generate a steady hum of noise. It is simply breathtaking in scale.

Advisers in their separate booths are usually clustered into groups of 12, with several responsible to one supervisor,

> as far as the eye can see. On the horizon, you can barely recognise the dots in their two-tone dens as human beings. They are worker ants. . . . Staring out over this factory of the 21st century . . . I couldn't decide whether the scene before me had been dreamt up by angels or demons.

The *Channel 4 News* report also confirmed that the nature of the work and the layout of the workplace allowed only minimum contact between advisers, who were physically isolated from each other and could only communicate with each other at the start and end of a working shift.

**An aggressive management work ethic**

The *Channel 4 News* report claimed that advisers at the Scottish call centre could not leave their work-stations without a supervisor's permission, had to raise their hands for a drink of water which was brought to them by their supervisor; and that any time spent in the toilet or on a meal-break was deducted from their paid hours of employment. Enquiries about an allegedly aggressive management style were rejected by a call centre management spokesperson; however, two advisers who had helped in secretly filming work arrangements in the Scottish call centre were later dismissed for refusing to take part in an internal company inquiry aimed at revealing the identity of the Channel 4 informants. The local MP later confirmed that he intended raising a question in the House of Commons about the company's work practices and *Channel 4 News* also reported that the Scottish Health and Safety Executive would be conducting its own formal investigation. It was subsequently reported that the call centre company had lost a valuable contract with a leading international telephone company because of the bad publicity arising from the Channel 4 report. Other call centre companies were quick to dissociate themselves from this criticism and pointed out that they were providing work, often in run-down areas, where high unemployment had prevailed before their arrival.

**The risk of burn-out**

An independent study carried out for the European Commission by the University of Newcastle and the Tavistock Institute[22] reported in January 1999 that women advisers employed at telephone call centres suffered 'burn-out' after six months and left their jobs with 'repetitive brain strain' after a year, due to continuously receiving telephone calls through a headset on an automatic system which sapped their motivation and eventually forced them to quit. The women interviewed were required to 'smile down the phone' for firms offering telephone banking, holidays, bathroom suites or double-glazing; and worked in huge computerised centres with up to 2,000 advisers in one room. According to this study, Britain has the biggest telesales force in Europe, with 3,560 centres employing 163,000 workers, mainly aged between 20 and 30 years, and the total is expected to exceed 3 per cent of the working population by 2001. Many respondents enjoyed the job at first but found the work repetitive, continuous, intense and low paid. Staff turnover is very high and most left after a year to take a few months off before taking a job with another call centre until burn-out occurred again. Few opportunities for promotion occurred as the number of supervisors was small and the nature of the work meant that interaction with management and other advisers rarely occurred. Ten years ago there were no call centres in Europe and the EU wished to explore experiences of those employed in this potentially huge area for employment which was predicted to grow up to 2005.

**Overtime work on public holidays**

The nature of work in the service sector is that people often have to work overtime at 'anti-social' hours, especially on public holidays. For example, the late Cardinal Basil Hume and the Anglican Bishop of Liverpool, James Jones, drew attention in January 1999 to the increasing numbers of people who were obliged to work over the previous Christmas period. Many of these service sector workers were in low paid employment in call centres and retail supermarkets, and relied on overtime to increase their take-home pay. This is confirmed by EU findings which show that low paid workers in the UK work almost twice as much overtime as in other European countries. The church leaders argued that the way that some people are made to work is very destructive of family life and people who lead companies ought to be more responsible. However, Ruth Lea, Head of Policy at the Institute of Directors, insisted that the churchmen were 'out of touch' and 'should accept that Britain was a multi-cultural society with many non-Christians happy to work over the festive period'. She added: 'At the end of the day employees want their company to do well, otherwise there will be no jobs at all, and don't forget they do get paid' (*The Guardian*, 4 January 1999, p. 7). Many of the big supermarkets insisted that employees had freedom of choice concerning working hours over Christmas and other public holidays.

A leader in *The Independent*[23] concluded that both church and business leaders had right on their side. The bishops were right to conclude that there was more to life than work. Hours of work had risen in Britain; overtime and weekend working were more prevalent than ever before, resulting in Britons working harder than any other Europeans. Social needs were not being met, however, and the number of divorces, the increase in single parenthood and a general civic malaise were damaging the fabric of British society. However, business leaders were right to point out that there were many reasons why families break up and it was certainly not due to people simply working harder. Laws rightly existed to prevent people being worked to exhaustion. No one should have to work longer than they feel they can. Those who wished to work on public holidays should still be able to. But the right to those holidays should be retained. Working longer hours is not necessarily a sign of avarice; it usually springs from the oldest and most laudable moral urge: to protect and nurture one's family. Nor is offering employment over holidays wrong: it gives opportunities to those who desire more flexibility in when they go to work. The challenge is to find a balance between those moral aims, and the right to a personal life, which can sustain civic duty.

The above concerns about Britain's call centre industry are confirmed in a recent study by Callaghan et al.[24] which describes these workplaces as 'hellish places, with employees treated as robots' who are required to work under a 'system built on intense pressure, obsessive control, and huge contradictions'. The main contradiction at the heart of the process was between quality and quantity. 'Customer service is pushed relentlessly throughout training. But the reality of the day-to-day work is quantity. Information is gathered on every keystroke and it is reported back every day, every week.' Two contrasting futures are forecast for call centres. Either they will up-scale people, 'giving them more interesting technical and product skills', or,

> if they want to keep things the same, they have to expect that there will be a quick turnover and . . . cut back on the resources they invest in training. The easy line is that call centres are hellish places, but they are bringing employment to areas that have no jobs.

Note
*Teleworking* refers to any work in flexible locations and at flexible times using computers and usually entails communication with the public via the telephone or the Internet, as part of a service provided by organisations.

**Questions**

1 In the case of advisers employed by call centres, what arguments would you put forward (a) in support of and (b) against the general criticism by church leaders that those who lead companies should act in a more responsible manner towards their low paid employees?

2 What arguments would you use to defend the claim of the employers mentioned in the case study that they are meeting their social responsibility to the local community by creating jobs as teleworkers in areas of high unemployment?

3 What examples would you cite to support the contrary argument that the introduction of new technology, in providing jobs as teleworkers, is inequitable because the work is repetitive, stressful and low paid; and exploits the fears of redundancy and unemployment in the local community?

4 Provide reasons why you (a) agree or (b) disagree with the Head of Policy at the Institute of Directors' response that the church leaders were out of touch in their criticism of companies requiring employees to work longer than their EU counterparts over weekends, Christmas and other public holidays.

**5** Explain why you (a) support or (b) reject *The Independent* leader writer's conclusion that both church and business leaders had right on their side in their attitudes towards the employment conditions of low paid British workers.

## Notes and references

1. Rogerson, S., Computer and Information Ethics, *Encyclopaedia of Applied Ethics*, vol. 1, New York, Academic Press, 1998, 563–70.
2. Parker, D., Rules of Ethics for Information Processing, *Communications of the ACM*, 11, 1996, 198–201.
3. Johnson, D.G., *Computer Ethics*, Englewood Cliffs, NJ, Prentice Hall, 1985.
4. Bynum, T.W., *Information Ethics: An introduction*, Oxford, Blackwell, 1997.
5. Maner, W., *Science and Engineering Ethics*, 2(2), 1996, 131–54.
6. Davis, E.R., Computer Technology, *International Encyclopaedia of Ethics*, ed. J.K. Roth, London, Fitzroy-Dearborn, 1995, 200–2.
7. De George, R.T., *Moral Issues in Business*, New York, Macmillan, 1990, 287–306.
8. Kutper, T.K., Privacy, *International Encyclopaedia of Ethics*, ed. J.K. Roth, London, Fitzroy-Dearborn, 1995, 704.
9. Spinello, R.A., *Ethical Aspects of Information Technology*, New York, Prentice Hall, 1995.
10. Weiss, M.J., Freedom of Information Act, *International Encyclopaedia of Ethics*, ed. J.K. Roth, London, Fitzroy-Dearborn, 1995, 330–1.
11. United States Dept. of Justice, Office of Information and Privacy, *Freedom of Information Act Guide and Privacy Act Overview*, Washington, DC, Government Printing Office, 1992.
12. Sutphen, C.E., Computer Crime, *International Encyclopaedia of Ethics*, ed. J.K. Roth, London, Fitzroy-Dearborn, 1995, 77–178.
13. France, E., *Our Answers: Data protection and the EC Directive 95/96 EC*, Wilmslow, Office of the Data Protection Registrar, 1996.
14. Mullins, L.J., *Management and Organisational Behaviour*, 5th edn, London, Financial Times Pitman Publishing, 1999, 49–53, 635.
15. Peters, T., What Will We Do for Work?, *Time Magazine, Visions 21: Our World*, 29 May 2000, 60–5.
16. Rawe, J., What Will be the Ten Hottest Jobs?, *Time Magazine, Visions 21: Our World*, 29 May 2000, 60–5.
17. Parker, S.B., Swope, S. and Baker, B.E., eds, *Ethical Conflicts in Information and Computer Science*, Wesley, Mass., QED Information Sciences, 1990.
18. Parker, D.B., *Crime by Computer*, New York, Charles Scribner's Sons, 1976.
19. Rogerson, S. and Bynum, T.W., eds, *A Reader in Information Ethics*, Oxford, Blackwell, 1997.
20. Collins, W.R., Miller, K.W., Spielman, B.J. and Wherry, P., *Communications of the ACM*, 37, 1994, 81–91.
21. Stanford, P. and Salter, T., Call Centres: The numbers game, *The Independent Magazine*, 4 January 1999, 13–16.
22. Phone workers' 'brain strain', *The Guardian*, 6 January 1999, 5.
23. The social costs and personal benefits of working on holidays, leader in *The Independent Review*, 4 January 1999.
24. Callaghan, G., Thompson, P. and Mathews, J., Help me! I'm on a helpline, *The Independent Open Eye Magazine*, 6 June 2000, 2–3.

# Moral Compass exercise

The Moral Compass instruments below are divided into two questionnaires, which should be evaluated using the 7-point Lickert scale shown in Box A. The simple Moral Compass contains the eight statements shown in Box B. The detailed Moral Compass includes the additional eight statements shown in Box C. Each statement corresponds with one of the ethical theories summarised in Chapter 4.

**Instructions**

1 Decide whether you wish to complete the simple or the detailed Moral Compass instrument.

2 Read each statement carefully before recording your response, using the 7-point Lickert scale shown in Box A below.

3 Record your scores for each part of the instruments in the Moral Compass section in the Appendix at the end of the book, where the corresponding ethical theories are shown.

**Box A**

| Strongly disagree | Disagree | Slightly disagree | Neither agree nor disagree | Slightly agree | Agree | Strongly agree |
|---|---|---|---|---|---|---|
| 1 | 2 | 3 | 4 | 5 | 6 | 7 |

## Box B

**S.1** For those in business, even honesty is a financial speculation.    1 2 3 4 5 6 7

**S.2** Good business? That's simple – it's acquiring other people's money.    1 2 3 4 5 6 7

**S.3** The effective manager knows that, as in sailing, business success
lies in steering every moment by the wind.    1 2 3 4 5 6 7

**S.4** Wages are a measure of the dignity that a fair society puts on a job.    1 2 3 4 5 6 7

**S.5** A sufficient rule is to follow your own instincts controlled by
the moral standards of the society in which you live.    1 2 3 4 5 6 7

**S.6** Trade unions are about individuals and the right of an employee
to express his/her opinion to a boss.    1 2 3 4 5 6 7

**S.7** The purpose of every organisation is to achieve consensus by
integrating specialised work into a common task.    1 2 3 4 5 6 7

**S.8** Only work that is the product of inner compulsion can have
any spiritual meaning.    1 2 3 4 5 6 7

## Box C

**S.9** A shrewd manager should always anticipate threats and choose
the least dangerous option.    1 2 3 4 5 6 7

**S.10** The most unfortunate people are those who do the same job
over and over again; they deserve the shortest hours and the
highest pay.    1 2 3 4 5 6 7

**S.11** Poverty is a business issue because many living below the poverty
line are part of the workforce.    1 2 3 4 5 6 7

**S.12** If an organisation's culture and the values of a community clash,
the community must prevail or else the organisation will not make
its social contribution.    1 2 3 4 5 6 7

**S.13** Industry's purpose is the conquest of nature in the service of
mankind.    1 2 3 4 5 6 7

**S.14** There is nothing intrinsically wrong with the aggressive pursuit
of money.    1 2 3 4 5 6 7

**S.15** Business is more agreeable than pleasure; it interests
the whole mind more deeply.    1 2 3 4 5 6 7

**S.16** What I want is power. Kiss 'em one day . . . kick 'em the next.    1 2 3 4 5 6 7

# PART III

# Groups

# 8 Employment issues

*All men are equal – all men, that is to say, who possess umbrellas.*

E.M. Forster, *Howards End*, 1911, ch. 11

## Learning objectives

After reading this chapter you should be able to:

- examine the relationship between employment and the civil rights of employees in organisations;
- evaluate moral arguments for and against a fair, legal minimum wage;
- explain the arguments that influenced the adoption and modification of the right to free association, to form trade unions and take strike action, in the USA and UK;
- consider the arguments that have influenced the adoption of more rigorous health and safety legislation in the UK and EU over the past 25 years;
- examine the reasons for the increasing emphasis on reducing the risk of physical violence at work;
- explore how legislation supporting Sunday working in the UK allows certain employees to withdraw their labour in specified industries;
- consider how the principle of equitable rights at work is investigated and enforced by industrial tribunals in the UK.

## Introduction

Employment policies in Britain have been subjected to numerous changes due to different political interpretations since World War II and ethical aspects of the underlying civil liberties are often set aside. The frequent redefining of employment law has, however, coincided with the rise of a better-informed, democratic society in the UK, as in other developed countries. As a result, ethical aspects of the 'employment at will' contract between the employer and individual employee have been re-evaluated from a group perspective. As the right to free association has gained wider acceptance, basic human rights relating to a just minimum wage, hours of work, overtime payments, the right to strike, improved health and safety regulations and protection from violence, etc., have been introduced into the workplace. Recognition of these rights has mostly emerged from collective bargaining between employers and trade unions, although governments have also sometimes intervened in tripartite negotiations with employers and employee representatives.

## Employment and human rights

Employment rights in the EU and USA are linked to widely accepted human rights in both the United Nations Universal Declaration and its European Convention counterpart. Britain, like the USA, is a signatory to the UN Declaration and also a founder member of the European Convention on Human Rights that was enacted in 1950. At a national level, Britain has also introduced the Human Rights Act 1998 which came into force in October 2000. Interest in the relationship between employment and human rights is unsurprising as democracy would probably be under threat in a modern industrialised state if human rights were neglected and an excessively wide gap developed between rich and poor. This is because in societies where basic human rights have been implemented, most people acquire wealth through employment. For example, in the United States, it has been estimated that wages and salaries amount to over three-quarters of all market transactions, with the remaining quarter almost equally shared between remuneration from self-employment and retained profits and savings from business organisations.

People still have to survive, whether in or out of paid employment, and supporters of human welfare rights believe that all persons, regardless of status, have a right to the basic economic resources needed to maintain their personal well-being and that of their dependants. Social anthropologists suggest that this moral imperative has its origins in traditional societies which recognised an obligation to meet the essential economic needs of all other members of the community. This is a view supported by all the world's great religions discussed in Chapter 3, and also underpins the humanistic idea of a community obligation which perhaps explains why most Western European countries adopted the political philosophy of a welfare state after World War II, committed to the following principles:

- All persons have equal moral worth regardless of economic circumstances.
- The primary causes of poverty are ultimately accidents of birth, social location, lack of capabilities or economic cycles. Therefore, there is a moral obligation to help others meet their basic needs.
- The basic needs of food, shelter, education and healthcare must be provided as necessary for survival and development.
- Greed and personal pleasure are irrational goals if they deprive others of the resources necessary for their human survival and development.
- Moral obligation aside, it is in the self-interest of individual members of a community to ensure that the economic subsistence of other members occurs.
- Fulfilling the welfare rights of others helps to improve the quality of life by reducing crime, class antagonisms and conflicts, and provides a healthy, well-educated population.

## Employment rights

The list of basic employment rights summarised in Box 5.2, p. 120, is derived from 'employment at will' ethical and legal principles which seek to define an acceptable relationship between employers and employees. Employment is regarded as the outcome of a contractual relationship, freely arrived at by both parties, which may be terminated 'at will', subject to specific terms and conditions in the contract not being violated by either party. To avoid this, it is necessary to consider legal and moral differences between the right to employment and the right to work.

## The right to work

The UN Universal Declaration of Human Rights states that 'Everyone has the right to work, to free choice of employment, to just and favourable conditions of work and the protection from unemployment' (Article 23, para.1). At first glance, it would appear that the right to employment and the right to work are one and the same thing. That is until the related question is asked: 'Who has responsibility for providing the necessary employment?' Supporters of Adam Smith's *laissez-faire* view of a free market economy would argue that it is irrational to expect every employer to undertake moral responsibility for providing work for every unemployed person, and still be expected to operate at a profit. Similarly, those responsible for the effective management of public sector institutions might add that it would be unreasonable to expect them to absorb the unemployed in bureaucratic jobs without the cost being reflected in increased taxation, inflation, or perhaps even devaluation of the national currency. In short, the UN Universal Declaration supports a utilitarian standard which, in seeking to benefit the majority, risks treating the individual unjustly, unless a clear distinction is made between the right to work and the right to employment.

## The right to employment

Confusion probably exists because the right to work is often viewed as both a negative and a positive right. In the former sense, it refers to work as an activity through which an individual expresses a vital part of what it is to be a human being. Both utilitarians and socialists support this view of work as a negative right because it implies that no other person, institution or government is entitled to deny this moral right to any human being, providing the work in question is lawful. The alternative view of work as a positive right assumes that each individual is morally entitled to membership of the community where they were born or live. Among the benefits of belonging to a community is the right to pursue gainful employment, providing legal constraints set by society are not contravened. Libertarians would argue that community membership does not mean that each individual has an automatic right to employment. This view prevails in most EU countries and in the USA where the right to employment means that governments through their various agencies, along with businesses and entrepreneurs, may all offer employment to individuals, or even undertake to help them find suitable work, but without giving any binding commitments that they will always be successful.

## The right to a fair wage

In addition to provisions in the United Nations Declaration, the European Convention on Human Rights also explicitly refers to the individual right to a fair wage. It should be noted that both declarations owe much to the earlier US Fair Labor Standards Act, which was introduced by the Roosevelt Administration in 1938 in response to a fall in real wages in the USA following the Great Depression. This Act authorised government to regulate wages and hours of work and limit the use of child labour, in order to eradicate unfair competition and the exploitation of labour by unscrupulous employers. The Act was a 'watered down' version of earlier legislation introduced by President Roosevelt in 1933 to regulate prices, wages, hours of work and other labour conditions, which were also abused during the Depression, but this legislation was rejected as unconstitutional by the US Supreme Court.

Amendments passed by the US Congress were upheld by the Supreme Court in 1941 and finally implemented in 1944. This Act introduced a minimum wage, subject thereafter to annual review by a congressional committee, and also authorised overtime pay of one and a half times that of regular pay after 40 hours' work per week were completed by the employee. It also eliminated the employment of children (i.e. those aged under 16 years) with certain exceptions. An important amendment to the Act occurred in 1963 when equal pay for equal work, without regard to sex, was approved. The Fair Labor Standards Act has been cited in some detail for two important reasons. First, it undoubtedly came to be seen as landmark legislation in the USA, where it was recognised that the US President and Congress had a responsibility to act as the guardians of economic and social justice in ensuring improved employment conditions. Secondly, many of these changes in employment legislation were adopted in most post-war European countries – although Britain dragged its heels on implementing a minimum wage for almost 50 years – and also in other industrialised nations in the southern hemisphere such as Japan and Australasia.

## UK minimum wage legislation

The reasons why Britain delayed introducing a national minimum wage until the National Minimum Wage Act 1998 and supporting Regulations (Statutory Instrument 1999, Number 584) were introduced, is a topic which is probably best left to historians and employment law specialists. Like the prototype American Fair Labor Standards Act, however, the UK legislation provides for payment of a national minimum wage to most workers over the age of 18 who work, or mostly work in the UK, regardless of their occupations. The Low Pay Commission is authorised under the Act to report to the Prime Minister and Secretary of State on any part of the legislation, after first consulting with employers and organisations of workers' representatives. The Commission is also required to ensure that any recommendations on the national minimum wage must consider the impact on the competitiveness of the UK economy.

The notion of a minimum living wage is not without its critics. Libertarians reject arguments supporting a fair or a just wage in favour of the minimum living wage which is determined by the market. For them, employment occurs in a market in which labour should be treated as any other commodity required by buyers and offered by sellers. If there are too many employers, then the price of labour rises; conversely, when there is a surplus of labour, then wages will fall. This argument necessarily assumes that governments, trade unions and employer associations will keep their distance and allow the market to rise or fall, thereby providing labour with a living wage. Clement[1] reports that the minimum wage in the USA was increased to $4.25 per hour in April 1991 after remaining unchanged at $3.35 for 10 years. Research on the effects of this change on the fast-food industry in New

Jersey revealed that unemployment rose most in the lowest paying firms, even though the USA was undergoing a recession at the time. Unfortunately, no follow-up studies were completed to establish whether the unemployed left the fast-food industry because they managed to find similar or higher paid jobs elsewhere in other industries.

Ethically, as De George[2] notes, supporters of the right to a fair minimum living wage recognise its link with the right to life which, only in extreme circumstances, can be denied to another human being. Recognition of the individual's right to life, necessarily presupposes respect for each person as a human being and for the individual's right to support him or herself and dependants. As noted above, the ethical justification is based on the Marxist argument (see Chapter 3) that the labour market is biased in favour of the employer, as a buyer, who has more power, resources and savings than the unemployed individual, as a seller, because the latter has limited time in which to obtain suitable employment at a fair rate of pay to provide for dependants. All too often, this leaves the individual open to exploitation by any unscrupulous employer which, in a modern democratic society, can only be eradicated by the intervention of governments, trade unions and employer associations.

Finally, supporters argue that intervention should be welcomed for two reasons: first, it provides the necessary checks and balances (by use of reliable measures such as the cost of living, average wage, unemployment rate, interest rate, exchange rate and rate of inflation, etc.), which will allow the labour market to adjust incrementally so that a fair and just living wage is achieved. Second, research evidence indicates, if appropriate external support is provided, the long-standing decline of run-down communities can be reversed as civil society reasserts itself in terms of reduced crime and improved standards of education and health, from which profit-seeking and public sector organisations can only benefit.

## The right to free association

The United Nations Declaration also states, first, that everyone has 'the right of peaceful assembly and free association' (Article 20, para. 1), which is later qualified to state that 'No one may be compelled to belong to an association' (Article 20, para. 2), before going on say that 'Everyone has the right to form and join trade unions for the protection of his interests' (Article 23, para. 4). The history of the rise, and recent partial decline, of trade unionism in Britain and mainland Europe over the last 100 years is a specialist subject beyond the scope of this book. However, attention should be drawn to developments in US labour relations legislation which were either accepted or rejected in Europe.

For example, another positive response to the US Depression led to the National Labor Relations Act (also known as the Wagner Act) being introduced in 1935. The Act was an unusual attempt to seize the high moral ground. It sought to eliminate industrial strife by outlawing strikes. Rather than antagonise employees, it became popularly known as the 'Magna Carta' of labour because it also sought to eradicate unfair labour practices, encouraged collective bargaining and sought to introduce equal bargaining power for employers and employees. A national labour regulation board was also created to administer the Act by providing transparent processes for the selection of employee bargaining representatives. It prohibited employers from interfering with union formation and recruitment and recognised the concept of a 'company' union for the first time. Discrimination against union members, refusing to recognise collective bargaining procedures, or retaliation against union members who filed charges of unfair labour practices, were all prohibited.

The Wagner Act was not without its fierce critics and, after 10 years of intense lobbying, employer representatives finally persuaded the US Congress to amend the 1935 legislation with the Labor and Management Relations Act in 1947. The new Act reflected employers' fears about the possible spread of communist ideology among the workforce by its strong support for a free enterprise system which led to the banning of 'closed-shop' union membership agreements, the prohibition of secondary strikes and picketing, an 80-day injunction, or 'cooling off' period, on all emergency disputes and, more controversially, a legal requirement that all trade union officials should publicly renounce any communist affiliations or beliefs before being allowed to take up office.

It should be noted that the moral rights of individuals to freedom of association, to join trade unions and to engage through their union representatives in collective bargaining with employers, were upheld in both of the US Acts. Furthermore, apart from the requirement that union officials should publicly renounce any communist affiliations and beliefs, many of the provisions in the 1935 Wagner Act and the amendments in the 1947 Act have been either introduced or repealed by successive British governments since the end of World War II. For example, in Britain an employee has the moral right to join a trade union and should not be refused a job, dismissed, harassed, or chosen for redundancy because of being a member or wishing to join a trade union. However, an employee also has the moral right not to join a trade union and his/her employment opportunities should not be affected in any way as a result of exercising this right in the workplace.

A member of a trade union also has the moral right to take part in trade union activities including the recruitment of members, collection of subscriptions and attendance at meetings. Any form of industrial action, for example, going on strike, is not considered a form of trade union activity. All trade union activities must take place either outside the employee's normal working hours or at a time agreed with the employer. An employee has no moral right to be paid for this time off work unless this is specified in their contract of employment. However, relevant employees have a legal right to take time off work with pay for the following activities:

- to carry out specified duties as a trade union official;
- to carry out approved duties as a trade union health and safety official;
- to look for alternative work if faced with redundancy;
- to receive ante-natal treatment and care.

In addition, the majority of employees have the right to time off work, although not necessarily with pay, for the following activities:

- to perform civic duties such as those of a Justice of the Peace, a local authority councillor or a school governor;
- to care for their children, usually under 5 years of age, who may be sick;
- to deal with unexpected problems with dependants, such as a breakdown in child-minding arrangements, where a dependant includes anyone who normally relies on the employee.

## The right to strike

As De George[2] observes, relations between employers and trade unions involve not two, but four parties, namely, employers, unions, government and the general public. In evaluating the morality of the right to strike, the principles of role theory (Mullins[3]) are pertinent since they reinforce the point that the persons who make up these constituencies are human beings, with rights and responsibilities, and do not cease to be so merely because they adopt different roles in society. As individual persons, they are entitled to respect on the understanding that they recognise a moral obligation to do what is right and avoid doing what is wrong. In terms of an 'at will' contract of employment, individual workers have the right to strike, which is extended collectively to the members of a legally recognised trade union, or association, of which an individual employee is a member. However, there are two obvious exceptions to this principle:

- a no-strike agreement is included in the 'at will' contract;
- strike action does not put members of the public at risk.

The latter proviso is more likely to occur in public sector organisations, where members of the public would be seriously inconvenienced if members of the police, armed services or emergency services were to withdraw their labour. To ensure that their moral right to strike is protected in the UK, should negotiations with management break down, mutually acceptable provisions for independent arbitration are made, which allow the statutory review board to evaluate any claims and investigate any disputes before recommending settlement arrangements. These arrangements are common in the public sector so that vital services are not disrupted. The aim of such third-party arbitration is to ensure that the moral rights of both employers and employees, or management and unions, are identified and respected so that solutions can be negotiated which will lead to peace, social justice and stability being maintained or swiftly restored.

## The right to health and safety at work

Although Health and Safety at Work legislation was consolidated in Britain in 1974, there was no structured approach in the European Community before 1989 when Directive 89/391 was adopted as a Framework Directive to introduce measures that encourage improvements in the health and safety of people at work. Mainly because employees live in a welfare state in which a free-at-the-point-of-use health service is provided nationally, there is a tendency to give greater priority to safety rather than health matters in most organisations. However, this assumption was suddenly challenged when the issue of HIV/AIDS attracted national attention in the early 1990s.

**HIV/AIDS in organisations**

The HIV virus attacks the human immune system, which is the body's defence against disease. A person who has HIV may display no symptoms for years until their immune system is unable to cope and they may develop a range of illnesses including cancers. At this point, the person is said to have AIDS. Various anti-HIV drugs, used in 'combination therapy' may slow down the effect of HIV on the immune system. However, Terence Higgins Trust research[4] indicates that of the 14,719 people in the

UK who had developed AIDS just under three-quarters (10,633) have died. This is from a total of 30,001 who were originally infected with the HIV virus. The highest ever total of 2,896 new cases was reported in 1996 which, the Trust concludes, 'shows that the problem of HIV is not going away'.

From an employment standpoint, according to Murphy[5], ethical considerations of social justice do not permit employers to test all job applicants for HIV/AIDS, on the assumption that a positive identification would make an individual unfit for employment. As far as the USA is concerned, however, he adds that the interest in testing is strongly influenced by the goal of reducing health insurance costs to a minimum. There is no duty to inform an employer on the part of potential employee, or for a medical professional to warn the employer about a job applicant's condition, as medical ethics in both the USA and Britain have always given greater priority to the issue of confidentiality in all healthcare matters.

Murphy notes that there is nothing in US anti-discrimination law that stipulates that an employer must hire applicants with HIV/AIDS, but neither can they refuse employment simply because an applicant is suffering from HIV/AIDS. Equally, people with HIV/AIDS can be dismissed if it can be shown that they are incapable of doing their jobs properly. From an ethical standpoint, however, the prevailing view is that the protection of people with HIV/AIDS in terms of gaining access to suitable employment should take precedence over the the immediate economic interests of employers. That said, this should not be at the expense of neglecting the legal requirement for all medical professionals, like managers of organisations, to report cases of HIV/AIDS infections as sexually transmitted diseases under the AIDs (Control) Order 1988 (SI 1988, No. 1047).

**The Framework Directive**

This places a more general obligation on employers to safeguard the health and safety of their employees 'in every aspect related to their work' and a hierarchy of preventative measures shown below is provided as a guideline for fulfilling this duty:

- avoidance of risks;
- evaluation of risks that cannot be avoided;
- combating risks at source;
- adapting the work ergonomically to suit the worker;
- adapting to include technical progress;
- replacing dangerous with non-dangerous or less dangerous processes.

The overall aim of these measures has been to develop a coherent accident prevention policy which covers technology, organisation of work, working conditions, social relationships, and the influence of any other factors related to the working environment, primarily from a utilitarian perspective which ensures the maximum health and safety benefits for the greatest number of members of an organisation by ensuring the following:

- Collective prevention measures are given priority over individual prevention measures.
- Appropriate instructions are given to all employees.
- Appropriate protective and preventative services are developed.
- First aid, fire fighting and evacuation of employees, serious and imminent danger needs are identified and provided.

- Consultation and participation of all employees is initiated.
- Training of experienced employee representatives is implemented.
- Health surveillance and monitoring is introduced.

The provisions in the Framework Directive were enacted in UK law under the Management of Health and Safety at Work Regulations 1992 (SI 1992, No. 2051). However, many employers were already fulfilling their responsibilities under the Health and Safety at Work Act 1974 (HSWA). The major difference was that employers had to undertake the additional duty of care to their employees of formally assessing hazards and their attendant risks, by recording their findings and bringing these evaluations to the attention of all employees. This systematic approach led to 14 'daughter' Directives being adopted up to 1998 which incorporate expert advice, often from external organisations, for implementation in Regulations that affect almost every aspect of the working environment.

## The right to protection from violence in the workplace

The employer's duty of care does not end by adopting a utilitarian policy aimed at providing the comprehensive list of health and safety measures summarised above, as there is an additional moral responsibility under the employment at will contractual arrangements to ensure that all reasonable steps are taken to protect all employees from the increasing risk of violence in the workplace. In Britain, for example, it is probably not realised that 25 per cent of all violent crime occurs at work and, according to the Suzy Lamplugh Trust[6], the number of assaults on employees by the public has doubled since 1991.

The most frequent incidents of violence include bullying and harassment of staff which occurs in service sector organisations, such as retail supermarkets, banks, building societies, hospitals, social security benefit offices and pubs; although increases have also occurred in schools and garages. In terms of understanding the problem so that staff can be provided with the necessary protection, it is first necessary to define what is meant by violence. Work-related violence generally includes any incident in which a person is abused, threatened or assaulted in circumstances relating to their work.

The Trades Union Congress (TUC) has identified employees in certain industries and public services as being more at risk from the members of the public, although physical attacks on employees are comparatively rare and most incidents involve verbal abuse or threats. The latter may cause individuals to suffer as much stress and anxiety from innuendo and rude gestures as they would from physical assault. Moreover, the nature of the service provided can influence an employee's perception of a 'violent' incident. For example, staff employed in betting shops or pubs will typically have encountered more foul language and aggressive behaviour than those employed in university reception areas or public libraries; and are more likely to have developed coping strategies, otherwise they would be less likely to remain in their jobs.

Employees most at risk from the threat of violence at work are those who provide care, information or advice, handle money or valuables, inspect personal belongings, enforce laws, work with potentially violent people, work on their own or are employed in the public services. The type of interaction in which violence is more likely to occur usually involves the provision of a service, caring, education, cash transactions, delivery/collection services, controlling the behaviour of others and representing authority. With prevention in mind, it is advisable for employers to ensure that all risks to employees have been assessed so that preventative measures can be introduced that will reduce the possibility of violent incidents and also minimise the effects of stress and anxiety on abused employees afterwards.

Although the incidence of workplace violence has undoubtedly risen, there is some uncertainty about whether this may be due to the introduction of new regulations in the 1990s which requires all such incidents to be reported. What is not questioned is that the severity of workplace violence has intensified and the use of weapons has become more common than a decade ago. One reason is that robberies in the retail sector have increased because these are probably seen as 'softer' targets now that preventative measures, such as video surveillance, have improved at banks and building societies. Longer trading hours at retail supermarkets have also contributed to the increase in workplace violence; however, school teachers are also more likely to be assaulted by pupils and parents than was previously the case. Similarly, National Health Service employees are reported to sustain about the same number of violent assaults as they are likely to be injured from accidents at work.

Studies by the Suzy Lamplugh Trust and the HSE on aggressive behaviour at work indicate that the main causes of violence are fear, humiliation and frustration, which trigger off aggressive behaviour due to prejudices, and biases, as well as the degree of stress the individual may be under at the time. Abuse of alcohol or drugs, a lack of adequate facilities and poor staff training also militate against the perpetrators and sufferers of aggressive behaviour from devising adequate coping or avoidance strategies. These findings led to the recommendation that risk assessment of possible aggressive behaviour should include a professional evaluation of possible 'triggers', based on the regular analysis of past incidents and consideration of future changes, which are aimed at reducing workplace violence.

## Sunday working in England and Wales

Since 26 August 1994, shops in England and Wales have been permitted to open on Sundays and shop workers have certain rights if they are asked to work on Sundays, which mostly apply to people employed in retailers, supermarkets, or in the betting industry. A shop worker is classified here as an employee who under the terms and conditions of his/her contract of employment is, or may be, required to work in or about a shop, which is open on a specified day to serve customers. People who work in betting shops or for bookmakers at racecourses are also included. For legal purposes, shop workers may include managers, office staff, warehouse staff, shelf fillers, cashiers, counter assistants, cleaners and canteen employees. Exceptions include any employees of a catering business such as a pub, restaurant or café, who may not be classified as shop workers and are therefore not protected from having to work on Sundays.

Any shop worker who started working for his or her employer before 26 August 1994 is classified as a 'protected worker', who does not have to work on Sundays if he or she does not wish to, on grounds of conscience, or for other reasons which need not be disclosed. If an employer tries to dismiss a protected worker because of a refusal to work on Sundays, the employee can automatically lodge a claim for unfair dismissal which will be upheld by an industrial tribunal. Protected employees are entitled to this protection, either individually or as a group, regardless of the length of individual employment prior to August 1994, their age, or whether employed in a full-time or part-time capacity. The moral right not to work on other days in the week, for example, those normally set aside for religious worship in non-Christian communities, subject to prior agreement with an employer, is also recognised under EU law.

Although custom and practice often results in additional overtime pay being paid to employees who work over weekends, there is no legal requirement for any employer to pay an employee more than their customary wages or salary for working on Sundays. Any basic or extra rates of pay are subject to agreement between the employer and employees, either individually or collectively, as specified in the relevant contract(s) of employment.

## Enforcing rights at work

In the UK, industrial tribunals exist as legal bodies which hear complaints about employment rights. A tribunal comprises an independent, legally qualified chairperson, and two other members representing employers and trade unions. If an employee wishes to challenge whether his/her employer is providing his/her rights at work, he/she can complain to an industrial tribunal. Many of these cases are raised directly by trade unions on behalf of individual members, although it is also possible for individuals to raise issues by themselves. Industrial tribunals usually deal with the following issues:

- the written statement of terms and conditions of employment;
- disputes about maternity rights;
- disputes about unpaid wages;
- disputes about sex discrimination/equal pay;
- disputes about race discrimination;
- disputes about disability discrimination;
- some disputes about health and safety at work.

## Synopsis

- Employment rights in most industrial countries are based on widely held welfare rights stated in the United Nations Universal Declaration or the European Convention on Human Rights, or based on traditional practices in individual countries.
- Welfare rights entitle all persons, regardless of status, to the basic economic resources needed to maintain personal well-being and that of any dependants. This moral imperative recognises that society has an obligation to meet the essential economic needs of other members of the community, which is supported by all of

the world's major religions as discussed in Chapter 3, although the right to work does not necessarily mean that the individual has the right to employment.

■ Employment rights are usually based on 'employment at will' ethical and legal principles that seek to define an equitable relationship between employers and employees, often through collective bargaining with trade unions or staff associations.

■ The moral status of this contractual relationship is that it should be freely entered into by both parties, and may be terminated 'at will', subject to specific terms and conditions in the contract not being violated.

■ The ethical justification for the 'employment at will' contract is based on a balance being achieved between the proprietary rights of employers to employ or dismiss whomsoever and whenever they wish with the utilitarian goal of producing greater wealth and higher living standards for employees in the community.

■ The aim is to achieve a system of voluntary exchange which enables employers and employees to collaborate as buyers and sellers to produce socially desirable goods and services.

■ The 'at will' contractual arrangements increasingly recognise that employees have a moral right to peaceful assembly and free association, which enables employees to form and join trade unions for the protection of their collective interests, providing no one is compelled to belong to any association on grounds of conscience, etc.

■ Employment rights include a fair minimum wage, the restricted employment of child labour and equal pay for equal work regardless of sex, which are all based on the principle that each human being is entitled to equal treatment in society.

■ The principle of a fair or just wage is rejected by libertarians who believe that the basic living wage should be set by a market of buyers and sellers without interference from governments and other vested employer or employee interest groups.

■ The right to health and safety at work places a general obligation on employers to safeguard their employees 'in every aspect related to their work', by the evaluation and avoidance of risks to the general well-being of employees at work.

■ Employees also have the moral right to protection from violence at work, including bullying and harassment of staff especially in service sector organisations such as retail supermarkets, banks, building societies, hospitals, social security benefit offices and pubs; and also in schools and other educational institutions.

■ Protected employees, mainly in the retail sector, also have the moral right not to work on Sundays on grounds of conscience, or for other reasons which need not be disclosed. If an employer tries to dismiss a protected worker because of a refusal to work on Sundays, the employee can lodge a claim for unfair dismissal.

■ Requests not to work on other weekdays by members of non-Christian religious communities are also upheld under EU law, subject to prior agreement between employees and their employer.

■ Independent industrial tribunals in Britain arbitrate on cases relating to a wide range of alleged cases of unfair employment or dismissal conditions, which are mostly raised directly by trade unions on behalf of individual members, but may be raised by private individuals.

## Review and discussion questions

**1** How would you distinguish between viewing the right to work as a negative or a positive right?

**2** What is the difference between the right to work and the right to employment?

**3** Explain what is meant by freedom of association and under what conditions this would give an employee the moral right to strike.

**4** Give several examples of the sort of health and safety risks that an employee is morally entitled to be protected from by an employer.

**5** Give several examples of the sort of violence at work that the employee is morally entitled to be protected from by the employer.

**6** Under what circumstances would a 'protected employee' be entitled to decline to work on Sundays on grounds of conscience and what legal rights would he or she be entitled to if disciplinary action were taken against him or her by an employer?

**7** What legal arrangements are in place in the UK to ensure that an individual's moral rights in a contract of employment are not exploited?

## Case study
## Health and safety at Sellafield

The safety record of the British Nuclear Fuels Ltd (BNFL) reprocessing plant at Sellafield in Cumbria first came under attack in an exclusive article by the science editor of *The Independent*, Stephen Connor, in September 1999. Connor reported that Health and Safety Executive (HSE) inspectors had been sent in to the BNFL plant following allegations that serious safety lapses had occurred. The Sellafield plant employs 10,400 people, half of whom depend on the chemical reprocessing of used nuclear fuel rods, which entails separating radioactive waste products from usable uranium and plutonium. The process is regarded as potentially one of the most dangerous to be carried out under manufacturing conditions and the safety of the workforce, local community and wider public takes priority over long-term economic conditions.

Things started to go awry at Sellafield in September 1999 when a leaked report that workers had falsified quality control records on shipments of nuclear fuel to Japan led to a visit by the HSE inspectorate, which reported in February 2000 on 'systematic management failures' in British Nuclear Fuels, the state-owned operator of the Sellafield plant. Five developments that threaten the future of the nuclear reprocessing industry in Britain are discussed below.

**The uncertain growth of the nuclear reprocessing industry**

The nuclear reprocessing industry has a short history and is a by-product of the post-war 'Nuclear Age' of the 1950s when the West vied with the USSR to produce increasing quantities of plutonium for use in nuclear weapons. This surge left additional nuclear fuel available which nuclear experts argued could be safely used in power stations at a time when the production of domestic electricity was reputedly 'too cheap to meter'. However, the need for an alternative source of energy to coal and gas was seen as a strategic priority not just in Britain, but also in France, where both governments were anxious to maintain cheap energy supplies. Nuclear capacity was developed at Sellafield and at La Hague, on the Normandy coast, primarily because of concerns about the availability and price of uranium which peaked during the 1960s and 1970s at five times higher than today's levels, falling from over $40 per lb. to under $8 per lb. between 1977 and 1999.

The case for nuclear reprocessing began to be questioned about twenty years ago when the US government decided against recycling nuclear fuel because of concerns that it would only increase the risk of nuclear proliferation. This left Britain and France as the leading countries with commercial nuclear reprocessing plants, although Russia, Japan, China and India are known to have entered the field at a time when the cost of commissioning power stations fuelled with cheap natural gas also began to fall. This resulted in programmes to build a new generation of 'fast nuclear reactors' being dropped; however, plans went ahead to open BNFL's Thorp reprocessing plant at Sellafield in 1994 at a cost of £1.85 billion.

Reprocessing capacity was increased by approximately 800 tonnes (50 per cent) of spent nuclear fuel on the previous output of Sellafield's 1964 Magnox plant at approximately the same time that Cogema, the French state-owned company, opened two plants at La Hague with a total capacity of 1,600 tonnes. Reprocessing costs are expected to fall until about 2005–2010 because the end of the Cold War will mean that the combined output of Russia, Japan, China and India should produce a further 1,800 tonnes. Meanwhile, a large surplus of nuclear weapon-grade plutonium exists that nobody is sure what to do with, but BNFL hopes to persuade the UK government to allow it to reprocess this as Mox (mixed oxide nuclear fuel) and thereby secure its commercial future for the next 15–20 years. However, trial consignments to Japan, Germany and Switzerland have recently been the subject of complaints from the nuclear 'watchdogs' in these countries.

**Environmental concerns**

Environmental groups like Friends of the Earth and Greenpeace have been opposed to the use of nuclear power for over fifty years since shortly after the first atomic weapons were tested in the USA. Without engaging in a detailed discussion of the cost/benefit aspects of nuclear fuel, this form of energy is known to be cheaper than alternative energy sources, but experts all agree that the short- and long-term risks to human health and the environment are disproportionately higher. Not surprisingly, therefore, the Irish, Danish and Icelandic governments have all registered formal requests with the UK government for the closure of the Sellafield plant, and they point to an increase in the incidence of certain types of cancer in their countries which are directly affected by effluent discharged from the reprocessing plant into the Irish Sea. The failure of the UK government to acknowledge these nuclear hazards obviously weakens its own hand in registering complaints about similar discharges into the English Channel from the two French reprocessing plants located on the Normandy coastline.

**Quality assurance issues** The need for stringent quality assurance procedures arises directly from the environmental safety concerns discussed above, which have not been helped by complaints that BNFL has failed to monitor quality procedures relating to overseas shipments of reprocessed nuclear rods to Japan, Switzerland, Germany and Sweden. As mentioned above, the first of these involved the Japanese nuclear safety authority which registered a complaint that the quality records on a shipment of Mox reprocessed fuel had been falsified. This report was followed by a further complaint, this time from HSK, the Swiss equivalent of the UK HSE inspectorate, which reported concerns that computer data and product specifications were missing for a consignment of Mox nuclear fuel which had recently been loaded into the Besnau 1 nuclear reactor in northern Switzerland. The Swiss authorities confirmed that, though records were missing, there was no record of falsification as had happened in Japan, adding that the incident was a blow to Swiss confidence and trust in BNFL and that they 'are not satisfied with what happened because there were people in the Sellafield facility who didn't do their jobs correctly. If things like this happen you lose confidence' (*The Independent*, 24 March 2000).

Meanwhile, BNFL management and a UK government delegation had visited Japan but without being able to persuade the nuclear safety inspectorate to reverse the decision to return the Mox shipment to Sellafield. This decision came as a huge blow to BNFL since Japan is their largest customer for reprocessed nuclear fuel with an order book of approximately £12 billion at the start of 1995 which, assuming current quality problems can be resolved, is likely to account for about one-third of Sellafield's production until the Japanese nuclear plant is completed at Rokkashamura after 2005. The immediate response of BNFL was to cite workforce failures for the Japanese and Swiss fiascos, but this left the media and the government unimpressed. Not surprisingly, the latter called for an immediate HSE inspectorate report on safety and quality standards at the Sellafield plant and summoned its management to appear before a House of Commons Select Committee to answer charges of negligence.

What proved to be a damning HSE inspectorate report, supported by the equally critical Select Committee findings, was anticipated by a further report in *The Independent* (7 March 2000) that BNFL had deliberately lowered its safety standards at Sellafield to reclassify a substandard batch of Mox nuclear pellets as satisfactory in order to meet an outstanding order. BNFL immediately stated that its safety standards had not been compromised but confirmed that yet another example of poor quality control had been uncovered. The government Nuclear Installations Inspectorate (NII) had already defended BNFL's decision to issue false data on previous Mox batches, but admitted that it had been 'kept in the dark' about the unsatisfactory pellets in question.

**The response of BNFL's stakeholders** Severe criticism from the government and the media was reinforced by an announcement on 21 March that the Ministry of Defence had decided to review the 10-year £2.2 billion contract offered to BNFL to operate Britain's nuclear weapons factory at Aldermaston because of concerns about management failures and safety lapses at the BNFL Sellafield plant. This decision was welcomed by the MP for nearby Reading who claimed that his constituents would rather that the Aldermaston plant was run by the cartoon character, Homer Simpson, than by BNFL. Further bad news was reported in *The Independent* on 24 March when the Swiss HSK nuclear safety inspectorate announced that it had banned further shipments from the Sellafield plant following critical reports from the NII which concluded that BNFL lacked a 'high-quality management culture'.

Switzerland joined Sweden and Germany by banning nuclear imports following revelations that BNFL employees falsified quality control data on Mox fuel pellets. The German Environment Minister had confirmed two weeks earlier that the import ban on Mox fuel would remain in force until 'it can be established without doubt that all safety standards are maintained at Sellafield'. As a result, the NII gave BNFL senior management two months to publish a strategy for improving safety or risk closure of the Sellafield nuclear waste reprocessing operations. Meanwhile, a BNFL spokesperson stated that the Swiss HSK inspectorate decision was 'unfortunate' as the NII audit had shown that there had been no falsification of the Swiss nuclear fuel consignment, but confirmed that safety remained the company's 'first priority'.

**Continuing safety problems at Sellafield**

The safety priority claim was thrown into greater doubt by further revelations later in March that the robot arms in the Mox reprocessing plant had been sabotaged by unknown members of the Sellafield workforce, which caused a temporary closedown of operations and led the trade union to take the unprecedented step of calling on fellow members to identify the culprits pending a police investigation. Media coverage of this incident led British Energy, BNFL's biggest customer, to insist on savings of up to £1 billion on contracts to reprocess nuclear fuel. BNFL confirmed that it had yet to be paid by British Energy for any of the £6 billion contracts which were due to run until 2010, but would not admit that it was under threat from UK or overseas customers who were seeking to renegotiate or cancel contracts, although it is known that the German government is planning a staged withdrawal from reliance on nuclear power and has publicly questioned the long-term viability of reprocessed nuclear fuel. Japan is less committed to withdrawal but is already planning to reduce its dependancy on UK supplies over the next five years.

The government is also thought to be privately opposed to further development of the reprocessed Mox fuel market and has encouraged industry competition which has already led to electricity prices falling below the cost of nuclear generated power. The industry regulator has also revealed that, to cover its costs, British Energy needed to charge 2p per kilowatt hour (kWh) compared with recent electricity costs of 1.8p per kWh, and it was only to be expected that the company would examine its nuclear contracts to see if costs could be reduced to compensate for lower market prices. Further indications of the government's position were reported on 30 March when the Energy Minister, Helen Liddell, admitted to MPs that events at Sellafield had been a 'setback' which had forced the government to postpone its plans to partially 'privatise' BNFL for an estimated £1.5 billion because of continuing safety fears about the company.

A BNFL-led consortium would, however, be allowed to run the Ministry of Defence's nuclear defence facility at Aldermaston, a decision which was immediately criticised by local politicians who raised fresh fears about the safety of the workforce and the local community. They were only partially reassured by the Prime Minister who stated that:

Ministers have made it very clear to the chairman of BNFL that we want to see big changes in the way that BNFL is run and managed. [However] I do think it important to emphasise to people that the Health and Safety Executive has given safety clearance to reprocessing.

Several days later, *The Independent* reported that BNFL would announce a major management shake-up at its Sellafield plant in an attempt to restore damaged confidence after the scandal over faked safety records. The overhaul was expected to include the sacking of junior managers and supervisors, the removal of others to different departments and the replacement of almost all the workforce employed in the Mox reprocessing plant where the data falsification had occurred. Further departures at the executive level were expected following publication of the NII-requested review by the BNFL chairman, and the finance director resigned following savage criticism of BNFL's accounts by the Select Committee which was due to issue its final report in 2001. This departure failed to satisfy the Cabinet minister and MP for the Sellafield region who called for the whole BNFL board to be dismissed, as they were more interested in getting rich quick from the BNFL privatisation than in effective management of the company. *The Independent* later confirmed (3 April) that up to eight managers and supervisors at Sellafield faced disciplinary action and two were thought likely to lose their jobs. Five process workers had so far lost their jobs although one was later reinstated.

*The Independent* continued its campaign against the Sellafield nuclear plant and in a separate front-page leader (31 March 2000) urged the government to face the awkward truth that

> reprocessing has no future. It is dangerous, polluting and uneconomic. That does not mean that the entire Cumbrian plant must close . . . but the imperative of preserving jobs alone cannot come before safety, the environment and the public finances. . . . You do not need to understand the . . . reprocessing industry to know that the Mox plant should be closed down. The facts are, first, that Sellafield has been leaking pollution since it was built . . . in the 1950s; second, it cannot guarantee the degree of safety society has the right to demand of an industry in which the risks can be catastrophic; and, third, it will never make money as a commercial venture.

The leader closed by recommending that BNFL should remain in the public sector and that its experienced staff should be employed on the huge job 'of cleaning up the nuclear power industry of the former Soviet Union, for which Britain could earn the world's gratitude . . . it would mean that this generation bequeathed one fewer problem to the next.'

BNFL's woes continued throughout 2000 when a report entitled 'Going Forward Safely' was leaked to the media which proposed a 'complete realignment of senior management' and the appointment of a team of experts to act as independent safety assessors. Up to 15 managers, supervisors and other staff due to be sacked as part of a major purge of the company's middle management appealed and, depending on the outcome, were likely to be dismissed, demoted or transferred (*The Independent*, 4 April 2000, p. 2). Five weeks later, the American nuclear weapons plutonium plant at Hanford, Washington, cancelled a multi-billion dollar contract because of doubts about BNFL management after an original project quotation of $7 billion suddenly rocketed to $15.2 billion (*The Independent*, 10 May 2000, p. 2). Finally, the Carlisle Crown Court fined BNFL a total of £75,000 in June for its sixth breach of health and safety regulations at its Sellafield plant during the past decade, when a spillage of nitric acid left two workers injured and one fire fighter suffering from inhalation of toxic fumes (*The Times*, 3 June 2000). A government decision on the proposed new BNFL Mox plant is still awaited at the time of writing and will probably not be taken until after the 2001/2 General Election.

**Questions**

1 What arguments would you raise in support of the contention that the moral right of the BNFL employees to a safe working environment has (a) been provided and (b) not been provided by the company?

2 What moral and socioeconomic arguments would you raise (a) in favour and (b) against the argument in *The Independent* leader (31 March) that the Mox nuclear processing plant at Sellafield should be closed down?

## Notes and references

1. Clement, B., Who Pays the Meanest Wages to Whom, News Analysis, *The Independent*, 20 September 1995, 17.
2. De George, R.T., *Moral Reasoning in Business*, New York, Macmillan, 1995, chs 15 and 16.
3. Mullins, L.J., *Management and Organisational Behaviour*, 5th edn, London, Financial Times Pitman Publishing, 1999, 470–4.
4. Terence Higgins Trust Annual Report, 1997.
5. Murphy, T.F., AIDS, *Encyclopedia of Applied Ethics*, vol. 1, New York, Academic Press, 111–22.
6. Suzy Lamplugh Trust Press Release, 1999.

# 9 Discrimination and equal opportunities

*We have talked long enough in this country about equal rights. We have talked for a hundred years or more. It is time now to write the next chapter, and to write it in the books of law.*

US President Lyndon Baines Johnson, speech to Congress, 27 November 1963

## Learning objectives

After reading this chapter you should be able to:

- explain the meaning of discrimination, in terms of segregation, stereotyping and prejudice; and of equal opportunities, in terms of equality and justice;
- explore the origins of racial discrimination and wage discrimination, and legal remedies that are intended to eliminate their unfair practices;
- understand the history of sexual discrimination and its impact on different approaches to sex equality;
- examine how sexual discrimination is reinforced through sexism, sexual abuse and harassment; and the legal remedies that are intended to eradicate these practices;
- examine the origins of discrimination against the disabled and consider legal remedies that are intended to ensure equal opportunities are provided in employment;
- explore the origins of ageism, its impact on employment, and the reasons why these practices are likely to change early in the twenty-first century.

## Introduction

Discrimination is regarded as unethical because it violates human dignity and autonomy and often leads to the withdrawal of rights that should be available to all members of society. Most developed countries introduced equal opportunities legislation over thirty years ago to remove historically entrenched discrimination against people based on their country of origin, race, religion, sex and physical disability. In order to eradicate these different forms of discrimination, legal remedies usually entail, first, ensuring that negative rights are not withheld from individuals, groups and institutions. Secondly, that positive rights are also restored by requiring employers to demonstrate that equal opportunities are provided. Legal issues aside, the ethical evaluation of discrimination would be incomplete without first exploring the related concepts of segregation, stereotyping, prejudice and inequality, which can lead to conflict in organisations and also violence in the wider community; and can easily be extended to include the disabled and the aged in society.

# Discrimination

Discrimination is a multi-faceted activity that comprises one or more of the constitutive concepts of segregation, stereotyping and prejudice.

## Segregation

Segregation refers to the separation of groups of people by custom or law on the basis of differences in race, religion, gender, age, wealth or culture. Segregation is usually permanent and needs to be distinguished from acceptable temporary separations of people for functional or cultural reasons; for example, male and female toilets, hospital wards, primary and secondary schools, prisons and universities. Segregation invariably involves some form of discrimination by one dominant group against a weaker party. Here, discrimination refers to the actions and customs which the more powerful group adopts to restrict the behaviour and opportunities of the subordinate group. Examples may include the provision of superior housing and schools, on the one hand, and limited employment opportunities, lower earnings and inadequate healthcare, on the other. More extensive restrictions may dictate where the subordinate group is allowed to eat, sleep, take exercise, buy land, own property, or run a business. Segregation may even restrict the use of public transport and access to civic buildings and to public officials, as happened in South Africa prior to 1994.

## Stereotyping and prejudice

Segregation is usually the outcome of a long-standing conflict of interests between rival groups in society and occurs as one party secures more power, resources and influence than the other. Negative, uncooperative attitudes towards the weaker group are reinforced through what the US political writer Walter Lippman (1889–1974) described as 'stereotyping' behaviour (i.e. after the metal type-set used to produce numerous copies of the same material using early twentieth century printing presses). This repeated pattern of behaviour reinforces the prejudices of both groups, where *prejudice* refers to the prejudgement of people, objects and situations, on the basis of stereotypes or generalisations that persist even when the facts demonstrate otherwise. These prejudices may lead the dominant group to use a mixture of force, law and custom to suppress its less powerful rival. Such acts are often justified by claims of superior intelligence, skills, inventiveness, cultural heritage, moral and physical courage over weaker groups, as happened in Nazi Germany before and during the Second World War.

Those who are suppressed often respond by displaying suspicion, fear, dislike and violence towards the dominant group because it possesses more wealth, political power and privileges. These advantages are exploited to confirm the dominant group's belief in its own superiority at the same time as they arouse a sense of inadequacy, frustration and injustice in the subordinated group. Differences between groups are often reinforced by the ostracism, punishment or expulsion of members who violate accepted codes of behaviour, usually by engaging too closely with outsiders, since loyalty to one's group is regarded as of paramount importance.

## Equality

Equality is a belief that every individual has the same innate value, status or class and that all human beings are entitled to the same basic legal, economic, moral and social rights in a just society. This view is at odds with the notion of justice defined by Aristotle in his *Nichomachean Ethics* as 'treating equals equally and unequals unequally' (V5). However, this definition raises more awkward questions than it answers. For example, how are different people to be graded as more equal/unequal than others without seeking the expert advice of a psychologist, sociologist, medical specialist and a bank manager?

A reliable scale of relevant and irrelevant characteristics or criteria is needed before the notions of equality and inequality can be separated in a consistent manner. For example, one applicant's proven ability to play darts is an irrelevant criterion in choosing between two equally qualified candidates for the next head of the World Trade Organisation, whereas a detailed understanding of macroeconomics is a relevant criterion for this post. Yet suppose the latter outstanding candidate is rejected because she has hammer toes or is tone-deaf? These would not only be irrelevant criteria but, according to Aristotle, some method of rectification would also be necessary to ensure that the rejected candidate received natural justice.

This far-fetched example aside, it should be apparent that the concepts of justice and human equality are central to the study of applied ethics in the real world, especially when the rights of minority groups are involved. Otherwise notions of moral principles, values, rights, duties and responsibilities would be meaningless, unless these were based on the premise that each human being is entitled to be treated equally. This view of equality is open to criticism on two levels. First, in terms of *meaning*. Here, a problem arises because equality can be defined from an individual standpoint as 'the condition of having equal dignity and rank as others' or 'of being equal in power' and, collectively, to describe 'a society operating with fairness and equity'.

The second problem with equality, alluded to above, is the *empirical evidence* from hard-nosed, reliable studies of human behaviour that individuals are profusely 'unequal' in intelligence, skills and wealth, etc. Libertarian critics of equality cite this evidence to justify their preoccupation with the individual definitions of equality, which support the notion of equal freedom for every person. Utilitarians and socialists, on the other hand, are concerned about the collective definition and with the provision of equal welfare for society as a whole. Tension between equal welfare and equal freedom is probably most apparent in the politics of democratic nations in which one government will seek to place restrictions on the economically dominant groups in society in its pursuit of equal welfare, only for its opponents to introduce policies aimed at securing equal freedom when they obtain power.

Ethically, however, libertarians seek to justify their political actions by defending the *negative rights* (see Chapter 5) of the individual. Their critics take up the alternative position of insisting that these negative rights are best guaranteed by providing specific *positive rights* for previously victimised minority groups. As noted above, these views on equality and justice may have been aired since classical times. Nevertheless probably the most notable sea-change in their legal application occurred in the USA when the Civil Rights Act was passed in 1964. At a stroke this legislation introduced a large raft of negative and positive rights to minority groups that had previously been discriminated against because of race, colour, religion, sex or national origin.

As is noted below, most developed countries have either introduced, or will enact their own versions of the American legislation. In Britain, for example, the Human Rights Act 1998 will prohibit any abuses of negative rights that threaten life or permit torture, slavery and forced labour. The denial of the rights to freedom of thought, conscience, religious belief, expression, assembly and association will also become illegal. The positive rights to protection of property (i.e. a safe environment), education, free elections and freedom to marry, are also included under the Act, which came into force in October 2000. The inclusion of more negative than positive rights arises because the positive welfare rights to food, shelter and other aspects of a safe environment are already provided under existing UK legislation.

Acts of discrimination, either as segregation or stereotyping of other human beings, have been illegal in developed nations since equal opportunities legislation was introduced during the 1970s and include the following areas:

- racial discrimination;
- sexual discrimination;
- discrimination against the disabled.

Ageism/age discrimination legislation, introduced in the USA, has yet to be enacted in most EU countries. However, it is discussed below because this subject seems likely to pose difficult moral choices for the ageing populations of Western nations early in the twenty-first century.

## Racial discrimination

As Jackson[1] and Hayward[2] note, racial discrimination is not limited to individuals, and two of its most pervasive forms in the West up to forty years ago were legal and institutional discrimination. As noted above, racial discrimination became illegal in developed countries when equal opportunities legislation was introduced about thirty years ago. Institutional discrimination has been less easy to eradicate and refers to any form of unequal treatment based on race that is entrenched by social custom in institutions and leads to the different forms of segregated behaviour and prejudice discussed above. Jackson provides an apt example of social prejudice in the USA where most women on welfare (family income support) are white, yet 'the stereotype persists of the typical female welfare recipient as a black woman with a brood of children'.

Although acts of prejudice and discrimination have probably been directed for centuries against every racial minority in Europe, the USA and on every other continent, undoubtedly the most cruel and entrenched discrimination has been experienced by those originally from the African continent and probably the most blatant way that equal opportunities were denied to them and other disadvantaged groups in organisations was by wage discrimination.

### Wage discrimination

Wage discrimination has been defined by Jackson as the payment of different wages to various groups for reasons unconnected with their skills or actual performance.

Reasons provided by managers for reported discrepancies range from actual to alleged differences in experience, intelligence, education and on-the-job training. Reasons cited by above average employees include occupational choice and a reluctance to abandon lower performing peers, even if this results in refusing additional training or promotion to a higher paid position with more responsibilities, such as a supervisor.

## Racially-based wage discrimination

Actual evidence of wage discrimination in the UK is hard to obtain as unscrupulous employers will not readily admit to breaking the law. However, in the USA, Skillen[3], reports that 'institutionalised' wage discrimination was still being imposed against African American employees nearly twenty years after the courts declared this practice to be illegal in the early 1970s. This is confirmed in a 1994 *Wall Street Journal* survey which reports that only one in seven black American families received incomes from employment of over the $50,000 benchmark during the previous year compared with more than one in three white families. Attempts to improve living standards were believed to have been frustrated most by racial prejudice, as findings revealed that 39 per cent of black entrepreneurs reported that their businesses had been hurt by being minority owned, compared with only 22 per cent who thought the latter had helped and 35 per cent who said it had made no difference.

Mobility also failed to alleviate the situation for black Americans who moved to another town to find better-paid work but were hindered by being rejected for mortgages at a rate 2.4 times higher than that of their white counterparts, according to a 1992 Federal Reserve Board Report. The cumulative effect of these and other constraints on family life indicate that a black child born in the 1980s had only a 6 per cent chance of living with his/her biological parents until the age of 17 in the late 1990s, compared with the 30 per cent chance of a white child born at the same time. Finally, individuals attempting to benefit from further education have to cope with the expectation that about 70 per cent of black American students at four-year colleges drop out and fail to qualify, compared with 45 per cent of their white counterparts.

## Race relations legislation

The prevention of racial discrimination in employment was first enacted in Britain under the Race Relations Act 1976. Amendments were introduced in the Race Relations Codes of Practice Order 1983 (SI 1983, No. 1081), the Employment Act 1989, the Courts and Legal Services Act 1990, the Race Relations (Remedies) Act 1994, the Race Relations (Prescribed Public Bodies) (No. 2) Regulations 1994 (SI 1994, No. 1986) and the Employment Tribunals (Interest on Awards in Discrimination Cases) Regulations 1996 (SI 1996, No. 2803).

The aim of the above legislation is to prevent discrimination in the field of employment on racial grounds which results in the victimised person being less favourably treated than other employees on the grounds of colour, race, nationality, or ethnic or national origins. The terms of employment covered by the above legislation include the advertisement, offer and terms of employment; access to opportunities for promotion, transfer, training or any other benefits, facilities or services; and extend to mode of dismissal of employees. The Acts also set up a Commission for Racial Equality with the general responsibility of working towards the elimination of discrimination and the promotion of equality of opportunities and improved relations between different racial groups. One of the Commission's main responsibilities is to issue codes of practice containing practical guidance for employers.

## Equal opportunities and sexual discrimination

As noted above, the big shift in equal opportunities legislation in the USA, which spread to Europe during the 1970s, was brought about by the Civil Rights Movement which led to the emergence of the Women's Rights Movement accompanied by the rapid development of an ever-widening field of rigorous academic research and debate. This field is already so vast that the non-specialist can attempt little more than a general survey of key topics based on the detailed writings of specialist scholars such as Kaplan[4], Range[5], Tong[6], Johnson[7], Dodds[8], McKenna[9], Boehlke[10], Taylor[11], Grimsley[12], Bohren[13] and Vandendorpe[14]. Individual analyses summarised below cover issues such as sexual discrimination, sexual equality, women's ethics, sexuality and sexual stereotypes, sexual abuse and harassment, and how managers need to understand the myths about sexual harassment before confronting hard-core harassers in their organisations.

With issues affecting business ethics and governance in mind, attention is drawn to Dodds' (ibid) writings which identify the ethical values and practices that need to be changed in social institutions before the following forms of sexual discrimination are abolished:

■ Women constitute half of the workforce but earn less than two-thirds of male earnings, and are overwhelmingly concentrated in low wage jobs.
■ Women are the targets of violence and harassment by men, both inside the home and in organisations; and are often subjected to further harassment when they report the initial abuse, which results in a lack of justice for women.
■ This lack of liberty for women is seen as a denial of their moral right to be regarded as persons in and of themselves, whereas in a moral society women would be entitled to the same rights as men both within the family and in the wider community.

### Gender-based wage discrimination

Wage discrimination against female employees in organisations was imposed for most of the twentieth century and occurs because employers regard women as more prone to periodic absences from work. The latter are the result of childcare responsibilities and also because women are more likely to leave their jobs for long periods, or permanently, to have children. From the employer's standpoint, these contingencies made women 'less valuable in the long run', even when their daily performance at work was identical to that of men. When questioned further on this point, employers defended their right to invest less in workers who are unlikely to remain as long with the organisation, or repay any investment in extra training, etc. In later studies which compared the stated reasons for wage differences with actual practice, the findings were mixed as half of the differences between men's and women's wages could be explained by 'objective factors'; the remaining differences possibly occurred 'as a result of discrimination'.

## Sex equality

The provision of similar rights, such as wages, is referred to as sex equality by Dodds, who notes that its historical development has resulted in three different uses, as follows:

- men and women are the same in all relevant characteristics and capacities;
- the distinct capacities and characteristics of men and women are equally valuable;
- men and women merit equal treatment and sex difference alone does not justify differential treatment.

**Women and men are the same**

This traditional view dates back to Socrates who claimed that there are no specifically female biological or psychological characteristics that would prevent women from taking on all the activities of political leaders (guardians). Natural capacities are distributed equally among men and women, although Socrates concluded that women as a group are weaker in the exercise of human capacities than men as a group, but have the same basic nature (although man's is more perfected?). For Socrates, childbirth and child-rearing are not legitimate obstacles to women engaging in training for public life and the responsibilities of political leadership. The view that men and women are of equal capacity and moral worth and ought to be treated equally influenced the liberal political views of John Stuart Mill (1806–1873) and Harriet Taylor (later Mill) (1807–1858).

As a utilitarian, Mill argued that, by treating women as equal to men, the whole of society would benefit. Nineteenth century laws that excluded women from various equal opportunities, such as exclusion from universities and colleges, paid employment, property ownership in marriage, and from receiving an inheritance, should be changed. Harriet Taylor held more radical views than Mill on the issues of women's self-sufficiency and responsibility, arguing that women should not be dependent on men. They should also have equal opportunities in education and for securing gainful occupations to provide alternatives to marriage, enhance their self-sufficiency, and enable them to assume responsibility for their children.

**Men and women are different but equally valuable**

This approach recognises that significant differences exist between male and female characteristics but rejects the view that these provide grounds for regarding feminine characteristics as of less value than those associated with masculinity. Historically, the view that men and women are complementary and differ both naturally (e.g. biological differences and differences in reproductive roles, strength, etc.) and in their roles was first proposed by Jean-Jacques Rousseau (1712–1778). He argued that woman's nature complemented man's and that men and women should be educated to pursue a civic and domestic life according to nature.

This patriarchal view of society advocated a different education for boys which would equip them to participate equally and dispassionately in public affairs with other men in running the state on behalf of a fraternity of fellow citizens. Privately, each male should be entitled to rule and enjoy his home and family life in the intimacy of his wife and children. Because of their biology, women were regarded as closer to nature and less rational. They could not separate universal principles from socially acquired prejudices and were not equipped to be citizens. Girls should therefore be educated to be good daughters, wives, mothers; and, as protectors of received morality from society, which could not be challenged, they should inculcate these values in their children and adorn the lives of men by being obedient wives in raising their children.

Mary Wollstonecraft's *The Vindication of the Rights of Women* (1792) refuted Rousseau's views on education by arguing that it was women's poor education, not a natural difference in rational capacity, that caused women to act as emotional rather than as rational beings, since women's capacities for rationality and virtue equal those of men. Once guaranteed the right to an equally rigorous education, women would exhibit the same capacity for rationality as men. Women's disadvantaged status in society reflected their inferior education and the lack of intellectual opportunities open to them. Wollstonecraft's criticism of women receiving a different education was less radical, as she accepted that women's reproductive capacities required them to adopt a different role in the exercise of rationality and virtue. Women's rationality should therefore be expressed in the raising and education of children, for which they need to be well educated so that independent, rational thought could be inculcated in their children as an alternative to being led by passion and prejudice.

**Cultural feminism**  Although the 'different but equally valuable' view of sex equality is widely criticised, it still finds limited support from some cultural feminists. Mention was made in Chapter 2 of the separate research of the Harvard psychologists Lawrence Kohlberg (1981) and Carol Gilligan (1982). When Gilligan repeated her research, she found that girls approached mature ethical decisions by applying principles which they considered to be of higher ethical value than the abstract rules of justice attributed to boys in Kohlberg's studies. She concluded that, in applying an 'ethic of care', girls sought to preserve relationships with others by considering the needs of the individuals involved; showed concern for what others thought; and regarded any enhancement of the emotional and physical well-being of others as an essential factor in every ethical decision.

These research findings have since been interpreted in both a positive and a negative way by supporters of women's rights. The positive interpretation is that the 'ethic of care' findings enable women to identify with efforts to establish international peace, racial harmony, equal opportunities for the disadvantaged, and concern for the environment. Critics insist that this interpretation of the 'ethic of care' findings merely supports the reinstatement of feminine virtues which historically restricted women to caring roles in employment and the narrower ambit of home and family, as supported by Rousseau and Wollstonecraft. Others also regard the former interpretation of the 'ethic of care' as a simplistic account of women's capacity for moral reasoning. They argue that women are as adaptable as men in responding to different moral situations and apply the 'ethic of care' when appropriate; and other types of ethical thinking, including rational analysis in the defence of justice, in different situations. Carol Gilligan supports this last view and argues that both men and women are able to take up a different ethical 'voice', depending on the context and their different experiences as individuals.

**Equal treatment in place of differential treatment**  The third sense of sex equality addresses notions of justice that affect the distribution of publicly valued benefits and opportunities within society. Equal treatment requires that people with the same entitlement to a benefit are treated alike in law, in terms of access or restraints. This means that any bias based on gender considerations is eliminated from the decision about the outcome. Supporters of this perspective also insist on the need to focus on particular cases rather than be distracted by statistical generalisations. For example, the possibility that men as a group perform differently from women as a group when different activities are compared is irrelevant. The key issue is whether a particular woman or man is better able to perform a specific task, based upon an even-handed assessment of their individual capabilities and experience. The question of ensuring equal treatment for women and men surfaces when decisions have to be taken about staff promotions in organisations. Senior managers often have to demonstrate that suitably qualified women applicants have not been overlooked because male employees have always been appointed to the vacant position in the past. This practice is usually referred as the presence of a 'glass ceiling' in the organisation, which is discussed in more detail below.

## Socialist feminist ethics

Socialist feminist ethics are derived from the Marxist perspective discussed in Chapter 3. Supporters view the imbalance of power in society as due to economic conditions which, if changed, would create a more just society in which women would cease to act, or be perceived, as the possessions of men. Arguments in favour of equal rights are therefore rejected as long as women lack the economic means to achieve greater equality. This includes the attention that liberal reformers give to the individual's right to equality in civic and employment opportunities because these deflect attention from the two main areas of oppression that directly disadvantage women: namely, capitalism and the patriarchal nuclear family.

Women's involvement in a capitalistic paid workforce, like that of working-class men, is seen as both alienating and oppressive. The over-representation of women in poorly paid, subordinate jobs compared with men merely confirms the oppressive nature of capitalism. For socialist feminists, the real division of labour is sexual in character since women, whether in low paid employment or not, are also burdened with unpaid domestic duties and responsibilities for childcare (see Box 9.1).

---

**Box 9.1**  **How most UK families managed on a single wage in 1993**

A survey by the UK life insurance company Legal & General calculated that the cost of paying someone else to do a housewife's work in the home was over £18,000 per annum, based on a 71-hour working week. This amount exceeded the average earnings of a train driver, plumber and the salaries of 70 per cent of the UK working population in 1993. The majority of respondents (47 per cent) in the survey of 1,001 married women were not in paid employment and had no direct income other than 'housekeeping money' received from their husbands and state allowances towards the upkeep of their children. Women in part-time jobs (35 per cent) averaged 59 hours work per week, while those in full-time employment (18 per cent) did 49 hours of domestic work, on top of an average 40-hour working week.

(*Source: The Independent*, 3 February 1993)

---

Attempts to reduce discrimination against women in organisations through equal opportunities legislation are acknowledged but with the proviso that these fail to expose capitalism's patriarchal exploitation of the economically weaker members of society both in organisations and in the home. This inequity is further compounded by men, who often compensate for being at the bottom of a hierarchy in the workplace, by seeking to assert their dominance over women at home. Before equality can emerge which will enable women to act and be treated as rational, autonomous individuals in society, socialist feminists believe it will be necessary for women to change their self-image through education. Societal reforms proposed by socialist feminists extend to the family, the home, the media and all socio-political and cultural institutions in society. Specific reforms of relevance to profit-seeking organisations include passing legislation to limit the growth and economic power of conglomerates and promoting the growth of worker-owned businesses in which all members share profits equally.

## Discrimination against women

The three main forms of discrimination against women in organisations are:

- sexism;
- sexual abuse and harassment;
- sexual stereotyping.

### Sexism

Boehlke[10] states that 'sexism as ideology tends to legitimate and mask patterns of constraints and inhibitions applied to the life chances of modern women. . . . It denotes a breach of the humanist conviction that all individuals ought to be recognized as unique personalities.' In terms of career progression, the appointment of women to senior management positions in organisations has been very slow. The number of women managers in the UK rose from approximately 2 per cent in 1973 to approximately 20 per cent in 1998, according to the Equal Opportunity Commission, and includes managers at all levels in the hierarchy. In the USA between 1 and 2 per cent of senior management positions in the corporate sector are filled by women. Transnational corporations such as Shell (UK) Ltd have also undertaken to increase the number of senior managers five-fold, from 4 per cent to 20 per cent by 2002/3. Explanations for this slow progress include:

- the 'glass ceiling';
- a 'fear of success';
- a 'women's culture'.

### The 'glass ceiling'

This euphemism refers to any informal barrier that frustrates attempts by women to obtain positions at the highest level of authority in private sector or profit-seeking organisations. The presence of these barriers is an indirect statement on the entrenched sexist culture that prevails in such organisations whose managers could not openly reject applications from suitably qualified women for a senior post on the grounds of gender without breaking the law. A probable explanation is that employees in most organisations establish formal and informal networks based on shared values, experience and tradition. 'Opinion leaders' tend to use informal networks to support the erection of barriers like the glass ceiling to prevent aspiring 'outsiders' from gaining senior positions, from which they might change the sexist culture and reduce the power of its supporters in the organisation.

**A 'fear of success'**

The absence of significant numbers of women in senior management posts is attributed to the supposed inhibiting role that a 'culture of women' has had on their career advancement as a group. This 'culture of women' is reputedly characterised by a 'fear of success' because women's traditional gender-role expectations have socialised them into practising 'success avoidance', which entails an unwillingness to assume positions of power and authority in organisations. The major drawbacks with generalisations of this sort are the absence of reliable supportive evidence, and the impact of sexual stereotyping, as discussed by Boehlke[10] and Vandendorpe[14] below. Unless the latter is eliminated, it is difficult to envisage how reliable research can be undertaken. Until this problem is resolved, it has to be assumed that basic differences between the sexes in the general population have no significant part to play in investigating the attributes of 'successful' managers.

**A 'women's culture'**

A rival explanation for the low incidence of women in senior management posts is based on the notion of a specific 'women's culture', as mentioned above. The underlying premise is that women do not 'fear' success because they have assimilated a different understanding of what constitutes achievement, which is generally critical of the dominant, market-driven culture of the 'successful life' aspired to in modern profit-seeking organisations.

## Sexual abuse and harassment

Taylor[11] defines sexual abuse and harassment as 'any interaction between two or more individuals with sexual implications or overtones in which at least one of the individuals involved is devalued as a person'. He adds that there must also be a distinction between the perpetrator(s) and the victim(s), which indicates that the interaction is neither solicited nor wanted by the victim(s), and is inappropriate either because of the setting in which it occurs or the assumed relationship between the perpetrator(s) and the victim(s). Such an action raises the following ethical issues:

- The moral worth and dignity of the victim as a person is devalued.
- Personal freedom is invaded by inhibiting the victim's ability to pursue whatever activities she was engaged in prior to the harassment.
- Gender inequality is reinforced by the incident.
- The legitimate distribution of power, authority and control, without which few organisations would function effectively, is seriously threatened by such incidents.

Since the vast majority of reported incidents of sexual harassment involve female victims and male heterosexual perpetrators, who hold positions of authority over victims, this assumption has been retained above, although there is also evidence of male and female perpetrators and victims of sexual harassment, who may be either heterosexual or homosexual. Specific forms of sexual harassment include:

- sexist remarks or jokes that stereotype or devalue a particular gender;
- unsolicited attention, including unwelcome flirtations;
- suggestive body language;
- verbal or physical sexual advances including pinching, fondling, etc.;
- explicit sexual propositions such as direct requests for sexual encounters;
- sexual coercion or bribery, including implicit or explicit promises of rewards for agreeing to, or threats of sanctions or punishment for refusing, a sexual encounter.

Grimsley[12] and Bohren[13] advise senior managers in organisations to investigate incidents of sexual harassment early to prevent possible legal action. Grimsley adds that most incidents are caused by 'hard-core . . . serial offenders. Most men don't harass anyone. But a few do it a lot.' These perpetrators are known to other employees and, if not apprehended, will continue in their activities on the assumption that they will not suffer repercussions if caught. Bohren identifies six myths about sexual harassment which permeate most organisations, as follows:

- It's not a problem here.
- It's human nature: they'll work it out.
- Women harass men as much as men harass women.
- If there's no intent to harass, the perpetrator is not liable.
- It's hard to determine guilt; it's one person's word against another's.
- There's not much they can do to us.

## Sexual stereotyping

Vandendorpe[14] defines sexual stereotyping as 'the assignment of emotional and ability characteristics to all men or women, solely on the basis of their physical sexual identity'. Ethical issues arise because discrimination and victimisation are encouraged, mostly against women, based on unreliable generalisations which diminish their personal autonomy. Sexual stereotypes are based on the notion that all the members of a gender are alike in personality, interests and capabilities; and form a homogeneous group.

The feminine stereotype comprises the characteristics of passivity, submissiveness, emotionality, modesty, low sexual interest and physical weakness. The masculine stereotype includes the characteristics of aggressiveness, interest in achievement, dominance, rationality, independence, high sexual interest and physical strength. Some forms of sexual stereotyping are accepted by society, especially in advertising and marketing, and these are discussed separately in Chapter 10.

## Sex discrimination and employment legislation

In the UK, the Sex Discrimination Acts 1975 and 1986 make it illegal to discriminate against any person on the grounds of his or her sex in the fields of employment or education. The Act also makes it illegal to discriminate in the provision of goods, facilities, services or premises. In the field of employment only, the Act also makes it illegal to discriminate against married persons on the grounds of marriage. Both Acts operate in conjunction with the Employment Protection Act 1975, the Race Relations

Act 1976, the Employment Act 1989 and the Courts and Legal Services Act 1990. Provisions exist under the first two Acts mentioned above for the Equal Opportunities Commission to conduct formal investigations, and impose penalties and other legal remedies when alleged cases of discrimination are proven. It is also authorised to issue codes of practice containing practical guidelines for employers to prevent discrimination and encourage equality of opportunities for all employees.

Separate legislation also exists to make harassment unlawful in the UK under the Harassment Act, although this legislation was primarily intended to make 'stalking' and racial harassment illegal as cases of alleged sexual harassment can be brought before a tribunal under the authority of the Equal Opportunities Commission.

## Discrimination against the disabled

The history of discrimination against disabled people dates back to classical times when Spartan parents were allowed to let a deformed newborn child die of exposure. A similar practice was adopted in Ancient Rome where disfigured children could be legally drowned by their parents. Prior to the twentieth century, disabled people were either ridiculed or treated with suspicion. A fortunate few were employed as jesters by the aristocracy in medieval Europe, whereas the majority were hidden away at home, sometimes to avoid being burnt as witches and, later on, were often disowned and locked away in workhouses or other institutions. The development of rehabilitation techniques and the discovery of antibiotics led to a major change in public attitudes approximately sixty years ago when it became apparent that disabled people could be enabled to lead fuller and more productive lives than was previously supposed.

The ethical arguments against discrimination against the disabled are similar to those discussed above in the sections on racial and sexual discrimination. Segregation and stereotyping often lead to the withholding of negative rights such as physical security, autonomy, freedom of thought and expression, and privacy. In addition, the positive rights of adequate medical care, education and employment without wage discrimination, may also be withheld unless guaranteed under appropriate legislation.

Mergenhagen[15] reports how the disabled have responded to provision of the positive right of appropriate employment under recent US legislation. Since then, 15 million workers with moderate or severe disabilities, that do not interfere with their lives enough to prevent them from accepting employment, have boosted productivity and morale in organisations which far outweigh the legal requirements of accommodating their needs. Over 52 per cent of the 29 million American disabled aged between 21 and 64 were in work in 1994. These include 64 per cent of those with a substantial impairment of one or more major life activities which affected their vision, hearing, speech, or capacity to walk, climb stairs, or lift and carry light objects. Of these, two-thirds were typically not disabled at the time of their employment and had suffered impairments associated with age, such as arthritis, or severe injuries in car and other transport accidents. The remaining one-third of disabled employees included people born with disabilities like cerebral palsy. Employment of people with severe disabilities is more problematic although the study shows an increase from 21 to 26 per cent between 1991 and 1994.

Between 1986 and 1995, the number of US firms employing disabled persons increased from 62 to 64 per cent. Most of the latter work in part-time services, rather than manufacturing jobs, mainly because of their impairments. The main incentives for hiring them include their work attendance, commitment, interactions with co-workers, productivity and initiative. Between 60 and 100 per cent of the employees surveyed were 'very satisfied' on each of these job-related factors but only 40 per cent were as satisfied with their interactions with customers, which may have been due to the latter's discomfort/prejudice at being served by a disabled person.

## Legislation

Shaw and Barry[16] note that discrimination against the disabled was made illegal in the USA under the Americans with Disabilities Act 1944, almost thirty years before racial and sexual discrimination were similarly treated. The reason was to ensure that injured veterans returning home from World War II were not excluded from the labour market because of a disability. Several Acts have been introduced since then including the Americans with Disabilities Act 1990 which influenced UK and other EU legislation in extending equal opportunities legislation to disabled people in most developed countries.

British organisations have to comply with the requirements of the Disability Discrimination Act 1995, by ensuring that equal opportunities are provided for those of the UK's six million disabled people in their employment. Under the Act, and the Disability Rights Commission Act 1999, a National Disability Council and a Commission have been established to advise the Department of Trade and Industry (DTI) on the training needs of disabled people; and issue appropriate codes of practice in the latter case. Preparation for employment is provided by the Employment Rehabilitation Service (ERS) which operates assessment and training centres to assist disabled people towards employment. It also advises employers with disabled staff on aids and equipment, occupation health, ergonomics, etc.

## Ageism/age discrimination

Abel[17] defines ageism as 'the practice of either prejudice or discrimination against a particular age group, and generally involves the promotion of false stereotypes about the members of that group', adding that 'An ethic of justice calls for the elimination of ageism, since age discrimination inhibits the fair and accurate determination of each person's true potential.'

Although certain age groups have probably always been subjected to unfair treatment, the concept of ageism, or age discrimination, is apparently a relatively recent social phenomenon in the USA. Discrimination against the aged has a longer history in Europe. In Britain, for example, when poor married couples of advanced years could no longer support themselves through manual work in the nineteenth century, husbands and wives were separated and spent their declining years in male and female workhouses. With rapid improvements in medical care, however, during the last century, a pervasive youth culture developed in the United States in which old people were frequently devalued and denigrated. Although the term 'ageism' is still used primarily to describe society's negative view of the elderly, most social scientists now believe that other age groups, such as that of young children, can also be subject to ageism.

## Discrimination against the elderly

Prejudice against the elderly appears to be the strongest form of ageism in the United States. Many researchers have discovered pervasive but erroneous beliefs that all old people are senile, cranky, physically unattractive, weak, and without sexual desire. Many Americans have an extremely stereotyped view of the elderly in which old people are seen as useless individuals who place both an emotional and financial burden on the rest of society. Abel (ibid) believes that the numerous derogatory terms that are used to describe the elderly, such as 'coot', 'geezer', 'old hag', 'old buzzard' and 'over the hill', are merely a reflection of the negative view that many Americans have towards elderly individuals.

In Western society, elderly minority women experience a triple oppression because of stereotypes and discrimination. Such terms fly in the face of research conducted by gerontologists, who study ageing and the needs of the elderly. In a review of research on the aged, psychologist David Myers, quoted by Abel, concluded in 1992 that many elderly individuals are physically healthy, socially active and mentally alert. Although most individuals experience some decline in mental and physical abilities with advancing age, the vast majority of older adults remain capable of living happy and productive lives. Stereotypical beliefs about the frail and lonely elderly are often based on worst-case scenarios, and they should not be applied to the whole population of aged individuals.

## Practical concerns

In addition to developing a poor self-image because of the negative social stereotypes that abound in our society, many elderly individuals experience discrimination in practical matters as well. Perhaps the most blatant example of this is the common practice of mandatory retirement at the age of 60 or 65, which forces many older adults to stop working when they are still competent and talented. While many organisations have begun to question this practice, it is common for healthy individuals to be forced from their professions simply because of their chronological age. There is a growing awareness in Britain, other EU countries and the USA that ageism not only contradicts the democratic ideals of fairness and equal treatment for all, but the welfare costs of early retirement are rising steeply as people live longer. Apart from the moral imperative that a society which strives to promote justice must treat people in an equitable fashion, regardless of their chronological age, demographic trends indicate that all Western governments will have to introduce radical changes in social welfare policy towards the elderly early in the twenty-first century. The alternative, if current policies prevail, is that the tax burden of the anticipated diminishing proportion of the population in full-time employment would have to rise to unacceptably high levels over the next two decades.

## Synopsis

- Discrimination has a long history in most communities and is a multi-faceted activity that denies negative rights to people through the practices of segregation, stereotyping and prejudice which can, for example, result in wage discrimination against minority groups in organisations.
- Opinions have differed since classical times, less about the inequity of denying the individual's right to equality and justice, than about whether these should be restored as positive rights that guarantee equal opportunities for minority groups in organisations.
- Sexual discrimination also denies negative rights to women, which are reinforced through gender-based wage discrimination and the employment of women in predominantly low paid jobs in organisations.
- Sex equality, as the provision of equal rights, has historically been denied to women by the reluctance of those in positions of power and influence in society to recognise that men and women merit equal treatment, as sex differences on their own have never justified discrimination against women employed in organisations.
- Sexual discrimination against women in organisations may also take the form of sexism, sexual abuse and harassment or sexual stereotyping behaviours, which are all illegal and may lead to the imposition of various penalties if senior management fails to ensure that codes of practice are upheld which should eradicate these activities.
- Ethical arguments over discrimination against the disabled are similar to those on racial and sexual discrimination. Segregation, stereotyping and prejudice can lead to physical security, autonomy, etc. being withheld and the loss of medical care, education and suitable employment without wage discrimination unless these are guaranteed by law.
- Ageism encourages discrimination against particular age groups and has led to loss of employment for people under the legal retirement age. However, changes in the birth and mortality rates are expected to reduce welfare benefits in developed countries, which will probably lead to this discriminatory practice being eradicated.

## Review and discussion questions

**1** What are the three main types of behaviour that may lead to the withholding of negative rights when discrimination occurs?

**2** Why are equality and justice regarded as important concepts in the restoration of positive rights as a way of eradicating discrimination?

**3** What part has wage discrimination played in denying equal opportunities to minority groups in organisations?

**4** Explain how the three main uses of the term 'sex equality' have been interpreted to eradicate discrimination against women in organisations and in the wider community.

**5** What are the three main forms of discrimination women may have to contend with as employees in organisations?

**6** What are the three common explanations why slow progress has been made in the erad-ication of sexism in the employment of women in senior management positions?

**7** On what grounds should discrimination against the disabled be regarded as unethical?

**8** What reasons would you give for supporting the view that ageism is likely to be made illegal in most developed countries during the next decade?

## Case study
## Sex discrimination in UK higher education

Wage discrimination against full-time women employees has not yet been eliminated, according to Eurostat, the European Union's statistical office, which reported that women's wages were 76.3 per cent of men's gross hourly full-time earnings in 1999, excluding bonuses, in the 15 EU countries. Amounts ranged from a minimum 68.0 per cent in Greece to a maximum 89.9 per cent in the former East Germany. Brit-ain was in tenth place with average earnings of 73.7 per cent, 2.5 per cent below the EU average, and behind Denmark, Sweden, Luxembourg, Belgium, Finland, West Germany, France, Italy and Spain. The Netherlands was in a surprising fourteenth position behind Austria, Ireland and Portugal (*The Independent*, 10 June 1999).

These findings are supported by a government-backed study which revealed that an average woman will earn almost £250,000 less in her lifetime than a similarly qualified man, even if she has no children and therefore takes no maternity leave that might disrupt her career progress. The TUC called for equal pay laws to be strengthened so that employers are forced to carry out pay audits by gender. Equal opportunities campaigners await a government response to new evidence that women suffer heavy pay discrimination, by compelling employers to prove they pay men and women equally and refusing to do with business with those who do not. The Equal Opportunities Commission, which also supports pay audits, called for legal reform to shorten the lengthy employment tribunal process so that women are able to raise concerns over equal pay anomalies more swiftly.

The report, 'Women's Incomes over the Lifetime', revealed that the pay differen-tial between men and women is as high as 20 per cent, and that women pay this large price simply because of their gender. For example, a professional woman graduate will earn £143,000 less than a similarly qualified male over a lifetime's employment, even if she has no children. Motherhood will cost her an additional £19,000, while having children will cost an unqualified woman worker £285,000 over her working life. The Ministers for Women, Baroness Jay and Tessa Jowell, admitted women were still being hit by a 'female forfeit'. The report also challenges longstanding myths that women's incomes were lower than men's because they took time off to have children.

The Equal Opportunities Commission chairperson, Julie Mellor, called on the government to show leadership by tackling the male/female gap in the public sector in institutions which depend on government grants or contracts. She stated: 'The government should insist that taxpayers' money is not spent paying suppliers who do not pay women equal wages.' She added: 'Twenty-five years after the Sex Discrimination Act was introduced, women are still paid less for equal work and earn less over a lifetime than men, even if they never have children.' The TUC proposed that a body such as the central arbitration committee should be given powers to look at pay structures in general. The TUC particularly wants action to address pay inequality among the lowest paid women workers, who suffer discrimination as members of traditionally low paid sectors such as the caring professions and nursing. The Equal Opportunities Commission supports this proposal and states that, without action, the pay gap would remain stuck at 20 per cent.

Another study by the government's Women's Unit revealed similar deep-rooted inequalities which indicated that an average mother of two children forgoes 55 per cent of her potential lifetime earnings which amounts to an estimated £230,000. According to Baroness Jay, the causes of this 'forfeit of pay' begin before women reach the age of 20 and occur mainly because they do not receive the same career advice as boys. It was also clear that pay inequalities were not always linked to educational qualifications but more to a lack of career information at school. This hides the 'cost of being female' which only became apparent later. Baroness Jay added: 'There is something about being a woman that means you suffer a forfeit on pay which is depressing. There is a built in disadvantage for women, which increases even further when they have children.' The minister added that government ministers would aim to improve information for and advice given to teenage girls and that an improvement in their financial literacy would also be sought so that they could set up their own businesses. Steps would be taken by the Treasury to encourage banks and insurance companies to lend money to encourage more women entrepreneurs.

The differences between government words and deeds are probably no more apparent than in the British higher education sector which is highly dependent on direct funding by the taxpayer. However, disparities between male and female graduate earnings continue to widen and show few signs of being eradicated. To obtain an appointment as a junior lecturer at a UK university, male and female graduate applicants are usually over 25 years of age and hold a master's degree in their specialist field; an increasing number have also been awarded a PhD, or are within sight of completing this qualification in the foreseeable future. Junior lecturers' posts are public appointments in the sense that advertisements appear in leading newspapers, academic journals and also increasingly on the Internet, along with broad terms and conditions and relevant pay scales for successful applicants. What is objectionable, in view of longstanding equal pay legislation, is that female junior lecturers are appointed at salaries at least 10 per cent lower than males of the same age who possess the same academic qualifications. Furthermore, these differentials are not only maintained but actually widen as male and female academics are progressively promoted to lecturers, senior lecturers, principal lecturers, readers, professors and even to the highest post of a university vice-chancellor.

Most vice-chancellors earn over five times more than a junior lecturer, depending on the university, and there is a big variation in the salaries paid to vice-chancellors. Figures published in the education supplements of *The Times* and *The Independent* in February 2000 indicate that the salaries of vice-chancellors ranged from £76,000 (University of London) to £252,000 (London Business School). The average salary paid to the vice-chancellors of over a hundred British universities in 1999 was almost £125,000. Vice-chancellors also received a 4.9 per cent increase for the year ending in July 1999, compared with a 3.5 per cent award to lower paid academic staff.

The University Vice-Chancellors' Committee has criticised the low salaries paid to academic staff but, according to the Association of University Teachers (AUT), despite all the rhetoric, the vice-chancellors are more concerned with their own financial positions than those of others. The AUT argues that, in the absence of an independent academic pay review board, little change is likely to occur in the pay differentials between academics and vice-chancellors. Their concerns need to be understood within the context of three major changes in higher education in Britain since the early 1990s:

■ the creation of new higher education corporations;
■ the impact of the new research assessment exercise (RAE);
■ the gender-based discrimination in vice-chancellors' pay.

**The new higher education corporations**

The widening differential in pay awards between academic staff and the managers of these institutions began soon after British universities and former polytechnics were 'restructured' as higher education corporations under the Further and Higher Education Act 1992. The Privy Council also authorised specific institutions to alter their names and include the word 'University' in their new titles. As a result, all the new corporations were able to award their own degrees, apply for government funds based on their published research output and increase their consultancy arrangements with public and private sector organisations. These consultancies were intended to achieve the related objectives of increasing contact with the non-academic world and contributing 'added value' to the UK economy, which would enable government to reduce its contribution to the rapidly expanding higher education sector. University revenue would also be increased and part of the consultancy fees could be used to supplement the incomes of the academic staff involved.

Shortly before the new Act came into force, academic staff at most new universities were required to sign new contracts of employment in return for an *ex gratia* payment of £1,000. Contracts specified minimum employment hours, including required teaching, course administration and research or consultancy commitments for each staff member. At the same time, a formal division of labour was introduced between university management and academic staff in addition to the existing separation of functions between the latter and the administrative staff, who were mostly female, worked a fixed 40 hours per week and were also less well paid. The new three-tier division of labour between management, academic and administrative staff left university vice-chancellors, their deputies, faculty deans, and heads of department, including those responsible for providing services such as computing, personnel and library services, at the apex of an organisational pyramid which excluded academic and administrative staff.

There was still much unease with the rapid pace of change and the *ad hoc* nature of the reorganisation strategy. As noted above, this created a new university management tier which was responsible for implementing an organisational structure, mostly recommended by outside consultants, and based on private sector models of which few of the new university 'executives' had any direct experience. Attempts to address internal unrest were further exacerbated when a 'matrix' structure was superimposed on the first structure, overlapping the top (management) and middle (academic) tiers of the new hierarchy. This matrix structure included the new post of Programme Area Director (PAD) in each department with overall responsibility for the introduction of new standardised versions of each degree programme, coordination of staff timetables, staff appraisals and the resolution of student problems, etc.

Each PAD worked alongside the departmental head (HOD) and was directly responsible to the deputy vice-chancellor for academic affairs. New subject leaders were also appointed in each department with joint responsibility to both the HOD and PAD for monitoring the teaching and research activities of colleagues in their specialist fields. As the 'budget holder', the HOD was also responsible to the dean for the management of each department. This meant the PAD had no financial resources but had to negotiate these with the HOD. Furthermore, the new subject leaders received no extra remuneration for their additional responsibilities.

These changes were supplemented by the introduction of annual performance appraisals based on management-by-objective (MBO) principles. Appraisals discriminated against new female staff who, as junior lecturers, had few opportunities to carry out personal research which, in turn, meant that they were unable to supplement their low starting salaries with paid consultancies because of lecturing commitments, administrative duties such as course management and the expectation that they would also act as student tutors.

At a time when allegations of 'sleaze' in public life were attracting media attention, not all university vice-chancellors and their executive boards displayed appropriate prudence. Many had already been awarded substantial increases in remuneration and added perks such as executive cars, free housing and generous entertainment and overseas travel arrangements with the approval of the university governors. Some were also allowed to retain paid part-time appointments on the governing boards of other public institutions such as hospital trusts. The vice-chancellors of two new universities were forced to resign after whistleblowers reported financial improprieties.

The AUT opposed these changes in organisational structure but, unlike the larger National Union of Teachers, lacked the political clout to influence either the Conservative government or the Labour opposition before the 1997 election. The union's main concern was that academics specialising in key subjects like computing, electronic engineering and accounting were leaving to take up employment in the private sector, or else took early retirement only to be recruited elsewhere on a part-time basis. The net effect eight years after the 1992 Act was implemented was that four times as many academics aged over 50 years were employed in some departments than staff under 35 years. The lack of 'new blood' was acute in some education departments where the school teachers being trained are now better paid than their higher education lecturers, whose pay has fallen behind by 30 per cent since 1992 (*The Independent Education Supplement*, 27 April 2000, p. 11).

**The new research assessment exercise (RAE)**

Another policy approved under the 1992 Act was the introduction of a research evaluation exercise, which was first carried out at universities by independent peer groups in 1992 and was intended to be repeated every four years. The aim of the RAE system was to introduce a more transparent, independent procedure for ensuring that government funding of university research grants was based on merit. What was probably not anticipated was the extent to which these evaluations would create a competitive 'head hunting' culture in universities which drew unfair comparisons with the recruitment practices of private sector employment agencies. Various universities that had received low RAE ratings in 1992 entered the 'transfer market' by buying in specialist academics with a higher RAE rating from a rival institution. These activities were still in place in 1999, in anticipation of the RAE assessment in 2000. For example, London Business School (LBS) paid six academics more than £150,000 and three more earned over £210,000 from public funds. In 1998, one unnamed LBS academic earned over £220,000 and was the highest paid in the UK (*The Times Higher Education Supplement*, 28 January 2000, p. 10).

**Gender-based discrimination in vice-chancellors' earnings**

The additional payments to attract and retain leading academic researchers had a corresponding impact on the earnings of university vice-chancellors, providing these were not women. For a start, at the beginning of 2000, only 12 of the 168 vice-chancellors and principals of the new higher education corporations were women. The highest paid female was sixty-eighth in the salary rankings, earning less than half of the highest paid British vice-chancellor. Three of these 12 women were among the seven lowest paid in their field. If anything, these disparities in earnings between male and female vice-chancellors have widened since 1992. For example, three of the female vice-chancellors appointed since then receive salaries below those of their male predecessors (by 12.3 and 27.3 per cent in two cases).

At the same time, the salaries of newly appointed male vice-chancellors pulled away by almost the same percentage points. For example, the new heads of four London-based universities were appointed at salaries of 11 to almost 15 per cent higher than their predecessors. A similar new appointee at a university in the Midlands received 20 per cent more than his predecessor. Other leading vice-chancellors received awards three or four times more than an average of 4.9 per cent, which followed a similar rise in 1998. Overall, 94 vice-chancellors and 480 academics were paid over £100,000 in 1999, which was almost double that for 1998, whereas the total earning more than £50,000 was over 5,400 or 15 per cent more than in 1998.

These disparities have been criticised by both the AUT and Natfhe unions, which represent academic staff at British universities. On the issue of gender-based discrimination, an AUT spokesperson said: 'For a woman to be appointed vice-chancellor is evidence of her success. For these excellent individuals then to meet discrimination on the basis of their sex, which would appear to be the case, is shocking and utterly reprehensible.' The head of the universities section of the lecturers' union Natfhe added: 'It does seem as if the endemic discrimination against women goes right to the top. The secretary of state's [for education] letter to funding councils, which requires institutions to implement equal opportunities policies, is underlined by these figures.'

On the issue of the wider disparities with academic staff's pay, various academics interviewed by the *THES* made the following comments:

As long as vice-chancellors have these increases, they don't feel the pressure to fight for the rest of university staff. . . . I would find it embarrassingly difficult to spend that amount of money (when) posts are being left vacant because there isn't enough money to fill them. . . . They have got their pay rise; we don't know when we will get ours. This is a source of irritation to staff. . . . I don't begrudge his salary – on every possible occasion he has said that academic staff should be paid more. . . . Staff in HE remain very despondent. To see vice-chancellors receive a pay award far ahead of ours on a salary that is already much greater than ours adds to that despondency. (*THES* Analysis Report, 28 January 2000, p. 10)

Signs that the government has called the universities to heel were visible in May 2000 when vice-chancellors agreed to overhaul recruitment and promotion procedures, including formal quotas for black or women staff which reflect the population as a whole. A new monitoring group will be set up by the Higher Education Funding Council for England to redress pay differentials and equal opportunities policies, although no mention is made of how the estimated £200 to £400 million needed to fund these changes will be provided (*The Independent*, 8 May 2000).

**Questions**

**1** What reasons would you give for (a) supporting or (b) rejecting the AUT call for an independent academic pay review to be established for the higher education sector in Britain?

**2** As a member of a selection panel that wishes to appoint a younger, less experienced female successor to replace a retiring male vice-chancellor, who has run the local university successfully for almost 20 years, what reasons would you give for (a) supporting or (b) opposing her appointment if the candidate were to insist on being paid the same salary as the retiring vice-chancellor?

**3** As a member of another selection panel that wants to appoint a well-known academic as a successor to a vice-chancellor who has taken early retirement after the local university has achieved a mediocre RAE rating for the third time in over eight years, what reasons would you give for (a) supporting or (b) opposing the proposal that his successor receive a salary 22 per cent higher than that of the retiring vice-chancellor?

## Notes and references

1. Jackson, C.C., Racial Discrimination, *International Encyclopaedia of Ethics*, ed. J.K. Roth, London, Fitzroy-Dearborn, 1995, 231–3.
2. Hayward, J.L., Racism, *International Encyclopaedia of Ethics*, ed. J.K. Roth, London, Fitzroy-Dearborn, 1995, 720–5.
3. Skillen, A.J., Racism, *Encyclopaedia of Applied Ethics*, vol. 3, New York, Academic Press, 1998, 777–89.
4. Kaplan, L.D., Feminism, *International Encyclopaedia of Ethics*, ed. J.K. Roth, London, Fitzroy-Dearborn, 1995, 312–15.
5. Range, L.M., Sexism, *International Encyclopaedia of Ethics*, ed. J.K. Roth, London, Fitzroy-Dearborn, 1995, 791–2.
6. Tong, R., Feminist Ethics, *Encyclopaedia of Applied Ethics*, vol. 2, New York, Academic Press, 1998, 261–8.
7. Johnson, P., Sexual Discrimination, *International Encyclopaedia of Ethics*, ed. J.K. Roth, London, Fitzroy-Dearborn, 1995, 797.
8. Dodds, S., Sexual Equality, *Encyclopedia of Applied Ethics*, vol. 2, New York, Academic Press, 1998, 615–32.

9. McKenna, E., Women's Ethics, *International Encyclopaedia of Ethics*, ed. J.K. Roth, London, Fitzroy-Dearborn, 1995, 937–9.

10. Boehlke, P.R., Sexuality and Sexual Stereotypes, *International Encyclopaedia of Ethics*, ed. J.K. Roth, London, Fitzroy-Dearborn, 1995, 795–8.

11. Taylor, S.C., Sexual Abuse and Harassment, *International Encyclopaedia of Ethics*, ed. J.K. Roth, London, Fitzroy-Dearborn, 1995, 792–3.

12. Grimsley, K.D., Confronting Hard-Core Harassers, *The Washington Post National Weekly Edition*, 27 January 1997, 6–9.

13. Bohren, I., Six Myths of Sexual Harassment, in *Business Ethics Annual Review 1994/95*, Guilford, Conn., Dushkin Publishing, 1994, 66–9.

14. Vandendorpe, M.M., Sexual Stereotypes, *International Encyclopaedia of Ethics*, ed. J.K. Roth, London, Fitzroy-Dearborn, 1995, 794–5.

15. Mergenhagen, P., Enabling Disabled Workers, *American Demographics*, New York, Ithaca, July 1997, 36–42.

16. Shaw, W.H. and Barry, V., *Moral Issues in Business*, 7th edn, Belmont, Calif., Wadsworth, 1998, 424–6.

17. Abel, S.C., Ageism, *International Encyclopaedia of Ethics*, ed. J.K. Roth, London, Fitzroy-Dearborn, 1995, 21–2.

# PART III | Moral Compass exercise

The Moral Compass instruments below are divided into two questionnaires, which should be evaluated using the 7-point Lickert scale shown in Box A. The simple Moral Compass contains the eight statements shown in Box B. The detailed Moral Compass includes the additional eight statements shown in Box C. Each statement corresponds with one of the ethical theories summarised in Chapter 4.

### Instructions

1 Decide whether you wish to complete the simple or the detailed Moral Compass instrument.

2 Read each statement carefully before recording your response, using the 7-point Lickert scale shown in Box A below.

3 Record your scores for each part of the instruments in the Moral Compass section in the Appendix at the end of the book, where the corresponding ethical theories are shown.

### Box A

| Strongly disagree | Disagree | Slightly disagree | Neither agree nor disagree | Slightly agree | Agree | Strongly agree |
|---|---|---|---|---|---|---|
| 1 | 2 | 3 | 4 | 5 | 6 | 7 |

## Box B

**S.1** Business ethics amounts to changing your behaviour to conform with the beliefs and practices of those you need to keep happy.     1  2  3  4  5  6  7

**S.2** People are seldom so harmlessly engaged as when they are working to become rich.     1  2  3  4  5  6  7

**S.3** Anyone who completely trusts others in business is asking for trouble.     1  2  3  4  5  6  7

**S.4** People at work should manage their lives unwastefully, aware that harm to one would mean harm to all.     1  2  3  4  5  6  7

**S.5** Ethical behaviour not only differs in different business communities, it is not the same at different levels in any organisation.     1  2  3  4  5  6  7

**S.6** A business should be organised like a home where each parent has a separate task, but also ensures that the family plays its full part in the community.     1  2  3  4  5  6  7

**S.7** Only if entrepreneurs offer constructive solutions to problems in society, which are also ethical, will they enjoy freedom of action in future.     1  2  3  4  5  6  7

**S.8** S/he who dies rich, dies disgraced.     1  2  3  4  5  6  7

## Box C

**S.9** A prudent manager cannot and should not be expected to keep his/her word when it is to his/her disadvantage.     1  2  3  4  5  6  7

**S.10** A business that makes nothing but money is unlikely to bring out the best qualities in its managers or employees.     1  2  3  4  5  6  7

**S.11** The trouble with the profit system is that it always has been highly unprofitable for most people.     1  2  3  4  5  6  7

**S.12** We have to distinguish between the creation of wealth, from which the community benefits, and the extortion of wealth, from which the community suffers.     1  2  3  4  5  6  7

**S.13** The growth of big business is merely the survival of the fittest – like a rose grown in splendour and fragrance after the early buds around it have been sacrificed.     1  2  3  4  5  6  7

**S.14** The pursuit of gain is the only way we can serve the needs of others whom we do not know.     1  2  3  4  5  6  7

**S.15** It is better to be a tyrant over your bank balance than over your fellow citizens.     1  2  3  4  5  6  7

**S.16** Those who act according to moral rules are idiots and blunderers, unable to take advantage or learn from life.     1  2  3  4  5  6  7

# PART IV

# The external environment

## Learning objectives

After reading this chapter you should be able to:

- understand what is meant by marketing ethics from a utilitarian and a libertarian perspective; and explore potential conflict areas involving product safety, responsibilities to consumers, privacy and respect for the individual;
- discuss ethical issues in marketing communications; manipulation and coercion of vulnerable consumers; and ethical decision making and responsibility;
- evaluate various aspects of responsibilities to consumers involving price fixing, the ethics of selling, warranties and guarantees; and explore how the rights of the individual, as a consumer, are protected;
- outline ethical issues in marketing including misleading or false advertising; shocking or indecent materials; telesales and the invasion of personal privacy; misleading PR communications; and the payment of bribes to secure business;
- discuss the impact of manipulation, coercion and paternalism on vulnerable consumers; and the allocation of responsibility to ensure that appropriate moral remedies are implemented.

## Introduction

Marketing is the most visible functional activity of profit-seeking organisations. This may explain why it is also regarded as the least ethical because of its use of advertising, sales promotions, marketing research and public relations practices. Ethical questions are mostly raised about advertising which is derived from the Latin word *advertere*: 'to make publicly known'. Supporters would claim it has fulfilled this task ethically in helping to raise the living standards of millions of people across the developed world during the twentieth century. They would add that if its content is honest, then advertising, like free speech, is a negative right which should not be banned or censored in an open society. Critics allege, however, that advertising not only encourages people to spend excessively on goods and services they could survive without, if greed and selfishness were not promoted by the media, but it also often misleads and deceives consumers, patronises women and exploits children and other minority groups.

As an academic discipline, marketing is barely seventy years old yet its influence has been so pervasive in what Galbraith[1] describes as 'the affluent society', that more has been published on this subject than on any other business or management topic. Definitions of marketing alter according to its applications although all are linked by the activities of buying or selling goods and services. As De George[2] puts it emphatically: 'Once goods are made, they must be sold. Marketing covers this process.' Unfortunately, the Achilles' heel of marketing as an academic discipline is that it falls somewhere between an art and a science and, even when market research is based on reliable statistical analysis techniques, markets can rarely be predicted with certainty. Not surprisingly, claims to be able to increase or second-guess market demand are often refuted where it matters most – in the marketplace. The need for marketing ethics arises because some practitioners may decide to manipulate market research data or other information in an unlawful or disreputable way to minimise the risk of failure.

## Marketing ethics

Richardson[3] defines marketing ethics as 'the application of ethical evaluation to marketing strategies and tactics.' It involves judgements about what is morally right and wrong for marketing specialists in organisations by seeking to ensure ethical practices are applied in the areas of consumer research, product pricing, promotion and distribution strategies for marketing products and services. Marketing ethics emerged in response to a combination of individual, societal and environmental factors that increased public awareness of the need for more responsible business activities. This was because adverse publicity about business often included revelations of unethical marketing behaviour leading to unsafe products, price fixing, deceptive advertising, legal liability, dubious warranty arrangements and unreliable after-sales services.

How these problems arose, or were handled, was seen to reflect the ethical attitude of managers in different organisations towards consumers. One firm might typically accept the need to balance its business interests with the rights of the consumer, believing the latter's loyalty, even dependence, on the goods and services provided was vital for the continuing success of the organisation. Managers in another company, on the other hand, might have rejected the notion that they had any social responsibilities in a market-driven economy, believing that the individual consumer always had a choice which would be exercised if the company's goods and services were unsatisfactory. These rival views are explored in the following summary of utilitarian and libertarian perspectives on the role of the company and the consumer in a modern market-driven society.

## Utilitarian and libertarian views on consumerism

Many of the issues raised in marketing ethics were first discussed in the writings of two eminent economists, Galbraith[1] and Hayek[4]. Galbraith drew a major distinction between an 'impoverished society' and an 'affluent society' which still underpins discussions about 'Third World countries' and 'developed nations'. Hence, in an impoverished society, supply is always behind the demand for basic goods and services related to the survival needs of food, energy and habitat whereas in an affluent society, this 'urgency of wants' has been satisfied. Those wishing to profit from the production of goods and services can only prosper if higher order wants and desires are created and gratified in members of the population, hence the notion of a 'consumer society'.

Yet these wants and desires are not 'innate' and people can, but may not wish to, do without them, as anyone who has given up smoking or lost weight on a diet would confirm. Two explanations are offered by Galbraith for why people learn to cultivate these wants and desires. First, as members of a gregarious species, people constantly compare themselves with others and feel envy, perhaps even shame, which fuels the need in them to keep up with their more affluent neighbours. Second, most people are influenced in this pursuit by marketing and advertising techniques, the main aim of which is to create new, and sustain existing, wants and desires for products and services.

The role of advertising is therefore critical in sustaining an affluent society and Galbraith's key theoretical assumption is that, in an impoverished society, demand constantly exceeds supply, whereas in an affluent society, technology becomes integrated with more efficient production techniques to ensure that supply exceeds demand. Manufacturers must therefore persuade people to 'consume' this excess demand by advertising their products and services until a 'dependence effect' is created. For example, as in the case of people who become so fond of fast food and fizzy drinks that essential vitamins may be excluded from their diets.

Galbraith makes two further points about the affluent society relevant to marketing ethics. First, since wants and needs are artificially created through advertising, the resulting goods and services purchased often have no utility to society, in the sense that they provide no benefits of lasting value to society. Secondly, because it is more efficient and profitable for manufacturers to concentrate on the supply of goods and services, the provision of education, welfare, health and security (i.e. police and fire services) tends to be neglected or regarded as a public responsibility. For example, government agencies advertise for teachers, probation officers, nurses and police constables and not the leading companies in the proposed iX European Stock Exchange index. These public services have to be paid for as taxes from the public purse. Not everyone likes, or is required, to pay taxes, so successive governments have to ration public services or risk loss of popularity and political power. Galbraith's analysis concludes with a utilitarian critique that, in an affluent society, marketing and advertising lead to a shift in resources away from areas of benefit and need to the greatest number of people, by promoting goods and services of no intrinsic benefit which gratify only the immediate wants and desires of individuals in society.

Hayek[4] refutes Galbraith's analysis by stating that even if our wants and desires arise as a result of marketing and advertising techniques, it cannot be claimed that their value to the individual is without urgency or importance. Moreover, if aggregated, society benefits considerably (e.g. from the new jobs and the increased wealth created), even if this demand is artificially stimulated. He extends this argument by questioning the notion that these artificially created wants and desires are so exceptional by noting that even the aesthetic feelings that characterise a civilised society are also 'acquired tastes'. That is to say, people do not have innate desires for art, music or literature. As an example, he notes that a writer does not wait until a demand arises for a book before writing it: on the contrary, the book is written first and, hopefully, demand follows later.

Hayek also draws attention to Galbraith's ambiguous use of the word 'dependent', in his claim that marketing and advertising make consumption dependent on production. In fact, the *Oxford English Dictionary* gives five different meanings for the word 'dependent'; two of which are irrelevant here. The three other meanings of dependent are:

- contingent on or determined by or conditioned by something else;
- resting entirely on someone or something for maintenance or support or other requirement;
- obliged to do something or unable to do without something maintained at another's cost.

The first of these meanings of dependent presents no problems for Hayek who accepts Galbraith's analysis that people buy goods and services either to keep up with friends and neighbours, or because of an interesting product promotion or sales campaign. However, the two part company over the second and third meanings of dependent. Hayek rejects the notion that manufacturers place restrictions on what consumers can purchase and then manipulate them by advertising to ensure that they actually purchase these goods or services. On the contrary, from a libertarian standpoint, individual consumers always should have a choice. For him, governments and other agencies have no right to intervene in the way the market works, other than to ensure minimum public safety and legal safeguards, so that this individual freedom of choice is always preserved.

## Potential conflict areas in marketing ethics

The difficulty with both of these viewpoints is that morally questionable behaviour on the part of manufacturers and marketing practitioners may interfere with the way either version of the market economy is supposed to operate in the following areas:

- product safety;
- responsibilities to consumers;
- privacy and respect for the individual;
- ethical issues in marketing communications;
- manipulation and coercion of vulnerable consumers;
- ethical decision making and responsibility in marketing.

### Product safety

Potential ethical problems covering all aspects of product safety start at the product development stage with the interaction of marketing professionals and operations management specialists. Integrated activities may include the concept generation of new products, screening, design evaluation, prototyping and the environmental impact analysis of final product designs and packaging (Slack *et al.*[5]). Further involvement with operations management specialists may extend to organising pilot trials, the setting of quality standards, branding decisions, and the sensitive issue of the relationship between the product life-cycle and planned obsolescence.

As Richardson[3] observes, ethical problems arise whenever marketing professionals propose or condone the use of 'misleading, deceptive, and unethical practices' in production or packaging processes. In the 1990s, this practice often resulted in unsubstantiated claims being made about products that appealed more to health-conscious, environmentally concerned people than to other consumers. Ethical behaviour occurs when safe, approved product development techniques are used to provide a product quality that meets the specified requirements and general expectations of consumers, by use of brand names that accurately communicate basic information about the product in packaging that realistically depicts its size, contents and other essential characteristics.

The transportation and storage of perishable products, in particular, may raise ethical problems if agreed distribution procedures, such as a first-in first-out (FIFO) policy, are ignored, leading to possible public health or safety hazards if product shelf-life or sell/use by dates are exceeded. A more serious prospect is the risk that product deterioration is not accidental or the result of indifference, but occurs because 'planned obsolescence' is built in at the design stage with the aim of cutting costs by persuading the consumer to purchase a potentially dangerous product. Some cases of planned obsolescence are acceptable to society – newspapers, calendars and diaries are normally discarded when they are out of date; however, there is less tolerance of medicines and drugs, for example, being sold after the specified expiry date.

Consumers are also entitled to feel aggrieved if planned obsolescence results in premature wear or damage to expensive items of clothing, or when fashion changes occur too rapidly (e.g. the frequent changes of the home and away 'strips' of English Premier League football clubs which, at over £40 per shirt, are exorbitantly priced for most adolescent supporters). Similar sources of complaint involve dubious design or other functional changes to products such as personal computers, cars, mobile phones and household furniture. Independent bodies like the Consumers Association argue that this sort of planned obsolescence often leads to resource shortages, price rises, increased waste (of unfashionable goods) and environmental pollution. Their concerns are rarely addressed by marketing specialists who argue that planned obsolescence is in response to consumer demand for change which also contributes to the national economy by increasing sales revenue and maintaining employment. This account is questionable in UK retailing where the 'lead time' (elapsing between the placing and delivery of orders) for Christmas toys, which are usually imported, is over 18 months, not one Christmas but two ahead.

## Responsibilities to consumers

**Consumerism**
A whole raft of legislation has been introduced in the USA and EU countries since the 1960s to protect the rights of consumers from possible exploitation by more powerful suppliers in the marketplace. An important contributor to the movement known

as consumerism is the civil rights activist Ralph Nader (see Chapter 1), whose book *Unsafe at Any Speed* (1965) identified dangerous design features of the Chevrolet Corvair car, which led to major changes in US legislation. The thrust of consumerism is to focus attention on ways of restricting the power of manufacturers by campaigning for legislation to ensure that their responsibilities to consumers are met in areas such as product safety, fair pricing and honest advertising.

Nader and like-minded civil rights activists approached the daunting problem of how best to challenge leading suppliers, especially manufacturers and retailers that were subsidiaries of giant corporations, to prevent exploitation of individual buyers. They approached this problem by founding consumer organisations such as the Center for Auto Safety, Public Citizen and the Health Research Group. Another strategy was to establish various buyer-owned cooperatives to promote safer products, lower prices and more honest disclosure in advertising. A further aim of the movement was to draw public attention to the growing complexity of labelling of many consumer products, which was thought to prevent individual buyers from making informed judgements before purchase.

## Price fixing

Philosophers have disagreed since classical times about the notion of a 'just price', which is fair to both producers and consumers alike. Nevertheless, price fixing is a criminal offence in the USA, UK and other EU countries. It usually occurs following a secret agreement by the suppliers or sellers to charge the same price for a product or service to consumers. On both an ethical and a legal level, the practice is regarded as inequitable because it exploits and misleads consumers who have less power and information than suppliers in bargaining over prices. Price fixing occurs because it is profitable to suppliers who are able to exploit the consumers' lack of knowledge about fixed costs, overheads, switching and storage costs, etc., which enable suppliers to manipulate prices so that profits can be maximised.

Of all the issues raised by consumer organisations, price fixing has probably become the most regulated area of public policy in most Western nations since it was first made illegal in the USA over 100 years ago. In particular, the Sherman Anti-trust Act 1890 forbade all contracts and combinations of business (as cartels), or conspiracies between suppliers, which acted against the public interest in restraint of trade. Precisely what constitutes a restraint of trade has been decided periodically by the US courts, as in the case of the ruling which led to the break-up of the Standard Oil monopoly in 1911, mentioned in Chapter 1 and the case study to Chapter 3, which reputedly left John D. Rockefeller and his fellow directors wealthier than beforehand. Conceivably, the recent US court ruling to break up the Microsoft Corporation may well leave Bill Gates and his associates even more prosperous.

The extent to which more efficient pricing policies are the direct result of consumer 'watchdog' monitoring (e.g. by the Consumers Association) and government monitoring, rather than the effects of direct competition among suppliers, is difficult to establish. Unethical pricing at the point of sale is easier to control because intervention on behalf of consumers in the UK is delegated to local authority inspectors. Their responsibilities extend to such anti-consumer practices as price discrimination, price fixing, predatory pricing and other misleading actions such as the switching of labels, non-disclosure of unit prices at display points and inflating prices to allow for bogus 'sale mark-downs' at a later date.

Specific questions have been raised about the ethics of pricing decisions relating to products which are regarded as necessities such as basic food items, children's clothing, household items, lighting and heating for the aged, and pharmaceutical products. For example, a continuous battle is waged between purchasers and the multinational manufacturers of healthcare products over the high prices of new drugs for life-threatening illnesses such as cancer, coronary problems and HIV/AIDS. Bulk purchasers such as health authorities are required to ensure that the taxpayer is not overcharged as a result of covert price fixing by manufacturers. The latter often seek to justify their pricing policies, however, by insisting that the profits from one successful drug have to carry the research and development costs of previous commercially unsuccessful products.

**Ethics of selling**

The selling of goods and services has also exercised the minds of moral philosophers and theologians such as Saint Thomas Aquinas (see Chapter 4) since the Middle Ages. Economists, led by Adam Smith, have argued that when a buyer and a seller with equal knowledge of a product reach agreement and a transaction occurs in the marketplace, the situations of both buyer and seller are improved; otherwise, one or the other would withdraw from the transaction. Nevertheless, since both buyer and seller are seeking to maximise their positions, with one seeking the lowest and the other the highest price, it is to be expected that each will try to take advantage of the other, sometimes unfairly. Left to market forces, the 'just price' will mainly depend on whether the buyer and seller have equal knowledge and the same interest in completing the transaction. In a modern context, however, products and services have become so diverse and some manufacturers, as sellers, have grown so massive, that to talk of equal knowledge and power between the supplier and individual buyer in a global market is, frankly, fatuous. This imbalance informs much of the criticism by consumer groups of transnational corporations which is discussed in Part V.

The ethics of any sale are initially linked to the safety and appropriateness of the product or service purchased in the transaction and the related issue of product liability. The latter should be answered by the question: who is responsible and liable for any damage suffered by the individual or society due to this product or service? In the past, this question was covered under common law according to the principle of *caveat emptor* (let the buyer beware). Both the buyer and seller were assumed to be equals and, once the transaction was completed, the buyer was held to be legally and morally responsible for the product, including any harm it might cause to a third party. Since World War II, first in the USA and later in EU countries, responsibility and liability for the product have increasingly been placed on the manufacturer. The ethical justification for this shift in legal responsibility is that the manufacturer, as seller, has more knowledge than the buyer about the product. The seller is also regarded in law as better placed to prevent harm from occurring, and also has more resources to bear the financial liability should such harm occur than the buyer, especially when the latter is an individual consumer. In short, manufacturers are increasingly expected to anticipate potential hazards or possible misuse of their products by customers and take appropriate preventative measures beforehand.

**Warranties and guarantees**

With this shift in legal responsibilities, assurances needed to be given to consumers as enforceable warranties and guarantees that their purchases would meet certain minimum standards. Otherwise, in their absence, as Sobczak[6] observes, some sellers might choose to lie about the quality of their products. The meanings of the terms 'guarantee' and 'warranty' are morally equivalent, if not strictly legally synonymous, in the normal meaning of a business transaction. For example, in Britain and in the USA, the legal term 'warranty' appears in contracts and sales transactions, whereas the word 'guarantee' is more commonly used in everyday language. Both terms imply, however, that some form of assurance is given to the buyer by the seller about the quality, or other standards, of the purchased product or service for a stated minimum period.

Warranties can be oral but increasingly take the form of written statements. Some warranties are implied and remain in force even though they are not directly communicated to the buyer by the seller, who has some protection and can specify that the product or service is warrantied only for 'reasonable use', which is usually specified as an attached warning or in the instructions for use. The effect is that the seller accepts no ethical responsibility for any harm that may occur if the product or service is not used in the specified way. Ethical and legal concerns often overlap in this area of deciding how a warranty should be interpreted and many consumer complaints or legal actions about product liability hang on the precise meaning of 'reasonable use'.

In the UK, warranties and guarantees are covered under a raft of consumer protection legislation which is different in Scotland from that in England and Wales (e.g. as in the Contract (Scotland) Act 1997). Warranties are covered under contracts and buyers' protection legislation in the Hire-Purchase Act 1964, the Misrepresentation Act 1967, the Supply of Goods (Implied Terms) Act 1973, the Consumer Credit Act 1974, the Sale of Goods Act 1974, the Sale of Goods (Amendment) Act 1994, and the Sale and Supply of Goods Act 1994. In the above legislation, the major terms of any contract are referred to as the conditions and the minor terms as the warranties, under which the injured party is entitled to claim damages. In the USA, written warranties are covered by the Magnuson-Moss Warranty Act (1975).

As a final point, it should be noted that the ethical responsibility of the seller, or manufacturer, to provide and abide by the conditions of a warranty normally applies to new products only; and consumers are afforded less protection in both the UK and the USA when they buy used goods, particularly if the goods are specifically sold 'as is' or 'as seen'. In such transactions, the above-mentioned *caveat emptor* principle applies.

## Privacy and the consumer

**Consumer privacy** Two important types of privacy were mentioned in Chapter 7, namely employee privacy and consumer privacy. Spinello[7] identifies consumer privacy as an expanding subject that covers the information compiled by data collectors such as marketing firms, insurance companies and retailers; the use of credit information collected by credit agencies; and also the rights of consumers to control information about themselves in commercial transactions. The increase in commercial transactions based on extensive sharing of personal data has important ethical implications because it can lead to an erosion of privacy that undermines the autonomy of individuals and their capacity to control major and minor aspects of their own lives. All organisations involved in such activities have a legal and moral responsibility to ensure that the privacy rights of the individual are upheld.

Consumer privacy focuses on the activity of acquiring personal information about individuals (e.g. as potential clients or actual customers), which may be acquired voluntarily in an interview, or bought and sold through a business transaction in which the identity of the individual must remain confidential. Client privacy is of paramount concern in the relevant UK, US and EU data protection legislation. In the case of the non-commercial collection, collation and storage of data on consumers, the concept of client privacy is equally important. All medical, educational, employment and criminal records, where applicable, are subject to the same mandatory privacy constraints. Spinello also identifies the issues that need to be addressed to ensure the confidential protection and movement of consumer (and client) data as follows:

- the potential for data to be sold to unscrupulous vendors;
- the trustworthiness and professionalism of data collectors;
- the potential for combining data in new ways to create detailed, composite profiles of individuals;
- the difficulty of correcting inaccurate information once it has been reproduced in many different files.

## Ethical issues in marketing communications

Christie[8] identifies the following ethical issues that arise in marketing communications as 'common concerns':

- misleading or false advertising;
- shocking, tasteless or indecent material in marketing communications;
- telesales calls and junk mail that invade personal privacy;
- misleading PR communications;
- payment of bribes to secure business.

**Misleading or false advertising**

As Galbraith noted, advertising plays a hugely important sociological and economic role in the different forms of market-driven capitalism adopted in most developed nations. In the USA, for example, Farhi[9] reports that just over a decade ago, nearly $120 billion was spent annually on all forms of media advertising. This was almost $500 per head of population which exceeds the total US government estimated spending on all forms of public and private education. The comparison is apposite because as a rule of thumb, if advertising is truthful and informative and complements formal education, objections are usually based on an ideological rejection of capitalism. When advertising is found to be misleading, false or intrusive, however, ethical and legal questions are appropriate about the rights of individual consumers and the powerful role of business in a democratic society. For example, Draper[10] criticises 'the persistent bad faith' of much American advertising which, according to Shaw and Barry[11], takes the form of ambiguity, concealment of facts, exaggeration and psychological appeals as described below.

*Ambiguity* is ethically unacceptable because it attempts to misinform the consumer through indirect deception. In developed countries, codes of practice are accepted by most companies, which are monitored by regulatory bodies such as the Advertising Standards Authority (ASA) in Britain and the Federal Trade Commission (FTC) in the United States. Examples of ambiguous advertising are legion and range from claims that eating certain brands of 'light', low-calorie bread will lead to 'loss of weight' (how the weight of the bread consumed leads to weight loss is never explained), to claims in the USA by the makers of Listerine that the mouthwash effectively fights bacteria and sore throats, which were untrue, and led to the powerful FTC forcing the manufacturers to run a costly nationwide TV disclaimer campaign.

*Concealment of facts* usually takes the form of a company excluding unflattering details from independent surveys about the quality, price or shelf-life of their products, or suppressing other facts about poor service. The practice is more common than generally realised and an advertising agency insider informed the *Washington Post*[12] that the usual thinking in planning a campaign is first to establish what can be said, true or false, to sell the product. The second step is to agree how to say this effectively and get away with it. The aims are to ensure that those who buy the product will not feel let down because what is promised fails to materialise and also that any advertisement escapes censure by the FTC.

*Exaggeration* refers to the misleading advertising practice of making claims for products and services without supporting evidence. Christie[8] distinguishes between a deliberate intention and what David Ogilvie, the advertising executive, calls 'puffery', which is the harmless use of superlatives in advertisements. Two examples should clarify the differences. First, not even the most die-hard Scunthorpe United supporter is taken in by shouts of 'Super Scunny is magic!' from fellow fans on the terraces. On the other hand, claims by cosmetic conglomerates that their skin-care products are 'anti-ageing' cross the line between puffery and deception, not just because they are intended to mislead, but because independent research indicates that such claims are often believed by those who are anxious to halt the ageing process.

*Psychological appeals* in advertising refer to attempts to persuade consumers by emotional means rather than by appeals based on reason. Examples include advertisements that appeal to a need for power, prestige, or an unfulfilled gratification or sexual fantasy, by offering stereotypes of masculine or feminine behaviour. Other techniques sentimentalise the roles of children, the family, grandparents, in-laws, neighbours, or household pets and rely on psychological appeals which are unethical simply because they promise experiences which cannot be delivered.

**Shocking, tasteless or indecent material**

This includes any materials that offend public standards in the opinion of religious leaders, educationalists, professional bodies, government or the media, which are normally 'censored' by the advertising regulatory body in the country concerned. A recent example was the Benetton billboard campaign which achieved notoriety by including photographic material that tried to catch attention with what some regarded as shocking and tasteless subject matter.

**Telesales calls and junk mail**

It is easy to share the concerns of Spinello[7] about unjustified intrusions on individual privacy from the increase in telesales calls and junk mail which have probably caused more annoyance than satisfaction to members of the public. Precisely how name lists containing addresses and other personal details on unsuspecting people come to be sold is rarely disclosed by institutional sellers or purchasers. One version is that the data chain starts when local authorities, which can legally hold data on householders, sell this to interested market research agencies, which use it for legitimate purposes before selling name lists to third parties. At the end of an unseen chain are unsolicited companies that pester householders by cold calling or with junk mail in an effort to sell their goods and services. The unethical invasion of privacy is prohibited under current UK data protection legislation and regulations exist to ensure good commercial practice. Individuals are also entitled to have their names omitted from the bought-in lists.

**Misleading PR communications**

Christie[8] describes the purpose of PR as 'to create and manage relations between the firm and its various publics', which raises the potential issue that there 'must always be a temptation in so doing to place undue emphasis on the positive aspects of the firm's actions'. There is no shortage of examples in which this policy has 'flattered to deceive', as in the case of the UK rail companies mentioned in an earlier case study (Chapter 2) which stressed their efficiency and use of the latest technology at the time of their launch, only to be criticised for not spending money on automated braking systems which could have avoided death and injury to their passengers during a major train accident in 1999. No doubt with this sort of example in mind, Christie stresses the need for PR firms to take an 'enlightened view of [their] long-term self-interest'. This entails gaining public trust to avoid being charged with making false and misleading statements when things go wrong 'if they are to do any good for their clients at all'.

**Payment of bribes to secure business**

The issues of employee fraud and white collar crime have already been discussed in Chapter 6 and these forms of unethical (and unlawful) behaviour obviously extend to marketing professionals as well. Illicit activities may range from the bribing of purchasing managers with small 'gifts' at Christmas to large 'kick backs' (the free painting of a purchasing manager's house by a paint company, naturally in return for placing a large order, and also paid holidays abroad, are examples which, when discovered, resulted in the dismissal of the employees involved). The moral issue involved is not complicated and the taking of a bribe is unethical because another party (e.g. the company or its shareholders) has to pay more for an order than it would have done had the bribe been offered as an above-board discount.

IBM's business conduct guidelines[13] tackle this problem head-on by stating that 'Gifts between employees of different companies range from widely distributed advertising novelties, which you may both give and receive, to bribes, which unquestionably you may not.' This statement is followed by examples of acceptable behaviour covering free meals, entertainment and even transport to overseas factory locations, before the question of gifts, services and entertainment is raised as follows:

> In the case of gifts, services and entertainment, however, there is a point of unacceptability. The difficulty lies in determining where that point is, unless, of course, laws make that clear. One way to approach the question is to recognise that the purpose of both gifts and entertainment is to create good will. If they do more than that and *unduly influence* the recipient or make the person feel obliged to pay back the other company by giving it business, then they are unacceptable.

## Manipulation and coercion of vulnerable consumers

Few would disagree with De George's[2] observation that TV advertisements aimed at pre-school children in the USA are a clear case of coercion which cannot be condoned. Christie[8] adds that issues such as coercion and truth-telling lead directly to questions about the special requirements of vulnerable groups in ethical market communications campaigns. For example, in many countries stricter controls are imposed on the content and timing of TV advertisements intended for children. Christie adds that this is based on 'an enhanced concern for the potential of advertisements and other promotional materials to delude and disturb these audiences'.

The libertarian critic, ever concerned about ensuring the freedom and right to be left alone of each individual, might raise hypothetical questions about how justified is this concern to protect the vulnerable groups in society. Christie, quoting a report in the *Guardian* (Liz Buckingham, 20 April 1996), notes that UK children have a disposal income of £1.6 billion per year, with an indirect influence over a further £8 billion. They are also

> significant consumers of TV (very high proportions have their own set) and seem to have much better advertising recall than adults. Parents . . . could be forgiven for feeling that they are being held to ransom . . . [when] . . . in Europe, the focus is on the ethics of advertising to children, but, in the UK, advertisers are homing in on the opportunity.

UK developments appear to be following US trends rather than those in continental Europe as, according to Shaw and Barry[11], US children aged 4–12 years receive or earn the dollar-equivalent of over £13 billion per year, of which nearly £11 billion is spent on snack foods and toys. Charren[14] adds that 'The two things sold to children most on TV are toys and food.' He states that 98 per cent of the food advertising is for 'products children don't have to eat, non-nutritive things. Now in fact they're designing foods that would never be on the market if it weren't for television and its ability to sell them.' These UK and US examples acknowledge the power of TV advertising to exploit the susceptibilities of children and provide support for the civil rights ethical principle that all members of a democratic society, if not directly discriminated against, should be protected against possible manipulation and exploitation by those with more power and resources at their disposal such as manufacturers and television conglomerates.

De George also criticises subliminal advertising as manipulative because it influences people's choices without their knowledge and, therefore, without their consent. This criticism is extended to the use of subliminal messages such as 'Don't steal' or 'Don't shoplift' in music tapes played in departmental stores and supermarkets, even though US research indicates that theft is lower than in other stores as a result. De George's ethical stance is based on the libertarian argument that because the customers do not know the content of the subliminal message, they have no way of deciding if it is moral or otherwise. In short, the individual's right to privacy extends to morally acceptable messages against shoplifting, which should not be broadcast without their knowledge or informed consent. No more than it would be ethical, for example, to alter the content of the subliminal message with the aim of manipulating unsuspecting customers to purchase, say, slow-moving stocks of concrete garden gnomes.

## Ethical decision making in marketing

**Paternalism**    Although De George[2] makes the point that 'anything that is illegal to manufacture, and sell to the general public cannot legally be advertised', he acknowledges that there are contentious areas such as those involving cigarette smoking and the sale of alcohol where public health issues may clash with individual freedoms. Yet he defends the role of the American FTC or the Advertising Standards Authority in the UK against the charge of paternalism, even though libertarian critics would insist that, unless advertising is actually dishonest and therefore illegal, consumers cannot be coerced by legal advertising messages into buying anything that they do not really want.

On the question of cigarette smoking, De George accepts that the question of whether to smoke or not is simply a matter of choice or preference. In fairness, however, he was writing before the revelation that cigarette companies had been systematically deceiving the public for years (see the case study in Chapter 4). Philip Morris Corporation, for example, spent over $800 million annually on advertising at a time when cigarette manufacturers were being criticised for manipulating so-called 'vulnerable' groups, including young cinema audiences in EU countries; and also women and upwardly mobile African Americans in the USA. Similar criticisms have been levelled at brewing companies for targeting young, inner city males and females in the UK as well as African Americans in the 18–25 age group.

Both examples reveal dilemmas that arise in applied ethics sometimes before the public becomes fully aware of the relevant facts so that the law can be changed. This raises awkward questions about how civil liberties (e.g. not being subjected to the effects of passive smoking) are to be reconciled with the individual's freedom of choice (i.e. whether to smoke or not). Another emerging social issue questions the ethical responsibilities of brewing companies in addressing the increase in alcoholism in UK males and females in the 18–25 age group (*ITN* Report, 10 May 2000), when licensing hours have also recently been extended. What is the appropriate role of other members of the public? Should they merely turn the proverbial 'blind eye', or risk being accused of paternalism and intruding on the individual freedom of others, by drawing attention to the frequency and content of advertisements for beer and other alcoholic drinks, mostly on TV, that are directly targeted at this age group?

All of the above examples fall under the heading of promotion in marketing, which is subject to the most scrutiny from an ethical standpoint, because advertising, personal selling and other promotional activities are the primary methods employed in marketing communications (Fill[15]). Despite the importance most marketing professionals attach to communicating product and service information to the public in an ethical way, promotion is the most visible of marketing activities and, however unfair it may be to rely on stereotyping as a response, the reputation of marketing will be damaged as a professional discipline whenever cases of misleading and deceptive advertisements, or dubious sales tactics, are reported by other members of the media.

## The allocation of responsibility and moral remedies

De George[2] identifies five groups that are ethically responsible whenever some advertising practices are adjudged to be immoral. With the UK in mind, a sixth group needs to be added since the ASA is a separate body from government, unlike the more powerful Federal Trade Commission (FTC) in the USA, which was created in 1914. The six groups are:

- the producer or manufacturer;
- the marketing company/advertising agency;
- the media (e.g. TV, newspapers, etc.);
- the general public;
- the body responsible for upholding standards (e.g. the ASA);
- the government.

The problem is how to apportion moral responsibility whenever unethical advertising practices occur. For example, the producer can be held morally responsible for manufacturing offending goods (or services), but not entirely. After all, it could be said that both the marketing company and the TV authority or newspaper owners could/should have refused to accept the advertising contract. Hence, De George asserts that the general public do not act immorally when they look at immoral advertisements for how could they object, without having had the experience? Nor do they have any moral responsibility to take action afterwards; as, indeed, most people in the UK do not. He adds that they perform a public service when they make their feelings or perceptions known, should they decide that an advertisement is untruthful, misleading or deceptive.

Since bodies like the ASA are required to monitor advertising in Britain to ensure that all parties comply with agreed codes of practice, it would be morally responsible for acting upon any breach of standards that is brought to its attention.

The government's role in a democratic society should ideally be that of an 'arm's length regulator' which would allow the agencies mentioned above to apply a rigorous system of self-regulation over their various activities. However, government could exercise its elected right to intervene as regulator whenever grounds existed for concluding that the code of practice was not sensitive enough to deal with individual or more widespread complaints from the public about possible malpractice, otherwise government should avoid having to intervene unduly and thereby prevent honest advertising making a contribution to economic growth from which the rest of society would benefit. After all, in ethical terms, advertising is a form of free speech and qualifies as a negative right. It should therefore not be denied in an open society unless it disseminates lies or distorts the truth for private gain or some ideological purpose that limits the freedom of choice of other members of the public.

Three other types of restraint on the marketing activities of business are also pertinent. First, various industries and business associations, which include marketing companies, already exercise self-restraint by the adoption of company- and industry-wide codes of conduct. Second, various 'watchdog' organisations (e.g. the Consumers Association) are effective in protecting consumers' interests and in drawing public attention to examples of alleged inferior or defective goods and improper behaviour by suppliers. Third, TV programmes like *Blue Peter* which focus on the interests of children, provide a valuable public information service role by broadcasting their viewers' concerns, as consumers, in the public domain so that corrective action can be taken.

In ethical terms, the above arguments address both Kantian concerns about the importance of marketing respecting the rights to privacy and autonomy of the individual, and the utilitarian argument that advertising should be employed to disseminate information leading to the increased economic benefit and welfare of the rest of society. As Christie[8], quoting Thompson, observes:

> For marketeers, adopting a more caring orientation offers an opportunity to become ethical innovators within their organization. In most firms, those in marketing positions are closest to consumers, in terms of direct interaction and knowledge of their lifestyles. One role for marketeers would be to regard themselves as more explicit advocates of consumer interests – both immediate and long term.

Further information on these and other related issues appears in Fill[15].

## Synopsis

- Marketing ethics is the application of ethical evaluation to marketing strategies and tactics, involving judgements about moral right and wrong for marketing specialists in ensuring ethical practices are applied in product pricing, promotion, distribution, and research strategies to the marketing of products and services.
- The utilitarian approach to consumerism notes that wants and needs are artificially created through advertising and the resulting goods and services purchased have no utility to society. As it is more profitable for manufacturers to supply goods and services, provision of public services tends to be neglected and must be provided by government because, in an affluent society, marketing and advertising help shift resources away from areas of benefit to the greatest number of people in society towards those which gratify the immediate wants and desires of individuals.
- The libertarian approach to consumerism is that the individual consumer should always have choice, as governments and other agencies have no right to intervene in the way the market works, other than to ensure minimum public safety and legal safeguards, so that individual freedom of choice always flourishes.
- Potential conflict areas in marketing ethics may arise in the areas of product safety, responsibilities to consumers, privacy and respect for the individual, ethical issues in marketing communications, manipulation and coercion of vulnerable consumers; and ethical decision making and responsibility in marketing.
- Ethical issues that arise in marketing communications include misleading or false advertising, shocking, tasteless or indecent material in marketing communications, telesales calls that invade personal privacy, misleading PR communications, and the payment of bribes to secure business.
- The six groups that are ethically responsible whenever some advertising practices are adjudged to be immoral are the producer or manufacturer, the marketing company/advertising agency, the media (e.g. TV, newspapers, etc.), the general public, the body responsible for upholding standards (e.g. the ASA), and the government.

## Review and discussion questions

**1** What is the case against the use of subliminal advertising methods to stop shoplifting by customers in supermarkets?

**2** What examples could you give (a) for and (b) against the argument that planned obsolescence leads to resource shortages, product waste and environmental pollution?

**3** What are the main reasons why price fixing occurs?

**4** How would you respond to the argument that so-called vulnerable groups like school children should not be protected from certain forms of advertising as the right to choose is a fundamental right of every person?

**5** What are the main arguments for and against paternalism in advertising?

**6** How should moral responsibility for unethical advertising be allocated in a modern developed country?

## Case study
## British national lotteries, 1569–2000

**Introduction**

Lotteries probably began in Asia over 3,000 years ago and have existed in Europe for over 500 years. Since then, their popularity has spread almost worldwide so that there were 165 registered national lotteries when the British lottery started in 1993. Lotteries are most popular in the USA, Canada, Italy and South America, although all EU countries except Luxembourg now run them. Italy has 13 national lotteries but Spain's *El Gordo* is the largest in the EU with £100 million in prizes. Germany has the largest 'super jackpot' prize of over £15 million. Prizes are limited by law and the amount designated for charitable purposes, which ranges from 21 per cent in The Netherlands to 73 per cent in France, is also regulated.

The first British national lottery was introduced in 1569 and proceeds were used in the eighteenth century to build the British Museum and pay for fighting the Americans in the American War of Independence. Lotteries were banned, however, in 1826 because civil servants were found to take bribes to rig results. The National Lottery Bill was approved by Parliament in October 1992, after being fiercely opposed by the UK gambling industry, which included combined lobbying by horse racing, football pools and casino interests. There was also sustained criticism from religious and citizen support groups which is discussed below.

The government finally agreed to relax all UK gambling laws and eight consortia submitted tenders to run the proposed national lottery in November 1993. Richard Branson's bid attracted carefully canvassed media attention by pledging all profits to charity and other 'good causes', although the National Lottery Bill forbade promises to give away all profits from being taken into consideration by the Lottery Commission in deciding between rival tenders. What appeared at first to be an unnecessary proviso was vindicated later when the Commission revealed that the Branson bid was only the fourth most cost effective of the eight tenders evaluated.

This tender was finally awarded to the Camelot consortium which included specialist printing, gambling, electronic communications, computing and retail distributing expertise provided by De La Rue, GTECH (USA), Racal Electronics, ICL and Cadbury Schweppes, respectively. Camelot secured a seven-year contract to run the lottery in July 1994. The consortium spent £10 million on promoting its bid and £40 million, the biggest UK advertising campaign, in launching the lottery. An estimated 40 million adults saw 13 'It Could be You' TV commercials between 4 and 19 November; and over 45 million £1 tickets were purchased by 20 million people for the first lottery which was drawn on BBC1 television. This was the first step in the estimated sale of 32 billion £1 lottery tickets which would be bought by 80 per cent of the UK adult population over the next seven years. Of the predicted £32 billion revenue, £9 billion would go to good causes, taxes would total £3.7 billion and Camelot's share would exceed £16 billion, of which 28 per cent would be allocated as prizes leaving projected profits of approximately £1.6 billion.

**Monitoring the national lottery**

The European lottery industry is worth a massive £40 billion annually and, as the EU's twelfth largest industry, is not surprisingly subjected to rigorous monitoring controls. These came into force in 1991 when a German company tried to pre-empt UK plans by exporting a German lottery which was banned by the UK government. The German firm took its case to the EU Court of Justice which ruled that a lottery should be classified under the single market's freedom of goods and services framework. Britain appealed in 1992 and the EU Court upheld its plea that a member-state could ban any goods or services that threatened the 'social or moral standards' of its population. An OFLOT ombudsman was subsequently appointed to ensure fair play and even-handedness by all parties engaged in the lottery; and he outlawed the import of non-stop TV lotteries from the USA before approving Camelot's decision to introduce instant scratch card weekly lottery tickets in March 1995.

**Those in favour of a national lottery**

The UK government remains generally in favour of a national lottery as, in addition to the predicted £3.7 billion in direct taxes mentioned above, it also expected to receive £500 million in extra taxation from other related business activities for the seven years ending in 2001. The government also plays a key role in decisions about the disposal of £1.8 billion annually on good causes. The Camelot consortium was expected to make the estimated profits of £1.6 billion per year over the same period. The UK leisure and tourism industry will also benefit as research reveals that most of the one million or so weekly winners spend their prize money on leisure, travel and luxury goods. The advertising industry has already received £40 million from the launch of the lottery and extra revenue will remain around £900 million for the seven years because the reluctant middle classes have to be won over if the target of 80 per cent lottery players is to be reached in the UK.

BBC TV paid Camelot a large undisclosed amount to stage the weekly lottery draw which, at its peak, attracted over 20 million viewers (i.e. about half of the viewing population) who mostly watch the Saturday rather than the midweek lottery draw. The precise benefit of the national lottery is hard to establish as BBC revenue depends on a licence fee approved by Parliament. However, an increase in the viewing public is thought to be a contributory factor in the licence fee review process. At the time of the launch, National Heritage was expected to gain an extra £550 million annually for the upkeep of national parks, stately homes and other tourist attractions. The Millennium Commission was to receive a further £500 million each year for special projects such as the Millennium Dome, although critics argued that the money would be better spent on providing smaller local services such as crèches and other facilities for the young and the old.

Other beneficiaries were to include the Arts Council which would receive another £500 million annually for extending national opera, music, theatre and galleries. The Sports Council expected to receive an extra £125 million annually for improving sports facilities around the UK. Finally, the Charities Board was to dispense small awards of approximately £500–2,000 to over 150,000 small charities, although there was a delay in installing the necessary IT systems which held back the first awards for over 12 months.

**Those against the national lottery**

The British are the heaviest gamblers in the EU and opposition from the gambling industry, which stood to lose almost £5 billion annually to the national lottery, has already been mentioned. As a result of fierce lobbying from the football pools, betting shops, casinos and slot machine industries, the government finally agreed in 1994 to relax the 1976 Gambling Act by allowing greater access to gambling facilities for a larger sector of the population. Somewhat surprisingly, moral opposition to these concessions on top of a national lottery was less forthcoming from the larger Christian churches than from the Salvation Army, Presbyterians, Methodists, Plymouth Brethren and Islamic groups, which remained resolutely opposed to all forms of gambling. It should be noted, however, that these moral objections were also based on direct experience of the social consequences of excessive gambling on the poorer sections of UK society from which these religions draw many of their members.

Voluntary organisations also opposed the national lottery because experience abroad indicated that they end up a poor second to large prestigious projects like national opera, parks, theatres and galleries, in terms of attracting resources. Since they depend directly on charitable contributions, voluntary organisations tend to collapse abruptly rather than decline gradually if their financial base is threatened. Small registered charities anticipated fewer public/corporate contributions as a result of the national lottery, amounting to about £270 million per year. Anti-gambling bodies, such as Gamblers Anonymous, feared that a large sector of the UK population would become addicted to the lottery and social life would suffer as they spend money they cannot afford. This concern is based on US research which shows that almost two-thirds of all lottery revenue is regularly staked by only 20 per cent of the population, of whom a further two-thirds are employed in blue collar/working-class jobs. Although OFLOT reports indicate that an average of less than £2.70 is spent weekly on the UK national lottery, data on the anticipated higher spending by poorer members of UK society is not available. This expected trend is supported by the UK retailing and drinks industries which have reported losses of about £500 million annually as poorer punters have tended to cut back on impulse buying of small treats in favour of buying lottery tickets.

The reasons why people buy lottery tickets are too diverse for detailed discussion here but presumably range from a 'harmless flutter, as a bit of fun' to a compulsive pursuit of the elusive first prize. With the latter in mind, professional gamblers express disinterest in the national lottery, as the odds of winning the jackpot of about 14 million to 1 are seven times higher than the unfavourable 2 million to 1 odds of winning the 'treble chance' offered by the leading UK football pools company. Even the odds of winning a £1,500 lottery prize at 55,491 to 1 are nearly 40 times greater than the odds of 1,368 to 1 of winning £1,296 by picking two correct consecutive numbers for a £1 stake on the roulette table at any gambling casino. These hugely unattractive odds aside, the average investment loss on the lottery is 55 per cent, which means Camelot receives £1 each time a punter loses and pays out only 45p on average each time correct numbers are predicted.

**A change in policy**

The election of a Labour government in 1997 saw the retention of the national lottery but changes were introduced, reportedly based on 'the views of those who play and those who apply the funds'. However, the formula by which 28p of every £1 spent on a lottery ticket goes directly to good causes was retained. The OFLOT regulator was replaced by the National Lottery Commission in 1999 and the number of beneficiary bodies was extended to six national organisations, namely the Arts Council, the English Sports Council, the Heritage Lottery Fund, the Millennium Commission, the National Lottery Charities Board and the New Opportunities Fund. The latter two bodies aim to fund community involvement; the alleviation of poverty and disadvantage; green spaces and sustainable communities; cancer treatment and care; and lifelong learning initiatives.

Other policy changes include a shift in focus away from big building projects to smaller activities involving more people; easier access to funds by less wealthy, locally based organisations; support for applications committed to sustainable development and reduction of economic and social deprivation; more delegation of decisions about how funds should be allocated; and the launch of an 'Awards For All' programme of grants up to £5,000 for approved small community projects.

Tenders to run the national lottery after July 2001 included bids from Richard Branson, who persuaded Bill Gates to join his consortium, and Camelot. The latter consortium re-submitted its bid despite reports that sales of lottery tickets fell 5.6 per cent from £5.5 billion in 1997/98 to £5.2 billion in 1998/99 due to 'lottery fatigue'. Camelot's profits dropped from £86.5 million to £70.1 million and amounts given to good causes fell from £1.57 billion to £1.49 billion. However, the consortium claimed that this increased its allocation from 28.0 to 28.6 per cent; and that it expected to donate £10 billion to good causes, £1 billion more than the original target, by the time its licence expires in September 2001. Ever alert to adverse public opinion, Camelot also reported that the controversial high earnings of its directors had been reduced from £2.08 million to £1.52 million and the highest paid director received £482,000 in 1999 compared with £636,000 in 1998 (*The Independent*, 2 June 1999, p. 4).

Critics of the national lottery acknowledge these changes but still raise moral objections to what they regard as dual taxation on the less well-off, the main supporters of the lottery, who subsidise projects in which they have little interest, which are promoted by more prosperous sectors of society who buy less than 20 per cent of lottery tickets. Another major objection is that there is little public recognition by government authorities or direct support of a minority of the poorest in society who become compulsive punters and incur debt as a result of spending money they cannot afford on lottery tickets. Lorenz[16] observes that any form of gambling can lead to addiction, and research in the USA has shown that lower income people of all ages prefer less expensive forms of gambling such as lotteries and bingo. The Lottery Commission has since reported that the average stake of UK lottery players is less than three pounds per week.

**Questions**

1  What reasons would you give for (a) retaining or (b) withdrawing the national lottery after the expiry of the original contracts in 2001?

2  What response would you give to critics who insist that all the arguments in favour of the national lottery are based on so-called economic benefits which fail to address the moral principles for opposing this form of gambling which exploits the poorer members of UK society?

## Notes and references

1. Galbraith, J.K., *The Affluent Society*, 3rd edn, New York, Houghton Mifflin, 1976.
2. De George, R.T., *Moral Issues in Business*, New York, Macmillan, 1995, 217–41.
3. Richardson, J.E., Marketing and Ethics, *International Encylopaedia of Ethics*, ed. J.K. Roth, London, Fitzroy-Dearborn, 1995, 529–30.
4. Hayek, F., The *non sequitur* of the 'Dependence Effect', *Southern Economic Journal*, April 1961.
5. Slack, N., Chambers, S., Harland, C., Harrison, A. and Johnston, R., *Operations Management*, 2nd edn, London, Financial Times Pitman Publishing, 1998, chs 4, 5, 6, 7 and 8, 107–311.
6. Sobczak, P., Warranties and Guarantees, *International Encyclopaedia of Ethics*, ed. J.K. Roth, London, Fitzroy-Dearborn, 1995, 923–4.
7. Spinello, R.A., *Ethical Aspects of Information Technology*, New York, Prentice Hall, 1995.
8. Christie, R., The Ethical Context, in *Marketing Communications: Contexts, contents and strategies*, ed. C. Fill, 2nd edn, London, Prentice Hall, 1995, ch. 3, 47–69.
9. Farhi, P., *San Francisco Chronicle*, 9 May 1989, C.5.
10. Draper, R., The Faithless Shepherd, *The New York Review of Books*, 26 June 1986, 17.
11. Shaw, W.H. and Barry, V., *Moral Issues in Business*, 7th edn, Belmont, Calif., Wadsworth, 1998, 479.
12. *Washington Post Health Supplement*, 8 January 1984.
13. *IBM Business Guidelines for Employees*, IBM (UK) Ltd, Havant, Hants, UK, 1993, 2.
14. Charren, P., in W.H. Shaw and V. Barry, *Moral Issues in Business*, 7th edn, Belmont, Calif., Wadsworth, 1998, 479.
15. Fill, C., *Marketing Communications: Contexts, contents and strategies*, 2nd edn, London, Prentice Hall, 1995, chs 18–19, 359–92.
16. Lorenz, V.C., Gambling, *Encyclopedia of Applied Ethics*, New York, Academic Press, 1998.

# Environmental protection

*The concerns of environmental ethics begin with the food on our plates.*

Tom Regan, *Introductory Essays on Environmental Ethics*, New York, Random House, 1984, 3

## Learning objectives

After reading this chapter you should be able to:

- explore the origins of environmental ethics and its attempts to resolve problems arising from the relationship between humans and the environment in an ethical way;
- consider whether individuals only have a moral obligation to comply with environmental legislation, and the consequences of rigorous legislation being withheld because of short-term higher costs and only longer-term benefits;
- consider the moral implications of defining pollution and the need to distinguish between intentional and unintentional pollution;
- examine whether irreversible damage to the biosphere can be controlled without preventing the legitimate economic needs of a growing world population;
- consider how sustainable industrial development could be achieved in industrialised countries without jeopardising economic growth in developing countries;
- explore ethical aspects of charging organisations for the amount of pollution they produce relative to the environmental damage caused, as a variation of the 'polluter pays' principle.

## Introduction

Two notable research studies from the 1970s, which influenced subsequent discussion of the likely impact of environmental changes on world development, also reached opposite conclusions. Meadows and Forrester's[1] 'pessimistic model' suggested that, without major changes in socioeconomic and environmental policy, global non-renewable resources would be depleted within less than 100 years. Kahn *et al.*'s[2] 'optimistic model' concluded that, whereas 200 years ago, the Earth's population was relatively small, poor and at the mercy of nature, 200 years from now it would be 'numerous, rich and in control of the forces of nature'. Paradoxically, human behaviour received less attention in the design of both models compared with its critical role in the socioeconomic and political systems anticipated one or two centuries from now. This suggests that managers are likely to become more concerned with how, rather than whether, attempts to raise global living standards can be reconciled with society's obligations to future generations. In short, how will aggregate changes in individual values, beliefs and behaviour ensure that existing economic and political institutions can accommodate these considerable environmental uncertainties in a reasonable and harmonised way?

## Organisations and the environment

The environmental movement emerged in the early 1960s to challenge the view that, although human beings have always exploited nature in what was assumed to be a vast and enduring biosphere, the belief that lasting harm would not be inflicted was no longer plausible. On the contrary, individuals, groups, organisations, civil society, governments and the global community needed to become aware that our planet is becoming steadily warmer as its protective ozone layer begins to disappear, essential forests upon which our weather systems depend are also rapidly being destroyed, and pollution is increasingly contaminating the air, water and land required to sustain human life. Those who insisted that the environmental case was being overstated were reminded that half of the change in the biosphere caused by humans has occurred since World War II. Despite the introduction of new environmental protection laws, managers of profit-seeking organisations could no longer assume that compliance with this legislation was sufficient as surveys indicated that over three-quarters of respondents stated that the environmental reputation of a company affected what products they would buy in the future.

## Environmental ethics

Purdy[3] states that environmental ethics emerged in the late 1980s as 'a standard of conduct based on moral principles that supports a holistic, biocentric view of the relationship of humans with the environment'. Its main aim is to apply ethical principles to resolve problems and challenges pertaining to the relationship of humans with the environment. This is considered to be essential because humans have already transformed or manipulated half the ice-free ecosystems on the planet; and have also made a significant impact on most of the rest. In addition, people have systematically reduced the number of other species on the planet by pollution, hunting, or through the destruction of the natural habitat. Hoffman *et al.*[4], quoting former vice-president Al Gore, note that 'The fact that we face an ecological disaster without any precedence in historic times is no longer a matter of any dispute worthy of any recognition', and raise three fundamental questions about the relationship between the two major players, business and government:

1  What obligation does business have to help with our environmental crisis?
2  What is the proper relationship between business and government, especially when faced with a social problem of the magnitude of the environmental crisis?
3  What rationale should be used for making and justifying decisions to protect the environment?

## Should business help with environmental protection?

The answer seems so obvious as to make the question unnecessary to those who make an immediate connection between the increase in environmental pollution and manufacturing output, etc. However, not all business ethics specialists are in agreement. Bowie[5], for example, argues that:

> Business does not have an obligation to protect the environment over and above what is required by law; however, it does have a moral obligation to avoid intervening in the political arena in order to defeat or weaken environmental legislation.

Hoffman *et al.* (ibid) disagree with Bowie on both points of this argument. First, they note that Bowie's assertion that business should merely avoid breaking the law on environmental matters is directly linked with Friedman's statement that the social responsibility of business is to make profits (see Chapter 1). Bowie supports this view by arguing that 'an injunction to assist in solving societal problems . . . makes impossible demands on the corporation because, at the practical level, it ignores the impact that such activities have on profit.' In short, if consumers are not prepared to meet the cost and use environmentally friendly products, then it is not the responsibility of business to correct this market failure.

On the second point of the business community having a moral obligation not to undermine environmental legislation, Bowie's argument appears to be based more on expediency than on ethical principle. He points out that politicians in the USA are already reluctant to approve environmental legislation which has short-term high costs and only long-term benefits, therefore 'corporations [should not] try to have their cake and eat it'.

Hoffman *et al.* however, see dangers in the strategy of encouraging business to adopt the view that good environmentalism is good for business. They are also unconvinced that the rationale that good ethics is good business is a proper one for business ethics, because 'one thing that the study of ethics has taught us over the past 2,500 years is that being ethical may on occasion require that we place the interests of others ahead of or at least on a par with our own interests'. This implies that the ethical thing to do may not be in our own self-interest. Which begs the question: what happens when the right thing to do is not in the best interests of the business community?

## Responsible action towards the environment

Hoffman *et al.* and De George[6] separately identified related rationales for deciding on what grounds responsible action should be adopted towards the environment. Hoffman[7] calls these:

- the minimalist view, or principle; and
- the naturalistic view.

De George approaches the problem in terms of risk assessment, as indicated below.

## The minimalist view/principle

The minimalist principle is to refrain from causing unwarranted harm, as failure to do so would, according to the libertarian argument, violate the moral right of the individual not to be harmed by another's actions. Bowie, for example, invokes this principle above when he argues that business only need refrain from causing damage to the environment in terms of existing law. Hoffman *et al.*[4] argue, however, that the harm-avoidance principle places a further moral obligation on organisations to find methods of *prevention*, so that harm does not occur to the individual in the first place. But what of the environment? The arguments put forward by both Bowie and Hoffman *et al.* share the common humanistic ground of acknowledging that only human beings have moral rights because of their unique value as human beings. These moral rights are not extended to trees, mountains, rivers, lakes, etc., since, as Hoffman *et al.* note, non-human things are valuable only if they are valued by human beings.

**Individual safety and acceptable risk**

De George (ibid) approaches the subject of environmental protection by identifying four related perspectives on safety and acceptable risk which are derived from the minimalist principle:

**The rational evaluation of risk**

This position is based on the rationale that, just as individuals have the moral right not to be harmed, they also have a right to know when they are at risk of being put in harm's way. That is to say, with environmental protection issues in mind, people are entitled to be informed by organisations responsible for manufacturing or storing dangerous chemicals or other toxic substances of the risk involved should the worst case situation occur.

**The nature and source of risk**

In addition, people are entitled to know not only when they are at risk but also the source and nature of the risk involved so that they can rationally evaluate the consequences. The rationale is that, denied this information, they cannot evaluate the risk before deciding whether they wish to take it or not. If the risk is a constant one (e.g. environmental noise pollution from living near a major international airport), then the individual can take corrective action, such as installing sound-proof insulation and double-glazing to shut out the excess noise; seeking compensation from the airport authority for the inconvenience; or simply moving to a quieter environment.

If the risk occurs only in certain extreme conditions (e.g. the risk of fire in living near to an oil refinery), then the individual has the right to know what precautions have been put in place by the owner to minimise the possibility of this extreme case occurring, and also the contingency plans that would follow if a fire broke out, so that a decision can be taken about whether to avoid the risk, or to take it in the knowledge of the likely consequences should the worst case occur.

**The magnitude of the risk and how to deal with it**

The third position differs from the previous two mainly by degree in that the individual also has the right to know the magnitude of the risk being taken (e.g. will an oil refinery fire destroy my property or perhaps human life through smoke inhalation, etc.?) and, if this occurs, how should people deal with it, as it would be unethical of the refinery owner not to inform individuals and therefore put them at risk, however remote, without knowledge of how to cope in an emergency.

The alternatives to taking the risk

So that any risk may be evaluated rationally, the individual also has the right to know what alternatives, if any, are available. For example, living near an international airport has the inconvenience of environmental noise pollution mentioned above but this might be offset against the benefits of attractive employment prospects and an efficient transport infrastructure, compared with the quieter environment, reduced job opportunities and slower transportation system on, say, the island of Jura in the inner Hebrides.

## The naturalistic view/principle

Hoffman[7] notes that the minimalist principle stands in sharp contrast to its naturalistic counterpart which states that natural things in the world, other than human beings, are intrinsically valuable and are therefore entitled to moral rights. Obvious candidates for inclusion under the naturalistic principle would be all sentient species in the so-called animal kingdom and Singer[8] has put forward cogent arguments for over 25 years in favour of evaluating environmental ethics in terms of the treatment of non-humans.

Briefly, Singer raises the general question of how the effects of our actions on the environment on non-human beings should figure in our deliberations of what we ought to do. For him, this is a critical ethical issue because of our knowledge that animals can feel pleasure and pain and have a capacity for subjective experience. They can therefore be said to have interests, which we must not ignore. On the contrary, the moral principle of 'equal consideration of interests' should be extended to include non-human beings. Once accepted, this principle has widespread implications which include the moral imperative of abandoning the practice of rearing and killing other animals for consumption by human beings. The subject of animal rights is discussed in Chapter 13.

Both Hoffman and Singer adopt what is generally known as a *biocentric* ethical standpoint towards the environment as opposed to the *homocentric* standpoint, summarised in the minimalist view above. The literature on the former branch of environmental ethics has burgeoned since the 1970s and already contains several different moral perspectives. Stone[9], for example, a law professor, extends the notion of environmental rights to include the moral and legal principles that nature needs to be protected for its own sake, which is proposed from the moral point of 'making us far better human beings'. This would entail reversing the common law 'rightlessness of natural objects' to include natural rights for the environment including the extension of legal rights to forests, oceans and rivers, etc., by acknowledging an earlier stage in human development when 'we had to trust (and perhaps fear) our environment, for we had not then the power to master it'. Stone concludes that: 'we may come to regard the Earth . . . as one organism, of which Mankind is a functional part – the mind, perhaps, different from the rest of nature, but different as a man's brain is from his lungs'.

Related views that fall under the biocentric view of environmental ethics include the notions of ecology and the Gaia principle.

Ecology

Ecology is a branch of science concerned with the relationships living things have with each other and with their environment. Its main premise is that no organism, large or small, simple or complex, exists alone in the enormous variety of living things in the world. Whether a simple organism like a bacteria or a more complex plant or animal, each is dependent in some way on other living things, with which it inter-relates, or non-living things for survival and growth in its surroundings. Ecology is also an unusual science because of its underlying multidisciplinary methodology. It began as a branch of biology but has since widened its scope to include chemistry, physics and computer science, as well as geology, meteorology and oceanography, in an attempt to understand the complex interactions between the elements in air, land and water and their impact on physical environments and climatic changes such as acid rain and the greenhouse effect. This methodology is used to study the way the world is organised on the three main levels of:

1 populations;
2 communities;
3 ecosystems.

A population refers to a group of the same species that survives in an area at the same time, as distinct from a community, which is a group of animal and plant populations living together in the same environment. The ecosystem comprises the most complex level of organisation in nature, being a community in a living physical environment made up of climate, water, air, soil, nutrients and energy.

**The Gaia principle/ hypothesis**

The Gaia principle is attributed to the UK chemist and inventor, James Lovelock[10], and the US microbiologist Lynn Margulis. It proposes that the earth is a living entity whose biosphere is self-regulating, able to maintain itself by controlling its chemical and physical environment, of which the human race is simply part of a biocentric whole that depends on balanced relationships being maintained between human beings and other forms of life. The tropical rain forest is often cited as an example of the Gaia hypothesis, in which trees give off water through transpiration, adding humidity to the air that increases the frequency of rainstorm clouds which maintain the natural environment by watering trees and also by blocking out sunlight to keep the forest from overheating.

The hypothesis aroused both considerable scepticism and support. Critics reject it as unscientific whereas others think it may lead to research which should increase understanding of serious environmental problems such as the greenhouse effect and the possible destruction of species.

## The greenhouse effect

This theory was first proposed in 1896 when it was noted that the earth's surface temperature was increasing due to the absorption of reflected, infrared radiation by atmospheric 'greenhouse gas' emission which may drastically alter global climates. Ecologists claim that carbon dioxide levels in the atmosphere have increased by 2.5 per cent since the 1800s, while methane levels have increased by over 150 per cent over the same period. Both are thought to be due to the increased burning of fossil fuels (e.g. coal, oil and natural gas) and the clearance of forestry land for agricultural pur-poses to feed the rapidly increasing world population of over six billion people.

Greenhouse gases of water vapour, small amounts of carbon dioxide, methane, nitrous oxide, ozone and chlorofluorocarbons, are known to absorb reflected infrared radiation, which raises the atmospheric temperature. Without this increase, the earth's mean surface temperature would be about 17.3 degrees Celsius, rather than the observed average of 15 degrees Celsius. Therefore, the greenhouse effect makes the earth habitable. The observed warming is referred to as the 'atmospheric effect'; and is thought to be due to the human production of carbon dioxide, chlorofluorocarbons, nitrous oxide and ozone since industrialisation began. For example, the atmospheric carbon dioxide is increasing by about 0.3 per cent annually which closely correlates with the increased rate of fuel consumption.

## Global warming

Ecologists estimate that the earth's average surface temperature has increased by between 0.5 and 1.5 degrees Celsius since the 1800s, arguably as a result of concurrent human generation of greenhouse gases. Further increases, ranging from the lowest estimate of 2–5 degrees Celsius by the year 2020, to the highest increase of 3–8 degrees Celsius by 2010, are predicted if no action is taken. Ecologists add that even greater temperature changes have occurred many times in the past without any human activity, although the causes of repeated glaciation and melting of the polar ice-caps in the last million years are not fully understood.

Worst case scenarios predict that the major environmental effects of global warming will include the pole-ward shift of climatic belts, raising sea levels globally by as much as 6 metres by 2020, with accompanying changes in rainfall patterns, tropical storms and shifting animal and plant populations, which are all predicted to have a disruptive impact on current human activities. Any regulation or abolition of activities that may be responsible for global warming, such as the burning of fossil fuels, will entail massive social and economic changes. These in turn will raise major environmental ethical issues if only because of the substantial lack of consensus, both nationally and internationally, about the causes of and future courses of action likely to cope with the consequences of current, let alone future, global warming.

## Environmental pollution

Much of the blame for environmental pollution is attributed to commerce, particularly to manufacturing organisations, which are charged with polluting the atmosphere, discharging toxic substances into rivers as industrial effluent, and burying poisonous waste products, despite the vigilance of government and local authority environmental protection services in seeking to safeguard the public. The ethical problems with pollution, as De George[6] observes, are that first, its meaning has to be clearly specified as the term pollution is often used in a relative way; and second, a distinction has to be made between intentional and unintentional pollution.

Ecologists point out that, as far as nature is concerned, there is no strict meaning to the term pollution, which is often used in an anthropomorphic way. That is to say, human beings tend to define pollution in terms of how adversely they are affected by the contamination of water, air and land which damages their interests but without necessarily doing irreversible harm to the environment.

As far as pollution is concerned, the first ethical issue is to prevent or minimise any harm resulting from human activity that can reasonably be avoided. As noted above, the term pollution may be used in a relative way, usually in terms of the quality of environment required by a specific authority or community. In such cases, cost–benefit analysis can play a major role in determining the overall costs of environmental improvement, so that a decision can be taken about implementing a pollution control system at a specific cost, to return the environment to its original condition.

The second ethical issue raises more complicated moral and socioeconomic perspectives on environmental pollution. For example, it would be unethical today for any water company to install lead pipes to supply water to a local school because it is now known that lead residues may remain in the water which can cause brain damage to young persons in particular. Because of ignorance, however, this was not known for certain until long after many lead pipes were in place, and huge socioeconomic countermeasures had to be taken to eliminate this hazard to public health. Before the dangers were confirmed, there were no grounds for assuming that a water authority acted intentionally in an unethical way to cause harm to school children, although had any ignored the warnings of the Government Medical Officer about this danger, then this would have been another matter.

Moral judgements therefore have to reflect emerging scientific knowledge when issues of intentionality arise as it is possible that the use, or dumping, of small quantities of a particular contaminant may be found to have caused major pollution problems, when evaluated in aggregate, at a later stage. For example, asbestos was formerly used with the best social welfare intentions to retard the spread of fires in housing and public buildings, only for it to be discovered later that the release of fine particles of asbestos fibres into the air could be linked to the incidence of serious pulmonary illnesses, including lung cancer. Ethical judgements about environmental pollution in this case clearly had to be modified to reflect both the intentionality and the presumed social welfare benefits in installing the fire-retardant, plus the socioeconomic costs of withdrawing it from use when its huge potential to harm public health became known.

## Divergent views on environmental pollution

Depending on whether a minimalist or a biocentric ethical perspective is adopted, ecologists evaluate the assumed aggregative effects of environmental pollution in different ways. Many who adopt the latter standpoint argue that if human economic activity continues at the present rate, within a few decades humans will 'overshoot' the carrying capacity of the biosphere and some irreversible collapse will be precipitated. Some critics respond that the earth itself is in no such danger at the hands of humans. Others acknowledge the harm done to the biosphere but justify it on cost–benefit analysis grounds in terms of the unprecedented economic growth and development of technology in industrialised countries which they anticipate will spread as Third World nations are drawn into a new global economy.

## Sustainable development

This raises a major question, which has yet to be answered with certainty, about the possibility of preventing irreversible damage to the biosphere and accommodating the legitimate economic needs of a growing world population at the same time. A tentative answer appears in the Call for Action in the report of the World Commission on Environment and Development (1987)[11], which is cautiously optimistic providing a new paradigm for environmental ethics is created, based on shared common values that are accepted by governments and international agencies under the aegis of the United Nations General Assembly.

The World Commission advanced the principle of sustainable development (i.e. humanity ensures that it meets the needs of the present without compromising the ability of future generations to meet their own needs) on the basis that the world community agrees to proceed within limits ('not absolute limits but limitations imposed by the present state of technology and social organisation on environmental resources and by the ability of the biosphere to absorb the effects of human activities', p. 8). For these limitations to be achieved, far-reaching legal principles would also need to be adopted by the international community which ensure environmental protection and sustainable development on the basis that human development and protection of the earth's environment are inextricably intertwined.

## Sustainable development and industry

The World Commission noted that industry is central to the economies of modern societies as 'an indispensable motor of growth', as it is 'essential to developing countries, to widen their development base and meet growing needs'. To meet these expectations, however, industry 'extracts materials from the natural resource base and inserts both products and pollution into the human environment'. For industrial development to be sustainable over the long term, it would have to change radically in terms of the quality of development particularly in industrialised countries. This would have to be done without a quantitative limit, particularly in developing countries, which would need to be raised by a factor of 2.6 to bring them up to current industrialised country levels. Furthermore, in view of anticipated population growth, a five- to tenfold increase in world industrial output can be anticipated by the time the world population stabilises some time in the twenty-first century.

In the interregnum, an agreed coherent strategy is needed in industrialised countries which will establish:

- environmental goals, regulations, incentives and standards;
- a broader range of environmental assessments;
- the encouragement of action by industrial organisations;
- increased capacity to deal with industrial hazards;
- stronger international efforts to help developing nations.

Either before or since the World Commission Report was published in 1987, rigorous legislation has been introduced in industrialised countries, including the Environmental Protection Act 1990 and the Environment Act 1995 in the UK. This legislation empowers local authorities to adopt a systemic perspective on manufacturing organisations which seeks to evaluate how inputs such as raw materials, energy and water are transformed through specific industrial processes to yield outputs such as the designated products or services, and emissions to the air, to the water supply as industrial effluent and to the land. International environmental protection standards such as ISO 14001 are increasingly set to manage all aspects of outputs which can have a significant impact on the environment. Specific measurable objectives and targets are set so that improvements in pollution control can be monitored by applying preventative measures as part of an environmental management programme action plan.

Implementation of effective environmental protection programmes is also being supported by government interventions in the USA and EU countries which give tax incentives to companies for the purchase and use of pollution control equipment. The advantage of such tax incentive programmes is that it minimises government intervention in business and encourages voluntary action rather than more coercive measures to ensure compliance with legislation.

## The polluter pays principle

Another approach, still in its infancy, is the introduction of pricing mechanisms which are intended to charge organisations for the amount of pollution they produce relative to the environmental damage caused. This approach is a variation on the polluter pays principle, which is designed to offset the costs of cleaning up specific pollution on the agency responsible. Another successful, practical application involves manufacturing companies that have previously drawn clean, potable water at the start of their processes – only to pollute and return it as effluent, in need of purification by some local authority or water company – at no cost to themselves. It has been found, for example, that the pollution of effluent decreases rapidly merely by reversing the intake point, so that the company draws in its water supplies downstream rather than upstream, and would be the first to experience the residual effects of any contamination remaining in the water.

This latter approach is supported by ecologists and environmental scientists who are generally opposed to pricing mechanisms which have been interpreted as a licence to pollute as, indeed, has the introduction in the USA of 'pollution permits' which entitle some organisations to negotiate with government authorities for acceptable levels of forms of pollution emanating from their processes. In practice, however, although the advantages of the various forms of cost allocation are recognised, none is without its drawbacks mainly because of the huge diversity of different manufacturing processes that have emerged during the last 150–200 years. It is therefore likely that a mixture of regulations, effluent charges, pollution permits and other direct incentives will continue to be used in developed countries in the future.

## Sustainable production and consumption management

Welford[12] has proposed a 'six E-factors' approach for use by senior management to ensure that continuous monitoring of the key elements of a sustainable production and consumption strategy takes place so that progress and setbacks can be recorded for corrective action or further improvement. The six E-factors are:

- Environmental monitoring;
- Empowerment of staff;
- Economy of production costs, etc.;
- Ethical environmental management;
- Equity of relationships with stakeholders;
- Education and training.

McEwan *et al.*[13] have compiled a survey instrument for measuring environmental performance and sustainable development, with specific reference to IS0 14001 standards, which appears as Box 11.1.

---

### Box 11.1

### Survey instrument for measuring environmental performance and sustainable development of ISO 14001 programmes

#### 1 INTRODUCTION

Welford[12] presents a framework for achieving sustainable development that includes six policy areas and the related indicative tools which appear in the following survey instrument. Any business that seeks to implement sustainable environmental development policies would be expected to have an identifiable policy in each of these six areas, although it must be stressed that no firm will be expected to produce a perfect profile in each area. The aim of the survey instrument is therefore to identify progress in each area so that a degree of continuous improvement can be demonstrated over time.

#### 2 EVALUATION SCALE

| Strongly disagree | Disagree | Slightly disagree | Neither agree nor disagree | Slightly agree | Agree | Strongly agree |
|---|---|---|---|---|---|---|
| 1 | 2 | 3 | 4 | 5 | 6 | 7 |

#### 3 POLICY AREAS TO BE EVALUATED

**(i) Environment**

(a) Our working environment is being protected with minimum use of non-renewable resources.     1 2 3 4 5 6 7

(b) Environmental performance is monitored and measured on a regular basis.     1 2 3 4 5 6 7

(c) An environmental management system exists in the company which includes regular audit activity.     1 2 3 4 5 6 7

(d) Products are evaluated according to an approved life-cycle assessment.     1 2 3 4 5 6 7

(e) Products are redesigned regularly to reduce environmental impact.

    1  2  3  4  5  6  7

(f) Products also undergo a reliable functionality assessment to ensure the best way of providing product benefits is used.

    1  2  3  4  5  6  7

(g) Strong connections exist along our supply chain to ensure that all stages of the product's life-cycle are integrated.

    1  2  3  4  5  6  7

(h) Proper steps are taken to ensure that the use and disposal of our products is managed according to recognised standards.

    1  2  3  4  5  6  7

(i) Our company places great emphasis on local community initiatives to ensure that sustainable development is achieved.

    1  2  3  4  5  6  7

(j) Our company places much emphasis on local action to ensure that the health and safety of all employees and neighbours is protected.

    1  2  3  4  5  6  7

### (ii) Empowerment

(a) Every employee feels part of the process of empowerment.

    1  2  3  4  5  6  7

(b) Every employee is empowered to act on their own obligations and work together closely with other colleagues.

    1  2  3  4  5  6  7

(c) Strong participation exists in the workforce with respect to decision making, profit sharing and ownership structures.

    1  2  3  4  5  6  7

(d) Our company is open to new suggestions from any of the workforce.

    1  2  3  4  5  6  7

(e) Workers are rewarded for suggestions as well as for work done.

    1  2  3  4  5  6  7

(f) Human resources are valued by the company and workers are not treated as factors of production.

    1  2  3  4  5  6  7

(g) Employee rights relating to equal opportunities and individual freedoms are enshrined within the company.

    1  2  3  4  5  6  7

(h) In our company diversity is encouraged and not stifled.

    1  2  3  4  5  6  7

### (iii) Economy

(a) Our firm's economic performance is sustainable and provides for ongoing survival and the provision of employment.

    1  2  3  4  5  6  7

(b) Periodic new investment occurs in both physical and human capital through education and retraining.

    1  2  3  4  5  6  7

(c) Financial audits are extended to include a justification of profits through good business practices rather than cost-cutting exploitation.

    1  2  3  4  5  6  7

(d) Periodic new investment occurs in both physical and human capital through education and training.

    1  2  3  4  5  6  7

(e) Because our business relationships are mutually advantageous, stability exists in our supply chain.

    1  2  3  4  5  6  7

(f) Since jobs are central to sustainability, the provision and growth of employment is encouraged by our company.

    1  2  3  4  5  6  7

(g) The products we make are of good quality, durable and suitable for
the purpose for which they are intended.   1 2 3 4 5 6 7

### (iv) Ethics

(a) Our organisation has a clear set of published values which it reassesses
periodically through the social-audit process.   1 2 3 4 5 6 7

(b) Our company is at all times honest and open about its ethical values,
and provides evidence relating to any activities which are being challenged.   1 2 3 4 5 6 7

(c) We are a transparent organisation and have clearly defined relationships
with head office, subsidiaries, contractors and other agencies.   1 2 3 4 5 6 7

(d) Ethics in our organisation are not declarations of intent but exist in practice
as codes of practice, education, information and communication programmes.   1 2 3 4 5 6 7

(e) Our business activities are ethically justified because it can be shown that
we meet the legitimate concerns of the maximum number of our stakeholders.   1 2 3 4 5 6 7

### (v) Equity

(a) Equal rights and opportunities are made available to all of our employees.   1 2 3 4 5 6 7

(b) Trade with local suppliers and buyers along our supply chain operates
in an equitable manner.   1 2 3 4 5 6 7

(c) Our international trade is also equitable and does not act against
the interests and human rights of workers in developing countries.   1 2 3 4 5 6 7

(d) The revenue accumulating as value added from the sale of our products
is equitably distributed amongst our suppliers, at home and overseas.   1 2 3 4 5 6 7

(e) Initiatives exist which ensure that technology and know-how is transferred
to our historically disadvantaged suppliers, both at home and overseas.   1 2 3 4 5 6 7

(f) Sponsorship, charitable donations and development aid are also provided
to our historically disadvantaged suppliers, both at home and overseas.   1 2 3 4 5 6 7

### (vi) Education

(a) Our company recognises that education is at the heart of the sustainable
process, according to recognised standards.   1 2 3 4 5 6 7

(b) Sustainable development depends on being able to communicate the
challenge to stakeholders and educate them to live in a more suitable way.   1 2 3 4 5 6 7

(c) Our company has to accept its role as an educator because of its close
links with employees, suppliers and customers.   1 2 3 4 5 6 7

(d) Our company should provide suitable information and education to all
employees and to everyone purchasing its products both at home or overseas.   1 2 3 4 5 6 7

(e) We should work closely with non-governmental agencies and campaign groups,
through sponsorship, etc., to raise awareness of sustainable development.   1 2 3 4 5 6 7

© T. McEwan and R. Welford, 1999.

## Synopsis

- Environmental ethics emerged in the late 1980s as a holistic, biocentric view of the relationship between humans and the environment, which aims to resolve problems arising from this relationship in an ethical way.

- Some critics think that people only have a moral obligation to comply with environmental legislation, but this argument may be based on convenience rather than on ethical principle, as rigorous legislation may not be introduced because of its short-term higher costs and long-term benefits, allowing pollution of the environment without penalties.

- Although blame for environmental pollution is attributed to manufacturing organisations, the ethical problems of the meaning of pollution, which is often used in a relative way, and a distinction between intentional and unintentional pollution, should be clarified.

- Because there is no strict meaning to the term pollution, people tend to define it in terms of how their interests are affected by contamination which may do no irreversible harm to the environment.

- A major unanswered question is whether irreversible damage to the biosphere can be prevented while accommodating the legitimate economic needs of a growing world population at the same time.

- For industrial development to be sustainable over the long term, the quality of development, particularly in industrialised countries, would have to change radically but without imposing a quantitative limit on economic growth in developing countries.

- Unresolved economic and ethical issues include how to set equitable environmental goals, incentives and standards, introduce more environmental assessments, encourage self-regulation by industrial organisations; and increase international help for developing nations.

- One possible ethical approach would be to introduce pricing mechanisms which charge organisations for the amount of pollution they produce relative to the environmental damage caused, as a variation of the polluter pays principle, which offsets the costs of cleaning up specific pollution to the agency responsible.

## Review and discussion questions

1 Given that the 'pessimistic' and 'optimistic' models of environmental changes on world development cannot be fully tested, what criteria would you propose for evaluating whether one set of predictions is more reliable than the other?

2 In *What Price Incentives?* Steven Kelman[14] argues that companies should be issued with emission permits, to prevent excessive environmental pollution, as being more ethical than setting emission charges and other financial penalties when mandatory standards are exceeded. What arguments would you present in favour of or against this proposal?

3 How would you reconcile two alternative interpretations of the 'polluter pays' principle, known as 'buyer beware' (*caveat emptor*) and 'seller beware' (*caveat venditor*), in discussing possible links between the two national fuel protests and the widespread flooding in the UK during the period September to November 2000?

## Case study
## After Bhopal: the unsettled case of Cape Plc

Over 16 years have elapsed since what is widely regarded as the world's worst industrial accident occurred in December 1984 at the Union Carbide pesticide plant near Bhopal, India. A tank containing 45 tonnes of the highly toxic pesticide chemical methyl-iso-cyanide (MIC) exploded shortly after midnight and escaped into the atmosphere to form a dense cloud over an area with more than 600,000 inhabitants. The catastrophic outcome was that some 2,500 people died and another 150,000 casualties needed medical treatment in hospitals and emergency clinics. Most victims died from a condition equivalent to drowning after their lungs filled up with fluid in reaction to inhaling MIC. Others died of heart attacks or suffered blindness, permanent nasal or respiratory damage, concussion, paralysis, or epilepsy.

Casualties still crowded the Bhopal hospital at the rate of one per minute for many days after the explosion. The plant was built in 1969 on a green-field site outside Bhopal with the approval of the Indian government and the local authority. However, an expansion programme had been implemented six years later. This led squatters to move into temporary accommodation between the chemical processing plant and Bhopal. Before the expansion was completed, the local administrator requested moving the whole plant to minimise the health and safety risk to the new squatter population, but the request was rejected and the Bhopal official was dismissed instead.

**The Union Carbide response to legal suits for compensation**

The question of legal compensation for the victims of the Bhopal disaster was complicated when a law suit was filed by the Indian government, itself a major shareholder in the Union Carbide joint venture. The US conglomerate had been incorporated in India prior to independence in 1947, and was one of a few overseas companies to retain a majority 50.9 per cent stake in the joint venture as part of India's agricultural 'Green Revolution'. Soon after news of the disaster broke, US attorneys filed a class action suit against Union Carbide for $15 billion on behalf of the Bhopal victims, hugely exceeding a preliminary settlement offer to the Indian government by Union Carbide for an immediate $60 million, followed by a further $180 million over the next thirty years.

However, the Indian government decided to exert its independence by seeking punitive damages in a separate suit for damages filed in New York for 'an amount sufficient to deter Union Carbide and any other multinational corporation from the willful, malicious and wanton disregard of the rights and safety of citizens in those countries in which they do business'. The previously mentioned class action suit for $15 billion against Union Carbide was regarded as unrealistic as the corporation was only insured against contingencies such as the Bhopal disaster for a reported $200 million and could ultimately neutralise excessive claims by declaring itself bankrupt. Meanwhile, independent legal experts agreed that it could meet a settlement of between $250 million and $300 million but anything over $500 million would defeat its purpose by driving the conglomerate into receivership.

Even though Union Carbide's inquiry had concluded that the Bhopal plant was poorly managed and that various international safety procedures had been violated, the corporation succeeded in raising the consequences of its liability with the US government. Consultations followed with the Indian government after which the US courts ruled that any claims for compensation should be filed in India rather than in the USA. The full settlement agreement details were still unknown 10 years after the disaster when *BBC World News* reported that many Bhopal victims and other dependants had yet to receive compensation.

**The case against Cape Plc**

The international ramifications of the Bhopal disaster had a less publicised impact on the case brought against the UK multinational company, Cape Plc, in 1999. *The Independent* and *The Times* (5 July 1999) both reported how the British company planned to go to the High Court in London to try to block compensation claims by 2,000 workers dying of asbestosis.

These former employees of Cape Plc and residents of Prieska in the Northern Cape, where the company operated an asbestos processing plant, were exposed during the 1960s and 1970s to asbestos dust levels up to 35 times higher than the maximum level accepted in the UK. The claimants argue that the company must have known that its operating conditions in South Africa were unacceptable in Britain. A government health inspector had reported cases of children aged 12 years old who were suffering from the disease, which had probably influenced the decision by Cape Plc to pull out of South Africa.

Until 1979, Cape Plc used blue and brown asbestos mined in two areas of South Africa to supply its English factories at Barking and Hebden Mill. The worst type of asbestos disease is mesothelioma. This cancer, which attacks the lining of the lung or abdomen, does not respond to treatment. The pain is often uncontrollable and the patient usually dies within two years of symptoms being diagnosed.

The late South African physician and research pathologist, Dr Christopher Wagner (1923–2000) was first to diagnose mesothelioma tumours due to inhalation of asbestos particles in 1956, only for his preliminary paper to be rejected by a British medical journal in 1959 but published, after considerable informal criticism of editorial policy, in 1960. Since then, thousands of African miners have died but exact numbers are unknown because accurate records were not kept by the company. It is currently estimated that up to 3,000 people a year will die of this disease in Britain, where compensation for asbestos diseases is recognised by British courts. A similar compensation scheme was introduced by the new South African government after 1994 but amounts are small mainly because Cape Plc has closed down its operations and apparently withdrawn its assets from South Africa; and has yet to recognise any legal claims for compensation from its former employees.

On closing its plants in South Africa in the 1970s, the company left behind a legacy of incurable disease. One in seven of the population of Prieska suffers from asbestosis; and eight of the ten black miners who died during a five-year period after working in the nearby Koegas mine were diagnosed as suffering from the disease. One of the claimants, Cupido Adams, stated that he had sorted and packed asbestos with his bare hands and had never been issued with gloves or a safety mask He said:

The dust was everywhere. It lay an inch thick on the ground. There were no warnings. Children played in it. I lived half a kilometre from the factory but in order to drink had to scrape a layer of asbestos off the top of my water jar.

The High Court hearing is the latest in a series of attempts by Cape's lawyers to stop the cases coming to court in Britain. The company is trying to challenge a House of Lords ruling that the former workers in South Africa can sue for damages against Cape Plc in the British courts. Its main argument is that the House of Lords law lords based their judgment on the first five claimants, two of whom had since died, and they might have made a different decision if they had been informed about the other estimated 2,000 cases. Cape Plc wanted these claimants to sue in South Africa, although the claimants' British lawyers reckon that there is a strong chance that the South African courts would refuse to hear the case because it involves a company registered in the UK and not South Africa. Nevertheless, had Cape Plc been registered anywhere else in the European Union, its foreign workers would almost certainly have received adequate compensation by now.

From the start, Cape Plc has sought to have any compensation claims against it by South African citizens filed in South Africa rather than in England for the following commercial reasons:

- There has never been a group action suit filed in South Africa.
- No one has ever been compensated for an asbestos disease by a South African court.
- If a person dies from asbestos disease in South Africa, the claim does not survive for the benefit of the estate.
- Estimated compensation levels would be between 10 per cent and 20 per cent of payments awarded by British courts.
- South African claims must be started in several internal jurisdictions and consolidated at a later date.
- Other parties could also be joined in any litigation, such as other asbestos mining companies, insurance companies and local authorities, which would probably increase costs and delay judgment.
- Finally, by preventing cases proceeding in Britain, Cape Plc could recover the costs of defending any action in the English courts out of any compensation or costs awarded against it by the South African courts.

An unusual feature of the Cape Plc case is that it attracted the attention of prominent members of the British Labour Party and influential trade union leaders before the Court of Appeal ruling. In a letter published in *The Independent* (5 July 1999), Labour MP Ann Clwyd and MEP Glenys Kinnock, wife of the former Labour leader and at the time of writing deputy-president of the European Union, argue that British companies are trying to exploit a legal loophole to prevent cases from coming to court. 'We fear that the legal system is failing to deliver justice to people overseas who have suffered through the negligence of British companies', they write. Their letter is also co-signed by the general secretaries of three leading UK trade unions, two prominent academics at British universities and the World Development Movement and Action for Southern Africa which are supporting the complainants' action.

The claimants' lawyers are already dealing with a series of cases involving British companies registered in South Africa and have already won £1.3 million on behalf of 20 Zulu workers who contracted mercury poisoning in a factory operated by Thor Chemicals outside Pietermaritzburg in KwaZulu-Natal. A further case is being pursued on behalf of another 20 workers against the Margate-based British holding company which moved to South Africa in the 1980s after failing to satisfy the UK Health and Safety at Work regulations. These regulations are believed to be more rigorous than those applied elsewhere in the European Union and in North America, probably because of the indiscriminate use of asbestos during various 'building-booms' in the UK since World War II, resulting in a higher incidence of mesothelioma than in other industrialised nations.

In 1998, for example, a Canadian government submission to the UK Health and Safety Executive (*Financial Times*, 20 December 2000) challenged the banning of white asbestos in its regulations, arguing that workers, public health and the environment are not endangered when the substance is processed under current controlled conditions. The Canadian government statement continues: 'No scientifically credible comparative risk assessment can be made at the present time' over the dangers of white asbestos. Banning it will force the substitution of one substance that is 'stringently regulated and controlled' by alternative fibres and products (that is, mainly processed from blue and brown asbestos) 'which are not innocuous and whose toxicity can hardly be quantified empirically'. The Canadian government, which is supported by its mining companies and trade unions, concludes that: 'The prevention of future exposures will not alter the fact that many workers will suffer from mesothelioma as a result of exposures before stringent regulations were enacted' in the UK.

In a judgment handed down in November 1999, the Court of Appeal ruled that where a foreign forum was clearly the most appropriate for a group action of personal injury claims, the institution of the group action was a sufficient change of circumstances to entitle the Court of Appeal to reconsider the position of five claimants not in the group action, whose action had already been allowed to proceed by an earlier Court of Appeal decision. In all circumstances, the first action should be treated in the same way as the group action, and accordingly it was appropriate to stay both actions in the UK. In short, cases against Cape Plc should be filed before the South African courts, because claims against Cape Plc by the complainants had failed to give weight to the fact that negligence alleged against the defendants was distinct from any allegations which might be made against its South African subsidiaries.

The reasons for the Court of Appeal's ruling included:

- Although the basis of decisions and policies were taken in England almost everything else about the case occurred in South Africa.
- The South African courts were held in high repute and there was also in South Africa a legal profession with high standards and a tradition of public service.
- The plaintiff's solicitors were under an obligation to make their intentions clear (i.e. to proceed with a group action involving up to 2,000 South African claimants), but a tactical battle was being undertaken and neither party wished to bring out into the open before the courts the large number of claims which they were each aware was likely to emerge.

- The claimants could not complain if the issue as to which forum was appropriate (i.e. a South African or a British court) was now assessed in the light of the large number of claims which it was always hoped would follow upon their action.

Separate analysis by City financial experts concluded that Cape Plc would almost certainly have been driven into receivership had the cases of the 2,000 South African claimants been successful, with compensation on the level of that previously awarded to the 20 African employees of the UK-based Thor subsidiary in South Africa. Finally, *The Times* reported (5 October 1999, p. 17) that three months after the original judgment by the High Court in Britain, the South African Legal Aid Board, in a state of financial and organisational chaos, announced it will no longer fund personal compensation claims. This decision is partly because crime has spiralled in recent years, so the legal aid budget is largely earmarked for criminal defendants. The abolition means that, if cases ever go ahead in South Africa, lawyers there must fund them on contingency fees. Several legal firms have gone on record saying they will not contemplate such action, as it is not clear how clients or lawyers could be protected from adverse cost orders if the cases were lost or abandoned. The South African government has since decided to take up the case of the 2,000 claimants directly with the British government on the grounds that this group has now been denied the right to claim for financial compensation both in the UK and in South Africa, where Cape Plc has closed down its operations and allegedly transferred all its financial assets back to a holding company in Britain.

**Questions**

1 What precautions should be required of multinational companies like Union Carbide and Cape Plc to safeguard innocent citizens living in the vicinity of their subsidiary processing plants in overseas locations, and how should these standards be regulated?

2 What are the arguments for and against a developing country like South Africa banning a multinational company from manufacturing products within its borders which are regarded as too hazardous to public health in most industrialised First World countries?

3 How should equitable levels of compensation have been set for the loss of life or serious injury to Indian and South African citizens against the subsidiaries of foreign multinational companies, without creating bankruptcies, on the one hand, or trivial penalties, on the other?

## Notes and references

1. Meadows, D.L. and Forrester, J., *The Limits to Growth*, New York, Universe Books, 1972.
2. Kahn, H., Brown, W. and Martel, L., *The Great Transition, from the next 200 years*, New York, William Morrow, 1976.
3. Purdy, K.A., Environmental Ethics, *International Encyclopaedia of Ethics*, ed. J.K. Roth, London, Fitzroy-Dearborn, 1995, 267–70.
4. Hoffman, W.M., Frederick, R. and Petry, E.S. Jr (eds), *Business Ethics and the Environment: The public policy debate*, New York, Quorum Books, 1990.
5. Bowie, N., Morality, Money and the Motor Car, in *Business Ethics and the Environment: The public policy debate*, eds. W.M. Hoffman, R. Frederick and E.S. Petry, Jr, New York, Quorum Books, 1990, 89, 91, 94.
6. De George, R.T., *Moral Issues in Business*, 3rd edn, New York, Macmillan, 1990, 182–6.
7. Hoffman, M.F., Business and Environmental Ethics, *Business Ethics Quarterly*, 1991, April.

8. Singer, P., Not for Humans Only: The place of nonhumans in environmental ethics, in *Ethics and Problems of the 21st Century*, eds. K.E. Goodpaster and K.M. Sayre, Notre Dame, Ind., University of Notre Dame Press, 1979.

9. Stone, C.D., Should Trees Have Standing? Toward legal rights for natural objects, *Southern California Law Review*, 1972, 45.

10. Lovelock, J.E., *Gaia: A new look at life on Earth*, Oxford, Oxford University Press, 1979.

11. World Commission on Environment and Development, *Our Common Future*, Oxford, Oxford University Press, 1987, Pt II, ch 4.

12. Welford, R., *Hijacking Environmentalism: Corporate responses to sustainable development*, London, Earthscan, 1997.

13. McEwan, T., Petkov, D. and von Solms, S., Towards sustainable production and consumption in a South African paper mill, *Eco-Management Conference Proceedings*, University of Leeds, June 1999.

14. Kelman, S., What Price Incentives? Quoted by Tom Tietenberg, *Environmental and Natural Resource Economics*, New York, HarperCollins, 1992, p. 388.

# Moral Compass exercise

The Moral Compass instruments below are divided into two questionnaires, which should be evaluated using the 7-point Lickert scale shown in Box A. The simple Moral Compass contains the eight statements shown in Box B. The detailed Moral Compass includes the additional eight statements shown in Box C. Each statement corresponds with one of the ethical theories summarised in Chapter 4.

**Instructions**

1 Decide whether you wish to complete the simple or the detailed Moral Compass instrument.

2 Read each statement carefully before recording your response, using the 7-point Lickert scale shown in Box A below.

3 Record your scores for each part of the instruments in the Moral Compass section in the Appendix at the end of the book, where the corresponding ethical theories are shown.

**Box A**

| Strongly disagree | Disagree | Slightly disagree | Neither agree nor disagree | Slightly agree | Agree | Strongly agree |
|---|---|---|---|---|---|---|
| 1 | 2 | 3 | 4 | 5 | 6 | 7 |

## Box B

**S.1** When in Rome, fast on Fridays; elsewhere, adopt local customs to avoid attracting attention or giving scandal.

1 2 3 4 5 6 7

**S.2** If your moral outlook makes you miserable, then rest assured it's wrong.

1 2 3 4 5 6 7

**S.3** I decline utterly to be impartial. One has to look at the facts and consequences, then choose between the fire and the fire brigade.

1 2 3 4 5 6 7

**S.4** Companies should provide all employees with fair productivity bonuses and inclusion in share option schemes.

1 2 3 4 5 6 7

**S.5** Managers of multinational corporations should follow the moral principles of a host country where those of their home country do not apply.

1 2 3 4 5 6 7

**S.6** Modern organisations cannot consist of bosses and subordinates, but must be organised as teams that know their local environment.

1 2 3 4 5 6 7

**S.7** The purpose of any organisation is to integrate its specialised knowledge into a common task that achieves consensus in society.

1 2 3 4 5 6 7

**S.8** If doing what is ethical leads to the demise of a company, then so be it.

1 2 3 4 5 6 7

## Box C

**S.9** Never forget that to build an organisation on people, is to build on mud.

1 2 3 4 5 6 7

**S.10** To be ethical because it may increase your profits, is to be so entirely for the wrong reason.

1 2 3 4 5 6 7

**S.11** Trade unions are about individuals and the right of an employee to answer back to his/her boss.

1 2 3 4 5 6 7

**S.12** We must make the business world honest for ourselves, the community, and our children, before insisting that honesty is the best policy.

1 2 3 4 5 6 7

**S.13** I believe the power to make money is inherited, like a gift from God.

1 2 3 4 5 6 7

**S.14** Since we have each been equipped with a neck, each of us is surely supposed to stick it out in defence of a belief.

1 2 3 4 5 6 7

**S.15** 'Business is business', so it is said. That means anything goes; and the only rule is: 'Get ahead, and exploit your friends and your foes.'

1 2 3 4 5 6 7

**S.16** The public interest be damned: I'm working for my shareholders! (Of whom the speaker held the largest number of shares.)

1 2 3 4 5 6 7

# PART V

# Organisations in a global context

# 12 International business and the Third World

*Avarice and usury and precaution must be our gods for a little longer still. For only they can lead us out of the tunnel of economic necessity into daylight.*

John Maynard Keynes, Treatise on Money (1930), in *Collected Writings of John Maynard Keynes*, London, Royal Economic Society, 1971–9

## Learning objectives

After reading this chapter you should be able to:

- describe how economic growth and poverty coexist in industrialised countries, and consider how rival theories of distributive justice influence attitudes towards this imbalance and the more intractable problem of poverty in undeveloped countries;
- summarise attempts by richer countries to create international agencies for alleviating poverty and stimulating the economies of developing countries and the objections to some of these policies by non-governmental organisations (NGOs);
- distinguish between the notions of relative and absolute poverty and discuss the various moral obligations that the latter places on developed nations in providing development aid to undeveloped countries;
- evaluate the benefits and drawbacks of the investment strategy of international corporations in the world's poorer developing countries;
- explore the extent to which the rapid spread of the global economy has undermined the economic development of the poorest countries through the practice of 'triage' by inter-governmental institutions and international corporations;
- summarise the increasingly powerful role of non-governmental organisations against the exploitation of developing countries and review the need to alleviate poverty more rapidly in the undeveloped majority of countries in the Third World.

## Introduction

A recurring criticism of capitalism is that it reinforces the unequal distribution of wealth between a minority of industrialised nations and a majority of undeveloped countries mostly in the southern hemisphere. Admittedly, richer countries have responded by creating international agencies to accelerate development, although progress is hindered by huge debts, misuse of funds, civil unrest, and the exploitation of beneficiary countries by transnational corporations. Ethical arguments for assisting developing countries appear to be incontestible. However, moral philosophers disagree about whether this is a right of recipient countries, or a qualified obligation undertaken by richer nations. As a result, resources may be used to reduce relative poverty at home rather than for eradicating absolute poverty in the world's poorest countries.

## Poverty in the developed world

Admirers of America's robust federalism, open government and technological advancement, which has undoubtedly helped to raise living standards outside its borders during the twentieth century, must sometimes be baffled that so many of its own citizens live in dire poverty. Even if poverty is accepted as a relative term in the world's largest economy, it still baffles the imagination to learn from Shaw and Barry[1] that over one in six US workers earns poverty-level wages and nearly one-third of the unemployed fail to collect their statutory welfare entitlements. Greider[2] notes that tax legislation has been altered seven times since 1977, yet over 90 per cent of US families currently pay more tax than they did nearly 25 years ago. Government revenue has also fallen by $70 billion per year. As for the missing revenue, the main beneficiaries have been the large US corporations and the top 10 per cent highest earning families.

The *New York Times*[3] confirms that the top 1 per cent of US families own nearly 50 per cent of all publicly quoted shares, over 60 per cent of all business assets, nearly 80 per cent of bonds and trusts, and over 40 per cent of all non-residential property. The total assets of this elite, of which 98 per cent are white Americans, was an estimated $5.7 trillion in 1995, or about 70 per cent of the USA's total marketable assets. Admittedly, just under half of this wealth was inherited and accumulated over 150 years in many cases but the remainder was acquired by entrepreneurial activities since World War II. Hence, 20 per cent of all US families acquired over 49 per cent of the total national income, whereas the share of the bottom 60 per cent of families in 1995 fell to under 28 per cent, the lowest since the US Census Bureau began publishing data in 1947. Less accumulation of wealth has occurred in the UK where the top 50 per cent owned 92 per cent of Britain's total marketable assets in 1997, of which 17 per cent belonged to the richest 1 per cent of the population, leaving 8 per cent in the ownership of the other half of the population (*Social Trends*, HMSO, 1999).

## The pervasiveness of poverty

The underlying reasons for poverty cannot be understood without first considering wealth distribution as repeated studies show that extreme poverty coexists alongside huge wealth, not only in the USA and the UK, but also in other developed countries, although often to a lesser degree. Unfortunately, political explanations seem to provide unreliable forecasts of poverty. For example, President Clinton completed his second four-year term in office in late 2000, but *The Economist* (20 May 2000, p. 24) reports that:

> despite almost a decade of economic boom, around one in eight Americans – including almost one in five children – still lives in poverty . . . the poverty rate . . . dropped from a high of 15% in the early 1990s [when a Republican President was last in power] but it is still higher than it was in the 1970s.

The economic restructuring which has helped create over five million new jobs in the USA since the 1980s has also done little to eradicate poverty, even at the epicentre of the USA's information society, in Silicon Valley, where 'some of America's poorer people – the bottom fifth of the Valley's inhabitants – saw their incomes decline in the 1990s' (*Weekend FT Supplement*, 27 May 2000, p. 1). *The Economist* correctly identifies two socioeconomic problems that underlie America's modern poverty as the lack of skills in education and training, and the breakdown of family life, but this analysis singularly fails to mention the impact of libertarian values on the redistribution of wealth in both the USA and in the UK since the early 1980s.

## Widening income disparities in organisations

Reliable evidence exists for accepting that the spread of libertarian values has resulted in a steep stratification of incomes in private sector organisations in the USA and UK since the 1980s. For example, the pay of non-supervisory employees in the USA, adjusted for inflation, was at its lowest in the mid-1990s since the mid-1960s, whereas the earnings of both middle and senior managers increased spectacularly over the same period[2,3]. Furthermore, Eckhouse[4] confirms that the total remuneration of US executives (CEOs) increased from 42 times to over 140 times that of a typical production employee. Differentials were less vertiginous in the UK where the average income of the top 20 per cent clambered to only 19 times higher than the bottom 20 per cent of employees in 1996 (*Social Trends*, 1999); and a mere one-third of UK leading company CEOs have dared to award themselves salary and bonus increases of over 20 per cent, barely seven times the annual rate of inflation in 1999 (*The Independent Review*, 27 April 2000 p. 3).

Even in the less controversial field of eradicating child poverty, the USA and UK have worse records than other industrialised nations. The child poverty rate is 21 per cent in the USA which spends only 0.6 per cent GDP on basic income support for children compared with 1.6 per cent in neighbouring Canada[5]. Meanwhile, child poverty in the UK affected 3 million children each year from 1993 to 1996 compared with only 1.4 million in 1980. In short, nearly one-third of all UK children were in poverty compared with 13 per cent in Germany, 12 per cent in France and 24 per cent in Italy (Institute of Public Policy Research, www.independent.co.uk/links/, 17 March 2000).

Some might point to the historical inevitability of capitalism, which always creates 'winners' and 'losers', but this surely restates the offensive principles of Social Darwinism summarised in Chapter 4, and makes a mockery of the widespread opposition to fascism and apartheid earlier in the twentieth century. Shaw and Barry reject the view that these large inequalities in wealth and income are inevitable and cite the economies of Japan and Germany, both as capitalistic as the USA and the UK, where the distributions of incomes are far less extreme. For them, 'inequality of income is not some brute fact of nature, even in market-oriented countries' and 'how much inequality a society is willing to accept reflects both its moral values and the relative strength of its contending social and political forces' (pp. 97–8).

Explanations of why more unequal distributions of wealth and income occur in prosperous democratic countries like the USA and the UK are too complicated for full discussion in this book. What can be asserted, however, is that any answer will be incomplete unless it explores the different values and beliefs people hold about distributive justice, which are likely to influence their political and socioeconomic behaviour.

## The concept of distributive justice

The concept of justice has been an important branch of ethics at least since Aristotle, who noted that it invariably raises the interrelated notions of:

- individual rights;
- fairness;
- equality; and
- entitlement.

These issues are often discussed as *distributive justice*, which explores the appropriate distribution of social and economic benefits and related costs in any given society according to the following five principles:

1 *An equal share for each individual/collectivity.* This approach upholds the principle of equal benefits for each individual or family as, for example, when equal family allowances have been paid by successive post-war governments in the UK, regardless of differences in family income.

2 *A share according to the needs of each individual/collectivity.* This approach is based on the principle of targeting specific needs of individuals usually in cases where rationing is seen as necessary. For example, special offers in a supermarket may be limited to one item per customer to attract the largest number of shoppers and reduce complaints should stocks run out too early.

3 *A share according to the efforts of each individual/collectivity.* This approach supports the principle of recognising individual achievement, as in the case of a productivity scheme that rewards staff according to their individual outputs.

4 *A share according to the social contribution of each individual/collectivity.* This approach grants awards according to the social benefit of specific activities such as paid leave of absence for employees to attend local council or trade union meetings, or tax concessions when a firm organises specialised training for its employees not provided by its competitors.

5 *A share according to the merits of each individual/collectivity.* This approach supports the principle of rewarding recipients on the basis of individual merit or collective achievement, as in competitions when the winners receive most prize money, or when a company is awarded the Queen's Award for Industry in recognition of outstanding export achievements.

## Three theories of distributive justice

The approaches to distributive justice considered below have influenced the economic, political and moral values both domestically in richer developed nations, and externally in their relationships with poorer developing countries.

### A libertarian approach

Nozick's[6] libertarian theory of economic distribution asserts that individuals possess what he describes as 'Lockean rights' (discussed in Chapter 3). Acknowledgement of these rights imposes 'side constraints' on how individuals may behave towards other persons, so that each individual remains responsible for his/her own unique life without coercion from others. This is achieved through an entitlement theory of economic justice which allows each individual to own personal goods, property and money that have been fairly obtained. The individual is also entitled to dispose of them as he or she chooses, unless one or more persons have a prior claim to them due to violation of their Lockean rights.

This entitlement theory is derived from three interrelated principles:

1 *The original acquisition of holdings.* Following Locke, Nozick argues that property is a moral right since individuals are entitled to the products of their labour, as when personal assets are used productively and sold without others suffering from these transactions. This principle also applies to money which may be held/saved without deterioration, other than that due to inflation.
2 *The legitimate transfer of holdings to/from others.* Individuals may also acquire assets from others which they are entitled to hold if legally obtained. These include all purchases, exchanges, gifts received or donated, but exclude anything obtained by theft, fraud or violence.
3 *The illegal acquisition of holdings.* Nozick defines injustice as any violation of a person's rights which seeks to justify the illegal acquisition of holdings contrary to the above two principles.

Paramount in Nozick's entitlement theory of economic distribution is how possessions are acquired. If individuals are legitimately entitled to their holdings then economic distribution is just, regardless of actual distribution at any one time. Whether the distribution is just depends solely on how holdings were acquired. Property rights are derived from an individual's basic moral rights which take priority over all social or legislative arrangements imposed by society. Hence, Nozick rejects the notion of taxes imposed by government for redistribution purposes, such as the provision of family income support benefits for those on low incomes, or government (as opposed to individual) aid for, say, flood victims in Mozambique. Such actions are unjust because 'Taxation of earnings from labour is on a par with forced labour.'

## A utilitarian approach

Also discussed in Chapter 4, utilitarianism is concerned with the maximisation of personal happiness which should ultimately determine what is just or unjust behaviour. However, it is not easy to identify which activities will promote human happiness for want of a reliable standard of utility. John Stuart Mill[7] acknowledged that without a clear standard of justice, confusion about how to evaluate principles is inevitable. In discussing economic distribution, he asked whether it is just that talented workers should receive greater remuneration than less capable counterparts, noting that two valid answers are possible. From one standpoint, whoever did their best 'ought not in justice . . . be put in a position of inferiority for no fault of his own'. On the other hand, 'society receives more from the more efficient labourer . . . [whose] . . . services being more useful, society owes him a larger return for them'. If arbitrary distinctions between equally plausible answers were to be avoided, 'social utility alone can decide the preference'. A utilitarian standard is therefore essential for resolving any conflict between rival principles of justice.

Mill's analysis of the relationship between injustice and justice indicated that injustice involves the denial of rights to some identifiable person. It differs from other forms of immoral behaviour because the denial of individual rights may include loss of possessions, breaking one's word, or treating the person worse than he or she deserves; and less equitably than people without superior claims to the individual. What these examples share in common is 'a wrong done and some assignable person who is wronged . . . the specific difference between justice and generosity and beneficence [is that] justice implies something which is not right to do, and wrong to do, but which some individual can claim from us as his moral right.'

If injustice involves the denial of moral rights, it follows that to possess a right to something is equivalent to having a valid claim on society to protect an individual's possession of that thing, either by law, education or pressure of public opinion. Justice, for Mill,

> is the name of certain classes of moral rules which concern the essentials of human well-being [and] the essence of the idea of justice – that of a right residing in an individual – implies . . . the moral rules which forbid mankind to hurt one another (in which we must never forget to include wrongful interference with each other's freedom).

Ultimately, the attainment of justice is a matter of pursuing social well-being which is tied to the question of promoting happiness through economic distribution.

During the early nineteenth century, as Shaw and Barry[1] observe, most utilitarians supported the free trade and *laissez-faire* economics associated with Adam Smith (and since cherished by modern libertarians), in the belief that unregulated markets and free competition were most likely to promote the overall social good. Modern utilitarians generally reject the notion that human happiness would be maximised under a system of unregulated market capitalism, unless specific welfare arrangements are guaranteed. However, Mill's[7] proposals for dealing with domestic economic redistribution by ending industrial conflict between the workforce and the owners/capitalists remain relevant in modern technological society. He supported worker participation and the cooperative principle which he thought 'would combine the freedom and independence of the individual with the moral, intellectual and economical advantages of aggregate production'. Such a transformation was nothing less than 'the nearest approach to social justice and the most beneficial ordering of industrial affairs for the universal good, which it is possible at present to foresee'. This analysis exposes the prolix in much that is written today about 'empowerment'.

Modern utilitarians also favour a reduction of the wide disparities of income that characterise capitalist societies because of 'the declining marginal utility of money' which, in plain words, means that on average successive increases in purchasing power are unlikely to produce more happiness. For example, the benefits gained from buying one lawnmower are unlikely to increase threefold as a result of purchasing a third machine. This reasoning supports the utilitarian view of Brandt[8] that a more equal distribution of income from those with more to those with less is likely to increase the overall happiness of a society.

## An egalitarian approach

This approach is associated with the views of John Rawls[9], author of *A Theory of Justice*, which explores the concept of justice in relation to the ideals of equality and freedom. His initial analysis is based on the notion of a social contract discussed in Chapter 4, except that Rawls introduces the notion of an abstract social contract to establish principles of justice rather than present specific laws or other social arrangements. His hypothetical contract therefore describes persons who are in an idealised 'original position', which is not unlike the 'state of nature' starting point of the social contract.

Rawls further assumes that these persons in the original position all live behind a 'veil of ignorance', unaware of their age, race, gender; or whether they are rich or poor, idle, energetic, intelligent or stupid. They are also assumed to know nothing about their individual situation or what sort of society they will be entering once the 'veil of ignorance' is lifted.

These constraints are included to ensure that the principles persons choose to live under are fair so that they will not seek to gain any overt or covert individual advantage over others. Rawls arrives at these principles by rational analysis. For example, these hypothetical people will be reluctant to live under utilitarian principles intended to provide the greatest good for the greatest number, rather than for all, as some members of society will be excluded. These could include anyone who chose to implement this system in the first place. Rather, people in the original position would choose to adopt what is known in games theory as a 'maximin' rule, which states that the option should be chosen under which the worse that could happen is better than the worse under any alternative system. A period of 'reflective equilibrium' should convince people that each individual will care more about avoiding an unacceptable outcome (e.g. execution) than in achieving the ideal outcome (e.g. world's richest person), given that no one has advance knowledge of what a hypothetical society would be like once the 'veil of ignorance' is lifted.

Furthermore, after considering all the possible options in a rational and systematic way, people will finally choose the following two basic principles of justice:

- Each person has an equal right to the most extensive scheme of equal basic liberties compatible with a similar scheme of liberties for all.
- Social and economic inequalities are to meet two conditions: they must be (a) to the greatest expected benefit of the least advantaged and (b) attached to offices and positions open to all under conditions of fair equality of opportunity.

Under the first principle, Rawls defends the notion that every individual would be assured justice as equal treatment for all once the veil of ignorance is removed. As for the equally important claim of freedom, Rawls argues that the 'maximin' principle recognises that: 'each person possesses an inviolability founded on justice that even the welfare of society as a whole cannot override [and] the rights secured by justice are not subject to political bargaining or the calculus of social interests.'

Under the second principle, Rawls addresses the notions of social and economic inequalities. To redress social inequalities, positions in society should be viewed, not in terms of any differences between offices and positions, but as 'differences in benefits and burdens attached to them, such as prestige and wealth, or liability to taxation and compulsory service'. As an analogy, he notes that baseball players do not challenge the notion of different positions or the various privileges and powers invested in each position under the rules of the game. Similarly, a nation's citizens do not object to the offices of president, senator or governor, or to the special rights and duties associated with each different position. In short, the basic social structure, not the transactions between individuals, should establish justice as a cooperative project for the mutual benefit of society, and minimise the socioeconomic consequences of random natural differences between people.

Challenged by libertarian critics that this would reduce the larger entitlements of those who emerged from behind the veil of ignorance with more talents and other advantages, Rawls' response was that: 'the primary subject of justice is not, in the first instance, transactions between individuals but the basic structure, the fundamental social institutions and their arrangement into one scheme.' He added that inequalities are most likely to be eliminated under a liberal form of capitalism, which includes enough welfare provisions to eradicate the unjust effects of excessive disparities in income, although the economic justice could also be obtained under a system of democratic socialism.

---

**Box 12.1**     **Practical steps towards a more egalitarian community**

A small practical example of distributive justice was introduced years before Rawls' theory was published by nuns in a remote convent at Freshfield, 15 miles from Liverpool, which had to accommodate nearly 70 evacuee children at short notice for most of World War II. To begin with, pandemonium would erupt on most days as larger/older children would snatch bigger portions of food away from smaller/younger children. Some squabbles could not be stopped in time by the nuns, nor injustices corrected afterwards because of food rationing. Instead, they established order in a more subtle way by persuading the children, who sat on opposite sides of long dining tables, to 'serve or choose' two portions of food. Peace and justice were achieved as the children soon acquired the practical skills of brain surgeons and precision engineers in ensuring that each portion was exactly the same size.

---

## Evaluation of the three theories of distributive justice

### Arguments for and against the libertarian view

De George[10] discusses property rights and their use/distribution from rival standpoints beginning with the status quo perspective on resources which supports the libertarian views of Nozick. The latter analysis supports the position that people must start with the world as they find it, with its resources already divided up. Arguments about the past or present ownership are therefore futile since different societies create mechanisms for deciding when the ownership rights they recognise are violated. According to this historical view, justice and equity amount to abiding by accepted rules and procedures in a system which usually carries legal force to ensure that abuses are condemned.

Singer[11] rejects this libertarian perspective on economic distribution which 'leaves too much to chance to be an acceptable ethical view'. For example, he compares the moral claims of those who settled in the sandy wastes around the Persian Gulf without any foreknowledge of the oil deposits beneath, who centuries later are enormously wealthy, with those who settled on better land in sub-Saharan Africa and now live in absolute poverty. He also challenges the notions of property rights and the allocation of the world's resources, adding that utilitarians and egalitarians are opposed to the libertarian views on distributive justice. For him, the theory of rights advanced by Nozick means that, provided one's property and possessions are obtained without force or fraud, an individual is entitled to accumulate enormous wealth while others starve. The latter view is rejected as immoral by all the great religions summarised in Chapter 3 and Singer adds that libertarianism is in direct opposition to the natural law view of Aquinas summarised in Chapter 4 that: 'whatever a man has in superabundance is owed, of natural right, to the poor for their sustenance.'

## Arguments for and against the utilitarian position

In seeking to achieve the greatest good for the greatest number of people, supporters of utilitarianism accept that some form of cost–benefit analysis rationing is essential. Eradication of all poverty is, however, an enormous task and the 'benefits' of incremental reductions are warranted if the 'costs' of social unrest are minimised. Extending this reasoning globally may mean, as De George observes, that the claims of those nearby, afflicted by domestic poverty, are reduced or neglected. He explores the case for taking care of our own first, by noting that those who support this argument are also often sympathetic to the plight of all disadvantaged people but maintain that the first moral obligation is to look after families and the poor in their own countries before considering the huge burden of alleviating poverty overseas.

Singer accepts that kinship ties are stronger than citizenship but adds that it is difficult to see any sound moral justification for the view that distance or community membership make a crucial difference to our obligations to those further away. For him, any small degree of preference for kinship ties is 'decisively outweighed by existing discrepancies in wealth and property'. As an example, he notes that these discrepancies not only prevent poor developing countries from buying grain produced by developed nations, but also that their farmers cannot afford to purchase improved seeds, fertilisers, or the technology to drill wells for irrigation. This argument has since been powerfully repeated by V. Shiva[12] in the BBC Reith Lecture 2000; and some of the consequences are summarised below.

## Arguments for and against the egalitarian position

Miller's[13] and Singer's views complement Rawls' egalitarian position, although Miller's analysis is less detailed and lacks concrete examples. Instead, he supports the view that since all people are entitled to live lives of material and psychological prosperity, the grossly unequal distribution of prosperity in the world has to change. Singer, who adopts a utilitarian position, provides the following rationale to justify a more egalitarian approach towards the poorest nations:

- *First premise*: If we can prevent something bad without sacrificing anything of comparable significance, we ought to do it.
- *Second premise*: Absolute poverty is bad.
- *Third premise*: There is some absolute poverty we can prevent without sacrificing anything of comparable moral value.
- *Conclusion*: We ought to prevent some absolute poverty.

He argues that the problem is not that the world is unable to produce enough to feed and shelter its population but that insufficient welfare provisions are in place to eradicate the unjust effects of excessive disparities in income which lead to absolute poverty. For example, he cites the fivefold disparity between the average grain consumption in developing countries of 180 kg/annum compared with about 900 kg/annum in North America, where much of the grain is fed to animals to produce meat and dairy products. Singer concludes that severe poverty could be eradicated if adequate welfare arrangements were provided. He adds that: 'The principle seems uncontroversial . . . most non-consequentialists [e.g. Robert Nozick] . . . hold that we ought to prevent what is bad – serious violations of individual rights, injustice, broken promises, and so on – and promote what is good.'

In summary, it should be noted that, just as libertarians are critical of any attempt by utilitarians or egalitarians to tamper with any of the property rights of the individual, so egalitarians reject the utilitarian notion (inherited from an earlier acceptance of the classical free market economic distribution of wealth) that the pursuit of happiness through economic distribution may result in exceptions through the application of piecemeal moral principles. These distinctions are important to understanding prevailing attitudes towards redistribution in both the rich modern market economies of the First World and in the poorer developing countries of the Third World.

## Relative and absolute poverty

Following Singer, any discussion of the ethics of the First/Third World nations relationship has to consider differences between the relative 'domestic' poverty summarised on pp. 272–3 and the absolute poverty of the poorest Third World nations. As examples of *relative poverty*, lone pensioners and single parents are amongst the poorest people in Britain, considerably less prosperous than the CEO of a typical UK company. Yet the former are similarly less poor than the typical unemployed male Zulu in KwaZulu-Natal whose income, according to the 1996 South African Census, is less than £200 per annum. Their situation is described as relative poverty and the lone pensioner and single parent would need to transfer their assets and relocate to Durban, rather than Dulwich or Derby, before their relative UK poverty could be alleviated. Examples of relative poverty would include the families, people who fail to collect their welfare entitlements, deprived children, lone pensioners and single parents in roughly the bottom 15 to 20 per cent of most First World societies, but more likely in the USA or Britain.

However, according to Robert McNamara, former US Government Defense Secretary and World Bank President, *absolute poverty* is: 'life at the very margin of existence . . . The absolute poor are severely deprived human beings, struggling to survive in a set of squalid and degraded circumstances almost beyond the power of our sophisticated imaginations and privileged circumstances to conceive.' He adds: 'Absolute poverty is a condition of life so characterised by malnutrition, illiteracy, disease, squalid surroundings, high infant mortality and low life expectancy as to be beneath any reasonable definition of human decency.' He is quoted in Singer[11], who also cites the World Watch Institute estimate that 1.2 billion people, or over 20 per cent of the world's population, live in absolute poverty because of 'the lack of sufficient cash or kind to meet the most basic biological necessities of food, clothing and shelter'.

## Redistribution as a zero-sum game

Miller argues that the economic relationship between First World and Third World countries is predicated on a relationship of unequal exchange based on the premise that economic interaction is a zero-sum game. This implies that, as one nation acquires more wealth and becomes richer, another nation loses wealth and becomes poorer. For Kelly[14], this means 'wealth is made on the backs of the poor'. It follows that if the developed First World countries are hoarding wealth, which is generating poverty in the undeveloped Third World, poverty could be eliminated by redistributing the wealth from developed to underdeveloped nations. One remedy proposed by the UN is to decrease this inequality by redistribution of wealth through foreign aid, low interest loans and grants administered by agencies such as the World Bank Group and the International Monetary Fund which are discussed below.

## First, Second and Third World comparisons

### The First World

This term is falling out of use but refers to the Western capitalist countries and prosperous southern hemisphere nations such as Japan, Australia and New Zealand. China will very likely be recognised as a First World member country soon, as its GDP is expanding at over 7 per cent annually and it already holds foreign reserves of approximately US$155 billion (*The Economist*, 11 December 1999). Other Asian countries, known collectively as the 'Asian Tigers', such as Singapore, Taiwan, Malaysia and Indonesia, are recognised as emerging First World countries despite economic setbacks during the late 1990s. Economically, First World countries belong to larger trading blocs such as the EU, North American Free Trade Area (NAFTA) and the Association of South East Asian Nations (ASEAN) which were, politically, opposed to the communist system before the Cold War ended in the early 1990s.

### The Second World

This term is also nearly redundant, but is still applied to the former communist countries that comprised the Soviet Union and the COMECOM economic union, which were ideologically opposed to the First World for nearly 40 years during the Cold

War period. Since the fragmentation of the Soviet Union in the 1990s, former member-states such as Poland and Hungary have applied to join the European Union, others stress their independence and international importance, notably Russia and Ukraine, and some have aligned themselves more closely with Islamic fundamentalism.

## The Third World

This term is used inaccurately to group developing countries and over 40 undeveloped countries under the heading of the world's poorer countries in Asia, Africa and Latin America, with some countries in the Middle East. Most Third World countries were not aligned to either the First or Second World blocs during the Cold War period, despite occupying over 60 per cent of the world's land surface and containing 70 per cent of its population, with China and India as the two largest member-nations and Gabon, Guyana and Mauritius amongst the smallest. These widespread countries are less homogeneous than First World countries and necessarily include a wider variety of social, economic, cultural, political, and geographically diverse environments. Most Third World countries were colonies of First World countries from the eighteenth/nineteenth centuries onwards until achieving independence after World War II.

Pacione[15] observes that the weak economic systems in Third World countries are characterised by low agricultural productivity, an underdeveloped industrial base, limited technology and purchasing power, and reliance on too few export products. This makes their economies particularly vulnerable to fluctuations in supply and demand. There is a reliance on foreign investments, and the importation of industrial equipment. Per capita GDP is generally less than $3,000 and less than a few hundred dollars in the poorest countries (compared with $20,000 equivalent in the UK and $29,000 in the USA in 1997). The average income ratio between First and Third World countries exceeds 140:1 ($22,808 to $163 per capita).

Absolute poverty is therefore more pervasive than in First World countries and hard to alleviate because of the inability of poorer nations to repay interest (let alone capital) on international loans which exceed their combined education and health budgets in several African countries. As a result, welfare systems are inadequate or non-existent and these countries suffer high rates of mortality and malnutrition. Countries dependent on one or two main crops are vulnerable to famine whenever these crops fail. Efforts by First World countries to help conquer poverty through direct aid and debt relief are moderately successful, except as shown in Table 12.1, in the poorest African countries, which remain poorer than in the 1960s.

Demographic problems also beset Third World countries and diseases such as malaria, bilharzia and the HIV/AIDS pandemic in sub-Saharan Africa contribute to the low life expectancy at birth. The poorest African countries have also experienced more political instability than their Asian, Latin American and Middle Eastern counterparts, which has undermined their relatively inexperienced government administrations, encouraged corruption and civil wars, and promoted further inequities based on tribalism which concentrated wealth disproportionately amongst the ruling elites. Many of these regimes retain power only through the supply of arms from richer countries. Insufficient resources are therefore deployed on social programmes and education; and high unemployment occurs particularly among women. Because of

## Table 12.1 Balance sheet of human development

| Human progress | Human deprivation |
|---|---|
| **Life expectancy** | |
| Average life expectancy in the South increased by a third during 1960–87 and is now 80% of Northern average. | Average life expectancy in the South is still 12 years less than in the North. |
| **Education** | |
| Almost five times more children in primary education (480 m) in the South compared with the North (105 m). | Almost 100 m children of primary school age in the South do not attend school. |
| 1.4 bn literate people in the South compared with nearly 1 bn in the North. | Nearly 900 m illiterate people in the South. |
| Literacy rates in the South increased from 43% in 1970 to 60% in 1985. | Literacy rates are still only 41% in South Asia and 48% in sub-Saharan Africa. |
| **Income** | |
| Average per capita incomes in the South increased by almost 3% a year between 1965 and 1980. | More than 1 bn people in the South live in absolute poverty. |
| | Per capita income in the 1980s declined by 2.4% annually in sub-Saharan Africa and by 0.7% annually in Latin America. |
| **Health** | |
| More than 60% of Southern populations have access to health services in 1990. | 1.5 bn people in the South are still without primary healthcare. |
| Over 2 bn people in the South have access to safe, potable water. | 1.75 bn people in the South are still without a safe source of potable water. |
| **Children's health** | |
| Mortality rates of children under 5 years in the South halved between 1960 and 1988. | 1.4 bn children in the South die annually before 5 years of age. |
| Child immunisation in the South increased from 30% to 70% in the 1980s, saving an estimated 1.5 m lives annually. | Nearly 3 m children in the South die annually from immunisable diseases. |
| **Food and nutrition** | |
| Per capita average calorie intake supply increased by 20% between 1960 and 1985. | Over 16% of people in the South still go hungry every day. |
| Average calories supplied rose from 90% of total requirements in 1965 to 107% in 1985. | 150 m children under 5 (one in three) in the South suffer from serious malnutrition. |
| **Sanitation** | |
| 1.3 bn people in the South have access to adequate sanitary facilities. | Nearly 3 bn people in the South still lack adequate sanitary facilities. |
| **Women** | |
| School enrolment rates for girls have increased at more than twice the rate of that of boys. | The female literacy rate in the South is still less than two-thirds that of boys. |
| | The maternal mortality rate in the South is still 122 times higher than in the North. |

*Source*: United Nations Development Programme Report 1990, New York, 1992. Hewitt, T., 'Developing Countries, 1945–90', in *Poverty and Development in the 1990s*, ed. T. Allen and A. Thomas, Oxford, Oxford University Press 1992, p. 451.

these inequities, better-educated members of the population tend to leave, and Miller[13] notes that one-third of Africans with post-secondary education emigrated to Europe in the 1980s.

The disparity in the distribution of wealth and power between First World and Third World countries widened considerably from 1960 to 1990. The 1992 United Nations Development Programme reports that income disparities between the richest 20 per cent and the poorest 20 per cent of countries more than doubled during this thirty-year period. Economic activity in the control of total gross national product, world trade, commercial lending, domestic savings, and domestic investment by the richest 20 per cent of First World nations stood at between 80 and 95 per cent. The poorest 20 per cent of countries controlled between 0.2 and 1.4 per cent of the same economic activity. This massive disparity in economic activity persists despite the sustained efforts of numerous UN and other agencies to eradicate poverty in the poorest countries with the qualified assistance of the World Trade Organisation, which is periodically hampered by the unregulated activities of some international companies.

## International development and trade

### United Nations development agencies

The principal designated UN economic development programmes in aid of poorer member countries are coordinated by the UN Economic and Social Council (UNESC) which monitors the UN Development Programme (UNDP) and inter- and non-governmental organisations. The UNDP is funded by voluntary contributions from richer UN member countries, and its aims are elimination of poverty, environmental regulation, job creation and advancement of women. All UNESC policies are funded by the International Bank for Reconstruction and Development (IBRD), commonly known as the World Bank, and the International Monetary Fund (IMF). UNESC also holds joint consultations with the World Trade Organisation, which represents the interests of its First World founder nations and transnational corporations (TNCs). UNESC also coordinates its policies with non-governmental organisations (NGOs) funded by charitable donations; and philanthropic institutions, such the Rockefeller and Ford Foundations, which support rarely publicised development projects in the poorest countries. All of these organisations are ultimately responsible to the UN General Assembly's 185 member countries which fund the United Nations Organisation (UNO) although, in reality, the interests of leading First World donor countries are coordinated by the Organisation for Economic Cooperation and Development (OECD).

### The World Bank Group (IBRD)

The World Bank was approved at the Bretton Woods Conference in 1944 and formed in 1946. The bank is self-supporting and obtains funds from capital paid by member-states, sales of its own securities, factoring of its own loans, and repayments by beneficiary nations. Loans are made to member countries against bonds backed by pledges from other governments and repayment of previous loans to members. Loans amount to over $22 billion annually and in 1996 the IBRD classified economies as low income (average GDP per capita of $785 or less), middle income (between $786 and $9, 635) and high income (above $9,635).

Some critics complain that this leads to discriminatory policies against the poorest countries based on 'triage' which is discussed later in this chapter. The bank launched the International Development Association (IDA) in 1960 to make long-term interest free loans to developing nations. Some of these funds are raised by the International Finance Corporation (IFC) through contacts with what is now the World Trade Organisation to encourage private firms to invest in undeveloped countries.

## International Monetary Fund (IMF)

This institution was also approved at Bretton Woods, established in 1945 and was formed as an independent international organisation in an agreement of mutual cooperation with the UN in 1947. Its aims were to promote monetary cooperation by expanding international trade and exchange rate stability, and the removal of barriers through a multilateral payments system supported by IMF financial resources. These are subject to strict IMF economic conditions to ensure the revolving nature of IMF resources. The IMF has 175 member countries and is funded mostly by the USA, which provided one-third of its assets in 1947, the UK, Germany, Japan, France and Saudi Arabia. Supplementary drawing rights (SDRs) were introduced in 1970 to protect the gold and currency reserves of member-states. These can be traded directly with the World Bank or other trading nations to repay debts or arrange loans. The members with the largest drawing rights are first the USA, joint second Germany and Japan and joint fourth France and the UK. That said, Mexico, South Korea, Thailand, Russia, Ukraine and Indonesia all received major supplementary loans in excess of their SDR entitlements during the 1990s.

IMF activities often overlap with the World Bank's in terms of providing financial development assistance to poorer developing countries subject mainly to the approval of the leading First World founding nations. Hence, to qualify for loans, member-states must demonstrate a willingness to change from a command to a free market economy subject to stringent controls which have led to political unrest in recipient countries although there is some evidence that economic stability and growth has occurred in most debtor nations over the longer term.

## Organisation for Economic Cooperation and Development (OECD)

This is an organisation of the governments of the world's richest nations. OECD is currently negotiating the first ever international agreement that would bind transnational corporations (see below) to collaborate in eliminating the use of child labour and forced labour, both directly and indirectly by their suppliers and customers. The agreement, which is legally binding, has taken three years to negotiate, and will also require signatories to ensure that transnational corporations improve the environmental standards of their operations in undeveloped countries. Mexico is threatening to veto the new agreement for fear it may deter Americans from investing in its *maquiladorora* manufacturing region near the US border with Mexico. As a result of representations from Mexico and other developing countries, the US

Department of Commerce released a statement of Model Business Principles for US businesses trading globally which have been placed before the World Trade Organisation for adoption. These voluntary guidelines include the provision of a safe and healthy workplace; fair employment practices; avoidance of child and forced labour; avoidance of discriminatory practices based on race, gender, national origin or religious beliefs; and respect of right of association and collective bargaining principles. Additional guidelines include responsible environmental protection and practices, and the banning of illicit payments, unfair competition and political coercion in the workplace (*New York Times*, 27 May 1995, p. 17).

The OECD has also reached an international agreement to isolate up to 35 'harmful' tax havens which are required to abandon special status arrangements before January 2006. The OECD aim is to eliminate practices such as the huge growth of money laundering of deposits from organised crime, tax evasion in their country of origin by non-residents who invest in tax havens, and harmful tax competition between countries for international investment on the Internet. Because of the secretive nature of these transactions, tax revenue lost by OECD countries to tax havens is unknown but is likely to exceed hundreds of billions, if not trillions, of dollars worldwide. Of the 35 countries cited, the Channel Islands, Belize, the Virgin Islands and Gibraltar have been officially named as 'harmful tax havens', and have six months to agree on a timetable of tax reforms acceptable to the OECD countries.[16]

## The World Trade Organisation (WTO)

Increasing international trade led to the formation of the WTO in 1995 to succeed the General Agreement on Tariffs and Trade (GATT), which emerged as an interim agreement in 1948 while a new international trade organisation was being debated by the United Nations Economic and Social Committee (UNESCO). The organisation's charter was never ratified because of disagreements between rival political and economic blocs during the Cold War period. Hence, GATT 'Rounds' emerged as the *de facto* regime which met the political aims of the powerful First World economies and which have formulated new rules/procedures for regulating world trade over the last 50 years.

The economic purpose of GATT was to expand non-discriminatory international free trade through successive rounds of multilateral negotiations. Eight GATT rounds, starting in Geneva in 1947 and ending in Uruguay (1986–94), prepared the way for average duties on manufactured goods to be reduced from 40 per cent to 3 per cent by 2002. Because of the drawn-out Uruguay Round, GATT was replaced by the WTO as the legal and institutional trading system for creating binding contractual obligations on how member nations draft and implement international trade policy. Supporters claim that world trade has been placed on a more secure basis through liberalisation, debate and negotiation among member nations. WTO adjudication is also accepted as the means of settling trade disputes between nations. In 1999, the WTO administered 29 multilateral agreements between members covering trade in agriculture, textiles and clothing, financial services, government procurement, rules of origin and intellectual property rights. These arrangements applied to 134 member-states and applications for entry by a further 31 countries have still to be approved.

## Transnational corporations (TNCs)

These are defined by the *Cambridge Encyclopaedia* as 'large corporate enterprises spread across a number of nations, via subsidiaries and holding companies etc.' The term is interchangeable with multinational corporations to describe firms that have no 'national' economy with which they are closely associated because these corporations may appear to act against the interests of their 'home' economy by closing down factories, to open others in 'host' countries, as part of a global restructuring programme. TNCs were developed in First World countries and trade in their own domestic markets and overseas. However, a larger proportion are now being launched by Asian Tiger countries. Since 1980, their number has increased from about 7,500 to over 16,000 in 1997. The largest TNCs such as Exxon, Ford, Royal Dutch Shell, Microsoft and Vodaphone each have turnovers larger than the GNP of 80 per cent of the world's countries. They previously specialised in mineral and oil extraction and manufacturing but new TNCs specialise in global communications, computing systems, retailing, the media and agricultural services.

## Transnational corporations and the Third World

Each TNC is likely to have different strategic aims before or after deciding to invest in Third World countries and arguments for and against these strategies are summarised below. Before considering the various criticisms levelled against TNCs, it is worth noting that, for all their real or exaggerated failings, they also bring considerable benefits to many of the world's poorest countries, some of which are presented below:

- The introduction of new technology and capital investment to provide new employment opportunities and enhance the quality of life of people in the developing host country.
- The reduction of costs by training local labour to use new technology more efficiently than rival firms internationally or in the host country.
- Tariff reductions on the import and export of goods from the host country are beneficial if they enable value to be added which helps raise living standards in the poorer country.
- Legitimate methods of lowering production costs are a recognised means of ensuring the profitability and future viability of overseas investments.
- Increasing the profitability of a TNC by opening up new markets in an undeveloped country has always been regarded as good business practice.
- TNCs would be reluctant to invest in poorer countries where set-up costs may be high, unless legal ways of avoiding corporation tax on profits were available after paying lower taxes in poorer host countries.

### General criticisms of transnational corporations

- They seek to gain control over the supply of resources in the host country
- They pursue competitive advantage through lower labour and material global rivals.
- They pay lower tariffs on goods both imported by/and exported from the

- They avoid the higher production costs, and more rigorous labour/health and safety practices of the home country.
- They provide only basic training and staff development for employees in the host country.
- They increase their turnover by expanding overseas sales at lower costs in the host country.
- They pay reduced taxes in the host country and avoid paying corporation tax in the home country by transferring profits to a 'shell' company in a third 'tax haven' country.
- As resources diminish in the host country, they consider closing down their operations and moving on to another developing country.
- They rarely reveal transaction costs incurred from overseas investments so that profits are maximised by minimising tax payments in both host and home countries.

Particular criticisms are levelled against transnational agricultural services specialists:

- The new global food economy launched by TNCs has almost, according to Shiva[12], created an irreversible ecological and social catastrophe.
- TNC agricultural policies are forcing Third World farmers into a monoculture through the global marketing of hybrid crops.
- TNCs dominate new seed supplies which must be purchased annually by Third World farmers.
- Centuries-old biodiversity in the Third World is at risk of being destroyed by monoculture which increases yields of one crop but overall food production output begins to fall.
- Pesticides destroy insects that pollinate indigenous plants making Third World farmers increasingly dependent on TNC seed supplies.
- The global treaty on trade-related intellectual property rights (TRIPs) currently exempts TNCs wishing to patent seeds of staple Third World crops (for example, Rice Tec owns the patent on Basmati rice, allegedly denying the rights of Indian peasant farmers who developed the variety).
- Despite claims by Rice Tec that most patent rights will not be infringed, leaders of up to 70 Third World countries, led by India, have refused to implement the TRIPs protocol on the grounds that it will threaten Indian rice exports exceeding $US 200m. annually.
- Since over 220 patents on staple crops such as rice and turmeric are held by five global corporations, the fear in these 70 countries is that the TRIPs protocol will permit TNCs to impose 'unregulated' premiums on farming activities in the Third World.
- A related fear of these 70 countries is that one-sided treaties will be endorsed under the TRIPs protocol which will lead to dumping of crop surpluses by TNCs in the Third World.

## Distributive justice in action

### The libertarian perspective

From an ethical standpoint, libertarians would support TNC investment in poorer countries as a moral right since all individuals are entitled to the products of their labour by using their assets productively, assuming no others suffer from these transactions. Investment would be subject to beneficiary nations being selected where future benefits could be maximised without need of any financial support from intergovernmental institutions. As De George observes about Third World investment: 'our government has no direct obligation to other peoples. But we as individuals do.' Western critics, in favour of 'trade not aid' policies are also critical of both the IBRD and IMF agencies for failing to persuade indebted nations to adopt more stringent policies for improving their economies. They also attack the IBRD, in particular, for investing in projects which could be left to private TNC investment. De George observes sympathetically: 'Paradoxically, the rise of multinational corporations, the targets of so much moral condemnation, may pave the way for increased contact and community.' By which he is presumably referring to increased benefits to undeveloped countries of the sort summarised above.

## The utilitarian perspective

The modern utilitarian perspective on aid and development to the Third World is influenced by the writings of Singer who would want to see far more financial support from the First World for the greater good of the greatest number of people in the Third World. For example, he argues that, despite their larger financial commitments to supporting the UN since its inception, only a handful of First World countries offer generous financial support to the United Nations Development Programme (UNDP) in aid of the poorest countries. In particular, only Sweden, the Netherlands, Norway and some of the oil-exporting Arab states have achieved the UN target of 0.7 per cent of GDP as aid to the Third World. During the 1990s, the UK gave just over 0.3 per cent, Germany over 0.4 per cent, Japan barely 0.3 per cent and the USA gave a penny-pinching 0.15–0.2 per cent of GDP.

Singer is also critical of the practice of 'triage', derived from the wartime practice of dividing the wounded into those who will: (a) recover without attention, (b) benefit from medical aid and (c) will not benefit from medical assistance. Similarly, undeveloped UNO member countries are classified by the IMF as low, middle and high income groups, which links aid with the capacity to repay debts and has the cumulative effect of denying other sources of private sector finance for development purposes to the poorest nations. Such policies are morally questionable because they are based on First World 'opportunity cost' financial reasoning for selecting or rejecting Third World countries to receive financial aid, as though they were subjected to relative rather than absolute poverty, which we are all under moral obligation to help eradicate.

## The egalitarian perspective

An increasing number of those taking an egalitarian perspective reject the moral arguments of libertarians and share much common ground with Singer's utilitarian perspective on aid and development for the Third World. There is also evidence that their beliefs are being expressed more in action than in moral debates, as follows.

## Non-governmental international organisations (NGOs)

*The Economist*[17] reports that the number of NGOs has increased worldwide over four times from 6,000 in 1990 to more than 26,000 in 1999. The reason is probably as follows: 'the end of communism, the spread of democracy, technological change and economic integration – globalisation in short – has exacerbated a host of worries over the environment, labour rights, human rights, consumer rights and so on' (p. 22).

The agendas of many NGOs have become less predictable and only their strategists know whether the NGOs will democratise, or merely disrupt global governance. With the poorer undeveloped countries in mind, in the aftermath of the disarray at the 1999 WTO Conference in Seattle, *The Economist* goes on to say that the NGOs

> were a model of everything the trade negotiators were not. They were well organised. They built unusual coalitions (environmentalists and labour groups, for instance, bridged old gulfs to jeer the WTO together). They had a clear agenda – to derail the talks. And they were masterly users of the media.

Far more NGOs exist within national borders and the World Watch Institute reckons there are about 2 million such groups in the USA, about 1 million grassroots NGOs in India, and over 100,000 were formed in Eastern Europe from 1988 to 1995. More rapid international transport and communications enables NGOs to formulate common agendas and strategies for opposing unacceptable policies towards poorer undeveloped countries by inter-governmental institutions and global corporations. *The Economist* quotes a RAND study which describes NGO strategies as based on:

> new partnerships between groups in rich and poor countries. Armed with compromising evidence of local labour practices or environmental degradation from southern NGOs, for example, activists in developed countries can attack corporations more effectively.' (p. 24)

These coalitions have been labelled as an 'NGO swarm' with no 'central leadership or command structure; it is multiheaded, impossible to decapitate – and can sting a victim to death' (p. 24). *The Economist* concludes that:

> Unelected bureaucracies such as the WTO and directors of TNCs may complain that 'self-appointed advocates have gained too much influence', but others will be hugely reassured if representatives of Everyman in the more moderate NGOs find themselves seats at the negotiating table to put the case assertively on behalf of the poorest undeveloped nations.

As an example, the successful outcomes of the disruption by NGOs of the World Bank's 50th anniversary conference with its '50 Years is Enough' campaign in 1994, are likely to be:

- further treaties relating to patent rights should guarantee sustainable developments, such as indigenous biodiversified farming in Third World countries, and swingeing financial penalties on TNCs that contravene these rights imposed in their home country by the International Court of Justice under international law;
- legally binding treaties to eliminate child and slave labour abuse and environmental pollution in host Third World countries by TNCs before 2005;
- greater involvement of Third World countries and NGOs in IMF, WTO and TNC strategic decisions, following an IBRD policy change in 1997 since when: 'More than 70 NGO specialists work in the Bank's field offices. More than half of World

Bank projects last year involved NGOs. From environmental policy to debt relief, NGOs are at the centre of World Bank policy' (*The Economist*[17]);

- new strategic compacts of fundamental reform with the above organisations similar to the IBRD reforms of the delivery of regional programmes to ensure achievement of the basic mission of reducing poverty;
- effective devolved management in each recipient country and the promotion of good governance and anti-corruption strategies by all First World institutions similar to the 1997 IBRD strategic compact;
- elimination of 'harmful' tax havens by 2006;
- acceleration of debt-relief proposals, supported by Britain and the USA, in the Jubilee 2000 initiative to reduce the international debts of the poorest Third World nations.

## Synopsis

- Empirical evidence confirms that, despite increased economic growth, a widening gap between prosperity and poverty exists in most industrialised countries, and that this growth in relative poverty since the early 1980s coincides with a larger increase in absolute poverty in many undeveloped Third World nations.
- Many people in the West realise how relative poverty can blight the lives of single parent families and the old, despite government efforts to eradicate this condition. Yet most are unaware of the results of absolute poverty, i.e. malnutrition, illiteracy, disease, squalid surroundings, high infant mortality and low life expectancy, as life 'at the very margin of existence' is the norm only in some undeveloped countries mostly in Africa.
- Policies aimed at alleviating both relative and absolute poverty are often influenced by attitudes towards the rival libertarian, utilitarian and egalitarian theories of distributive justice. These differences need to be recognised in understanding why attempts by richer nations and international agencies to develop poorer countries are criticised.
- Transnational corporations (TNCs) are criticised for seeking to control resources; achieving lower labour/material/production costs; taking advantage of less rigorous health and safety practices; and paying lower tariffs on imports/exports, plus lower taxes than in their home country, often by transferring profits to a 'shell' company in a third 'tax haven' country.
- On the other hand, TNC policies benefit undeveloped countries by introducing new technology and capital investment; providing new employment opportunities; training local labour; opening up new markets; and enhancing the quality of life of people in developing host countries.
- In a capitalist society, TNCs would be reluctant to invest in poorer countries, where higher set-up costs occur, unless legal ways of avoiding corporation tax in home countries were available after paying lower taxes on profits in developing host countries.
- Disagreements between TNCs and international agencies, on the one hand, and the rapidly expanding non-government organisations (NGOs) sector, on the other, are likely to intensify over aid and development policies towards the world's poorer nations, but numerous successful collaborations and projects are underway in the Third World.

## Review and discussion questions

1 What arguments would you raise (a) in favour or (b) against the economic policies which have widened the wealth gap between the prosperous and those in relative poverty in most developed countries?

2 What additional steps could be taken by international agencies and transnational corporations to accelerate the alleviation of absolute poverty in the poorest undeveloped countries?

3 Summarise the key differences between the libertarian, utilitarian and egalitarian perspectives on distributive justice.

4 What is meant by 'triage' and what measures do you think should be introduced to eliminate this type of international transaction?

5 What should be done to (a) increase or (b) decrease non-governmental organisations' involvement in addressing the criticism that aid and development programmes offered by international agencies support the interests of transnational corporations at the expense of the poorest undeveloped countries?

## Case study
## HIV/AIDS in Sub-Saharan Africa

KwaZulu-Natal (KZN) Province on South Africa's eastern seaboard, the traditional home of the Zulu nation, is home to 8.4 million people, or almost 21 per cent of the 40.8 million population (1996 Census). The largest city, Durban, is the principal seaport on the African continent; and the Durban Greater Metropolitan Area (DGMA) is also the world's second fastest growing conurbation after Mexico City, with a population exceeding 4 million. Most of this rapid increase occurred during 1995 to 2000 due to the spread of 'squatter townships' after the long apartheid era was replaced by the new South African constitution in 1994. Over 30 per cent of the population is estimated to be suffering from HIV/AIDS.

KZN has the third highest unemployment rate (39 per cent) in South Africa, despite the DGMA's hefty contributions to the national and provincial economies. Average per capita income is $4,200 (UK: $22,000) and, because the main source of investment is still provided by the white population, wide disparities in wealth distort calculations of average incomes for the unemployed which were $2,765 and $2,075 for Zulu males and females compared with $5,185 and $3,455 for white males and females, respectively (1996 Census). Low income distribution among the unemployed provides only a partial picture of the daunting development backlog in KZN province. For example, nearly 1 million Zulu children in rural areas are without a formal education and a further 700,000 people are classified as 'functionally illiterate'. An additional 500,000 households live in traditional housing (kraals) without direct access to electricity or potable water supplies (*SA Sunday Times* report, 25 October 1998, p. 5). The United Nations Human Development Index/Gini Coefficient is 0.59 for KZN province, compared with over 0.92 and 0.95 for the UK and Canada, respectively (*SA Industrial Development Report*/Pietermaritzburg Spatial Development Initiative, 1997).

As if high unemployment, illiteracy and slow rural development, particularly in land reform, are not enough burdens for any undeveloped region, KwaZulu-Natal also has to contend with the added major problems of a high, politically motivated crime rate and the rampant spread of HIV/AIDS. Politically motivated crime has undoubtedly retarded economic development of tourism in South Africa. This is especially so in KwaZulu-Natal where more people have been killed since 1994 than in the whole of the former Yugoslavia (*SABC News* report, 3 October 1998). The historical background to these political killings is deep-rooted and difficult to unravel. Suffice it to say, that the Zulu nation is the largest ethnic group in South Africa which has failed to secure what its supporters regard as an equitable share of political and economic power. For example, in 2001 the African National Congress (ANC)-led government which had been re-elected for a second term of office since 1994 was dominated by the smaller Xhosa nation, to which both the former and the present state presidents, Nelson Mandela and Thabo Mbeki, belonged. In contrast, the Zulu nation remained split between support for the traditional tribal chiefs in the rural areas, who mostly support the Inkatha Freedom Party, and those in the urban areas who support the ruling ANC party.

Meanwhile, the HIV/AIDS pandemic which affects the populations of the 10 leading sub-Saharan African countries, is particularly prevalent in KZN province. Accurate infection rates are always out of date, but UNO/World Health Organisation estimates that there are almost 25 million cases in Africa of which over half are in sub-Saharan Africa. There are 1.7 million cases alone in Botswana and 85 per cent of the young men are expected to die before reaching adulthood. South Africa has over 2 million cases and, at the provincial level, 53 per cent of the beds in the University of Natal (UNP) King Edward Hospital, the largest in KZN province, were occupied by HIV/AIDS patients in 1998; and over one-third of women attending ante-natal clinics were also diagnosed as HIV positive. As a result, WHO experts estimate that the SA government will need contingency plans to cope with an estimated 2 million orphaned or abandoned children between 2001 and 2010. Smith[18] reports that epidemiological surveys for HIV prevalence over the past decade in KZN have shown an inexorable progression from 1.7 per cent in 1990 to 32.5 per cent in 1998 with some areas as high as 44 per cent. Recorded figures at the UNP's Sexually Transmitted Diseases Clinic reveal infection levels of 40 per cent in 1995, rising to 54 per cent in 1999 and stabilising around 53 per cent over the last three years.

Longitudinal studies on the rapid spread of the HIV/AIDS pandemic in sub-Saharan Africa will presumably focus on two consequences of the combined effects of apartheid policy and the employment strategies of transnational mining corporations. First, a major consequence of South Africa's 'separate development' policy up to 1994 was the relocation of thousands of African people in their 'traditional homeland' areas which, not unlike the Indian reservations in the USA in the nineteenth century, provided little employment in areas far away from the prosperous white-dominated conurbations. As the South African mining industry expanded, however, the major flaw with this policy was the shortage of a regular supply of cheap African labour. Hence 'Pass Laws' were introduced which allowed approved workers to be transported from traditional homeland areas to work the mines and live together for 3–12-month periods in hostels and compounds provided by the mining corporations, where polygynous behaviour occurred.

The effects of this policy led to the gradual decline of the 'Lobola' system in tribal areas where families were started before the African version of a Western 'marriage' took place. Women traditionally remained in the rural area with their parents and raised new offspring while the men were employed hundreds of miles away in a mining/industrial area primarily to earn enough for Lobola (traditionally by purchasing cattle) to be paid to the women's parents and also to support the couple's children. Secondly, the 1996 Census reveals that the combined effects of apartheid and the mining corporations' employment policies have resulted in the migration of African men to urban areas becoming a permanent feature of the South African economy, with penurious consequences on the economic stability of traditional homeland areas. Sixty-three per cent of African males under the age of 20 live in rural areas, but this total declines to less than 40 per cent by the age of 30 years. The trend only starts to reverse itself for men aged over 55, so that almost 70 per cent of males have returned to their homeland areas by the age of 70 years.

The socioeconomic consequences of this demographic change are that large numbers of African women have been abandoned in rural areas by their male partners as destitute 'single parents' without any employment prospects. This has become another permanent feature of the South African economy as the 1996 Census shows that 63 per cent of all African women were born in rural areas and almost three-quarters remain at home without access to income throughout the most economically active period of their lives. As a result, 50 per cent are unemployed against a national average of less than 30 per cent across South Africa. Many of these women and their children are also infected with HIV/AIDS as a result of sexual relations with their male partners, home on annual leave from the mining areas.

South Africa's policy towards the HIV/AIDS pandemic is understandably cautious as, after some 45 years of apartheid, the democratically elected administration is reluctant to impose policies which will restrict the freedom of its citizens. In calling for greater public awareness of the HIV/AIDS virus, and sympathetic understanding by employers of the needs of those affected, President Thabo Mbeki added that the Government regards it as one of several problems, including poverty, which are holding back development in the new South Africa. An anti-AIDS policy was implemented in 1996 and became a national issue when President Mbeki invited world experts to an international conference on the treatment of HIV/AIDS in Durban for advice and medical assistance in curtailing the pandemic. However, his subsequent rejection of the links between the HIV pandemic and AIDS infection was widely criticised by medical experts in South Africa and overseas.

What is rarely discussed in the Western media is the reluctance of most developed nations to offer more substantial financial assistance to sub-Saharan African countries in meeting the huge cost of importing drugs for treating HIV/AIDS sufferers. It is currently estimated that the cost of treating all the HIV/AIDS patients in Africa would exceed $40 billion. The estimated cost in Zambia is about $2 billion or two-thirds of the country's GDP. The USA, UK and Switzerland, all major pharmaceutical manufacturers, lead the countries which have held back from providing assistance in the form of drugs mainly because South Africa and its neighbouring countries are unable or unwilling to pay world prices for the necessary drugs to be imported and Western companies will not yet allow them to be manufactured under licence in sub-Saharan Africa. A second concern raised by Smith, which goes unmentioned by Western critics of Southern African policy, is that vaccine development to control HIV/AIDS has largely been carried out in the USA against the predominant clade B viral infection. There are mounting concerns that this vaccine may not be effective against the predominant clade C and less prevalent clade A viral infections in sub-Saharan Africa, which is why South Africa has launched its own initiative against the clade C virus. What is urgently needed is an anti-AIDS vaccine but no one can say when current research will produce this. Meanwhile, health education programmes are being introduced and Uganda has achieved considerable success with its programmes for schools, promoting safer sex with one partner and use of condoms.

It is a so-called economic fact of life that life-saving drugs are expensive, but *The Economist* reports that: 'Poor countries often have to pay the highest prices, according to a study by Health Action International (HAI), a consumer lobby group' (11–17 December 1999, p. 145). For example, fluconazole, which is used to treat fungal infections that complicate HIV infection costs only US$1,168 per 100 units in Italy compared with US$1,740 in South Africa. Lamivudine, also used to treat HIV, costs US$314/100 units in Belgium yet US$438/100 units in Zambia. According to HAI, one reason for the higher prices is the lack of competition in some domestic markets. Only one brand of fluconazole is available in South Africa and it costs over 30 times more than it does in India where at least 17 brands are supplied by international drug corporations. India, of course, has far fewer HIV/AIDS patients requiring treatment than in sub-Saharan Africa, where governments and sufferers cannot afford even the lowest prices charged for these drugs by international pharmaceutical corporations.

**Questions**

**1** What ethical arguments would you use (a) to justify and (b) to challenge the apparent reluctance of transnational pharmaceutical corporations to play a more active role in helping to eradicate the HIV/AIDS pandemic in sub-Saharan Africa?

**2** What changes would you recommend in the role of international agencies to ensure that (a) transnational pharmaceutical corporations do not operate at a loss, at the same time that (b) sub-Saharan African countries are not required to pay more than they are able to in their efforts to alleviate the HIV/AIDS pandemic?

## Notes and references

1. Shaw, W.H. and Barry, V., *Moral Issues in Business*, 7th edn, Belmont, Calif., Wadsworth, 1998, ch. 3, 95–138.
2. Greider, W.B., *Who Will Tell the People? The betrayal of American democray*, New York, Simon & Schuster, 1992, 80.
3. *New York Times*, 11 May 1992, C5, and 18 April 1995, A16.
4. Eckhouse, J., Pay Disparity Threatens US, *San Francisco Chronicle*, 5 June 1989, C1, and US Still Tops in Executive Pay, *San Francisco Chronicle*, 5 November 1990, C1.

5. Marshall, J., Child Poverty is Abundant in the US, *San Francisco Chronicle*, 6 October 1996, B2.

6. Nozick, R., *Anarchy, State and Utopia*, New York, Basic Books, 1974.

7. Mill, J.S., *Principles of Political Economy*, ed. Donald Winch, London, Penguin Books, 1970, 129–41.

8. Brandt, R.B., *A Theory of the Good and the Right*, New York, Oxford University Press, 1979, 312–13.

9. Rawls, J., *A Theory of Justice*, Cambridge, Mass., Harvard University Press, 1971.

10. De George, R.T., *Moral Issues in Business*, New York, Macmillan, 1995, chs 19–20.

11. Singer, P., *Practical Ethics*, Cambridge, Cambridge University Press, 1993.

12. Shiva, V., BBC Reith Lectures, London, May 2000.

13. Miller, J., Helping the Rich Help Themselves, *Dollars and Sense*, 147, June 1989, 17.

14. Kelly, M. *et al.*, Are you too Rich if Others are too Poor?, *The United Reader*, 53, September–October 1992, 67–70.

15. Pacione, M. ed., *The Geography of the Third World: Progress and prospect*, New York, Routledge, 1988.

16. Diana Coyle, OECD Takes Aim at 'Harmful' Tax Havens, *The Independent*, 27 June 2000, 22.

17. *The Economist*, Storm over Globalisation and the Battle in Seattle, 27 November 1999, 13, 23–8.

18. Smith, A., In Search of a Vaccine [for HIV/AIDS], *Focus Journal*, University of Natal, Durban, 11 (1), 2000, 21–2.

# 13 Ethical investment

*If we don't invest ethically, we may find we don't have pure water to drink, clean air to breathe, or healthy food to eat, let alone a good return on an investment.*

Peter Lang, *Ethical Investment: A saver's guide*, Charlbury, Oxford, Carpenter Publishing, 1996, p. x.

## Learning objectives

After reading this chapter you should be able to:

- explain what is meant by ethical investment and summarise its history as an alternative source of financial support for publicly owned companies and other organisations;
- describe how ethical investment was used by protest groups in the USA and Britain during the 1960s, and how some of these issues were adopted by some financial investment advisers during the 1980s;
- summarise the reasons why funds are withheld from one company, in favour of another, as negative and positive forms of ethical investment;
- evaluate moral arguments in favour of or against animal rights, vivisection and other ethically questionable activities as a basis for investment;
- describe the ethical issues behind decisions to invest in the social economy rather than in publicly quoted companies or financial institutions;
- examine the reasons why individual shareholders are often unable to influence the ethical policies of publicly quoted companies or financial institutions.

## Introduction

Surveys repeatedly show that an overwhelming majority of those polled want their money or pension fund contributions to be invested in socially responsible companies. Yet little is known about how respondents reconcile ethical questions on where their money should, or should not, be invested with the financial dilemma of what to do if a poor return on investment occurs. There is no shortage of ethical issues to choose from, although what is less clear is how to translate these into ethical investments. The latter may entail investing in a prosperous quoted company or financial institution with a heavily advertised ethical prospectus, only to find it difficult to question these at an annual general meeting. Otherwise, it may extend to small firms or housing associations in the lesser-known social economy with marginally worse financial prospects than the latest dot. com entrant to the high risk software and computer services sector.

## What is ethical investment?

Ethical investment is a term used when individuals or groups such as NGOs allow moral issues to influence decisions to withhold or place money with a publicly quoted company or a financial institution, in preference to another, for the joint purposes of supporting an ethical principle while gaining a profit. The practice has been known in Britain for over 150 years and prompted the Rochdale Pioneers to boycott alternative forms of business enterprise and invest their funds in the Cooperative Movement in 1832. Lesser-known forms of ethical investment were undertaken by members of the Society of Friends (Quakers), other non-establishment religions, and radical political groups, which withdrew their support of businesses that profited from Britain's more controversial military or social policies from the late nineteenth century down to the present day.

Modern forms of ethical investment were revived in the policies of 'protest groups' which concerned themselves with protecting the negative rights of individuals and communities during the early 1960s. For example, these movements opposed national governments, private sector companies and public sector organisations which either profited from or were slow to condemn such controversial issues as apartheid, nuclear weapons, the Vietnam War, environmental pollution, exploitation of child labour, or the 'hidden persuader' and 'built-in obsolescence' techniques for exploiting consumers which were key social issues at that time.

Since the 1980s, a minority of publicly quoted companies and financial institutions have joined the original NGOs in upholding the ethical investment banner. One leading promoter of ethical investment, the Cooperative Bank, only came into being after its parent organisation rejected the ethical ideals on the reinvestment of profits propounded by its original founders during the nineteenth century. The bank now promotes ethical investment 'with a clear conscience [that] may attract customers [but] in the competitive world of modern financial services, it would never be enough by itself to keep them satisfied'. Whether this is an example of a small organisation shrewdly exploiting social trends to gain market share from its larger conglomerate rivals only time will tell.

## Negative and positive forms of ethical investment

The first assumption to be made in discussing ethical investment is that an individual or group has no moral objection to the principle of obtaining reasonable rent, profit or interest from investing private assets which have been legally acquired. That aside, ethical investments are intended either to protect the civil liberties of other human beings, previously discussed under negative or positive rights; animal rights; or conservation of the natural environment. Ethical investment may therefore be *negative*, in withholding investment from an organisation because its policies fail to meet certain ethical criteria, or *positive*, because it does.

## Leading ethical investment issues

Negative investment is discussed first because there is a longer history of people withholding investment from companies which are directly or indirectly involved in the following business activities:

- alcoholic beverages production and distribution;
- animal rights violation;
- armaments manufacture and shipment;
- companies importing products from oppressive regimes;
- companies with poor employment practices;
- environmentally hazardous products or processes;
- gambling;
- genetic engineering and related biotechnology products;
- nuclear power and waste reclamation;
- production of pet foods;
- pornography or other sexually explicit materials;
- tobacco products and promotion.

This list could be extended by individuals or groups that want to boycott (and may seek to persuade others to protest against) organisations that act against their beliefs and values, which is regarded as legitimate behaviour in most mature democratic societies. However, such actions are usually conditional on the nature of the protest and also on representatives or supporters of the focal organisation being allowed to put their version of the dispute before the general public. Apart from a need to balance public order concerns with those of freedom of speech, the other main concern would be to ensure that investment is not withheld from an organisation that is carrying out legitimate activities which are not a threat to the political, economic, health, safety, moral or other civil rights of the rest of society at home or abroad.

## Positive criteria influencing ethical investment decisions

It would be inaccurate to suggest that public awareness of the importance of civil liberties and other related issues has not increased since the 1960s, if only because of the large increase in NGOs discussed in the previous chapter which concern themselves with a wide range of political, socioeconomic and cultural issues, ranging from eliminating the macro-ecological effects of a potential nuclear power/weapons disaster to the micro-world of genetic engineering and the unknown consequences of new developments for human beings and agriculture. Investors with concerns about these and other issues may be expected to invest in companies with the same values and beliefs on the following issues:

- conservation and environmental protection;
- ethical research and user-friendly technology;
- equal opportunities and ethical employment practices;
- improved public amenities and transport schemes;
- inner city renovation and community development projects;
- raising quality standards and public awareness;
- safety standards at work and in the community.

Most of the examples included as negative or positive criteria above have been raised in the text or the case studies in previous chapters. The main exception is animal rights, which is explored in detail below because of ramifications which affect the whole of society, through direct or indirect involvement in the food chain, even though the majority of people may not regard these issues as contentious aspects of ethical investment.

## Animal rights

Animal rights is a branch of ethics concerned with the application of rights-based ethical theories to non-human animals, which attempts to justify, or oppose, the actions of those who initiate political and other changes aimed at altering society's attitudes to and uses of animals. In practice, animal rights ethics has attempted to find common ground with both the utilitarian and libertarian rights-based traditions in moral philosophy. The modern movement to extend rights-based ethical theories to non-human animals emerged in the late 1970s and early 1980s, mainly through the contributions of two philosophers, Peter Singer[1] and Tom Regan[2], which are summarised below.

### The case for and against animal rights

Varner[3], Katen[4] and Auday[5] all cite examples of earlier 'animal rights movements' in theology, philosophy and politics in Europe which can be traced back to the writings of St Thomas Aquinas (1225–1274), who declared that it is not that cruelty to animals could dehumanise people, but that it necessarily does. Aquinas's view was opposed by Descartes (1596–1650), who justified the cruel treatment of animals on the grounds that because animals could not reason, they could not feel pain. This rationale was used to justify systematic cruelty to animals in Europe for over 150 years, until a change in ideas about animal rights began to gain ground and alter public opinion in Britain during the nineteenth century, and later in the USA.

### Changing public attitudes in favour of animal rights

Moves to ban cruelty to animals were first considered in the English parliament in 1800 when a bill to outlaw bullfighting in England was heavily criticised in *The Times* newspaper; and over 20 years elapsed before an act outlawing cruelty to cattle was passed in 1822. Public figures like Lord Shaftesbury (Anthony Ashley Cooper) and members of the Clapham Sect condemned the act of people taking 'unnatural pleasure' in the suffering of animals, which led to the foundation of the Society for the Prevention of Cruelty to Animals (SPCA) in 1824. The aims of the SPCA later met with Queen Victoria's approval and she condemned any civilisation to be unworthy of the name that condoned cruelty to animals. Her views were similar to those of the Nobel Prize dramatist George Bernard Shaw, who subsequently declared that it would be impossible to be cruel to animals without causing damage to one's own character.

Similar concerns in the USA led to the founding of the American Society for the Prevention of Cruelty to Animals (ASPCA) in 1866. More recently, animal rights groups, such as People for the Ethical Treatment of Animals (PETA), the Fund for Animals, the Farm Animal Reform Movement (FARM) and the Animal Legal Defence Fund, established themselves internationally primarily by basing their mandates on ideas borrowed from the philosophical debate on the use of animals in agriculture and science. Other protest groups such as the Animal Liberation Front (ALF) isolated themselves from popular support by seeking confrontation through 'direct action', in perpetrating illegal actions such as stealing/liberating laboratory animals and destroying scientific equipment and data.

## Traditional arguments in favour of animal rights

Ethical arguments supporting animal rights emerged in the late eighteenth century from contrasting areas of philosophy when the idealist, Immanuel Kant, and the utilitarian, Jeremy Bentham, separately condemned cruelty to animals on moral grounds. Kant argued that if people were indifferent to cruelty to animals, they would become insensitive to their own experiences of pain and suffering and ultimately incapable of conceptualising the impact of their cruelty on animals. This would ultimately make them indifferent to displaying cruel behaviour towards their fellow human beings.

Jeremy Bentham dismissed arguments defending cruelty to animals because they could not reason by arguing that the moral issue is not whether animals can or cannot reason, or are unable to imitate human behaviour such as talking, but whether they can suffer pain. Since there is ample evidence that animals do suffer pain, human beings cannot defend cruelty to animals, which is unethical in its own right, but also because it is not possible to isolate cruelty to animals, as behaviour, from cruelty to fellow human beings. Later, in the twentieth century, Kant's ideas influenced those of Tom Regan and Bentham's were taken up by Peter Singer.

## Modern arguments in favour of animal rights

As noted above, the views of modern animal rights activists have been heavily influenced by the ethical analyses of Singer[6] and Regan[7]. Singer's views on animal rights were first stated as a 'Principle of Equal Consideration of Interests', which he later modified by adopting a utilitarian position. Briefly, he argued that any defence of the moral rights of animals should be based on the proposition that certain ways of treating them cannot be justified in terms of promoting happiness. Singer did not oppose all uses of animals and conceded that if the human benefits of animal experimentation, or the use of animals in agriculture, outweigh the harm inflicted on animals, then such activities could be justified on utilitarian grounds. The key moral issue is *equal consideration of interests*, which, when applied to racial and sexual discrimination, made these morally repugnant because the perpetrators fail to give equal consideration to the similar interests of individuals from other races, on the one hand, or to the similar interests of men and women, on the other.

Comparable behaviour occurs when animals are subjected to cruelty, which Singer defines as 'speciesism', and rejects as morally indefensible because the members of one species (i.e. human beings) abuse, withhold and abrogate the rights of another species (i.e. animals) in pursuit of their own self-interests. Singer's analysis convinced many animal activists to accept that humans have no authority to usurp the rights of another species for their own purposes, because animals possess intrinsic worth and should be free to live without restrictions imposed by an intellectually superior species, as contained in Singer's question: is speciesism merely another form of blatant racism? By way of reply, he notes that what a human being and an animal share in common is sentience (i.e. consciousness that is capable of sensations and responding to stimuli), plus an interest in avoiding suffering. This capacity for avoiding suffering is a necessary and sufficient condition for moral standing to be recognised in humans and animals. However, science and agriculture are historically based on the principle of equal consideration of interests being violated, and no human being would be subjected to the systematic pain inflicted on sentient animals for relatively small benefits, as when pain and stress are inflicted on farm animals to produce nutritionally unnecessary meat.

Regan goes further than Singer in calling for the total abolition of the use of animals in agriculture and experimentation on moral grounds. He argues that, in order to possess moral rights, an individual must be not merely sentient but also a 'subject of a life'. This entails self-consciousness, beliefs, memories, desires, and a sense of its own future. Regan, like Singer, argues that probably all mammals are self-conscious, and that all birds, reptiles, amphibians and fish ought to be treated as if they have rights, if only out of moral caution (i.e. they should be given the benefit of the doubt until it can be proved that they do not possess 'subject of a life' characteristics). This moral caution would recognise that all subjects of a life have basically one moral right: the right not to be harmed on the grounds that doing so benefits others. If animals have moral rights, then neither their use in experiments nor slaughter can be justified in terms of the benefits accruing to humans. Similar arguments are used to justify vegetarian and anti-vivisectionist behaviour.

## Ethical arguments against animal rights

Frey[8], a utilitarian philosopher like Singer, criticises animal rights philosophies by expressing doubts about the usefulness of 'rights' as a moral concept. He is willing, however, to accept as a starting point Regan's argument that having rights implies having desires. Frey challenges the view that animals have rights because they are incapable of having desires as analysed by Regan. For Frey, having desires means being capable of holding various beliefs, otherwise conscious desires cannot be separated from mere needs, unless individual beliefs are also recognised. Animals lack beliefs, however, because they lack language. Since only sentences can be true or false, only creatures with language can think about sentences as being true or false. Hence, it follows that only creatures with language can have desires and therefore only animals with language can have moral rights. Frey concludes that neither the vegetarian nor anti-vivisectionist conclusions follow logically from the rights-based analysis presented by Regan. The scepticism of critics like Frey has been challenged by Griffin[9], a behavioural scientist, whose research on bat sonar supports arguments that mental experiences exist in animals.

## Animal experimentation

### The use of animals for research

As Auday notes, animal research is carried out with the positive aims of acquiring new knowledge that could benefit humankind, education and product testing. On the negative side, there are questions regarding the moral acceptability of subjecting animals to pain, suffering and sometimes death for the benefit of another species. The ethics of animal experimentation are related to the previously discussed issue of animal consciousness. In short, if animals are aware of fear and pain, then ethical behaviour would require that any human use of an animal is designed to minimise the animal's distress. On the other hand, if animals are not prone to such experiences, an ethical argument can be made out for using them more indiscriminately for research purposes rather than risk causing harm to a fellow human being.

The use of animals for research purposes in the West, also known as vivisection, dates back to the start of medicine in classical Greece, which advanced through the study of living organisms. With hindsight, experimental physiology, biology and comparative anatomy would not have emerged as independent disciplines without the knowledge gained from animal laboratory research. This is because, as Rupke[10] notes, there were no moral, legal or religious objections to vivisection prior to the nineteenth century when members of the English establishment became involved in the controversy. Over time, this led to the influential animal welfare movement during the 1920s and the eventual passing of the Cruelty to Animals Act 1976 in the UK, as the first law enacted to regulate animal research.

Similar developments in the USA have restricted the use of animals in both biomedical and social science research (e.g. psychology). According to Auday, the US National Research Council estimates that about 17 million animals are used for research annually, of which some 85 to 90 per cent are laboratory rats or mice. Primates, such as chimpanzees, make up less than 7 per cent of research animals. In comparison, the American Humane Association (AHA) reports that about 12 million unwanted animals are 'put down' every year. Comparative British data is not available at the time of writing.

### Modern arguments against animal research

As noted above, some animal rights activists assume that consciousness exists in both humans and animals, and that the latter should not be used by humans in any way. At the other extreme, others assume that the notion of animal consciousness is a human construct and that animals are, in reality, unfeeling creatures that can be used as human beings see fit. Regan[2] rejects the latter arguments, adding that even animal research intended to save human lives cannot be justified if animals have moral rights, as no one is justified in violating the latter for the sake of human advantage regardless of how great the presumed benefits. He adds that human beings sometimes knowingly disclaim their rights and accept the suffering or additional risks of participating in experiments, whereas animals cannot. Critics use the same argument, however, concluding that animals are incapable of communicating their feelings because these are not present in the first place.

Whereas Singer is not opposed to all forms of experimentation and would accept the need for some research under rigorously controlled conditions, to ensure that no pain is inflicted on another species which could be regarded as cruel and immoral, Regan argues that only those experiments that impose no new risks on the animals are acceptable. Critics observe that this arrangement would eliminate most, if not all, research experiments. The major purpose of new research would also be lost or seriously limited if enquiries were restricted to areas of known risk. Furthermore, if the risks were known in advance, there would be no need to substitute animals for human beings. Finally, by confining research to areas of known risk, slow progress would be made while the lives of perhaps millions of human beings would be put at further risk for want of more prompt research experimentation.

## Modern arguments in favour of animal experimentation

Fox[11] bases his defence of animal experimentation on an anthropocentric perspective on ethics which insists that rights and duties apply only among sentient beings capable of recognising reciprocal obligations, of which only human beings are capable. He adds that only human beings are capable of being full members of the moral community and, as a result, members have no direct duties to animals. However, cruelty must always be opposed, such as the deliberate infliction of unnecessary pain, because such actions make individuals more likely to inflict harm on their fellow human beings. Auday points out that Fox subsequently withdrew his main arguments in support of animal experiments; however, they are included here because they are still used by others to defend animal experimentation.

Fox's other arguments, however, are overlooked because of his 'recantation'[12]; namely, that the charge by animal rights groups that the scientific community has been reluctant to adopt humane animal research methods is inaccurate. For example, the AHA data mentioned above indicates a sharp reduction in the number of animals used and there is evidence that efforts are made to adopt procedures that minimise or eliminate the pain or suffering animals experience during experiments. Animal rights groups continue to maintain that much research serves no valuable purpose. Fox never disagreed that pain and suffering should be minimised whenever possible, but argued that the importance of a research project cannot be predicted until after it has been conducted.

## A pragmatic evaluation of arguments for and against animal experimentation

Paton[13] summarises the case for and against the use of animals in research as follows:

*Arguments for animal experimentation*:

- animals provide good models for understanding fundamental human processes;
- since animals are less complex organisms (both biologically and psychologically), they provide a good starting point for exploratory research;
- animals have shorter life-spans, which allows genetically transmitted traits to be studied more rapidly;
- scientists are able to control an animal's environment effectively, reducing the number of competing variables that make research so complicated;

- animals can be used for experiments that would be considered unethical (and unlawful) if performed on human beings.

*Arguments against animal experimentation:*
- inflicting pain and suffering on animals is unacceptably cruel and is therefore immoral;
- the outcomes of animal research make no positive moral contribution towards understanding the human condition;
- most animal research serves no practical human benefit that could not be achieved by other means, and is therefore unnecessary;
- the cost of harming animals in most cases does not outweigh the benefit to society;
- animals have intrinsic worth and deserve to live freely, unrestricted by the selfish motives of another species.

## Animal rights and ethical investment

The direct or indirect commercial use of animals is usually justified or opposed by reference to either negative or positive criteria as a basis for ethical investment in quoted companies. For example, positive 'replaceability' or 'damage limitation' arguments to justify ethical investment. The 'replaceability' argument maintains that if an animal is humanely treated and slaughtered before being replaced by another humanely treated animal, then the species is no worse off, whereas human beings benefit in utilitarian terms. Alternatively, the 'damage limitation' argument is used to justify activities such as fox hunting by maintaining that more damage (as a cost) would occur to the countryside if fox populations were not controlled.

Animal rights activists generally rely on Singer's rejection of the replaceability argument in condemning large-scale, intensive animal farming for two reasons. First, the humaneness of the living conditions, handling, slaughter and processing is inversely proportional to the huge scale of intensive animal agriculture involved. In short, the argument would probably only apply to small-scale animal agriculture. Secondly, both the 'replaceability' and 'damage limitation' arguments are criticised by Singer who argues that 'self-conscious individuals, leading their own lives and wanting to go on living' are not replaceable because when an individual animal dies, its desires go unsatisfied even if another replacement animal's desires are satisfied later. A case can be made out that all mammals are self-conscious, according to Singer, who argues that the replaceability argument would not apply to most types of farm animals which, unlike some fowl and fish, he regards as self-conscious.

## Intensive farming

This is also known as 'factory farming' and the publicly quoted companies involved, and those which supply products (e.g. feedstuffs) or services (e.g. transport), are criticised for what animal welfare groups regard as inhumane husbandry. Decisions to withhold investment in these companies are a response to the objections people raise against modern livestock production methods, which may include the addition of synthetic chemical hormones in feedstuffs to accelerate growth, and intensive processes which confine chickens, veal calves and pigs to unlit factory farming units.

## Mad cow disease

The origins of bovine spongiform encephalopathy (BSE), or mad cow disease, have still to be identified, although the addition of tainted animal parts known as 'scrapies' to feedstuffs probably played a part in the spread of the disease. Because of draconian measures imposed by the Ministry of Agriculture, Fisheries and Food (MAFF) since the early 1990s, which have driven many beef farmers into bankruptcy, the incidence of BSE in the UK fell from 37,056 cases in 1992 to 2,280 cases in 1999. A few cases, although still well below current UK numbers, have been reported in Portugal, Ireland and France (EU Commission, 2000). The probability of transmission of BSE to humans on a large scale is regarded as low but the extent of degenerative infection of brain tissue may take years to emerge and is unknown. Hence, the near collapse of the British beef market in the early 1990s as consumers chose alternative products and import bans were imposed by the UK's trading partners. Without undue pessimism, experts predict that the market is unlikely to recover fully if and when the disease is eradicated.

## Fox/badger hunting

Fox hunting in the UK was recently the subject of a public inquiry led by Lord Burns and is likely to be made illegal, or more strictly regulated, as a result of a free vote by MPs to ban this practice being passed in January 2001. At the time of writing this seemed unlikely to become law until after the next General Election. Badger hunting is already banned by law in Britain, although reportedly still carried out in remote parts of the UK.

## International protest movements against cruelty to animals

These are organised by NGOs such as Friends of the Earth, Greenpeace, the Ethical Consumer Research Association (ECRA), the Ethical Investment Research Service (EIRS), People for the Ethical Treatment of Animals (PETA), the Royal Society of Prevention of Cruelty to Animals (RSPCA) and the WorldWide Fund for Nature (WWF), which campaign either singly or collectively against investment in publicly funded companies to bring about a global ban on whaling; seal culling; the killing of dolphins by drowning in the southern hemisphere tuna trawling and in northern hemisphere sea bass trawling by international fisheries companies; the ivory trade and export of rhino horn from Africa for use in Asian countries for decorative art and aphrodisiac production; and the use of animals for the fur trade in mainland European countries.

## Other leading ethical investment 'target' industries

Three of the many industries falling under this broad heading include:

- alcoholic beverages distribution;
- use of additives in food production;
- the international arms trade.

## Alcoholic beverages distribution

Alcohol Concern, the UK pressure group, estimates that well over 25,000 people die annually from alcohol-related causes, and many more become alcohol-dependent to the extent that it causes serious damage to their working, family or personal lives, and often results in violent attacks on others and damage to private property. In addition, according to *The Ethical Consumer Guide to Everyday Shopping*[14] additives to beer production may include 'hydrochloric acid, caustic soda, plaster of paris, dimethylpolysiloxane and sulphites' (p.87). Sulphites provoke asthma in about 10 per cent of sufferers and, unlike in the USA, do not have to be labelled in the UK. The fact that these issues have failed to result in government action against what is rapidly becoming an internationally owned brewing industry which, admittedly, makes a massive contribution to the national exchequer, has led some concerned individuals to oppose investment in these companies on ethical grounds. An additional argument raised by the latter is that the brewing industry fails to contribute to the direct 'social costs' incurred (e.g. ambulance, hospital, police, courts, social services, etc.) as a result of the alcohol abuse displayed by younger members of society, in particular, who are targeted in TV advertisements, etc.

## Use of additives in food production

The independent Food Commission's survey of 358 children's food products found that 77 per cent were 'nutritional disasters' and contained excessive saturated fats, sugar, salt or artificial additives. Products advertised as 'healthy eating' such as flavoured fromage frais, yogurts and mousses contained between 22 and 30 per cent sugar, 11 to 15 times the amount recommended by international health authorities. Breakfast cereals also contained from 30 to over 45 per cent sugar; and the juice content of drinks such as cranberry juice was only 5 to 10 per cent cranberry juice and an added 90–95 per cent sugar and water. One popular cheese savoury snack also contained a high added saturated fat content of over 25 per cent.[15] *The Ethical Consumer Guide to Everyday Shopping* lists 15 different food products, ranging from baby food, baby milk and biscuits to tinned fruit and yogurt, manufactured and sold in the UK, in which the majority of brands available consistently exceed WHO standards on recommended sugar, salt, saturated fats and additive levels by considerable margins.

## The international arms trade

Opposition to investment in companies involved in the manufacture and supply of weapons, including combat equipment, is coordinated internationally by leading NGOs, and investment in these companies is condemned for several reasons. First, arms are often purchased to prop up oppressive regimes in undeveloped countries causing huge loss of life and holding back development projects. A successful example of NGO action led to the international ban on land mines in 1996. Second, arms are often used against a nation's own population. For example, many of the hand guns and rifles used in the USA were manufactured by Smith & Wesson, part of the UK conglomerate Tomkins, which is under pressure to sell this subsidiary because its UK shareholders oppose the gun culture in the USA in the wake of recent killings of children in US schools and public places. Finally, the selling of arms to other nations that either reject UN resolutions or engage in conflict with NATO forces raises the possibility of UN troops fighting rebel soldiers armed with the same weapons.

## Ethical investment in the social economy

Lang[16] introduces the useful term 'social economy' to distinguish between using negative criteria to withhold investment from ethically unacceptable companies and

---

**Box 13.1**

### (Perhaps not) everything you want to know about ethics at the Cooperative Bank

The Cooperative Bank[17] claims to be the 'only high street bank that promises its customers to invest their money according to their views and wishes', by giving them 'control of how their money is managed – more importantly through our Ethical Policy'. Before the latter was formulated, they talked to their customers 'in depth, to find out how they did, and didn't, want their money to be used'. Over the years, their Ethical Policy 'has gone from strength to strength, winning thousands of new customers' who are also provided with 'the most advanced "any time, anywhere" banking and financial services'. The Ethical Policy also lists international policies and industries in which customers have indicated their money should/should not be invested. Those which meet with customer approval include companies supporting positive human rights and ecological impact policies. Those from which investments should be withheld include armaments, tobacco product manufacturers and companies supporting animal testing, exploitative farming methods, blood sports and fur farmers. Regular consultation with customers occurs and the Ethical Policy can be developed accordingly.

What is less widely known is that the Cooperative Bank subsidiary, the Unity Bank, has no personal customers and invests solely on behalf of the trade union movement. Lang[16] reports that a marketing executive confirmed that, after consultations about ethical investment, the customers indicated that they expected the bank to invest only in UK industry. Their stated aim is to retain and create jobs on behalf of trade union members who work in the nuclear power/waste, tobacco, animal research, oil drilling, HGV road haulage and toxic chemicals industries. An ethical investment policy or environmental code of practice would clearly act against the interests of its TU customers. Yet only someone who had never known or witnessed the demoralising effects of prolonged unemployment would reject out-of-hand the Unity Bank's investment policy of trying to meet the legitimate socioeconomic needs of its members. A more convoluted moral argument concerns how the Cooperative Bank can reconcile its policy that its customers are entitled to 'a clear-cut set of promises about how we will invest their money and how we won't', with its decision not to include a clear-cut statement about the investment policy of the Unity Bank in its Ethical Policy statement.

the more constructive use of positive criteria which is 'likely to take you out of the stock market altogether, and into the world of small businesses, worker and housing cooperatives, housing associations, and the social economy where charity and business move ever closer together' (p. 15). Successful examples are cited of what are, admittedly, largely unknown small companies, cooperatives, housing associations, ecological trading companies, banks and investment funds (e.g. Triodos Bank and the Ecology Building Society) which are solely committed to ethical investment.

Attention to the social economy is apposite because it allows comparisons to be made between those organisations which have been established solely for direct investment, and to provide ethical investment opportunities in similar organisations, and the separate ethical investment offered by the leading UK financial institutions. Of the two, investments in the former amount to a tiny portion of the massive UK financial services market and there is no known reason to call their ethical policies into question. The same can also be said of designated ethical investment funds offered by UK mainstream financial service institutions; however, most of the latter organisations also, quite legally, offer numerous alternative funds which are invested in companies that fail to meet some of the ethical criteria discussed above.

## Ethical investment and the individual shareholder

As mentioned in previous chapters, libertarians are uncompromising in their support of the individual's personal liberty, privacy and property rights, which writers like Nozick and Friedman extend to individual shareholders in publicly quoted, profit-seeking companies. What has yet to be discussed with an equal single-mindedness is the disturbing difference between principle and practice, which occurs almost daily in the virtual powerlessness of the majority of individual shareholders in British companies. This is manifested, for example, in the conduct of annual general meetings at which the proposal of resolutions is restricted unless:

- the proposer is an individual shareholder with at least 5 per cent of the voting rights;
- the proposal is made by a minimum of 100 shareholders with individual holdings of £100;
- resolutions are filed in sufficient time for circulation to shareholders before the AGM, although details of the latter are often not circulated by the company secretary until a few weeks before the actual date of the meeting;
- the proposer(s) meet(s) the legal requirement of bearing the cost of circulating details of the resolution to other shareholders which, in the case of a transnational corporation, could be huge;
- the resolution secures the support of the 'block votes' of the larger shareholders, such as banks, insurance companies or investment trusts, whose ownership rights easily exceed that of individual shareholders;
- institutional shareholders waive their right to ask questions at AGMs in favour of individual shareholders, which rarely occurs.

## Synopsis

- Ethical investment occurs when individuals or groups allow moral issues to influence decisions to withhold or place money with specific quoted companies or financial institutions for the dual purposes of gaining profits while supporting an ethical principle.
- Ethical investment emerged over 150 years ago and was revived by protest groups in the USA and Britain during the 1960s, before being popularised by the financial services industry during the 1980s.
- Decisions to withdraw/withhold investments on ethical grounds usually occur because the policies, business practices or other activities of particular organisations fail to meet negative rights criteria supported by existing or potential shareholders. The management of non-contravening organisations may also have to demonstrate that their policies and other activities advance specific positive rights criteria before the support of potential ethical investors is forthcoming.
- Moral arguments in favour of or against animal rights and vivisection are important because resulting investment decisions may affect a wide range of commercial activities internationally, including intensive factory farming, the beef industry (BSE/mad cow disease), whaling, the ivory and rhino horn trades and the fur industry.
- Investors may have to decide between the rival ethical claims and practices of small businesses that operate openly in the social economy, and larger publicly quoted companies or financial institutions, which may offer conflicting ethical investment opportunities either through different subsidiaries, or by segmenting customers, to minimise the overall impact of any failure to meet accepted ethical investment criteria.
- The rights of individual shareholders, strenuously upheld by libertarians, are often neglected or ignored at AGMs by the informal influence and voting power of large financial institutions in many quoted companies.

## Review and discussion questions

**1** What reasons would you offer (a) in support of or (b) against the view that both negative and positive rights are applicable only to human beings and should not be extended to animals?

**2** What are the main arguments of Singer and Regan in favour of animal rights?

**3** What are the main arguments of Auday and Fox in favour of animal experimentation?

**4** What arguments would you raise (a) for or (b) against the introduction of a special 'social cost' contribution of 1p on each alcoholic drink, beefburger or packet of crisps, to go towards specific NHS projects for, say, reducing heart attacks or obesity?

**5** The British defence industry is the world's second largest exporter, providing direct and indirect employment for many thousands of people. What arguments would you put to the senior managers and the trade union members employed in such a company for (a) opposing or (b) supporting investment by the Ministry of Defence on ethical grounds?

## Case study
## Out of Eden: the introduction of GM crops into Europe

**Introduction**

Advances in genetic research over the last thirty years have pioneered the new, radical technology of genetic engineering, which makes it possible to replicate genes and insert these clones into selected organisms. Deoxyribonucleic acid (DNA) genes are the blueprint from which all proteins are made, which provide the hereditary material of all living matter. Several increasingly sophisticated genetic engineering techniques exist but probably the most simple method is the polymerase chain reaction (PCR) which allows millions of genes to be copied in a few hours. These genes are then allowed to recombine with the DNA of selected organisms so that in cases of successful cloning the inserted gene actively replicates the desired characteristics in the selected organism.

**The first GM crop experiments**

The first genetically modified (GM) crop trials were carried out on strawberries grown in California during the early 1980s. Most people are aware that a strawberry has a thin outer membrane (i.e. skin) which, if bruised by frost damage, for example, encourages the growth of a grey mould, *botrytis cinaria*. This accelerates deterioration and makes the strawberry unpalatable within a short period, depending on the ambient temperature (hence the name, as the berries were formerly cultivated on straw to protect them from ground frost). Genetic research revealed that certain bacteria encourage frost damage by allowing water to freeze more rapidly on the strawberry's surface. The reaction of opponents to the first GM experiments, who attacked the field trials, challenged sound economic and ethical arguments as the economic rationale supported the identification and removal of the frost-inducing gene from the surface bacteria in carefully controlled field trials. These experiments should be regarded as successful if they resulted in higher yields of less disease-prone strawberries which were more acceptable to consumers. The ethical argument supported the economic rationale for the research by noting that the resulting GM-modified bacteria carried no foreign gene but had merely had an existing one removed. As Lichtenstein (*FT Weekend*, 1–2 April 2000) enquired: 'How could this be dangerous?'

**The introduction of GM crops into Europe**

Public reaction has indicated that people were taken unaware by the introduction of GM crops into the food chain in the late 1990s. By 1999, for example, over two-thirds of all US soya beans were genetically modified, and cotton and maize crops are being transformed at almost the same rate. Connor (*The Independent*, 21 May 2000) observes that the four-year battle by environmentalists against the treatment of strawberries with genetically modified bacteria by the patent-holders, Advanced Genetic Sciences, was lost in the US courts in April 1987. The war against GM crops began on the same day, but has since shifted to Europe. The outcry against GM trials in Britain in 1999 appeared to be repeating the furore that broke out in the USA a decade earlier when GM life forms were first released into the environment; and the prolonged animosity between GM activists on the one hand and the scientific community and its commercial sponsors on the other, shows no sign of abating in Britain in particular.

**Current use of GM products**

GM soya beans have been used in the UK in most processed foods such as biscuits, ready meals and soft drinks for at least five years. *The Guardian* (24 May 1999) reported that safety tests for possible side-effects on humans and animals have never been carried out on this GM product for the toxic chemical herbicide it was designed to resist. This revelation added to the GM controversy which resurfaced when a letter was leaked to the media from the UK government's senior scientific adviser, in which he speculated that the commercial cultivation of GM crops could not proceed until at least 2003. In effect, this was a call for a moratorium. This was rejected by the government, which favoured a policy of allowing production to begin perhaps within a year of the proposed first round of farm-scale field trials. In 1999 fewer than 200 research trials – each occupying an area smaller than a tennis court – on land mainly owned by research institutes and universities, were being carried out in the UK. Three licenses have also been issued by the government agriculture minister for larger farm-scale trials so that the full commercial impact of growing GM crops can be assessed. These trials will all use GM crops developed by the US Monsanto Corporation.

**Reaction of food producers and supermarkets**

*The Independent* reported (10 June 1999) that UK food producers were in headlong retreat from the use of GM soya in their products after a consumer backlash against them. The removal of GM soya and maize derivatives from the manufacture of products such as chocolate biscuits, chocolate, dried baby foods, pizzas, bread, food flavourings, spreads, trifles, fish fingers and crisps and their replacement with non-GM additives was expected to raise the production costs by up to 10 per cent. Leading supermarket and retail chains including Tesco, Sainsbury, Asda, Safeway, Somerfield, Marks & Spencer and Iceland confirmed that they sold GM-based brands, but had started phasing these out between one and four months previously. All but one chain, Iceland, added that their own-label products also contained GM ingredients but that these would also be replaced probably for a two-year period until further research had been completed.

**The global impact of GM crops**

Connor reports that the USA, China, Canada and Argentina are the main countries where GM crops are being grown commercially. The UK is one of several EU countries set to join this group and various developing nations are likely to follow soon after. Connor concludes that the war against GM crops has been lost in the USA. The area of land where GM crops are being grown quadrupled between 1996 and 1997 from 6.9 million acres (2.8 million hectares) to 31 million acres (12.8 million hectares). This is equivalent to the area of England, although most of these trials occurred in the USA. The fight against GM crops has shifted to Britain and continental Europe because environmental activists there are prepared to risk prison sentences for vandalising experiments by destroying GM crops.

**The environmental argument**

Environmental activists seek to ban the release of any GM organism into the environment on the grounds that genetic engineering crosses a critical threshold in the biological life of the Earth, and risks altering the fundamental nature of life itself which, once initiated, probably cannot be halted or reversed. Dr Parr, a Greenpeace scientific adviser, argues that the risks to the environment are too great and can never be eliminated because the technology is inherently unpredictable. His conclusions reinforce the earlier findings of the 1989 authoritative inquiry into the likely consequences of releasing GM organisms, carried out by the UK Royal Commission on the Environment, and chaired by the previous government chief scientist. A key conclusion in the report stated: 'Unlike chemicals, biological agents can multiply in the environment. There is therefore a risk that once released, it will be impossible to control them.' Where experts like the current and previous chief scientific advisers differ from environmental specialists like Dr Parr is that they oppose an indefinite moratorium. Such a moratorium was considered and rejected by the Royal Commission in 1989 because experts concluded that it would prevent 'exploitation of the enormous potential GM crops offer' for improving the environment and public health especially in the developing world.

**Supporters of GM crops**

These include the following organisations and individuals:

- *Monsanto.* The company advocates the managed introduction of GM crops, which would not be brought in on an unlimited basis; and is unwilling to plant any crops commercially in the UK before 2001/2.
- *Scimac.* A body which represents the British Agrochemical Society, the National Farmers' Union and the Society of Plant Breeders and supports: 'the regulatory process that has to be gone through before any crops can be planted. We have consistently maintained there is no scientific basis for stopping these plants' use.'
- *HM government.* At the time of writing the Prime Minister, Mr Blair, is concerned about the effects of a ban on UK biotech companies when American corporations lead the field. Connor quotes him as informing a private meeting of Labour MPs: 'We are not going to destroy an entire industry'; and he told the House of Commons in February 1999: 'I do not think it sensible to impose a moratorium.' Mr Blair is strongly supported by Dr Cunningham, one of the few scientists in the Labour Cabinet, who points to the thousands of jobs that would be put at risk if a moratorium is imposed and argued in April 1999: 'GM crops have grown for 19 years in North America with almost no effects on biodiversity.' Mr Meacher, the environment minister, is thought to be the most sceptical member of the government, and understood to be willing to support a moratorium, if at all possible, although he lost the support of some Cabinet colleagues when he suggested that scientists with links to the biotech industry should be excluded from government committees with responsibilities for GM crop issues. Since then he has informed the House of Commons that: 'No crop from any of the first-year trials will enter either the human or animal food chains.'
- *The Princess Royal and the Duke of Edinburgh.* Both mounted separate defences of GM organisms in June 2000 which took issue with earlier criticism by the Prince of Wales (see below) and the Chief Rabbi, Dr Sachs. The Princess Royal stated in *The Grocer* magazine that: 'Man has been tinkering with food production for such a long time it's a bit cheeky suddenly to get nervous about it. It's a bit of an oversimplification to say there should be no GM foods. Life isn't that simple.' Her father took a similar line in proposing a vote of thanks to Dr Sachs at the annual St George's lecture in June who cautioned against the creation of 'genetically modified human beings' by noting that 'we have genetically modified animals and plants ever since people started selective breeding . . . People are worried about genetically modified organisms getting into the natural environment. What people forget

is that the introduction of exotic species – like, for instance, the introduction of the grey squirrel into this country – is going to do, or has done, far more damage than a genetically modified piece of potato.'

**Opponents of GM crops**

- *English Nature.* An advisory body to the government on the environment which is opposed to any commercial planting until after UK field and farm-scale trials have been evaluated as it does not believe that environmental impact studies carried out in the USA are adequate.
- *Friends of the Earth.* Opposes the commercial development of GM crops for a minimum five-year period because it will take that long to carry out and evaluate trials properly. Another concern is who owns the GM technology in future, currently owned by commercial corporations, as debate is likely to be dominated by economic and political issues rather than providing answers to key environmental questions.
- *Royal Society for the Protection of Birds (RSPB).* Is sufficiently concerned about cumulative effects on bird life to think there should be no commercial planting of GM crops in the UK until rigorous environmental testing is carried out and shown to have no harmful effects, which could take four years.
- *The Prince of Wales.* Raised his concerns in 10 questions in which he associated himself with the anti-GM foods lobby (*The Independent*, 2 June 1999). These are listed below.

The 10 questions raised by the Price of Wales provide a useful summary of the arguments:

1 *Do we need GM food in this country?* The anti-GM lobby's view is that no one needs or wants GM foods or crops other than the agrochemicals industry. The pro-GM foods lobby takes the opposite view and neutrals argue that, if it lowers pesticide levels and produces cheaper food with added nutritional benefits, GM foods should be welcomed.

2 *Is GM food safe to eat?* The anti-GM lobby argues that it is not, if seen in terms of wider environmental damage which could affect the health of everybody in the future. The pro-GM food lobby cites positive evidence from the USA and government chief medical and scientific advisers, which neutrals support but argue that each new food must be tested for adverse immune reactions and toxicity.

3 *Why are less stringent rules used to approve GM foods?* The anti-GM lobby argues it is because GM foods would fail normal safety tests carried out on new drugs, but the pro-GM lobby points out that the same tests cannot be carried out because GM food is, by its nature, an impure substance. Neutrals observe that new foods undergo more rigorous testing than traditional varieties and to suggest that clinical trials should be conducted on GM foods is unrealistic.

4 *What do we know about the environmental impact of GM foods?* The anti-GM lobby insists we know next to nothing, whereas the pro-GM lobby notes that no adverse effects have been reported in the USA where extensive trials have been in progress since 1991. The neutrals accept that there is a need for more research and argues that the UK farm trials should proceed.

5 *Will trials proceed without strict regulations in place?* The anti-GM lobby argues that the trials are for the benefit of Monsanto and the UK government and nobody can predict their outcome, whereas the pro-GM lobby points out that GM crops cannot be planted without government permission and its guidelines are mandatory. Neutrals agree that GM crop regulations are more stringent than generally realised and field trials will last for several years.

6 *How will consumers be able to exercise choice?* The anti-GM lobby insists that genuine choice will not be possible since contamination is inevitable if the farm trials proceed. The pro-GM lobby argues that all GM food grown in the UK will be separately labelled. Neutrals agree that proper labelling is the key but caution that this issue has been the undoing of the pro-GM lobby to date in the USA.

7 *If something goes wrong with a GM crop, who will be responsible?* The anti-GM lobby insists that all of us will have to pay for the mistakes of the few, as has happened with the BSE 'mad cow disease' crisis. The pro-GM lobby insists that 'the polluter pays' principle would allow growers to sue GM seed suppliers. Neutrals regard this as the weak link in the GM food chain and question how the supplier of a GM food consignment can be identified.

8 *Are GM crops the most effective way to feed the world's growing population?* The anti-GM lobby says no and that undeveloped countries want to improve their traditional farming methods instead. The pro-GM lobby partially accepts this argument but adds that peace and more efficient food distribution are needed to alleviate global poverty and that, realistically, GM crop development will occur first. Neutrals note that wars and greed are the historical causes of starvation and the introduction of GM crops is unlikely to change this aspect of human behaviour.

9 *What impact will GM crops have in undeveloped countries?* The anti-GM lobby argues that it will only worsen their situation by making the developing world more dependent on industrialised countries, whereas the pro-GM lobby maintains that real benefits could result from the introduction of pest-resistant crops. Neutrals argue that progress may be at the cost of making undeveloped countries more dependent on transnational corporations.

10 *What sort of world do we want to live in?* The anti-GM lobby is against the spread of a world dominated by transnational corporations that put profit before the environment and seek to promote corporate greed. The pro-GM lobby favours the creation of a sustainable agriculture and a balanced environment in which safe, cheap and nutritious food is available to all. Neutrals favour a rational future in which decisions are based on science and it is accepted that simple technological answers are not always available.

**The GM industry fights back**

The US biotechnology industry hit back against 'celebrity critics' such as the Prince of Wales in July 1999 when the president of the Biotechnology Association criticised Prince Charles and Hollywood stars for their opposition to GM crops stating that: 'They just don't know enough about the issues they use their star power to highlight.' Further criticism occurred in the UK when the chairman of the Nuffield Council on Bioethics dismissed the Prince of Wales' intervention as 'that of a nice man but [who is] utterly confused . . . He has very primitive ways of thinking. He talks about a choice of working with nature or an Orwellian future. Think about what life on a farm was like 75 years ago. . . . The idea that it was some primitive Eden we can all go back to – He must be absolutely cuckoo.'

**The debate widens**

The angry debate about GM foods surfaced at the Montreal World Trade Organisation (WTO) meeting in February 2000 when 175 countries agreed to debate a new protocol on food laws which would entitle WTO member-states to block the import of GM products from other countries. Meanwhile, doubts began to be raised in the USA about GM food safety claims when a legal challenge was filed against the US Food and Drug Administration in February 2000 for 'a deliberate ploy to deceive the world' that GM crops were substantially equivalent to normal crops, despite evidence that 11 of 17 experts on the US Task Force to assess risks had expressed disquiet about GM foods, only to be overruled (*The Guardian*, 29 February 2000). This argument was taken up by President Clinton at the Group of Eight (G8) meeting in Okinawa, Japan, in July 2000, when he criticised European leaders for moving too slowly on the promotion of GM foods. He defended the US position by stating: 'If we could get more of this golden rice [which is genetically modified and especially rich in vitamin A] out to the developing world, it would save 40,000 lives a day, people that are malnourished and dying.' Asked if GM food is safe, President Clinton replied: 'All the evidence that I've seen convinces me, based on what all the scientists know now, that it is.' Tony Blair, the UK Prime Minister, stated: 'This whole science of biotechnology is perhaps going to be for the first half of the twenty-first century what information technology was to the last half of the twentieth century.' Both leaders approved the G8 commitment to explore how to 'integrate the best scientific knowledge available into the global process of consensus building on biotechnology and other aspects of food and crop safety'. A G8 statement also referred to 'the potential risks associated with food' but without making any direct mention of biotechnology or GM foods.

**Question**

Evaluate the arguments in favour of or against the introduction of GM crops in Europe from the following ethical standpoints:

(i)   idealism;
(ii)  pragmatism;
(iii) utilitarianism;
(iv)  Natural Law.

## Notes and references

1. Singer, P., *Animal Liberation*, New York, Random House, 1990.
2. Regan, T., *The Case for Animal Rights*, Berkeley, University of California Press, 1983.
3. Varner, G.F., Animal Rights, in *International Encyclopaedia of Ethics*, ed. J.K. Roth, London, Fitzroy-Dearborn, 1995, 37–40.
4. Katen, T., *Animal Consciousness*, New York, McGraw-Hill, 1992.
5. Auday, B.C., Animal Research, *International Encyclopaedia of Ethics*, ed. J.K. Roth, London, Fitzroy-Dearborn, 1995, 36–7.
6. Singer, P., *Practical Ethics*, New York, Cambridge University Press, 1979 (revised edn, 1992).
7. Regan, T. and Singer, P., eds, *Animal Rights and Human Obligations*, 2nd edn, Englewood Cliffs, NJ, Prentice Hall, 1989.

8. Frey, R.O., *Interests and Rights: The case against animals*. Oxford, Clarendon Press, 1980.

9. Griffin, D.R., *Animal Minds*, Chicago, University of Chicago Press, 1992.

10. Rupke, N.A., ed., *Vivisection in Historical Perspective*, New York, Croom Helm, 1987.

11. Fox, M.E., *The Case for Animal Experimentation*, Berkeley, University of California Press, 1986.

12. Fox, M.E., Animal Experimentation: A philosopher's changing views, *Between the Species* 3, no. 2 (spring), 1987, 55–82.

13. Paton, W.D., *Man and Mouse: Animals in medical research*, Oxford, Oxford University Press, 1984.

14. *The Ethical Consumer Guide to Everyday Shopping*, Manchester, Ethical Consumer Journal, 1993.

15. The Food Commission, Guide to Children's Food, *The Times 2*, 31 May 2000, 3–4.

16. Lang, P., *Ethical Investment: A saver's guide*, Charlbury, Oxford, Carpenter Publishing, 1996, x, 86, 87–105.

17. The Cooperative Bank 2, Everything you want to know About Ethics, 360A(2) D300.

# PART V

# Moral Compass exercise

The Moral Compass instruments below are divided into two questionnaires, which should be evaluated using the 7-point Lickert scale shown in Box A. The simple Moral Compass contains the eight statements shown in Box B. The detailed Moral Compass includes the additional eight statements shown in Box C. Each statement corresponds with one of the ethical theories summarised in Chapter 4.

**Instructions**

1 Decide whether you wish to complete the simple or the detailed Moral Compass instrument.

2 Read each statement carefully before recording your response, using the 7-point Lickert scale shown in Box A below.

3 Record your scores for each part of the instruments in the Moral Compass section in the Appendix at the end of the book, where the corresponding ethical theories are shown.

## Box A

| Strongly disagree | Disagree | Slightly disagree | Neither agree nor disagree | Slightly agree | Agree | Strongly agree |
|:---:|:---:|:---:|:---:|:---:|:---:|:---:|
| 1 | 2 | 3 | 4 | 5 | 6 | 7 |

**Box B**

| | | |
|---|---|---|
| **S.1** | Crime in the poorer sectors of society is the sort of behaviour that is often considered perfectly legitimate in the business community. | 1  2  3  4  5  6  7 |
| **S.2** | The test of a vocation is the love of drudgery it entails. | 1  2  3  4  5  6  7 |
| **S.3** | Many are made unhappy and fail to advance in business by displaying a moral sense too early, before they have evaluated all the facts. | 1  2  3  4  5  6  7 |
| **S.4** | The best leader is not the best orator or efficient trader but one who integrates the experience of the organisation's members for the common good. | 1  2  3  4  5  6  7 |
| **S.5** | A loyal colleague anywhere in the world may know nothing about ethics but would always act in an honest, open and generous way. | 1  2  3  4  5  6  7 |
| **S.6** | In taking responsibility for employees' well-being, there's nothing wrong with paternalism, if it is fair, realistic, open and benign. | 1  2  3  4  5  6  7 |
| **S.7** | Societies, communities and families have leaders, whereas organisations have managers, whose job is not to command, but to inspire individuals. | 1  2  3  4  5  6  7 |
| **S.8** | Business is of trivial importance: love, truth of character, and aspirations, these are sacred to me. | 1  2  3  4  5  6  7 |

**Box C**

| | | |
|---|---|---|
| **S.9** | The wise manager uses every means of keeping employees under an obligation so that they cooperate and would never deliberately do anything to cause him/her an embarrassment. | 1  2  3  4  5  6  7 |
| **S.10** | I am unable to understand how any rational individual could attain happiness by exercising power over others. | 1  2  3  4  5  6  7 |
| **S.11** | Don't be surprised if poor people decide to steal or destroy their rich neighbour's goods in a society that only worships competition. | 1  2  3  4  5  6  7 |
| **S.12** | By providing workers with training, unions contribute to both social justice and higher productivity. | 1  2  3  4  5  6  7 |
| **S.13** | No policy is illegal if the leading 100 British businesspeople decide it should be carried out. | 1  2  3  4  5  6  7 |
| **S.14** | Idealists are individuals who help other people to become richer than themselves. | 1  2  3  4  5  6  7 |
| **S.15** | It is difficult but not impossible for an individual to practise strictly honest business conduct. | 1  2  3  4  5  6  7 |
| **S.16** | Whatever is not nailed down is mine, and whatever I can pry loose is not nailed down. | 1  2  3  4  5  6  7 |

# PART VI

# Managing values and beliefs in organisations

# 14 Organisational culture and stakeholder theory

*Nations are fast losing their nationality. The great and increasing intercourse, the exchange of fashions, and uniformity of opinions are fast destroying those peculiarities that formerly prevailed. We shall in time grow to be very much one people, unless a return to barbarism throws us into chaos.*

Washington Irving, *Journals and Notebooks*, October 1822

## Learning objectives

After reading this chapter you should be able to:

- explain the origins of the study of organisational culture;
- outline the links between organisational culture and stakeholder theory;
- summarise the main ethical arguments for and against stakeholder theory;
- consider the impact of stakeholder theory on new management perspectives in systems thinking, corporate strategy and organisational behaviour;
- discuss the findings of longitudinal research in Canada which introduced a stakeholder framework to evaluate the corporate social responsibility of participating companies.

## Introduction

Nearly three decades have elapsed since Daniel Bell's *The Coming of Post-Industrial Society* was published (1973), which predicted how technology and the conversion of theoretical knowledge into intellectual 'software', as a new principle of innovation, would reshape the technological and economic order of business on a global basis. As a result, the complex relationships between the socioeconomic structure of society and its culture could no longer be neglected by social scientists, just as the pivotal role of values and beliefs in specific cultures and their impact on change in society had to be recognised. As the 'global' economy emerged during the 1990s, these ideas had a growing influence on management thinking in areas such as organisational culture and the introduction of alternative flat or networked structures, based upon stakeholder and open systems perspectives, in the fields of corporate strategy and organisational behaviour. Meanwhile, longitudinal research from Canada (see p. 337) indicates that the ethical implications of adopting a stakeholder framework have had a positive impact on the corporate social performance of the participating corporations.

## Culture in society and organisations

### Culture in society

As a concept, culture is inseparable from the notion of human society which makes defining it a complicated task. Not surprisingly, Kroeber and Kluckhohn[1] discovered over 160 definitions which they grouped into three categories for convenience:

- a concept that separates human beings from non-human species;
- an amalgamation of mankind's historical social achievements; and
- knowledge that is capable of being communicated.

Provision is made under these three headings for explanations and comparisons of the beliefs, values, languages, behaviours and ways of life of past and present societies. References to the diverse art, inventions, rituals, technology, religions, politics and economic activities of different communities are also included. What binds these definitions together is a view that culture has always been shared by humans and transmitted across generations. Individual and collective learning has therefore been acquired through the family and community, and their educational and religious systems and, more recently, through the media. Although a culture is known to be assimilated in various ways, the outcome is assumed to be the same and mainly consists of similar patterns of thought and behaviour which are reinforced in society through private discussion and social pressure such as public events.

### Definition of culture

With so many definitions to choose from, Czinkota *et al.*'s[2] is included because it is concise and applied to international business. Culture is defined as: 'an integrated system of learned behaviour patterns, characteristic of the members of any given society'. They add that individuals learn the elements of culture as the 'right way' of doing things through acculturation. The elements of culture are also known as *cultural universals* and refer to every aspect of the total life of a society or smaller group of people, including:

| | |
|---|---|
| verbal language; | religion; |
| non-verbal language; | values and beliefs; |
| manners and customs; | political, economic and social infrastructure; |
| aesthetics and artefacts; | technology; |
| education; | community reference groups. |

## Culture in a business and organisational context

### Culture and the global economy

Most of the cultural universals in the right-hand column above are discussed in previous chapters and these are included to complement the traditional business disciplines through which people contribute to their own and society's well-being. Their inclusion also raises important questions about the future nature of paid employment.

What tasks will need to be performed? Where will these be carried out? What new training and skills will be required? And how will work be organised and decisions taken, etc.? The rationale for questions of this sort is that the widening reach of modern media has already brought about unprecedented change which has radically altered our view of the world, so that what was regarded by many as a vast, incompletely explored planet just a generation ago, is now regarded as a 'global village' in a new global economy.

The effects have been twofold. At one level, individual experiences constantly re-affirm the view that personal well-being depends upon our ties with family members, friends, colleagues at work and other members of the local community, as indicated in studies of the cultural universals in the left-hand column above. At another level, however, those of us who live in developed countries are also having to cope with all the complexities of being the members of the first 'information/post-industrial' society. How we learn to integrate both perspectives may be compared with suddenly having to explore the world by peering through the miniaturising and magnifying lenses of a telescope.

## Culture and the death of distance

Cairncross[3] confirms Bell's prediction that a rapid change in business orientations would occur as a result of the 'death of distance'. This useful metaphor is intended to convey the simple economic fact that geographic distance no longer determines the cost of communicating electronically. As a result, location is no longer:

> the key to certain business decisions; culture and communication networks will hold companies together, not rigid structures of control; new ideas and information will travel faster to the remotest corners of the world; and governments will find national legislation and censorship inadequate for regulating the global flow of information.

Economic historians point out that a global economy is not a new phenomenon. The former British empire ran one successfully during the late nineteenth and early twentieth centuries, and railways and telegraph systems helped bind this network together. What differs now, apart from the USA's predominance (see Chapter 3), is that electronic communications and technological innovations are exchanged almost instantaneously across a larger network of nations due to the 'death of distance'. As a result, how members of organisations respond to the different religious, ethical, socioeconomic and political values and beliefs of others, which may challenge the cultural universals alluded to in a company mission statement, has rapidly taken on a new importance. Because of the death of distance, these different viewpoints cannot be ignored for long without possible negative consequences. The need for managers to understand, reconcile and accommodate the legitimate concerns of rival stakeholders is therefore likely to become increasingly unavoidable in the future. The alternative is that failure to anticipate the impact of the values and beliefs of stakeholders on international corporate strategy could well undermine decades of attempting to develop successful organisations in the more culturally diverse, global economy of the twenty-first century.

Business administration and organisational behaviour are not the first disciplines that have had to adapt to these global changes. For example, Baerwald[4] describes how a reappraisal of the study of geography resulted in its focus being widened from providing answers to traditional 'Where?' questions. Instead, additional considerations had to include 'Why?' questions, about the reasons some resources are located in one region and not another; and 'How?' questions about changes in resource levels over time. Apart from acquiring knowledge for its own sake, answers to these enquiries also made a vital practical contribution to achieving more accurate economic forecasts and investment decisions.

The rationale for geography's changing role is easy to understand because it deals with concrete information about the physical world. By comparison, references to cultural universals are unavoidably vague. Perhaps the gap can be narrowed if the links between culture and business activity are regarded as a sort of 'mental geography' which seeks to map unexplored relationships between different peoples around the world. Exploration with a few, admittedly roughly drawn, maps has already begun in business and organisational culture.

## Business culture

Lockwood[5] and Hall[6] are credited as being first to study the relationship between culture and business success in international markets. Comparing the Japanese and US political economies nearly 35 years ago, Lockwood's observations are worth quoting in detail. Of US corporations, he writes:

> Hardly a country in Europe (or Canada or Latin America) fails to worry today about the 'corporate colonization' of giant American companies with seemingly limitless resources and know-how. Apprehensions seem to be more pronounced in Japan than in Europe. . . . Americans will have to respect such apprehensions as a valid concern over Japan's national integrity, and her fear of slipping into permanent dependence in the sphere of corporate enterprise. Self-confident as they are, and in possession of an industrial system three times that of Japan, they can expect increasing political difficulties unless they sensitize themselves to such feelings.

Of the emerging Japanese economy, he adds:

> The Japanese, for their part, . . . would do well to avoid the emotional cliches that abound in this realm of national economic policy. If they do, and if they examine realistically the policy alternatives open to both America and Japan, they will become less certain as to who is actually becoming dependent on whom.

Hall's subsequent study of the impact of culture on business activities led to the identification of international *high* and *low context cultures*. In high context cultures (e.g. Japan and Saudi Arabia) homogeneous views on nationality, religion, values and beliefs prevailed and the context of communication exchanges was of equal importance to what was discussed. Ceremony, body language, courtesy and gestures were often more valued than the details of any contract; what was left unsaid, more important than what was actually discussed. In low context cultures (e.g. the USA, UK and Germany), opposite behaviour was more prevalent and important information in any business discussion was conveyed in words and formal written records.

Comparing these cultural differences, Czinkota *et al.* add that Hall also predicted that international business contacts would act as a change agent, altering local culture over time. They cite the entry of McDonald's into Taiwan, formerly a high context culture, where the eating habits of the young have changed remarkably in a generation; and no doubt in the 108 other countries where the brand has been established during the last 25 years.

## Organisational culture

More recent observations on the relationship between business activity and culture include two influential studies of the dimensions of acculturation in a transnational corporation by Hofstede[7,8]; and a later study of managers in various developed countries by Trompenaars[9]. Hofstede defines culture as 'collective programming of the mind' and follows Hall in describing it as a multi-dimensional concept, which he reduces to four sets of opposite, interdependent dimensions, as follows:

- *low v. high power distance*, which measures the degree of inequity in organisations;
- *low v. high uncertainty avoidance*, which measures the extent that employees are disturbed by and seek to withdraw from unpredicted events;
- *low v. high individualism*, which measures the prevalence of an individualistic or collective culture in an organisation;
- *low v. high masculinity*, which measures the degree of masculine (assertive, 'me-first', competitive behaviour) and feminine (caring, group-oriented concern for others, the environment and the quality of life) behaviour of employees.

Hofstede classifies his findings by country into eight categories and his findings have probably attracted more attention in the USA and continental Europe than in the UK. The originality of his research cannot be faulted but, as with any 'universal' theory, the general conclusions are more controversial due to a questionable experimental design. By way of analogy, Hofstede's conclusions have been queried for the same reasons that a report on world football would be if it consisted of hundreds of interviews in numerous countries, with only Manchester United supporters. That said, detailed information on attributes of a single category of football supporters around the world is still a valuable contribution to what would otherwise have to be a massive, more representative research project.

Much of Trompenaars' analysis of international cultural variance is a reworking of an earlier joint study with Hampden-Turner[10] of the seven different 'cultures of capitalism' in 12 leading industrialised countries (the USA, Japan, Germany, the UK, Canada, Australia, France, The Netherlands, Italy, Belgium, Sweden and Singapore). Both works study cultural differences based on responses to seven sets of dilemmas (i.e. conflicts or tensions at work capable of being resolved). The aim was to identify management values which influence behaviour in an international context. These dilemmas were:

- *universalism v. particularism* (i.e. the use/non-use of codes, rules or laws, however imperfect, in dealing with exceptional cases);
- *analysing v. integrating* (i.e. is more effective management achieved by analysing phenomena as parts or integrating them into patterns or relationships?);
- *individualism v. communitarianism* (i.e. whether each individual's rights, etc., should prevail over serving the organisation as a community – see Chapter 4 for further discussion of these ideologies);

- *inner-directed v. outer-directed orientation* (i.e. reliance on our inner-directed judgements or adjustments to demands and trends in the world);
- *time as sequence v. time as synchronisation* (i.e. doing things fast in the shortest time as opposed to completing a task by synchronised coordination);
- *achieved status v. ascribed status* (i.e. status dependent on performance and achievement as opposed to status based on age or seniority, etc.);
- *equality v. hierarchy* (i.e. treatment of employees as equals or as occupying roles dependent on the authority/judgement of senior members of a hierarchy).

A summary of Trompenaars' findings also appears in Mullins[11]. The importance of his joint research with Hampden-Turner[10] is that clear national differences are identified in:

> the relative importance of those values necessary to wealth creation [which] typically are loaded with ideological fervour. . . . foreign cultures are seen as representing that other value, as subverting 'what we believe in'. This narrow view turns other cultures from commercial rivals into ideological adversaries with no concept of 'fair competition'. (p. 12)

In short, the contributions of Lockwood, Hall, Hofstede, Hampden-Turner and Trompenaars have established a sound basis for further studies of the impact of cultural universals on business activity. Specific research is called for into how the values and beliefs of managers of organisations in the leading industrialised countries can be reconciled with the different attitudes and behaviours of widely distributed constituencies of consumers and other stakeholders in the emerging global economy both in home and host countries.

## Stakeholder theory

### Origins

Stakeholder theory is regarded as a rebuttal of the well-known attack on the notion that business has a social responsibility, other than to make profits, associated with Milton Friedman. Uncertainty exists about the origins of stakeholder analysis in research and other organisational publications. Contrary to Freeman's[12] account, the term was used in business practice and strategic planning theory long before it was introduced at the Stanford University Research Institute in 1963, or its strategic management implications received fleeting attention from Ansoff[13] in 1965. Hence, Preston[14] reports that stakeholder analysis was carried out in the 1930s by the General Electric Corporation during the US Depression when shareholders, employees, customers and the general public were identified as the four 'major stakeholder' groups. Johnson & Johnson also described its customers, employees, managers and shareholders as 'strictly business stakeholders' in 1947.

### Stakeholder theory defined

Freeman defines a stakeholder as 'any individual or group who can affect, or is affected by, the achievement of the firm's objectives'. Stakeholder theory is presented as a series of challenges to the supposed primacy given to the shareholder by managerial capitalism. These challenges appear as:

- the legal argument; and
- the economic arguments.

The simple idea underpinning the agency theory of capitalism is that management is appointed as the agent of the owners of capital to pursue the interests of all shareholders, in return for controlling the organisation's activities. However, Freeman notes that the numerous changes in business and company law that occurred during the twentieth century have combined to make this original model of management capitalism untenable. According to Freeman: 'Such changes in the legal system can be viewed as giving some rights to those groups that have a claim on the firm, for example, customers, suppliers, employees, government, local authorities and management' (p. 410).

These changes raise the key question: in whose interest and for whose benefit should the firm be managed? The obvious answer is 'the shareholders'. Yet Freeman goes on to argue that 'the law has been progressively circumscribing this answer' by citing the following economic arguments.

**Free-riding**

The first economic argument against the agency model is failure to address the common problem of human frailty, or what Freeman calls the 'free-rider' problem (see Chapter 6). Simple examples of free-riding include the case of a firm that fails to repair a private road leading to its premises, which becomes a major factor in a subsequent serious accident. A second example involves a firm that fails to dispose of stale food from the staff canteen, or to cut the grass on its adjacent plot, which encourages rats to breed leading to a public health problem. Other examples of free-riding include firms that have neglected to treat effluents or chemical gases before discharging the former into the local water supply and the latter into the atmosphere, polluting both micro-environments as a consequence.

These examples of free-riding (so-called because they may be compared with failure to pay a bus or train fare) are usually referred to as 'externalities' by economists. In all cases, third parties and various government agencies have to intervene because free-riding by the firms prevents the greatest good being achieved by the greatest number of people in society. The point made by Freeman is that the market economy model is undermined by free-riding whenever government agencies have to resolve a problem through the taxpayer.

**Moral hazards**

A second economic argument raised by Freeman is the failure of the competitive system when the provider and consumer of a good or service pass on part of the cost to an unsuspecting third party. It used to be common practice in the catering industry for waiters to agree to some customers' requests for an inflated receipt for an inexpensive meal, in return for a generous tip, which allowed the customers to reclaim fictitious costs by fiddling expense claims submitted to their employers. This sort of behaviour is discussed in business ethics under the heading of 'moral hazards', because it interferes with the efficient running of the market economy as a source of inflation and mistrust.

**Problems with monopoly**

Finally, some firms also form cartels or 'price rings' which engage in the oligopolistic practice of submitting almost identical quotations or tenders (which are also inflated) for the same contract, thereby reducing/excluding genuine competition. If all goes to plan, the lowest tender secures the contract and a handsome profit is made. The secretive 'rules of the price ring' also require the winner of the last contract to submit the highest tender next time around so that each cartel member eventually secures a lucrative contract, often at the public's expense if a local authority is involved as the purchaser. This type of behaviour is discussed in ethics and economics under 'problems with monopoly' as it also undermines the efficiency of the market economy. It leads to mistrust and, when third parties or government agencies have to intervene on behalf of stakeholders in the public interest, even to criminal prosecution. Freeman, without pausing to consider the arguments of Burnham, Nader, and Berle and Means (see Chapter 1), concludes that: 'externalities, moral hazards and monopoly power have led to more external control on managerial capitalism. There are de facto constraints, due to economic facts of life, on the ability of management to act in the interests of shareholders' (p. 411).

## Bi-polar perspectives on stakeholder theory

As an incomplete description of human behaviour, stakeholder theory still needs to be refined so that its salient points are emphasised as there is a tendency to explicate the theory in terms of different bi-polar comparisons of stakeholders, as follows:

- narrow v. wide definitions;
- primary v. secondary stakeholders;
- internal v. external stakeholders.

Freeman and Reed[15] distinguish between narrow definition and wide definition stakeholders. The former include all groups/individuals who are crucial to the survival of the organisation, whereas wide definition stakeholders include only those who can affect or are affected by the organisation. The support of narrow definition stakeholders is obviously more crucial to the success of an organisation. Freeman presents various arguments in favour of equitable treatment of narrow definition stakeholders as follows.

Following Rawls (see Chapter 12), Freeman argues that the way to ensure that narrow definition stakeholders are treated fairly is to adopt the 'veil of ignorance' argument for all the parties to a contract. In short, if ignorant of the stakes involved, each party would be prepared to accept what is on the other side of the table if seats were reversed. This he calls the doctrine of fair contracts. To ensure appropriate 'rules of the game', Freeman proposes six ground rules based on the 'veil of ignorance' position, as follows:

- the principle of entry and exit;
- the principle of governance;
- the principle of externalities;
- the principle of contracting costs;
- the agency principle;
- the principle of limited mortality.

- *The principle of entry and exit* proposes that any contract between each stakeholder and the organisation must have clear points of entry, exit and renegotiation, so that all parties are aware of when an agreement exists which is capable of being fulfilled.
- *The principle of governance* proposes that the procedure for changing the rules of the game must be agreed unanimously, to ensure that no stakeholder is excluded by others, but retains the right to participate in the governance of the organisation.
- *The principle of externalities* proposes that when contracts between stakeholders A and B are agreed, costs cannot be imposed on C without the latter agreeing to become party to the contract. The principle is designed to ensure that no stakeholder is placed in the same unacceptable situation as C.
- *The principle of contracting costs* proposes that all parties to a contract involving the organisation must share the cost of contracting to avoid any single stakeholder gaining/losing at the expense/advantage of another.
- *The agency principle* proposes that any agent of the organisation must serve the interests of all the stakeholders without preference or prejudice.
- *The principle of limited mortality* proposes that the organisation must be managed as if it can continue to serve the interests of all stakeholders over time who, subject to exit conditions above, must accept that the continued existence of an effective organisation is in their interests.

Freeman also proposes three further principles for reforming the way that corporations should legally operate, as follows:

- *The stakeholder enabling principle* proposes that organisations shall be managed in the interests of their stakeholders.
- *The principle of director responsibility* proposes that the duty of care of directors shall be to use reasonable judgement in defining and directing the organisation's affairs according to the above stakeholder enabling principle.
- *The principle of stakeholder recourse* proposes that stakeholders may bring any action against the directors for failing to perform the required duty of care.

Freeman's explication of stakeholder theory is a coherent attempt to address the legal, economic and ethical shortcomings of the earlier model of management capitalism and merits further attention in three areas:

- It does not treat corporate governance, or the social responsibilities relating to narrow definition stakeholders, as separate management issues. Hence, it provides a logical alternative to the widely criticised *ad hoc* models of corporate governance which have been adopted in the USA and Britain since the early 1990s.
- It is based on the Kantian moral imperative, i.e. 'treat persons as ends in themselves', and advocates equal treatment of shareholder, customer, employee, supplier and community members' interests in a business context as a basis for good management practice.
- In seeking to ensure equal treatment of all stakeholders, by recognising their legal rights and moral obligations, it recognises the relevance of ethical pluralism (see Chapter 4) principles in an organisational context. The supposition is that this moral stance is better able to address cultural universal issues than other business ethics perspectives.

As Freeman notes, his proposals also adopt a normative stance which includes various statements of the 'managers ought to do X' variety. This leaves his analysis open to the criticism that there is no logical connection between how managers should/ought to behave and what they actually do in different business situations. Before dismissing his defence of stakeholder theory out-of-hand, however, it should be noted that Friedman's attack on the social responsibility of business (see Chapter 1) is open to the same criticism.

## The case against stakeholder theory

### Prioritising between stakeholders

Jackson[16] summarises an alternative 'multi-fiduciary' (where 'fiduciary' describes the trust and public confidence expressed by/towards another person) version of stakeholder theory by Goodpaster[17], which treats all stakeholder claims as if these are of equal importance. Goodpaster rejects this multi-fiduciary view as untenable because shareholders are ultimate owners of the company, and have contractual arrangements with management, which give them a special claim over other stakeholders. Sternberg[18] agrees with Goodpaster and distinguishes between management's ethical duties to advance shareholders' interests, striving to maximise the long-term value of the business, and also to be attentive to the expectations of other stakeholders. Her argument against stakeholder theory is worth quoting in detail:

> If stakeholder theory is taken seriously, it makes business impossible. And that is because the definitive stakeholder aim – balanced benefits for all stakeholders – precludes all benefits which favour particular groups. Business . . . as the activity of maximising the long-term owner value is automatically ruled out. So are the quite different aims of maximising value-added for customers and improving benefits for employees. (p. 89)

As Jackson notes, Sternberg distinguishes between the fiduciary responsibilities of managers to shareholders, summarised above, and the non-fiduciary obligations to other stakeholders, which are no different from the 'basic obligations' that each of us has to other individuals. Managers are therefore morally required to act within the accepted constraints of 'ordinary decency' and 'distributive justice'. Ordinary decency excludes deceit, theft, violence and coercing stakeholders into acting against their own interests. It also excludes other forms of illegality from which no one has 'moral immunity'.

Sternberg's view of distributive justice is closer to that of Nozick than Rawls (see Chapter 12), in proposing that the rewards of labour should be proportional to an individual's contribution to the declared outcomes of the business (i.e. if it is assumed management are more responsible for strategic decisions than other employees, rewards are justified when their policies succeed, but appropriate costs may be incurred when they fail). Sternberg adds that enlightened managers should also take into account the concerns of other stakeholders for the strategic reasons identified by Goodpaster, with the proviso that: 'Taking something into account' does not mean being accountable for it (p. 50). This statement prompts the question: why should a manager who fails to take a stakeholder's valid concerns into account be entitled to different treatment from the motorist who argues that: 'I took into account the car that was parked behind me, but am not accountable for the damage incurred after reversing into it through my careless driving'?

## Stakeholder theory and management theory

Ambler and Wilson[19] raise numerous concerns about stakeholder theory but acknowledge its central part in 'the debate on corporate social responsibility and ownership, and the role of organisations in society'. Missing from their analysis, however, is any discussion of the management capitalism perspective on company ownership (see the discussion of shareholders' rights in the corporate governance sections in Chapters 1 and 13), or the long-standing contribution of stakeholder theory in corporate strategy, organisational behaviour and human resource management. For example, most of the problem areas they raise about the determination of stakeholders, confusion of purpose, company success, and the distribution of benefits and power among stakeholders have already been explored in the field of corporate strategy, as noted below.

Hardly less important, however, is the impact of stakeholder theory on developments in the related fields of organisational behaviour and human resource management, which has been overshadowed to some extent by the wider acceptance of open systems theory in new paradigms on organisational behaviour since the 1970s. The connection between open systems theory and stakeholder theory is based on the notion of interdependency between the numerous sub-systems that comprise a dynamic open system so that the whole is assumed to be greater than the sum of the parts. Logically, where such interdependency exists, the rationale for retaining hierarchical structures is open to question. However, political economy issues are rarely decided on theoretical grounds and changes in the organisational structure of most Western companies came about as a result of what Sidelsky[20] describes as 'the creation of policy as well as of ideals and the unguided forces of technology', in what became known as the New Political Economy, which Bell[21] had envisaged as *post-industrial society*.

A major consequence of the coming of post-industrial society was a major restructuring of the workforces in industrialised nations, also known as 'downsizing', which led to a global shift in manufacturing from the northern to the southern hemisphere, as increasing numbers of people found employment in the service sectors of most developed nations. Just how accurate Bell's prediction was can be gauged from the data presented in Table 14.1. GDP data in 1970 would have shown the approximate

**Table 14.1 GDP by economic sector of selected industrialised countries**

| Country | Year | Services | Manufacturing | Agriculture |
|---------|------|----------|---------------|-------------|
| USA | 1997 | 75% | 23% | 2% |
| UK | 1995 | 66% | 32% | 2% |
| Germany | 1994 | 65% | 34% | 1% |
| Japan | 1994 | 64% | 34% | 2% |

*Source*: Collated from *World Books Encyclopaedia*, Chicago, 2000.

2:1 ratio of services to manufacturing output above reversed in favour of manufacturing to service sectors for the same economies.

Fukuyama[22] and Kets de Vries[23] argue that the traditional management hierarchy has since been modified by the increased flow of information and communication technology into organisations which has rapidly made authoritarian forms of organisation obsolete. In short, the most admired and successful US corporations since the 1980s, according to Kets de Vries, are those which have learnt how to reinvent themselves in order to deal with changes in the business environment. These self-renewing organisations are increasingly characterised by flat or networked management structures, in which shared values and the well-being of the corporation are promoted through what Kets de Vries describes as 'distributed leadership' and more participatory decision making processes.

## Impact of stakeholder theory on corporate strategy

These changes in the strategic management decision process were anticipated by Mason and Mitroff[24] who were also first to discuss the role of stakeholders in business policy making and corporate strategy when they defined a business firm as being conceived as 'the embodiment of a series of transactions among all of its constituent purposeful entities, that is, its stakeholders'. The latter stakeholders were previously defined as 'all those claimants inside and outside the firm who have a vested interest in the problem and its solution'. They also modestly acknowledge that they adopted the stakeholder concept from the systems analysis research by Rhenman[25] at the Tavistock Institute in London, published some 15 years before Freeman's[12] major work on the influence of stakeholder theory on strategic management, which identified the separate interests of internal and external stakeholders in particular.

### Internal v. external stakeholders

Strategic analysis is usually undertaken by identifying and comparing the key issues and objectives of the internal and external interest groups, which are both referred to as stakeholders in the organisation (Johnson and Scholes[26]). The contributions of these internal and external stakeholders are often evaluated separately using a range of techniques starting with SWOT (i.e. strengths, weaknesses, opportunities and threats) and PEST (i.e. political, economic, social and technological factors) analyses. In short, evaluation of the impact of stakeholder expectations on an organisation's objectives entails identifying key stakeholders, as individuals and groups, and assessing their expectations by mapping their interests before evaluating their power to influence the eventual choice of strategies by using cost–benefit analysis and DELPHI ranking techniques. Thus, most of the concerns raised by Ambler and Wilson[19] about stakeholder theory have been subjected to systematic analysis in corporate strategy for almost two decades.

## Stakeholder theory and organisational behaviour

### New perspectives on organisational hierarchies

Mullins[27] notes that major changes occurred in the traditional hierarchical structures of US and British organisations during the 1990s. Most of these were due to the introduction of Japanese management ideas by Western organisations, and the impact of technological and electronic telecommunication systems on mass production processes and business administration activities. These radical changes have led many organisations to restructure job designs, management communication systems and other key aspects of the working environment using one or more of the following systems. Due to space constraints, only empowerment and total quality management are discussed below, but the remainder are evaluated in detail by Mullins and by Slack et al.[28]

- empowerment;
- self-managed/flexible work-groups;
- quality circles;
- the McKinsey 7-S framework;
- the learning organisation;
- total quality management (TQM);
- business process re-engineering.

**Empowerment**  Many UK companies were persuaded to change their traditional organisational structures by the Department of Employment's initiative on Employee Involvement[29], and introduced empowerment programmes. Mullins notes that empowerment involves: 'allowing employees greater freedom, autonomy, and self-control over their work and responsibility for decision making'. Four ways of achieving empowerment are:

- participation, e.g. delegation of decision making;
- involvement, e.g. consulting employees for ideas and suggestions;
- commitment, e.g. through measures to increase job satisfaction;
- delayering, e.g. reducing the management levels following downsizing.

Some supporters regard empowerment as a new management theory because it stresses the role of managers as facilitators, rather than leaders, who devolve power and responsibility to employees to complete agreed tasks in autonomous groups. These principles are not new and occur in John Stuart Mill's writings on worker participation (see Chapter 12). More research on the benefits to stakeholders of empowerment is necessary as Mullins reports that a study of a Canadian life assurance company found no evidence to support predicted, rather than potential, benefits of empowerment. Meanwhile, self-managed/flexible work-groups, quality circles, the McKinsey 7-S framework, and the learning organisation have all succeeded in partially dismantling traditional hierarchical structures in organisations, resulting in improved communications and increased employee involvement, but without loss of productivity or profitability.

**Total quality management (TQM)**

Slack *et al.* describe TQM as a logical extension of the way that quality-related practice has progressed since the 1930s. Records show that this occurred in four stages, beginning with 100 per cent inspection of output, followed by statistical quality control sampling techniques and quality assurance costing and planning, before TQM was introduced in the West from Japan in the late 1980s. It is worth noting that the first three quality procedures lacked any employee involvement and relied on the 'scientific management' principles of F.W. Taylor (1856–1917) to implement quality standards. Efforts by US specialists to introduce the latter methods in Japan after World War II were unsuccessful, mainly because the 'them and us' principles of scientific management were contrary to the traditional Japanese organisational culture of *kaizen*, which Slack *et al.* define as follows (p. 693): 'Kaizen means improvement in one's personal life, home life, social life and work life. When applied in the work place, "kaizen" means continuing improvement involving everyone – managers and workers alike.' A TQM philosophy emerged instead which emphasised the following objectives:

- meeting the needs and expectations of customers;
- covering all parts of the organisation;
- including every member of the organisation;
- examining all costs associated with quality, especially the cost of 'failures';
- getting things 'right first time' by designing quality into all procedures;
- developing systems/procedures which support quality improvement;
- developing a continuous process of improvement across the organisation.

The success of TQM under manufacturing conditions is mostly associated with the simultaneous introduction of just-in-time (JIT) planning and control systems, to ensure delivery of specified products and services, only when needed by the customer. The salient point is that these improvements could not have been achieved, without higher costs, under traditional mass assembly line conditions controlled by scientific management principles. In short, empowerment of employees, elimination of boring repetitive tasks through job rotation, formation of smaller work-groups, redesign of tasks according to Japanese *kanban* procedures, and more employee involvement in management decisions, were essential for the TQM/JIT 'revolution' to succeed.

The main advantage of the 'open systems' perspective is that it successfully challenges the notion of a hierarchy as the most effective organisational structure for responding to the needs of internal stakeholders, such as employees, and external stakeholders like consumers. As a result, the general management distinction between external markets and communities, on the one hand, and hierarchies on the other, is no longer sustainable and, not for the first time, a self-fulfilling management 'science' model has been overtaken by the need to introduce changes in the organisation of people at work as a result of changes in technology.

## Primary v. secondary stakeholder groups

Clarkson[30] substitutes the notions of primary and secondary stakeholder groups in place of internal and external stakeholders, as mentioned above. Primary groups are those 'without whose continuing participation the corporation cannot survive as a going concern'. Secondary groups are 'those who influence or affect, or are influenced or affected by, the corporation, but they are not engaged in transactions with the corporation and are not essential for its survival'. Clarkson cites the media as a secondary stakeholder group with the capacity to mobilise public opinion for, or against, a company. Secondary stakeholder groups would also not be subjected to the Freeman doctrine of fair contracts, unlike primary stakeholder groups such as employees or suppliers. Otherwise, the differences between primary and secondary stakeholders are marginal and of little consequence.

## A longitudinal study of the management of primary and secondary stakeholders

Clarkson provides empirical evidence which challenges the major concerns of the critics of stakeholder theory, cited by Ambler and Wilson[19], who argue that 'organisations which try to benefit stakeholders . . . are not only at a huge competitive disadvantage, they are literally unmanageable', or disown the concept, wondering 'how it helps a Chairman decide what to do'. On the contrary, one of the propositions advanced for empirical testing by the Canadian researchers is that when a corporation is unable to continue as a going concern, it will be shown that one or more of the primary stakeholder groups has withdrawn from participation in that corporate system.

The Canadian research discusses conclusions obtained from a 10-year longitudinal study on the effectiveness of a stakeholder framework for analysing and evaluating the corporate social performance of major Canadian corporations in over 70 field studies from 1983 to 1993. Sixty-five of the largest companies in Canada participated in the programme including 10 major financial institutions, three each of the largest publishing and brewing companies and two each of the largest transport and steel companies, of which 20 companies remained in 1993. In addition, the largest electricity, gas, nickel, auto parts, paper pulp and telecommunication companies, four of the five largest oil and six largest retail companies also participated in the research study. The five main research findings are summarised below:

- None of the corporations experienced difficulty in identifying and dealing with its primary or secondary stakeholder groups.
- However, stakeholder issues and social issues needed to be distinguished because corporations and their managers were better able to manage relations with identifiable stakeholders than with the society as a whole.
- Analysis of stakeholder issues also needed to be conducted at the appropriate institutional, organisational or individual levels in the corporations.
- Analysis and evaluation of both the social performance of each organisation and the performance of individual managers was possible, as part of the task of managing the corporation's social responsibilities to, and its relationships with, its various stakeholders.
- The majority of corporations, whose executives had previously not identified stakeholder and social issues so comprehensively, found the task of evaluating the implications of relevant performance data with the interviewers to be worthwhile.

Corporate social performance is discussed in more detail in Chapter 15 as a concept for integrating corporate social responsibility, business ethics and corporate governance issues within a primary and secondary stakeholder framework.

## Synopsis

- The rapid growth of information technology and the emergence of a global economy have led to more awareness of the importance of the acculturation process through which the values and beliefs of different peoples influence the organisational culture of national and international businesses.

- The study of organisational culture coexists alongside the more contentious stakeholder theory, whose supporters argue addresses shortcomings in the traditional 'agency' model of management which, in reality, fails to recognise the fiduciary rights of individual shareholders and the multi-fiduciary rights of millions of new stakeholders in organisations who are simultaneously employees, shareholders, pension fund contributors and investors in unit trusts, etc.

- Critics of stakeholder theory contend that it fails to replace the classical 'agency' model of organisations which authorises managers to maximise the interests of owners/shareholders, while dealing with the legitimate concerns of other stakeholders as equivalent to those of other members of society, who are all entitled to 'ordinary decency', which excludes deceit, theft, violence and being coerced into acting against their own interests.

- Notwithstanding these rival arguments, stakeholder theory is compatible with the rise of self-renewing organisations, in response to the increased growth of global communications, which are characterised by less hierarchical management structures, distributed leadership and more participatory decision making processes.

- Stakeholder theory has already been successfully assimilated into corporate strategy, organisational behaviour and other business activities to establish more effective decision making and communications procedures with different internal and external stakeholders. Examples include the introduction of empowerment and total quality management programmes.

- Longitudinal research in Canada found widespread supportive evidence in favour of a stakeholder theory framework 'operationalised' as corporate social performance. Findings led to a proposition being advanced for empirical testing that when a corporation is unable to continue as a going concern, it will be shown that one or more of the primary stakeholder groups has withdrawn from participation in that corporate system.

## Review and discussion questions

1 What are the main difficulties to be overcome in the study of organisational culture?

2 Summarise the various constituents in Freeman's definition of a 'stakeholder' and give examples of and reasons why this list should be reduced or expanded.

3 Summarise the main arguments for and against stakeholder theory.

4 Explain what is meant by self-renewing organisations, and give examples of distributed leadership in any organisation with which you are familiar.

5 Discuss the argument that empowerment and TQM programmes are merely new management techniques for manipulating employees into believing that they have more control over their own activities at work.

## Case study
## Playing to win: the battle to televise Premier League football

**Introduction**

Early in September 1998, executives of BskyB and Manchester United Football Club held a joint press conference to announce that, after three months of secret talks, the TV company had made an agreed £623 million bid for the world's financially largest football club, and the most successful English team over the past decade. Days later Carlton TV, BskyB's main rival, announced it had started takeover talks during the same period with Arsenal, the second most successful English Premier League club. The prospect of the two leading Premier League clubs being taken over dominated the British media, and supporters of both clubs launched public protests against these moves. An action group, SUAM (Supporters against Murdoch), was formed to oppose the purchase of Manchester United by BskyB, a subsidiary of News Corporation, a transnational TV, newspaper and motion pictures corporation, run by the Australian, since naturalised American, media tycoon Rupert Murdoch.

Questions were raised in Parliament and in October the Minister for Trade and Industry decided to refer the BskyB bid to the Monopolies and Mergers Commission (MMC) for an independent ruling on whether the takeover was in the public interest. This decision had an immediate consequence as Carlton TV announced that it had decided to cancel takeover talks with Arsenal Football Club. The stated reason was uncertainty over the outcome of the MMC ruling but the more likely cause was that leading Arsenal supporters had refused to sell their shares to the pay-TV company. Between December 1998 and February 1999, the involvement of two other TV conglomerates in English football clubs was announced. The American-based NTL corporation made a £160 million bid for Newcastle United and the UK-based Granada Group purchased a minority stake in Liverpool Football Club.

Meanwhile, if the MMC referral was not a clear signal to BskyB of public opposition to its bid for Manchester United, then this message was emphasised in January 1999 when the independent Office of Fair Trading (OFT) started a case involving the BskyB pay-TV company and the Premier League in the Restrictive Practices Court. The charge was that BskyB had breached UK restrictive practices law by entering into a £670 million four-year contract in 1997 with the English Premier League. This deal gave BskyB exclusive rights to show 60 live football matches in the FA Carling Premier League, with highlights being shown later on Saturday nights via the BBC's *Match of the Day* programme.

**The growing support for Manchester United**

Those indifferent or opposed to football may be bemused at why the possible takeover of a leading football club should have attracted so much attention in the UK Parliament, courts and media. After all Manchester United may be the richest club but it is by no means the oldest or, until recently, the most successful English football team. At least 20 rival teams had been playing each other for over 50 years before the club was founded and a handful have won more League championships and FA Cup trophies than Manchester United. The club's huge international following and – since this support attracts huge revenue – financial wealth has its origins in the aftermath of a tragic plane crash at Munich in the early 1950s when many of its young players, known after the team's manager as 'The Busby Babes' were killed or seriously injured. The public sympathy and admiration for the courageous way that the club fulfilled its football commitments with a makeshift team formed the bedrock of its fanatical support, which is grudgingly acknowledged by rival UK supporters, and interest boomed, especially in the southern hemisphere, and particularly after Manchester United achieved repeated success in the FA Challenge Cup, English League and European Championship in the last decade.

**An illegal cartel**

The Restrictive Practices Court was asked by the OFT to rule whether the FA Premier League was operating an illegal cartel by negotiating collective exclusive deals mainly with BskyB but also with the BBC for the spin-off *Match of the Day* highlights. The OFT's case was that both deals acted against the public interest and if they were declared illegal, more fans could watch more live football matches at a lower cost. This was because the deal covered a mere one-sixth of the 360 Premier League football matches played in a single season. Those featuring Manchester United were televised most frequently and the club therefore received a disproportionately high 7 per cent, compared with the other 19 Premier League clubs, of the total revenue paid by BskyB and the BBC for exclusive rights to show the club's matches on television.

**The rationale for the BskyB bid**

BskyB sought to take over Manchester United because of the prospect of immediate large financial returns from being able to act as both a buyer and seller in what many regarded as a self-serving cartel. In short, as owner of Manchester United the pay-TV company would be guaranteed a large return on its investment as a pay-back on the revenue it had already paid for the exclusive right to show televised Premier League football matches. Additionally, as owner of the club, it could legally obtain bid details submitted by rival TV companies to televise Premier League matches after 2001; and raise/lower its bid accordingly to hold on to these exclusive rights. Commenting on the proposed bid, the respected media analyst, Raymond Snoddy, observed that: 'It is exclusive football rights followed by many other exclusive sports deals that, more than anything else, persuaded viewers to buy satellite dishes or take up cable television subscriptions.'

**The reaction of Parliament**

As if seeking to pre-empt a long drawn out hearing by the Restrictive Practices Court of a case widely regarded as a violation of the UK anti-monopoly legislation, over 100 MPs reflected public anger against the BskyB bid by signing an emergency 'early day motion' which called on the government to declare its opposition publicly against the proposed BskyB takeover of Manchester United. The government remained publicly unmoved but declared it would support both the ruling of the MMC and the OFT action in the Restrictive Practices Court. The public debate continued, however, as football and assorted media commentators lamented how the world's 'most beautiful game' could have been taken away from its millions of working-class supporters in the UK to become the exclusive property of a terrestial TV corporation, run by a 'foreigner' who, reputedly, had never watched a live football match, which now planned to ignore public sentiment and take over 'the most popular and arguably the best marketed football club on the planet' (*Financial Times*, 4/5 March 2000).

**The Murdoch empire**

*The Economist* (20 March 1999) reports that Rupert Murdoch's media empire, News Corporation, incorporated in Australia, is a global company comprising almost 800 subsidiaries, including 60 incorporated in tax havens such as the Cayman Islands, Bermuda, the Netherlands Antilles and the British Virgin Islands. The corporation's structure is designed to minimise tax payment and the most profitable subsidiary is News Publishers, incorporated in Bermuda, which in the seven years ending in June 1996 made around £1.6 billion net profit, but has no employees or any source of income apart from paper transactions with News Corporation subsidiaries. Mr Murdoch's main British holding company, Newscorp Investments, runs three leading national newspapers: the tabloid *Sun*, which has the highest circulation, and *The Times* and *The Sunday Times*. In addition, News Corporation also has a 40 per cent stake in the BskyB pay-TV channel.

*The Economist* reports that during the four years ending in June 1998, News Corporation reported consolidated pre-tax profits of A$5.4 billion yet only paid A$325 million in corporate worldwide taxes. That is, 6 per cent over a four-year period compared with the 31 per cent of its main media rival, the Disney Corporation. At the same time, basic corporation tax in the three countries where News Corporation operates – Australia, America and Britain – was 36 per cent, 35 per cent and 30 per cent respectively. A major contributor to News Corporation's tax-free activities is Mr Murdoch's British operation and *The Economist* reports that for the 11-year period 1988–1998 Newscorp Investments paid no corporation taxes on pre-tax profits of £1.39 billion. Putting the UK tax avoidance policies into perspective, *The Economist* notes that the Murdoch UK holding company would normally have expected to pay £350 million in corporation tax during the 11-year period, or sufficient to fund seven new hospitals, 50 secondary schools or 300 new primary schools.

Similarly, in the USA, the Murdoch empire also managed to minimise payments of corporation tax primarily by registering his subsidiary companies in the state of Delaware where there is no legal obligation to file publicly available company accounts. The apparent reason for the Murdoch aversion to paying similar taxes to other corporations is his anti-statist philosophy by which he justifies handing back little of his profits to governments and he employs various tax accountants and lawyers who have identified numerous loopholes in tax legislation enabling him to siphon off profits in the UK or USA and transfer them to the various tax havens mentioned above. Two possible threats to the anti-tax regime employed by Murdoch should be mentioned, one of which appears to have been resolved in the short term. Mr Murdoch has divorced his wife after a long marriage and it was rumoured in the newspapers owned by his rivals that he had to pay a huge settlement to buy her silence so that she did not 'spill the beans' to the Australian, US and British tax authorities on exactly how the complex system of moving profits between News Corporation subsidiaries actually operates. How long his ex-wife will remain silent about her former husband's tax avoidance schemes is an open question.

The second unknown threat is how Mr Murdoch, who is approaching 70 years of age, will divide his empire up between his children. *The Economist* (ibid) reports that the sheer complexity of the News Corporation structure baffles institutional analysts and deters investors, which has led to its share price underperforming on the US stock market for over five years. A low share price raises the cost of investment more than if financial transactions were more transparent. In the long run, warns

*The Economist*, doubts will arise about the sustainability of News Corporation's elaborate structure. Unless Mr Murdoch's children, whom he expects to run the corporation after him, are able to master (and willing to perpetuate) its arcane complexity, the empire will begin to fall apart.

**The DTI ruling**

In March 1999, the MMC gave its verdict on the proposed takeover to the government and a few weeks later the Minister for Trade & Industry announced that the BskyB plan would not be allowed to proceed on the grounds that the deal 'would reinforce the trend towards growing inequalities between the larger, richer clubs and the smaller, poorer ones'. The shares of football companies immediately fell. Manchester United's shares fell almost 33p to 182p compared with the BskyB bid price of 240p. Newcastle United shares fell almost 15 per cent and Celtic and Aston Villa shares also lost between 7 per cent and 10 per cent respectively. BskyB shares, for reasons discussed below, lost less than 0.5 per cent.

**Those in favour of the deal**

Commentators were divided on the merits of the government decision. Those in favour of the proposed takeover argued that the merger would have been good for fans, football and the Manchester United club. For British football fans, the 'Holy Grail' is for their club to win a European club competition; a challenge in which huge financial backing and success appear to be strongly correlated. Outside of the UK, other EU countries raise no objections to media conglomerates taking over football clubs; for example, the French Canal Plus pay-TV corporation owns the successful Paris St Germain football club. Silvio Berlusconi, a former Italian prime minister and owner of the very successful AC Milan and less famous Monza football clubs, also controls Mediaset, the leading satellite TV station in Italy. Similar deals apply in South America where football is very popular and club and national teams are also highly successful. The financial facts of football were inescapably gloomy. Most of the 90+ football clubs in England and Wales survived on bank overdrafts and would face financial ruin but for funding received either directly or indirectly from TV coverage. Even a very prosperous club like Manchester United raised less than 35 per cent of its revenue from the gate receipts of over 50,000 spectators attending live games at Old Trafford, its home ground.

**Those against the deal**

Opponents were delighted with the government's decision. They had viewed the proposed takeover with alarm as likely to raise the cost of attending 'the people's game' further beyond the reach of the largely working-class population which had traditionally supported English football. The foundations of the modern League and Cup competitions were established over 130 years earlier in the north of England. Clubs like Blackburn Rovers and Aston Villa owed their existence mostly to local entrepreneurs while others, like Everton and Sheffield Wednesday, which for years never played on Sundays and only on Wednesdays, respectively – so that church and football match attendance need never compete – were founded by local non-conformist churches. Romantic sentiment aside, there was a genuine populist opposition to the continuing erosion of 'civitas' (i.e. a sense of pride in and belonging to a local community, football team, place of worship, etc.) as a result of commercial exploitation by transnational TV corporations which SUAM members believed Mr Murdoch could never even begin to understand.

As ever, politicians were quick to jump on the populist bandwagon. The MP Mr Keen told *The Times* (10 April 2000): 'I think it refutes the allegation that Labour would not do anything which offended Rupert Murdoch.' Mr Cunliffe described the decision as 'A great victory for United's supporters . . . A great slap in the face for Murdoch and rightly so.' A former minister, Mr Clarke, commented: 'This is tremendous news for English football. It shows that there is a limit to what finance can buy in English football. It is a warning shot to the likes of Murdoch.'

**The impact on Manchester United**

The 1999 season saw Manchester United achieve the 'Treble' success by winning the English Premier League, the FA Challenge Cup and the European Club Championship. Despite this unparalleled success, the club was forced to raise its admission charges for the 2000 season and also attracted public criticism by changing its expensive 'strip', different for home and away matches, worn by supporters, for the eighth time in as many years. None of these financial decisions received as much censure as its decision to withdraw from the English Football Challenge Cup competition so that it could take part in the globally televised World Club Championship in South America, which it did without distinguishing itself. A further setback occurred when the club was eliminated from the European Club Championship competition. As for its future success, time will tell, although its directors cannot feel complacent about the need to buy international players at huge transfer fees and wages of up to £50,000 per week.

**The alternative News Corporation strategy**

Whatever disappointment Mr Murdoch and his BskyB executives felt about the failure to buy Manchester United was kept silent. City media analysts predict that the media giant is merely waiting its time. Meanwhile, BskyB announced (*Financial Times* (*FT*), 4/5 March 2000) that it had invested £40 million in Chelsea, another rival of Manchester United. Further reports revealed that BskyB now owned stakes ranging from 5 per cent to 9.9 per cent in six Premier League clubs, including Manchester United. The *FT* commented that Mr Murdoch would need to acquire shares in more than six Premier League clubs if his undeclared strategy was to use these minority stakes to block rival pay-TV policies which failed to meet with his approval. Other commentators speculated whether BskyB might be simply hedging its bets against the possibility that Manchester United might not maintain its position as the leading English football club in the foreseeable future. Meanwhile, News Corporation also diversified its media interests in June 1999 by purchasing three of the Berlusconi-owned pay-TV channels in Italy, and offering to buy a minority stake in the British Open Golf Championship which has a huge worldwide following.

The major BskyB coup was undoubtedly securing the new Premier League rights contract which comes into effect in August 2001. This cost News Corporation a massive £1.11 billion and the US cable TV operator, NTL, £328 million for a three-year period. The major loser in the new deal is the BBC which lost to ITV its right to show the long-established *Match of the Day* highlights. The BBC had to settle for second-best in having to pay £70 million as part of a separate BskyB £400 million deal with the Football Association to show the FA Cup matches and all the England home international matches. Although BskyB and NTL refused to comment, media pundits predicted that the full cost of watching televised football matches would rise the following season from £420 to around £1,000 per annum. NTL has no contract to show live football but will screen 40 live pay-per-view Premier League matches per season from 2001. Because of BskyB's firm grasp of the live televised matches for the next three years, interest levels in pay-per-view games will have to increase more than tenfold before NTL can break even. The long-awaited findings of the Restrictive Practices Court have yet to be published but, even if they rule that the Football League is operating as a cartel, no changes are likely until the next round of TV rights contracts expires in 2004.

**Questions**

**1** Summarise your reasons for supporting or opposing the News Corporation/BskyB campaign to win the Premier League TV franchise from the following ethical standpoints:
   (i)   idealism,
   (ii)  Machiavellianism,
   (iii) utilitarianism,
   (iv)  ethical pluralism.

**2** Explain why you would support one of the above (or another ethical perspective) in your evaluation of the News Corporation/BskyB strategy.

## Notes and references

1. Kroeber, A. and Kluckhohn, C., *Culture: A critical review of concepts and definitions*, New York, Random House, 1985, 11.
2. Czinkota, M.R., Ronkainen, I.A. and Moffett, M.H., *International Business*, 5th edn, Fort Worth, Dryden Press, 1999, 35.
3. Cairncross, F., *The Death of Distance*, London, Orion Business Books, 1997, xi–xiv.
4. Baerwald, T.J., Geographical Perspectives on International Business, in *International Business*, 5th edn, eds M.R. Czinkota, I.A. Ronkainen and M.H. Moffett, Fort Worth, Dryden Press, 1999, 21.
5. Lockwood, W.W., Political Economy, in *The United States and Japan*, ed. H. Passim, The American Assembly/Columbia University, Englewood Cliffs, Prentice Hall, 1966, 126.
6. Hall, E.T., *Beyond Culture*, Garden City, New York, Anchor Press, 1976, 15.
7. Hofstede, G., *Culture's Consequences: International differences in work-related values*, London, Sage, 1980.
8. Hofstede, G., National Cultures Revisited, *Asia-Pacific Journal of Management*, 1, September 1984, 22–4.
9. Trompenaars, A., *Riding the Waves of Culture*, London, Nicholas Brearley, 1993.
10. Hampden-Turner, C. and Trompenaars, A., *The Seven Cultures of Capitalism*, New York, Doubleday, 1993, 11–12.
11. Mullins, L.J., *Management and Organisational Behaviour*, 5th edn, London, Financial Times Pitman Publishing, 1999, 31–3.
12. Freeman, R.E., *Strategic Management: A stakeholder approach*, London, Pitman, 1984.
13. Ansoff, I., *Corporate Strategy*, New York, McGraw-Hill, 1965.
14. Preston, L.E., Stakeholder Management and Corporate Performance, *Journal of Behavioral Economics*, 19(4), 1990, 361–75.
15. Freeman, R.E. and Reed, D., Stockholders and Stakeholders: A new perspective on corporate governance, in *Corporate Governance: A Definitive Exploration of the Issues*, ed. C. Huizinga, Los Angeles, UCLA Extension Press, 1983.
16. Jackson, J., Business Ethics Overview, *Encyclopaedia of Applied Ethics*, vol. 1, London, Academic Press, 1998, 406–8.
17. Goodpaster, K., Business Ethics and Stakeholder Analysis, *Business Ethics Quarterly*, vol. 1, 1991.

18. Sternberg, E., *Just Business*, London/Oxford, Warner/Blackwell, 1994.

19. Ambler, T. and Wilson, A., Problems of Stakeholder Theory, *Business Ethics*, vol. 4, no. 1, January 1995, 30–5.

20. Sidelsky, R., *The World After Communism*, London, Macmillan, 1995, 134.

21. Bell, D., *The Coming of Post-Industrial Society*, London, Heinemann, 1973.

22. Fukuyama, F., Death of the Hierarchy, *Financial Times Weekend Supplement*, 12/13 June 1999, 1.

23. Kets de Vries, M., Beyond Sloan: Trust is at the core of corporate values, *FT Mastering Management Supplement*, Part 2, 2 October 2000, 14–15.

24. Mason, R.O. and Mitroff, I.I., *Challenging Strategic Planning Assumptions*, New York, Wiley, 1981, 43–5.

25. Rhenman, E., *Industrial Democracy and Industrial Man*, London, Tavistock Institute, 1968.

26. Johnson, G. and Scholes, K., *Exploring Corporate Strategy*, 4th edn, London, Prentice Hall, 1997, 195–205, 348–9.

27. Mullins, L.J., Empowerment, in *Management and Organisational Behaviour*, 5th edn, London, Financial Times Pitman Publishing, 1999, 652–4, 663–9.

28. Slack, N., Chambers, S., Harland, C., Harrison, A. and Johnston, R., *Operations Management*, 2nd edn, London, Pitman Publishing, 1998, 547–87, 760–94.

29. *The Competitive Edge: Employee involvement in Britain*, London, Department of Employment, 1994.

30. Clarkson, M., A Stakeholder Framework for Analyzing and Evaluating Corporate Social Performance, *Academy of Management Review*, vol. 20, no. 1, 1995, 92–117.

# Corporate social performance, ethical leadership and reputation management

*Human conditions and possibilities have altered more in a hundred years than they have in the previous ten thousand, and the next fifty may overwhelm us, unless we can devise a more adaptive morality.*

I.A. Richards, *Principles of Literary Criticism*, London, 1924, 24

## Learning objectives

After reading this chapter you should be able to:

- review the status of social responsibility, business ethics and corporate governance from both domestic and transnational standpoints;
- consider how the academic legitimacy of these subjects can be placed on a more secure footing in future;
- explore the concept of corporate social performance as a method of integrating social responsibility, business ethics and corporate governance developments, as a basis for conducting comparative international research;
- discuss the notion of ethical leadership from an altruism versus egoism perspective;
- examine how these issues affect reputation management and influence stakeholder perceptions of the ethical leadership of an organisation;
- consider the implications of ethical leadership on the reputation management of a company from both an enlightened self-interest and principled behaviour standpoint;
- identify various stakeholder issues which will probably emerge in the UK as a result of the global economy and adoption of the European Convention on Human Rights.

## Introduction

The concept of corporate social performance (CSP) has been successfully adopted by Canadian managers to evaluate economic, legal, ethical and other social issues within a stakeholder framework. Hence, the CSP model could be employed to integrate corporate social responsibility, business ethics and corporate governance, and also for further comparative research. If companies are to be managed responsibly, aspects of ethical leadership need to be examined from contrasting altruistic and self-interested standpoints. Both have important practical implications for the reputation management of companies which operate in a global economy and also have to comply with the European Convention on Human Rights, if the legitimate concerns of various stakeholders are not to be neglected.

## The status of corporate social responsibility, business ethics and corporate governance

### Corporate social responsibility

Davis and Blomstrom[1] put forward five propositions on social responsibility based on the premise that 'social responsibility arises from social power', which they justify by pointing to the immense social power wielded by the modern business corporation even in such loosely related social issues as the employment of minority groups and the control of environmental pollution. If this social power is assumed, they argue that an equitable relationship with the rest of society is essential, and should be based on the proposition that business bears responsibility for the consequences of its actions which affect the interests of others. In short, business activities cannot be treated merely as abstract economic decisions because all economic activity is inseparable from the overall socio-political system. These propositions are summarised below:

- In the long run those who do not use power in a responsible manner acceptable to society will tend to lose it.
- A responsible company will operate as an open system which receives inputs from society and discloses its subsequent operations to the public.
- The social costs and benefits of any business activity should be calculated accurately and evaluated before decisions are taken about whether to make the relevant goods or services available to the public.
- The full social costs of each product or service should be factored into the final selling price so that consumers pay for the effects of their consumption on society.
- Beyond these direct social costs, business organisations are responsible, mainly through their managers, for seeking social involvement in areas where their competence addresses major social needs in local communities, etc.

Taking each in turn, the key assumptions in the first proposition are that society entrusts business with a large portion of its resources to accomplish its mission; and therefore expects business to manage these resources as trustees in a wise and prudent manner. How people should ensure that business acts as a competent trustee is a vexed question in a democratic society which would prefer to seek compliance with voluntary codes of behaviour and revert to legal constraints only if these codes of practice fail to achieve the minimum requirements.

The second proposition assumes that profit-seeking organisations will constantly survey their business environments for indications of emerging needs and neglected wants in society. If the social costs of meeting these needs are high, it is assumed that the socially responsible business will postpone further involvement, preferably on a voluntary basis, until these costs can be reduced, with the option of mandatory action in fail-dangerous situations. The third proposition also presupposes that detailed social costs and benefits will be calculated before a decision is taken to proceed with a specific activity.

The fourth proposition assumes that a fair consumer price will be charged for any good or service in which relevant production, social costs and overheads have been included. The point is that, historically, society has often unknowingly had to pay the social costs of eliminating environmental pollution, rather than the original polluter. Here again, the problem should initially be addressed through voluntary codes of practice on the understanding that legal sanctions will be imposed if these are contravened.

The final proposition is the most controversial because of assumptions which are challenged by critics of the stakeholder theory perspective on corporate social responsibility. The rationale is that business, as a major social institution, should bear the same proportion of 'societal' costs as the individual citizen. A predictable response of the business community would be that it already abides by codes of practice and relevant legislation, approved by society, and pays its share of local rates and corporation taxes. Why should it have to incur more costs when, for example, society is already selective about those on whom it levies taxes? For example, children, the old and the infirm are not expected to pay the same as those who are in good health and in full-time employment.

The counter-argument is that business benefits from a better society and should contribute to the costs of resolving these problems. For example, the business community may initially turn its attention away from the problem of low educational standards. Yet supporters of communitarianism (see Chapter 4) would argue that business stands to benefit from gaining future access to better-educated employees and consumers. It is therefore not an unreasonable proposition that the business community should accept some responsibility for helping to develop and apply practical solutions to raise educational standards in areas where it possesses special expertise.

**Legal aspects of corporate responsibility**

Underlying these proposals is the further assumption that effective legislation will be in place in the event of a breakdown of voluntary codes of corporate social responsibility. Wells[2] notes that, in order for corporations to play a central role in developed economies, agreement needs to be reached about their social responsibilities in the following areas which have to be reconciled with prevailing legal constraints:

- Businesses should perform acts that promote society's good.
- They should also act to prevent the occurrence of social harm.
- They should maximise company profits within the limits set by law.

The concept of responsibility falls under two headings, namely, *social responsibility*, which deals with the purposes for which companies should act and the limits of their freedom to act, and *corporate responsibility*, by which liability is attributed to a company for actions done in its name. To avoid confusion between the two types of responsibility, Wells proposes that the latter is better rephrased as 'the responsibility of corporations'. The view that a non-human entity like a corporation can hold responsibilities and might incur legal liabilities or penalties, discussed in Chapter 1, is contentious and requires clarification. If an organisation possesses a corporate personality, is the term being used in a descriptive, moral or legal sense? The legal sense is easier to understand in countries where legislation is derived from Roman law since the separate status attributed to corporations was established because individual rights died with the person and, since some rights needed to continue, artificial persons were constituted, sometimes in perpetuity, known as 'bodies politic' and ' corporate'. Examples of the former in Britain include the government, th of Commons and Lords, and the opposition parties. More example corporate exist as religious, academic and commercial institutions. T differ legally from their members in enjoying rights and immunities in perpetuity which would otherwise disappear with the death of those individuals.

**Nominalist and realist views of corporations**

The practice of endowing corporations with a separate legal status is also contentious and opposing views are classified as either 'nominalist' or 'realist'. The 'nominalist' position, that corporations are merely collections of individuals, contrasts with the 'realist' view that the corporation has a separate existence, meaning and legal personality. These differences in viewpoint have an obvious importance in moral philosophy as it applies to business ethics and social responsibility in organisations. For example, if 'personhood' is attributed to human beings, then an organisation can be regarded as a person when it is seen as simply a collection of individuals. However, problems arise when a collectivity is regarded as an individual if this is taken to mean that it is an autonomous, indivisible entity.

The opposite view that corporations have a separate existence and are not collectivities of individuals raises the awkward question of whether they should be regarded as moral persons as well. If it is assumed that corporations are capable of moral actions, it follows that they are also capable of moral accountability, blame and criminal liability. Opponents of this view might ask how could it be legally or morally justified to charge a company employing 50,000 people with an offence when it would not be acceptable to charge the same number of spectators at a football match with a public order offence because the crowd included some rioting soccer hooligans? These opposing views of corporations are raised whenever loss of life occurs in public transport accidents which are followed by calls for the companies involved, or their employees, to be prosecuted with 'corporate manslaughter'.

**Evaluating legal and ethical issues**

As Henderson[3] notes, ethical issues emerge when perceptions of what constitutes human welfare receive or require clarification. In particular, ethical issues arise when laws or legal precedents are unclear or at variance with shifts in cultural values. He proposes that ethical and legal issues affecting an organisation should be codified and evaluated in the four quadrants of the framework presented as Figure 15.1.

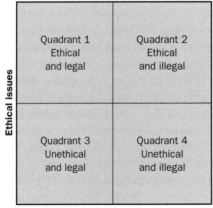

**Fig. 15.1 The classification of ethical and legal decisions in organisations**

Quadrant 1 shows ethical and legal issues which would normally take up the least time to review by management and other stakeholders because they could be shown to meet the acceptable governance and social responsibility criteria of all the parties. Quadrant 2 shows ethical and illegal issues which would be of greater concern to both management and the stakeholders of a company, if only because the latter's public reputation could be damaged unless the legality of the policy in question was established.

Quadrant 3 shows unethical and legal issues which would normally preoccupy management because of possible disagreements with concerned stakeholders. More specifically, although responsible stakeholders might be expected to acknowledge occasions when management had acted appropriately to establish the legality of its actions, the same stakeholders could also be expected to question the rationale behind other policies to ensure that the relevant unethical issues were more critically evaluated by management. Finally, Quadrant 4 shows unethical and illegal issues which, following the 'worst first' principle of time management, would normally claim the immediate attention of both management and stakeholders with concerns about the impact of these issues on the reputation of the company. Reputation management of a company is discussed in more detail below.

## Placing business ethics on a legitimate footing

De George[4] expresses concern about the need to legitimise business ethics, 'which grew out of religion's interest in ethics in business and management education's concern with social issues, [and] has become an interdisciplinary academic field', but business ethics are likely to advance or founder depending on the quality of joint and comparative research carried out on an international scale. Mahoney[5] adopts a broadly similar view. After noting that corporate social responsibility and ethical issues frequently overlap in organisations, he proposes that these topics should be investigated as a series of 'ethical business circles', expanding from the 'internal' to the 'external' activities of the organisation as follows:

- Internal business activities in the innermost circle include ethical issues affecting the relations between individuals and colleagues such as discrimination, confidentiality and loyalty, which have a direct bearing on employee relations with management. Company and shareholder issues would also be included in this circle, but could also be discussed where applicable in other ethical business circles.
- The second ethical circle focuses on the ethics of marketing, customer relations, and issues affecting the pricing and promotional policies of the organisation.
- The third ethical business circle involves relations with other companies such as suppliers and includes issues relating to payment and working with suppliers who may mistreat their workforces, as well as relations with other companies when matters such as mergers and insider trading, etc. arise.
- The fourth, outer ethical business circle deals with the company's relationship with the local community and may include issues relating to self-regulation, impact on the environment and responses to cultural diversity.

In passing, the reader might wish to reflect on the range and arrangement of topics discussed so far before deciding on the extent to which this sound methodology advocated by Mahoney has been followed in preceding chapters. Similar concerns to those raised by De George and Mahoney have also preoccupied specialists in corporate governance such as Lorsch and Graff[6] and Charkham[7], in the next section.

## International aspects of corporate governance

As a first step, Lorsch and Graff propose that an understanding of the different corporate governance systems in the major industrialised countries is essential, and they proceed by comparing the roles of corporate boards in the USA, the UK, Germany and Japan, noting that each nation utilises systems that reflect the decision making methods, ownership patterns and principal goals of their respective corporations.

### Corporate governance: Checks and balances versus networks

US and UK corporations, which are run in the context of a national belief in economic and political checks and balances, are contrasted with German and Japanese corporations, which are more concerned with promoting collective welfare. As a result, Anglo-American corporations tend to rely more on adversarial and litigious approaches to conflict resolution, operating in a regulated environment that limits consolidation of economic power and favours competition on an even playing field. On the other hand, German and Japanese corporations operate on a less adversarial basis which favours a longer-term view and an inclination towards more trusting and mutually beneficial relationships.

### Impact of global economy

As the global economy develops, however, it is anticipated that the emphasis on adversarial and litigious checks and balances in transnational corporations will give way to those sharing economic, political, religious and ethical values and beliefs, which are increasingly linked in coherent cultural networks. Just how rapidly these networks will emerge is uncertain, yet a prudent working hypothesis would be to assume that change is occurring rapidly, and for Anglo-American corporate boards to plan accordingly.

### Dispersed versus concentrated ownership

Developments in corporate governance reflect different perspectives on the ownership and management of companies which are supported by actual levels of share ownership in most developed nations. This trend was first observed nearly 70 years ago by Berle and Means[8], who identified ownership without appreciable control and control without appreciable ownership as the main way of distinguishing the behaviour of shareholders from that of managers in the modern corporation. Lorsch and Graff observe that this trend has increased in most developed countries but note that cross-shareholdings among affiliated companies still persist in Japan which enable owners to retain close involvement in the management of firms.

This phenomenon, known as *keiretsu*, was studied by Kester[9], who notes that one-third of the shares in a typical Japanese company are owned by banks, one-third by other related corporations, and one-third by the company's shareholders. He adds that 'This corporate networking achieves its highest expression in the "keiretsu" when a group of companies is federated around a major bank, trading company or large industrial firm.' In 1990, over half of Japan's listed companies belonged to such *keiretsu*. Charkham (p. 81) adds that not only do these shareholders form a stable core, supported by a complex web of reciprocal claims against each other, but they also abide by a strong tacit mutual agreement not to sell shares that are held reciprocally, which explains why over 70 per cent of Japanese shares are never traded on the Tokyo Stock Exchange.

This behaviour contrasts sharply with that of other countries such as the USA, for example, where the general public is extensively involved in the ownership of business so that over 53 million Americans owned shares either directly or as indirect institutional investors in 1994, amounting to approximately half of the total equity market (*NY Stock Exchange Fact Book*, 1994). Mutual funds, public and private pension funds, insurance companies and bank trust departments are the largest holders of shares on the New York Stock Exchange but, as Lightfoot and Kester[10] remark, public companies are usually owned by thousands of widely dispersed shareholders, chiefly because banks are prohibited by law from owning more than 5 per cent of the voting stock in any non-bank company or from controlling different types of company by any other means (p. 3).

Share ownership in Britain resembles that in the USA and Charkham (p. 283) reports that there are over nine million individual shareholders in the UK, most of whom invest indirectly through financial institutions along similar lines to the USA, with pension funds and insurance companies being by far the largest institutional investors. Because they are large in number, dispersed and generally disenfranchised in directly influencing the investment strategies of these large institutions, Anglo-American shareholders are relatively powerless to affect the policies of the companies in which their savings are ultimately invested on their behalf as either multi-fiduciary shareholders or multiple stakeholders.

As noted in earlier chapters, this problem goes to the heart of the debate about effective corporate governance and is recognised by Lorsch and Graff who note that these shareholders: 'have to rely on boards of directors to represent their interests. Their only real control over their own risk is their ability to buy and sell their holdings at a moment's notice – for stock is almost as liquid as cash.' However, even this control may not be readily available, in the case of investments in mutual trusts and pension funds. This Anglo-American tendency towards a share-owning democracy contrasts sharply with Germany where there are fewer than 700 quoted companies compared to over 3,000 in the UK and shares in German companies are also owned by far fewer shareholders. This is because, unlike the USA and UK, German banks are not as closely regulated in terms of their shareholdings and may own large blocks of shares in their own names as well as by acting as the custodians of individual shareholders. As Monks and Minnow[11] found, banks hold about 5 per cent of all shares in German companies but they vote for over 50 per cent of all shares because of their separate role as shareholder custodians (p. 292). Another feature of the investment policy of German banks is that they hold on to their shareholdings for longer periods than their Anglo-American counterparts.

## Shareholders versus stakeholders

The principal goals of corporations is another issue which separates Anglo-American businesses from their German and Japanese counterparts. According to Lorsch and Graff, the main aim of corporate governance in the USA and Britain is the creation and enhancement of shareholder wealth. However, as noted by Burnham and Nader (see Chapter 1), whether shareholder interests really prevail is open to doubt and this raises critical questions about the effectiveness of corporate governance guidelines in regulating the remuneration of company directors and other senior managers.

As Charkham[7] notes, the situation in Germany is more transparent due to the constitution, which states that:

> Property imposes duties. Its use should also serve the commonweal . . . That is to say, corporate governance in Germany is ultimately concerned with the long-term survival of a company from the standpoint of not only the owners, but also stakeholders including employees, suppliers, creditors and customers. (p. 10)

A similar situation applies in Japan where the aim of corporate governance is to ensure the continuing prosperity of the company. As Kester[9] remarks, the company is regarded as a 'family', comprised of:

> a coalition of stakeholders . . . holding a complex blend of senior and junior, short term and long term, conditional and unconditional, implicit and explicit claims against the company [whose] corporate growth tends to emerge as the common denominator among stakeholder groups – the one objective that nearly everyone can agree on as having a potential benefit. (pp. 76–7)

Ways of reconciling Anglo-American perspectives on corporate governance issues with those prevailing in Germany and Japan, particularly the rights of multi-fiduciary shareholders and the remuneration entitlements of managers as their 'agents', are likely to become more pressing agenda items as increased globalisation leads to more transnational takeovers in the twenty-first century.

## Corporate social performance

The integrative concept of corporate social responsibility presented by Carroll[12] is based on the following four principles:

- *economic responsibilities*, referring to the belief that business has an obligation to be productive and responsible to meet the consumer needs of society;
- *legal responsibilities*, referring to the need for business to indicate a concern that economic responsibilities are approached within the confines of written law;
- *ethical responsibilities*, reflecting unwritten codes, norms and values implicitly derived from society, which go beyond legal frameworks and can be undertaken or ignored;
- *discretionary responsibilities* of business that are volitional or philanthropic in nature and, as such, also difficult to ascertain and evaluate.

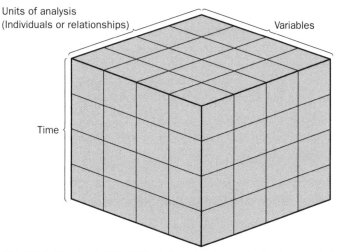

**Fig. 15.2 The Cattell (1952) data cube for analysing human behaviour**

Carroll's[13] methodology was previously proposed by Cattell[14] as a three-dimensional data cube for unrelated research in psychology, as presented in Figure 15.2. Cattell demonstrated how the impact of several multivariables can be investigated in field research, which was adapted to investigate longitudinal changes in corporate social responsibility in Canadian corporations by Clarkson[15], as summarised in Chapter 14. The first three responsibilities shown above, namely: economic, legal and ethical issues, were proposed by Carroll, with 'discretionary responsibilities' being investigated separately. The three variables are shown on separate faces of the Cattell data cube in Figure 15.3.

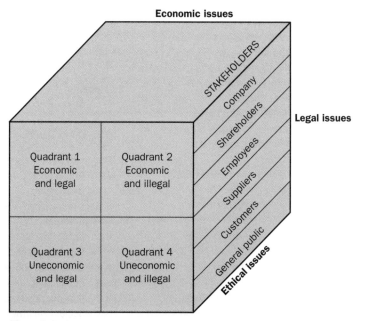

**Fig. 15.3 A stakeholder issue matrix**

The ethical issues face is subdivided to show the six categories of stakeholder identified by Clarkson and Mahoney[5]. Clarkson adds that, because it proved to be more suitable for testing in the field, Wartick and Cochran's[16] amended corporate social performance methodology was introduced during the last seven years of the 10-year longitudinal study. Typical ethical issues, investigated by Clarkson, which have previously been regarded as separate corporate social responsibility, business ethics or corporate governance concerns, are presented in Box 15.1.

---

**Box 15.1**

## Typical corporate and stakeholder issues

**1 Company**
1.1 Company history
1.2 Industry background
1.3 Organisation structure
1.4 Economic performance
1.5 Competitive environment
1.6 Mission or purpose
1.7 Corporate codes
1.8 Stakeholder and social issues management systems

**2 Employees**
2.1 General policy
2.2 Benefits
2.3 Compensation and rewards
2.4 Training and development
2.5 Career planning
2.6 Employee assistance programme
2.7 Health promotion
2.8 Absenteeism and turnover
2.9 Leave of absence
2.10 Relationships with unions
2.11 Dismissal and appeal
2.12 Termination, layoff and redundancy
2.13 Retirement and termination counselling
2.14 Employment equity and discrimination
2.15 Women in management and on the board
2.16 Day care and family accommodation
2.17 Employee communication
2.18 Occupational health and safety
2.19 Part-time, temporary or contract employees
2.20 Other employee or human resource issues

**3 Shareholders**
3.1 General policy
3.2 Shareholder communications and complaints
3.3 Shareholder advocacy
3.4 Shareholder rights
3.5 Other shareholder issues

**4 Customers**
4.1 General policy
4.2 Customer communications
4.3 Product safety
4.4 Customer complaints
4.5 Special customer services
4.6 Other customer issues

**5 Suppliers**
5.1 General policy
5.2 Relative power
5.3 Other supplier issues

**6 Public stakeholders**
6.1 Public health, safety and protection
6.2 Conservation of energy and materials
6.3 Environmental assessment of capital projects
6.4 Other environmental issues
6.5 Public policy involvement
6.6 Community relations
6.7 Social investment and donations

---

**Table 15.1 The reactive–defensive–accommodative–proactive (RDAP) scale**

| Rating | Posture or strategy | Performance |
| --- | --- | --- |
| **Reactive** | Deny responsibility | Doing less than required |
| **Defensive** | Admit responsibility but fight it | Doing the least required |
| **Accommodative** | Accept responsibility | Doing all that is required |
| **Proactive** | Anticipate responsibility | Doing more than required |

More than one method of evaluating the issues in Box 15.1 is available and the main advantage of Clarkson's RDAP scale presented in Table 15.1 is that it has been tested in a 10-year longitudinal empirical field study.

## Application of the corporate social performance (CSP) model

The Clarkson CSP methodology is less difficult to understand than may first appear. After all, ascertaining whether an ethical issue raised by a specific stakeholder might have economic or uneconomic consequences for a company could be readily calculated by an accountant or financial adviser. Similarly, whether an ethical issue might involve the company in legal or illegal activities could also be rapidly established by a company secretary or legal adviser. In short, any of the corporate or stakeholder issues presented in Box 15.1 could also be evaluated using the four-step procedure proposed by Sternberg[17]:

- clarify the underlying ethical question;
- establish its relevance to the company;
- identify any constraints (i.e. economic/uneconomic or legal/illegal, cultural, technical, etc.);
- evaluate available options to deal with the ethical question (i.e by use of a cost/benefit analysis which does not compromise company standards of distributive justice and 'common decency').

In advancing propositions for further empirical testing, Clarkson remarks that 'corporate performance is best evaluated on an industry-by-industry basis to reduce the number of variables when making comparisons' (p. 111). In the case of companies involved in chemical manufacturing, for example, use could be made of the survey instrument for measuring environmental performance and sustainable development as a relevant indicator of corporate social performance. Irrespective of what methodology is employed, the underlying assumption is that ethical leadership will be displayed by members of the company management team.

## Ethical leadership

The prospect of being able to evaluate corporate social responsibility, business ethics and corporate governance variables in a single data cube from the perspective of different stakeholders is of limited value, if the senior managers of an organisation are disinclined to display ethical leadership. Kanungo and Mendonca[18] stress this point and identify ethical leadership as vital in providing direction which will enable the organisation to achieve its declared aims and objectives. Ethical leadership behaviour goes beyond the routine management activities of procuring and allocating resources, monitoring and directing followers, and building group cohesion. It is manifested in assessing the followers' needs and expectations and influences them to work towards realising a shared vision, articulated by the leader for the benefit of the members of the organisation and its stakeholders. The leader's vision should therefore inspire and articulate the organisation's mission, which provides the rationale for the organisation's goals and objectives. It is also the task of the ethical leader to communicate the values and beliefs that influence and shape the organisation's culture and behavioural norms. From these are generated strategies, policies and procedures, supported by the moral principles and integrity that give legitimacy and credibility to the vision and sustain the organisation's culture and reputation.

## The harmful effects of unethical leadership

Kanungo and Mendonca remark that when the leader's moral integrity is in doubt, then the leader's vision, however noble, well crafted and articulated, is viewed with scepticism by the followers, loses its vigour, and is incapable of moving them to work towards its realisation in an ethical environment. They also state that the moral environment of an organisation depends on the moral calibre and behaviour of its members which, in turn, is largely determined by people in leadership positions. The manner in which leaders function in these positions of influence can directly contribute to the strengthening or the deterioration of the moral behaviour of members of an organisation towards each other and towards stakeholders in the wider community.

## The nature of leadership motives: altruism versus egoism?

Kanungo and Mendonca add that the overarching motive for ethical leadership is displayed in the altruism of the leader, motivated by a concern for others. This is characterised by actions which are guided primarily by the criteria of *benefit to others* even if these result in *some cost to self*. The underlying rationale or purpose for having a leader in a group or an organisation is to move it towards the pursuit of objectives that, when attained, produce benefits to the organisation, its members, stakeholders, and society at large. This view of the importance of altruistic as opposed to egotistic leadership is supported by Hogan *et al.*[19], whose research reveals that it is not enough that leaders are intelligent, industrious, and competent in their technical speciality if, despite these desirable qualities, they are also regarded as self-seeking, as this may lead to them becoming ineffective because they lack ethical qualities and are perceived to be 'arrogant, vindictive, untrustworthy, selfish, emotional, compulsive, over-controlling, insensitive, (and/or) abrasive' in their dealings with other members of the organisation.

## The five Ps of ethical leadership

Blanchard and Peale[20] identify five characteristics of ethical leadership which are based on virtue theory (see Chapter 4), as follows:

1 *Pride.* Without high self-esteem, the ethical leader will struggle to receive the esteem of other members of the organisation. Gaining the acceptance of followers is not sufficient if, in formulating strategies, the leader allows the desire for acceptance to compromise his/her vision of how the goals and objectives of the organisation should be achieved. Blanchard and Peale add that ethical leaders exhibit healthy pride, not vanity, noting that the dividing line between pride and vanity is thin because of the strong egotistic tendency in human beings, but ethical leaders recognise that inordinate self-love is a human vice and not a virtue.

2 *Patience.* Patience is needed because, as the leader works towards the realisation of the organisation's strategy, s(he) is certain to come across obstacles from the internal or external environment, or from the reluctance of the followers to accept and be committed to the vision. It takes time and effort to overcome such obstacles that are inevitable in a worthy and noble endeavour; hence the need for patience.

3 *Prudence.* The exercise of prudence enables the leader to assess the facts and circumstances surrounding decisions thoroughly, and display fortitude in developing the capacity to act positively when difficulties arise. Blanchard and Peale add that the patient leader, who is in the habit of exercising prudence and fortitude, will not be inclined to resort to unethical practices when things do not go as planned.

4 *Persistence.* The authors distinguish between displays of stubborn obstinacy and the commitment not to allow difficulties to weaken the leader's resolve to 'stay the course', by continuing to take the necessary steps to achieve agreed goals, even when these involve personal risk and sacrifice. It is perfectly human to justify unethical practices when one feels overwhelmed by insurmountable internal or external difficulties, but persistence lies in striving to overcome such difficulties because of a sense of duty to others.

5 *Perspective.* Perspective is described as the capacity to see what is really important in any given situation. The authors add that it is the product of reflection which is not possible unless one devotes some time each day to silence and view the latter as an untapped resource that is recommended by those assumed to be wise in all cultures. They do not view silence as merely refraining from noise but the cultivation of that inner silence which allows reflection on some higher purpose and the inner strength to question decisions without betraying a sense of responsibility towards others. Kanungo and Mendonca, Hogan *et al.* and Blanchard and Peale also regard ethical leadership as a key factor in the management of an organisation's reputation compared with that of rival companies.

## Reputation management

Fombrun[21] identifies a company's reputation, which is rooted in the perceptions of its employees, customers, investors, and other stakeholders, as its most important intangible asset. Research has shown it to be among the most important predictors of future success and explains why senior managers strive to induce and maintain favourable assessments of their company's reputation by both employees and outside observers. This is because of the perception that a good reputation is a reflection of a company's values and beliefs, which develop from the systematic management of activities throughout the company and result in increased employee trust, pride and commitment. Many approaches exist for understanding corporate reputations. The two most common perspectives are the pragmatic view of reputation as an expression of 'enlightened self-interest' and the view derived from virtue theory that reputation is an outcome of 'principled' behaviour.

## Company reputation as the outcome of enlightened self-interest

Fombrun identifies four elements in the instrumental, teleological view of reputation management: namely, the marketing, accounting, stakeholder and competitive advantage perspectives on outcomes.

**The marketing view**

This is based on the interchangeable use attributed by stakeholders to the terms 'reputation' and 'brand'. A company's distinctiveness and attractiveness to its customers is based on both brand 'recognition' and 'equity' as a result of investment in customer-oriented programmes that enhance loyalty, increase name awareness, and widen product associations. This branding process usually focuses on products, but marketing specialists also recognise how corporate brands (i.e. what Fombrun calls 'reputational halos') influence the preferences of customers. By linking the corporate name closely with favourable attributes such as quality, value, dependability, innovation, community-mindedness, good management and environmental concern, corporate branding is said to build a special relationship with target audiences which can motivate them towards forms of positive action in their local communities, etc.

**The accounting view**

Like brands, reputations are a form of goodwill which, as intangible assets, provide real benefits that are difficult to quantify. For this reason, conservative accounting policies in the United States currently do not capitalise intangible assets in financial statements, and the convention is for all activities and programmes concerned with developing brands and corporate reputation to be classified as expenditure during a specific financial year. Fombrun notes, however, that an increase in disparities in the accounting treatment of goodwill by transnational corporations, and concern over the misleading character of historical cost reporting in merger situations, has led to greater interest in ways of incorporating brand values and capital associated with corporate reputation development as assets in financial statements.

**The stakeholder view**

Corporate reputations describe perceptions about a company held by its internal and external constituents. Following Mahoney[5] and Clarkson[15], Fombrun distinguishes between internal constituents, which include a company's employees, managers and directors, and external constituents, which encompass its shareholders, customers, suppliers, host governments and the media. Stakeholder views contend that a company's reputation describes the net assessment that constituents make of a company's ability to meet their expectations.

**The strategic view**

Corporate reputations are also a source of competitive advantage because companies are able to develop a protected market position through ownership of relevant physical assets, or create a unique corporate culture which earns a good reputation for the organisation and the way in which it is managed. As a result, a corporate reputation is developed which acts like a barrier against rivals and like a protective shield against downturns and crises. Fombrun concludes that a strong corporate reputation can help a company to outperform rivals in existing businesses and outdo them in competing for new markets.

**Enlightened self-interest as a safeguard**

Fombrun also regards the development of a reliable corporate reputation as a safeguard against the increasing vulnerability of most organisations to attacks on their reputations. This is a particular problem for transnational corporations because of their increased size, product ranges and domain of their activities, which attracts the attention of traditionally disenfranchised stakeholders; many also operate in politically sensitive areas or with technologies that pose a significant environmental challenge. An additional area of vulnerability for transnational corporations is the increasing media coverage of the activities of large global companies due to the availability of more rapid communication which has made the diffusion of information and misinformation a relatively simple and inexpensive activity.

## Reputation as an outcome of principled behaviour

Fombrun (p. 830) states that companies, as recognisable institutions with a separate legal status, and their managers are expected to act responsibly simply because it is 'the right thing to do', 'just as the Bible prescribes a code of conduct for Christians, the Koran for Muslims, the Torah for Jews, the Upanishads for Hindi, so does a principled approach seek to enumerate the rules by which to judge the actions of a company' (see Chapter 3). From this perspective, reputation deservedly accrues to a company that acts in morally defensible ways. It adheres closely to a code of conduct that defends or upholds the basic human rights of all of its employees and consumers, as well as the property rights of its shareholders, and the political rights of the individual citizens in the communities and countries where it operates. A principled approach to reputation management therefore tries to articulate what Fombrun calls 'the sacred and symmetrical duties and obligations that all companies must demonstrate if they are to be seen as "legitimate" by the communities and the societies in which they operate'.

This principled approach calls on the managers of organisations to 'set the standard' of ethical business conduct for others to follow. This can be achieved via two main ethical routes: namely, through Kantian idealism or virtue theory and the practice of the virtues of honesty, integrity, respect, trust, responsibility and good citizenship (see Chapter 4). By way of a practical application, Fombrun adds that this latter approach has been adopted across the Lockheed Martin Corporation (Source: Lockheed Martin, 'Setting the Standard', Corporate Policy Document, June 1996).

## Tomorrow's Company

The RSA Interim Report[22] on the Tomorrow's Company Conference predicted that the 'social contract' between business and society will be transformed into a 'licence to operate', with licences being issued by stakeholders and the wider community with the aim of ensuring that only companies that are of benefit to society in general and individual stakeholders in particular would operate. This notion obviously presents a clear challenge to the prevailing management capitalism framework identified by Burnham and summarised in Chapter 2. In addition, as noted in the previous chapter, Fukuyama[23] and Kets de Vries[24] both argue that the traditional management hierarchy has already been modified as self-renewing companies adapt their decision making processes to accommodate the increased flow of electronic information into organisations. In short, hierarchical forms of organisation are reportedly seen as obsolete and being replaced by flat or networked structures based on shared values and more participatory democracy.

Before cries of 'O brave new world that hath such wonders in it' become commonplace, Parry's[25] study of political elites is worth recalling for its summary of the difficulties that have been encountered in attempts to devise a system of classical democratic organisation based on Rousseau's 'Social Contract' (see Chapter 4) of taking men as they are, and laws as they might be; i.e. 'with man's potentialities for political action and with laws which, while appropriate to man's capabilities, aim at establishing a framework for a freer and more moral society than had existed hitherto'.

Bachrach's[26] model is probably the most relevant here and advocates what Parry calls 'radical democracy' which would lead to democratisation of industry, not just to consultation but to direct participation in the decision making process. This would be achieved through a wider membership of the 'corporate constituency' as stakeholders with employees joined by shareholders (not though public ownership), suppliers and consumers. Trade unions should not be members of the managerial body because their duty is to act as an opposition party defending the rights of their members and promoting improved working conditions. This role, Bachrach argues, would be compromised by managerial involvement, as it cannot be assumed that the interests of an employee as a producer will inevitably coincide with his/her interests as a worker, otherwise union activity would be rendered superfluous.

Whether the introduction of flat, networked structures leads to ethical leadership in an increasingly pluralistic society, as advocated by Blanchard and Peale[20], is impossible to foretell. Meanwhile, if the RSA prediction proves correct and Tomorrow's Company becomes dependent on a 'licence to operate' provided by stakeholders, the performance of each company will increasingly be scrutinised in the public domain if only because their senior managers are not elected to their positions.

One solution proposed by Nader[27] is for society to create conditions of tolerable uncertainty for tomorrow's senior managers, as an alternative to government intervention. He declares

> I have a theory of power: That if it's going to be responsible, it has to be insecure; it has to have something to lose. That is why putting all economic power in the state would be disastrous, because it would not be insecure. If General Motors is sensitive at all, right now, with the tremendous dominant position it has, it comes from fear of losing something it has.

## The role of government

Notwithstanding Nader's reasonable argument that putting more economic power in the hands of the state would not lead to improvements in the corporate social performance of companies, it has to be noted that the present UK government has declared an interest in these developments by appointing a minister with special responsibilities for business ethics. As a result, more companies will presumably turn their attention to adopting business conduct, environmental audits and social responsibility guidelines, and publishing details of progress achieved for the benefit of their shareholders, employees, customers and other secondary stakeholders.

The implementation of voluntary codes of practice is likely to lead to the gradual removal of self-serving barriers that companies have erected to isolate corporate governance issues from the legitimate demands for more effective corporate social performance by a growing constituency of better-informed and more articulate stakeholders. The obvious alternative to unsuccessful voluntary codes of conduct would be for relevant legislation to be introduced by government in the public interest. Examples of issues where new laws are likely to be introduced in the public interest, if attempts to introduce more effective voluntary codes of corporate social performance are unsuccessful, include:

- A new charge of 'corporate manslaughter/killing' in cases where company directors and senior managers fail to accept full responsibility for serious breaches of health and safety legislation that result in loss of life of employees, customers, or other members of the public. (Concern about unsafe public transport systems is the subject of an earlier case study (see Chapter 2), but public attention is also likely to focus on the UK construction industry, which is open to the charge of 'putting profits above safety' after recording 86 deaths on construction sites, a 20 per cent increase, plus a rise in major injuries from 4,656 to 4,689, for the year ending in April 2000 (*The Independent*, 24 July 2000, p. 2)).
- The transfer of authority from non-executive committees to company shareholders for the annual approval of the remuneration packages of all directors and designated senior managers. In particular, the National Association of Pension Funds, whose members control over a quarter of the stock market, might be required to issue recommendations to other shareholders on matters relating to equitable awards to directors; and also on how to vote on crucial issues raised at annual general meetings.
- A statutory right to be granted to employees, or their legal representatives, to be consulted by the directors and senior management of companies, prior to takeover or merger offers, which could result in large numbers of redundancies.
- More rigorous consumer protection legislation authorising local trading standards officers to act more rapidly against unscrupulous businesses by imposing larger penalties for exploiting consumers through breaches of warranty, unsatisfactory after-sales service, charging extortionate interest on loans, or for paying less than the statutory minimum wage to part-time employees or for casual work done at home.
- Publication of interim government guidelines and codes of practice aimed at eliminating cases of racial and sexual discrimination at work until such provisions in the new UK Human Rights Act, as part of the European Convention on Human Rights, have been clarified in the courts.
- An effective moratorium on Third World debt which actually alleviates unfavourable economic conditions in these 'burdened societies', as proposed in John Rawls' *The Law of Peoples*[28].
- Implementation of effective EU legislation aimed at controlling the deposit of offshore funds by transnational corporations in tax haven countries, thereby gaining

unfair competitive advantage over rival companies by evasion or reduced payment of corporation tax, etc., in host countries.

## Synopsis

- Corporate social responsibility contains two broad rival perspectives: namely, social responsibility, which arises from social power, and corporate responsibility which comprises opposing 'nominalist' and 'realist' views on the legal status of a company.
- Contemporary business ethics shares common ground with corporate social responsibility in calling for more interdisciplinary collaboration and comparative research, which explores organisational issues as a series of ethical business circles, expanding from the 'internal' to 'external' activities within an emerging global economy.
- Corporate governance provisions differ between leading groups of developed nations such as the USA/UK and Germany/Japan, mainly in terms of share ownership by the general public, the role of banks, and the relative powerlessness of Anglo-American shareholders to influence management policy compared with their counterparts in Germany or Japan.
- Ethical leadership comprises altruistic rather than self-serving behaviour which is characterised by appropriate pride, patience, prudence, persistence and a sense of perspective.
- The management of a company's reputation may be approached from either an enlightened self-interest or a principled behaviour standpoint. The former involves evaluating good or bad reputation management in terms of the marketing, financial, stakeholder and competitive advantage outcomes. Principled behaviour views reputation management as the outcome of acting in a morally defensible way.
- The impact on UK companies of having to operate in the global economy and also comply with recently adopted human rights legislation is likely to raise new stakeholder issues which are probably best resolved through voluntary codes of practice rather than government intervention and rigorous regulations.

## Review and discussion questions

1 What are the main differences between Anglo-American approaches to corporate governance and those of other leading developed nations such as Japan and Germany?

2 Summarise the main elements in the five proposals on social responsibility.

3 What are the main components in the Henderson quadrant linking legal and ethical issues in organisations?

4 What are the six main stakeholder constituencies in the corporate social performance model?

5 Summarise the main elements of the different approaches to ethical leadership.

6 Explain the meaning of reputation management and summarise the main performance measures which are discussed in the enlightened self-interest perspective on an organisation's activities.

## Case study
## Calling high street banks to account: the case of Barclays Bank

**Introduction**

This case study deals with one of Britain's main high street banks over a five-month period and is based on articles featured in the leading 'quality' daily newspapers (i.e. *The Financial Times*, *The Independent*, *The Times*, *The Guardian* and *The Daily Telegraph*) from February to July 2000. The case focuses on Barclays Bank because it seems to have irritated its customers more than its high street rivals in what even Barclays Bank's chairman later admitted was a series of public relations disasters.

Sixteen banks, including five former building societies, are listed in the Financial Times/Stock Exchange banking sector and the big four high street banks are HSBC (with assets of over £66,000 million), Lloyds TSB (over £36,000 million), Royal Bank of Scotland (over £28,000 million) and Barclays Bank (almost £26,000 million) Possibly because it is the smallest of these banks, with the highest share price and lowest price/earnings ratio, Barclays senior management felt that they had to adopt a more ebullient attitude towards two issues that subsequently attracted widespread criticism: namely, cash machine charges and branch closures.

**Cash machine charges**

The public controversy over cash machine charges dates back to the government's decision in 1999 to appoint Mr Don Cruikshank, a former senior bank executive, to carry out a review of high street banking services in the UK. The first indications that the banks were at odds with Mr Cruikshank's findings occurred early in March 1999 when a delegation of leading banks, including Barclays, agreed to meet the Secretary of State for Trade & Industry (DTI) to discuss cash machine (ATM) charges. The main item on the agenda was the proposed imposition of increased charges when customers used the Link-ATM service, which enabled them to withdraw cash from their own bank from any cash machine that was part of the Link network. The network included 34 banks, building societies and other providers of financial services which City analysts divided into three broad groups: banks like Barclays, that wanted to charge users of their machines for withdrawing cash from accounts held with other banks; those adamantly opposed to this arrangement; and those that were neutral about imposing these transaction costs.

**Related issues**

The situation was complicated by three further issues. First, the DTI Secretary had announced a few days earlier that the high street banks could be compared to bandits for imposing higher surcharges on the public who used their ATMs to withdraw cash from accounts with other banks (a possible £2.50 surcharge on a minimum £10 withdrawal was proposed). Second, some UK supermarkets had already introduced an arrangement of offering cash to customers against production of their debit cards at check-out points, and the market leader, Tesco, warned that it would insist that banks imposing surcharges on its customers remove their ATM machines from its supermarkets. Finally, Mr Cruikshank had also announced that his enquiries indicated that ATM charges of over 30p were unjustified whereas banks like Barclays were insistent on a charge of at least double that, perhaps as high as £1 per transaction,

365

with higher surcharges for customers from other banks who used its cash machines. Mr Cruikshank clarified his position by stating that:

> The Link Board is not the place to discuss [bank] retail charges. These are the concern of the individual banks concerned . . . setting prices collectively through [the Link] scheme would run into problems with the competition authorities. The valid concerns that have been expressed about these prices should not be directed at Link, but at the individual banks concerned. (6 March 2000)

**The public response**

Public reaction to the introduction of ATM surcharges was obviously varied but overwhelmingly hostile. A typical reaction was that the main banks had persuaded customers to use cash machines by establishing the inter-bank Link-ATM system. Now they appeared to be abusing this near-monopoly position by surcharging customers who wished to use a convenient machine in the ATM network rather than travel possibly miles to locate one of their own bank's machines. Irritated customers saw this behaviour as typical of the high-handed attitude banks had towards their customers. Such a response was not without some justification as most people open accounts shortly after starting in their first jobs and remain with the same bank for life. Just how indifferent Barclays was to the needs of its customers is unknown. Nevertheless, it is hard to escape the conclusion that it was either oblivious or uncaring about their wishes, as the following examples of what the media regarded as public relations disasters involving Barclays Bank since September 1998 should indicate:

- *Public relations disaster number one.* Barclays was always likely to incur the combined wrath of the government and the City before its main high street competitors because it had acquired a reputation for unreliability since its reluctant admission in September 1998 that it had lost £250 million speculating on Russian bonds less than one year after informing City analysts that it had withdrawn from all high risk investment banking activities.
- *Public relations disaster number two.* A related fall-out in the Barclays boardroom had occurred in November 1998 when the highly respected CEO, Martin Taylor, resigned, allegedly because he had not been informed about all the bank's high risk investments overseas. Millions were wiped off the bank's share value overnight.
- *Public relations disaster number three.* A replacement CEO, Mr O'Neill, was appointed but resigned on the same day following doctor's orders after suffering a minor heart attack.
- *Public relations disaster number four.* The present CEO, Mr Barrett, appointed to replace Mr O'Neill, would probably also have been asked to leave – had it not seemed like one resignation too many – after nude photographs of his ex-wife were distributed on the Internet.
- *Public relations disaster number five.* Shortly after the government investigation began into allegations that high street banks were 'ripping off' their customers, Barclays exacerbated the situation by starting a widely publicised dispute with the Nationwide Building Society and unilaterally deciding to charge customers from other banks and building societies £1.50 per each Link transaction using its machines without informing other Link-ATM members.
- *Public relations disaster number six.* Barclays was also singled out for public criticism in mid-March when it announced its intention to desert dozens of rural areas

within the next few weeks by closing down 171 branches. This 'downsizing' was designed to save more than £1 billion over the next three years, on top of the £2.5 billion pre-tax profits reported in 1999, as closure of one in eleven of Barclays 1,900 branches went ahead on 7 April. According to Barclays, this change was a strategic response to a new trend towards Internet and telephone banking. The bank claimed to have 700,000 online customers with 4,000 new entrants per day. It claimed this was reflected in a fall in the number of customers using its branches from 56 per cent to 36 per cent over the previous five years.

- *Public relations disaster number seven.* What Barclays seemed to have overlooked was that its customers in rural areas would be most affected by its proposed cash machine charges especially if its branches were closed down. The bank seriously underestimated the public outrage at its decision. One MP, Mr Beith, informed the House of Commons that he had pleaded in vain with Barclays to defer its branch closures until after a pilot trial could be assessed to provide basic banking services in 270 rural post offices. The Minister of the Environment, Mr Mullin, was equally critical and called on the bank's customers in these areas to 'vote with their feet'. The planned closures were featured in national TV news programmes for several days as the public learned of places like Terrington St Clement, with a population of 3,000, which would be without a bank and residents of Swaledale in the Yorkshire Dales, who would be forced to travel 10 miles to use the banking services provided by a rival bank.

- *Public relations disaster number eight.* Barclays further irritated its customers by announcing two weeks after it planned to close up to 200 branches (171 within the next three weeks) that the salary of its chairman, Sir Peter Middleton, had quadrupled to £1.76 million in 1999. Furthermore, the new CEO, Mr Barrett, would be paid £1.35 million for a mere three months' work in 2000. Mr Barrett, an Irish-Canadian, subsequently misjudged the judicial nature of a televised House of Commons Select Committee meeting by stating he was worth this money, but without providing supportive evidence.

- *Public relations disaster number nine.* Instead of being candid with its customers and the general public about these pay awards, Barclays had done its best to keep details away from public scrutiny. Unlike its competitors, which post their annual reports to City analysts in the media, Barclays had released a brief announcement to the Stock Exchange newsroom on 15 March that its annual report was available on request. Two weeks later, it was struggling to keep up with demand as rumours about its internal difficulties during 1999 began to circulate. The director of corporate affairs attempted to justify the bank's position in a *Channel 4 News* interview, only to find that his attempt to browbeat the politely incisive Jon Snow back-fired embarrassingly. Thereafter, Barclays stopped giving public interviews and defended its position in hastily prepared, self-justifying video statements by its corporate affairs director.

- *Public relations disaster number ten.* The bank's widely reported difficulties in addressing customer concerns were compounded by the failure of its expensive 'Big Bank for a Big World' TV campaign. Made by Tony Scott, the director of the 1986 box-office success, *Top Gun*, the Barclays' advertisement showed the shaven-headed Oscar-winning actor, Sir Anthony Hopkins, portraying a corporate tycoon, leaving his luxury home and being driven around Los Angeles in a large limousine as he delivered some artless media-babble about 'big deals', 'big bucks', 'big banks' in a 'big world'. Meanwhile, back in the smaller world of Gwaun-Cae-Gurwen, near Swansea, in Wales, where Sir Anthony Hopkins was born, the local Barclays branch was due to close. The predictable public outcry led to the TV campaign being withdrawn at short notice and subsequently used as an example of a marketing promotion disaster on more than one business administration programme in the UK. Whether the campaign also prompted Sir Anthony Hopkins' later announcement of his application for US citizenship is not known.

**The Cruikshank bank review**

The Cruikshank report published in late March 2000 urged the government to oppose further consolidation in the UK banking sector, arguing that the personal current account and small and medium-sized markets were already too concentrated. This allowed the main banks which were operating a monopolistic system to act against the public interest. As an example, Mr Cruikshank criticised the recent takeover of NatWest bank by the Royal Bank of Scotland as their combined share of the small business banking services market in north-west England already exceeded 50 per cent. The barriers to entry in the UK banking sector were also too high, and government supervision was too lax, with the result that banks were able to 'write their own rules'. This had eliminated real competition in money transmission services, such as the Link-ATM network (i.e. the policies of the big high street banks dictated those of the other 34 member institutions). Customers were provided with insufficient information about financial alternatives and how their bank compared with rival services. For all the interest in Internet banking, traditional slow payment settlements prevail which failed to meet the needs of e-commerce customers.

**The Cruikshank recommendations**

The report was criticised by the British Bankers Association president, a former Barclays Bank chairman, as 'spin doctoring', but was generally welcomed by consumer associations, chambers of commerce and small business representatives. In particular, there was strong support for the main recommendation that a new payment systems regulator, PayCom, should be appointed to monitor money transaction systems between UK banks. Product regulation should be withdrawn, however, so that genuine competition could develop, as the four high street banks already held over 68 per cent of all UK current accounts. These banks were currently making an average 28 per cent return on equity which was at their customers' expense since the current cost of global capital was less than 17 per cent. To alter the system more in the customer's favour, further competition was needed for which the high cost of entry would have to be reduced by government regulation. Retail banks should no longer be supported by the Bank of England and, if poorly managed, must be allowed to go bust. New transparency measures should be introduced under the auspices of the Financial Services Authority (FSA) and reviewed by the government at two-year intervals to ensure greater transparency. More consumer involvement, information from banks, and greater power through involvement in the FSA were essential. Finally, Mr Cruikshank was particularly scathing about the attitude of banks towards their customers. The prevailing wisdom was that people were more likely to divorce than to switch bank accounts. As a result, there was a financial culture of 'Everything that moves, charge them for it!' This resulted in the need for far-reaching changes in credit card charges, the bank clearing system, cash machine charges and interest rates, which were all in need of radical reform after years of making high, unjustified profits at the customer's expense.

**The banks' response**

Within 10 days of the report's publication, high street banks and building societies bowed to public pressure by withdrawing the two-tier system whereby customers using the Link cash withdrawal system paid a surcharge for withdrawals from another Link member bank. Meanwhile, at the Barclays Bank AGM in late April, *The Independent* (27 April 2000) reported that the chairman:

> humbly apologised for closing 171 village branches, admitting that 'our executive and PR has not been of the best' before unveiling a plan to work with the Post Office in providing basic banking services close to 155 of the affected areas.

The new national preoccupation with calling banks to account was far from over. In late May, for example, *The Times* reported that high street banks were on a collision course with the government following revelations that they were making excessive profits of about £5 billion or 'cheating each customer of £136 a year' by paying a 'measly 0.1 per cent interest on the £85 billion left in current accounts by customers'. An unpublished report leaked to *The Times* by a rival UK bank showed that Barclays, NatWest, Lloyds TSB and HSBC were the main perpetrators of this spurious practice.

By the end of June 2000, the high street banks realised that they were fighting a losing battle against their customers and early in July announced that cash withdrawal charges would be withdrawn at the earliest opportunity. By then, shares in the four high street banks had fallen to their lowest values in over a year. Possibly slower to learn the cost of irritating its customers, Barclays Bank announced in mid-July that it would unilaterally introduce a two-tier interest rate system which penalised customers who were slow to pay their bills or exceeded overdraft arrangements. According to critical consumer affairs groups, the bank had apparently failed yet again to consider the social consequences of its policies by introducing a divisive arrangement which would benefit its richer customers at the expense of its poorer account holders, who traditionally struggle more to settle their accounts on time.

**Question**

Evaluate the activities of Barclays Bank from the perspectives of (a) ethical leadership and (b) reputation management.

## Notes and references

1. Davis, K. and Blomstrom, R.L., Five Propositions for Social Responsibility, *Business Horizons*, June 1975, 19–24.
2. Wells, C., Corporate Responsibility, *Encyclopedia of Applied Ethics*, New York, Academic Press, 1998, 653–60.
3. Henderson, V.E., The Ethical Side of Enterprise, *Sloan Management Review*, 23, 1990, 37–47.
4. De George, R.T., The Status of Business Ethics: Past and future, *Journal of Business Ethics*, 6, 1987, 201–11.
5. Mahoney, J., *Mastering Management*, London, Financial Times Pitman Publishing, 1997.
6. Lorsch, J. and Graff, S.K., Corporate Governance, *International Encyclopedia of Business and Management*, ed. M. Warner, London, Routledge, 1996, 772–81.
7. Charkham, J., *Keeping Good Company: A study of corporate governance in five countries*, Oxford, Oxford University Press, 1994.

8. Berle, A.A. and Means, G.C., *The Modern Corporation and Private Property*, New York, Macmillan, 1932.

9. Kester, W.C., *Japanese Takeovers: The global contest for corporate control*, Boston, Mass., Harvard Business School Press, 1991.

10. Lightfoot, R.W., and Kester, W.C., Note on Corporate Governance Systems: The United States, Germany and Japan, Harvard Business School Case No. 292–012, 1992, 3.

11. Monks, R.A.G. and Minnow, N., *Corporate Governance*, Oxford, Blackwell, 1995.

12. Carroll, A.B., A Three-dimensional Conceptual Model of Corporate Social Performance, *Academy of Management Review*, 4, 1979, 497–506.

13. Carroll, A., Amoral Management: The ethical challenge of the 1990s, *Ethics Today*, Washington, Ethics Resource Center, 1996.

14. Cattell, R.B., The Three Basic Factor-Analytic Research Designs: Their interrelations and derivatives, *Psychological Bulletin*, 49, 1952, 499–520.

15. Clarkson, M.B.E., A Stakeholder Framework for Analysing and Evaluating Corporate Social Performance, *Academy of Management Review*, 20(1), 1995, 92–117.

16. Wartick, S.L., and Cochran, P.L., The Evolution of the Corporate Social Performance Model, *Academy of Management Review*, 4, 1985, 758–69.

17. Sternberg, E., *Just Business*, London/Oxford, Warner/Blackwell, 1994.

18. Kanungo, R.N. and Mendonca, M., *Ethical Dimensions of Leadership*, Thousand Oaks, Calif., Sage, 1996.

19. Hogan, R., Murphy, G.J. and Hogan, J., What We Know about Leadership Effectiveness and Personality, *American Psychologist*, 49(6), 1994, 493–504.

20. Blanchard, K. and Peale, N., *The Power of Ethical Management*, New York, Fawcett Crest, 1988.

21. Fombrun, C., Reputation Management, *Encyclopedia of Applied Ethics*, New York, Academic Press, 1998.

22. Royal Society of Arts, *Tomorrow's Company: Interim report*, RSA publication, February 1994.

23. Fukuyama, F., Death of the Hierarchy, *Financial Times Weekend Supplement*, 12/13 June 1999, 1.

24. Kets de Vries, M., Beyond Sloan: Trust is at the core of corporate values, *FT Mastering Management Supplement*, Part 2, 2 October 2000, 14–15.

25. Parry, G., *Political Elites*, London, Allen & Unwin, 1980, 141–58.

26. Bachrach, P., *The Theory of Democratic Elitism*, Boston, Mass., Little, Brown, 1967, 96.

27. Nader, R., Urging Business Change, *The New York Times*, 24 January 1971, section 3.

28. Rawls, J., *The Law of Peoples*, Cambridge, Mass., Harvard University Press, 1999, 15, 38, 90, 105–13.

# Moral Compass exercise

The Moral Compass instruments below are divided into two questionnaires, which should be evaluated using the 7-point Lickert scale shown in Box A. The simple Moral Compass contains the eight statements shown in Box B. The detailed Moral Compass includes the additional eight statements shown in Box C. Each statement corresponds with one of the ethical theories summarised in Chapter 4.

## Instructions

1 Decide whether you wish to complete the simple or the detailed Moral Compass instrument.

2 Read each statement carefully before recording your response, using the 7-point Lickert scale shown in Box A below.

3 Record your scores for each part of the instruments in the Moral Compass section in the Appendix at the end of the book, where the corresponding ethical theories are shown.

### Box A

| Strongly disagree | Disagree | Slightly disagree | Neither agree nor disagree | Slightly agree | Agree | Strongly agree |
|---|---|---|---|---|---|---|
| 1 | 2 | 3 | 4 | 5 | 6 | 7 |

## Box B

**S.1**  If someone asks: 'What's two and two?' follow the advice of the great impresario who enquired: 'Are you buying or selling?'     1 2 3 4 5 6 7

**S.2**  If greed means large profits, I'm selfish enough to buy all the shares, and at a premium price, of anyone who complains.     1 2 3 4 5 6 7

**S.3**  All decisions should be taken at the lowest level in the hierarchy. After all, the Charge of the Light Brigade was ordered by an officer who was elsewhere at the time.     1 2 3 4 5 6 7

**S.4**  Business only contributes to the public good if it is efficient, successful, profitable, and also socially responsible.     1 2 3 4 5 6 7

**S.5**  Good business is implementing what is socially responsible at home and abroad without losing your job or ruining the company.     1 2 3 4 5 6 7

**S.6**  Envy serves the valuable social function of making the rich moderate their habits for fear of losing what they have accumulated.     1 2 3 4 5 6 7

**S.7**  To ensure fairness, the remuneration policy for all the directors and employees in a company should first be approved by independent, non-executive directors.     1 2 3 4 5 6 7

**S.8**  Business is a great civiliser, for ideas have always been exchanged as goods have been traded, and will continue so in the global economy.     1 2 3 4 5 6 7

**Box C**

| | | |
|---|---|---|
| **S.9** | Those who enable another to become powerful through their shrewdness, or use of force, risk ruin because both of these qualities are feared most by powerful new leaders. | 1  2  3  4  5  6  7 |
| **S.10** | If managers are careless about basic things – telling the truth, respecting moral codes, proper professional conduct – who can believe them on other issues? | 1  2  3  4  5  6  7 |
| **S.11** | Public and private sector organisations become more corrupt than individuals because they have more power and resources, and are also less amenable to disgrace and punishment. | 1  2  3  4  5  6  7 |
| **S.12** | Business and the community must cooperate more because commitment to a high level of ethical business behaviour has deteriorated almost in direct proportion to a decline in societal values. | 1  2  3  4  5  6  7 |
| **S.13** | The ultimate effect of protecting people at work from the consequences of their errors is to overload the organisation with time-servers. | 1  2  3  4  5  6  7 |
| **S.14** | In matters of personal conscience, the views of the majority have no place. | 1  2  3  4  5  6  7 |
| **S.15** | I don't like work, no one does, but I like what is in work – the chance to find yourself, your own reality, for yourself and not for others – a private feeling no other person can ever know. | 1  2  3  4  5  6  7 |
| **S.16** | If you don't drive your business and those you employ, you will soon be driven out of business. | 1  2  3  4  5  6  7 |

# Appendix:
# Calculating your Moral Compass scores

## Simple Moral Compass

**1** Enter the scores you recorded for each statement, S1 to S8 inclusive, in the appropriate box below.

|          | S1 | S2 | S3 | S4 | S5 | S6 | S7 | S8 |
|----------|----|----|----|----|----|----|----|----|
| Part I   |    |    |    |    |    |    |    |    |
| Part II  |    |    |    |    |    |    |    |    |
| Part III |    |    |    |    |    |    |    |    |
| Part IV  |    |    |    |    |    |    |    |    |
| Part V   |    |    |    |    |    |    |    |    |
| Part VI  |    |    |    |    |    |    |    |    |
| **Total** |    |    |    |    |    |    |    |    |

**2** Check that all your scores have been inserted for each Part (I to VI) and that the box is fully completed.

**3** Calculate the totals for each score entered under columns S1 to S8.

**4** Plot each total on the scale provided against the appropriate ethical theory in the simple Moral Compass diagram (Figure A), using the following key:

S1 = Ethical relativism    S5 = Moral pluralism
S2 = Hedonism              S6 = Natural law
S3 = Pragmatism            S7 = Social contract
S4 = Utilitarianism        S8 = Idealism

**5** Insert your four highest total scores in the following box:

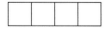

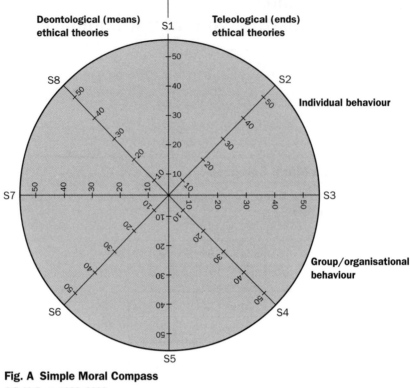

**Fig. A Simple Moral Compass**
© T. McEwan 1993, 2000

## Detailed Moral Compass

**6** Plot each total recorded in (4) above on the scale provided in the detailed Moral Compass diagram (Figure B).

**7** Enter the scores recorded for each statement, S9 to S16, inclusive, in the appropriate box below.

|          | S9 | S10 | S11 | S12 | S13 | S14 | S15 | S16 |
|----------|----|-----|-----|-----|-----|-----|-----|-----|
| Part I   |    |     |     |     |     |     |     |     |
| Part II  |    |     |     |     |     |     |     |     |
| Part III |    |     |     |     |     |     |     |     |
| Part IV  |    |     |     |     |     |     |     |     |
| Part V   |    |     |     |     |     |     |     |     |
| Part VI  |    |     |     |     |     |     |     |     |
| **Total** |   |     |     |     |     |     |     |     |

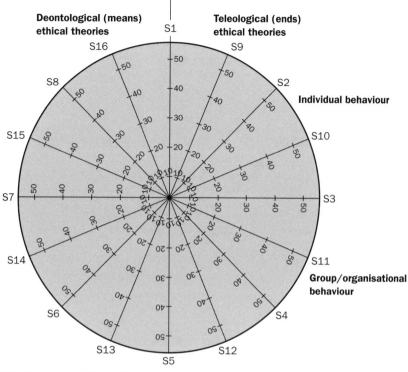

**Fig. B Detailed Moral Compass**

© T. McEwan 1993, 2000

**8** Check that all your scores have been inserted for each Part (I to VI) and that the box is fully completed.

**9** Calculate the totals for each score entered under columns S9 to S16.

**10** Plot each total on the scale provided against the appropriate ethical theory in the detailed Moral Compass diagram (Figure B), using the following key:

S9   = Machiavellianism     S13 = Social Darwinism
S10 = Virtue ethics           S14 = Libertarianism
S11 = Socialism                S15 = Individualism
S12 = Communitarianism    S16 = Ethical egoism

**11** Insert your four highest overall total scores recorded in the detailed Moral Compass in the following box:

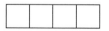

**12** An optional final step might involve comparing your total scores with those of fellow students or colleagues and discussing the reasons, values and beliefs which influenced each person.

# Index

*Note: due to space restrictions text within the synopsis, review and discussion questions, the case studies, notes and moral compass exercises at the end of each chapter has not been indexed.*